MANUAL FOR
TODAY'S MISSIONARY
From Recruitment
To Retirement

Marjorie A. Collins

William Carey Library

Pasadena, California

Published by William Carey Library
1705 N. Sierra Bonita Ave.,
Pasadena, California 91104

ISBN 0-87808-204-2

Cover art by Mary Lou Totten

Printed in the United States of America.

Library of Congress cataloging in Publication Data

Collins, Marjorie A.
  Manual for today's missionary

  (Missionary candidate aid series)
  Bibliography: p.
  1. Missionaries--Handbooks, manuals, etc.
I. Title. II. Series.
BV2091.C64 1986 266'.0023 85-27603
ISBN 0-87808-204-2

Lovingly and gratefully dedicated
to my dear friend and faithful intercessor,
ELEANOR LASIER ROWE, R.N., Ed.D.
whose life is a constant challenge to me
by her giving and witnessing. Without her
support and encouragement, this volume
could not have been written.

MISSIONARY CANDIDATE AID SERIES

Contents

v

SECTION II RUNNING THE RACE: Field Experience

SECTION III CONTINUING THE RACE: Furlough

Foreword

This is a book specifically and crucially for missionaries, or those already in candidacy. However, it is much more than that. No volume can give you a better "behind the scenes" look at the life of a missionary than this one. Many people are already indepted to Marjorie Collins for her earlier books on the missionary life. In this latest book every chapter takes up a specific aspect of the missionary task from the early stages of candidacy through to retirement.

To be sure, the book was not written for the purpose of giving "would be" missionaries a behind the scenes look at the life of a missionary. But inasmuch as it does, in fact, take up all the various complexities at every step of the way, there is probably no book that gives a more honest insight into that reality than this one. Students will be especially interested in this manual.

But not just missionaries and would-be missionaries will be interested in this book. It also gives tremendous insight into how people in the local churches can participate in the care and the feeding of missionaries, and gain maximum enjoyment in following their exciting and sometimes difficult task. It shows mission committees and mission-minded people in the congregation just what it is that they can do that will allow them to participate in the overall mission cause by understanding the missionaries themselves.

There is no other book in print which will provide the kind of information and help you will find here.

Ralph D. Winter
U.S. Center for World Mission

Preface

This book is meant to be a practical guide for those who are involved in missionary service or are looking forward to it. It is designed to be used as a textbook in Bible Schools/Colleges and Seminaries; a reference book for pastors, youth workers, libraries; an orientation tool for Mission Boards and other sending agencies. It is also a manual for those who are already missionaries.

The questions which follow each chapter should be thought through carefully and answered as honestly as possible (as a group or individual endeavor). Only by thinking through these issues and finding the answers will it be possible to absorb some of the shocks which will be experienced in your quest for God's will and purpose for your life. There will be uphill climbs, plateaus of impatience, and times when the trail downward looks very tempting and pleasant. But God can and will overrule in all the circumstances of your life. This book may help you through some of those difficult times.

Having chosen Him and His way, your life will be filled with joy,responsibility, and the anticipation of unknown tomorrows. You have already proven the faithfulness of God in your experience. You know He is directing you each step of your way. And you stand expectantly,waiting for the beginning of the next phase of your Christian service.

This book, first of all, will acquaint you with many of the details that will need to be cared for during your time of walking in "no-man's land" as an accepted missionary candidate. It will cause you to stop and ask questions concerning yourself and your ministry. It will tell you some of the pitfalls you must avoid. It will guide you concerning matters which you must care for during the weeks and months before departure for the field. And it will encourage you in maintaining a close and consistent walk with the Lord.

Secondly, you will catch a glimpse of what commitment to the Lord through missionary service is like as you seek to fulfill the Great Commission in a country which is foreign to you. You will discover ways to make your ministry most effective. You will learn how to cope with common problems. You will find yourself referring to these chapters many times in the days ahead.

Thirdly, you will find guidelines which will help you plan for and best utilize your time(s) of furlough and assist you as you prepare to return to your field of service. You will also have opportunity to evaluate your work and witness.

Lastly, you will be brought face-to-face with the reality of retirement with its benefits and blessings. How to prepare for it, how to enjoy it, how to have a continuing ministry during it, and how to face the future are subjects explored.

May God grant you quietness of heart and mind, whether you are looking to Him to lead you to the field of His choice, to bless your overseasministry, to refresh you through furlough periods, or to provide you with a happy and fulfilling period of retirement.

"And whatsoever ye do in word or deed, do all in the name of the Lord Jesus, giving thanks to God and the Father by him."
Colossians 3:17

Marjorie A. Collins
October, 1985

PART I
ENTERING THE RACE
Preparation

1
Considering The Mission Field

Many of you are seeking God's leading in your future ministry. You are earnestly desirous of allowing your talents, gifts and abilities to be used to their highest good in the cause of missions. You are looking for His positive direction to a Board, a field, a ministry, and a people to which you can give not only your best for the Master, but also receive satisfaction from the ministry into which you enter. Lesser pursuits will result in frustration—no matter how high the position or how tempting the wages.

For the first time you may be seriously considering missionary service. You have felt the peace of God flood your heart as you have made that decision to become a missionary. You are going to pursue this course unless God closes the door by specific circumstances about which you are currently unaware.

But there are questions you want answered. The first may very well be, What is a missionary? Others follow naturally. What Board should I choose? What field is of particular interest to me? What type of ministry do I want to perform? About what people group am I most concerned?

WHAT IS A MISSIONARY?

Although the word "missionary" can be defined in many ways, from "an individual with a mission", to "one who is sent", to "an individual who serves overseas", perhaps one of the best definitions has been given by Dr. Terry C. Hulbert:

> A missionary is a supported worker who is involved in the expansion of the church in a culture other than his own.[1]

By being a supported worker," it is implied that the missionary

---

Hulbert, Terry C. **World Missions Today**. Wheaton, IL: Evangelical Teacher Training Association, 1979, p.92.

has been approved by churches and Christian individuals who believe God has put His hand on this person to represent Jesus Christ. These individuals are willing to back their approval with financial, material, and prayer support.

The "expansion of the church" is not indicative of a reaching forth of a home church to replicate itself in another geographical location. Rather, it is the multiplication of disciples to add to the Church — the entire body of believers — resulting in an expanded population of adherents to Christian faith and practice. The special concerns of a mission agency, as compared to other Christian organizations, is the initial planting of the church where no stable beachhead has yet been established, or the rearing of that church in its own missionary (not merely evangelistic) vision.

Some confuse the fact that all believers are called to be witnesses (Acts 1:11), whereas very few are chosen to be apostles (sent ones). To understand what this text is teaching, we must not confuse our verbiage. As with so many other once strongly "Christian" words which are now being utilized by the secular press and the world at large (e.g., the expression, "born again") the word "missionary" has come to mean little more than one who tells somebody else something and has a purpose in doing it. But our definition includes the focus, "in a culture other than his own," implying where Christ has not yet been named effectively. This means cross-cultural experience and not simply giving a word of witness to neighbors who are part of our own people. Paul distinguishes on this same basis between Peter's ministry to his own people, and Paul's to people not his own (Galatians 2:7).

WHERE TO START

Once you sense your call to the cause of missions, you will want to read as much as you can concerning missions, write to missionaries, become actively involved in any mission programs your local church may offer, attend missionary conferences, have interviews with mission executives whenever possible, become acquainted with those of other cultures in your local colleges, universities and neighborhood, and, in general, try to understand what your maximum contribution to the cause might be.

One exciting prerequisite to the aforementioned consideration is to study a world atlas. If you are to immerse yourself in a global cause it might be embarassing to be fuzzy about geographical locations of the world, capital cities, rivers, seas, mountains, etc. How long has it been since you've looked at a current world map? Could you immediately locate Mozambique, Surinam, the Comoros Islands, Bhutan, Senegambia, Kuwait? What about the cities of Medellin, Islamabad, Tegucigalpa, Luanda, Bangkok, Lae? Do you know what countries border on the Sudan, Paraguay, Gabon, Afghanistan, Austria?

Does not true concern drive you to these real places? Is it not logical to know something about the areas of the world available to you and to others you may be able to attract to the cause? Should you only consider serving in Brazil or Japan because you have heard so much about them and know where they are?

As you speak with personnel from mission boards, they will tell of their work in countries of which you may have never heard. In order to inquire and receive information intelligently, you should have some idea of the world as a whole. Such knowledge opens up far more possibilities for selecting a field where you and others are needed and where you can contribute the most for the sake of extending the church of Jesus Christ.

How well can you pray for the starving hordes in the Ogaden, or for those left homeless because of a typhoon in Chittagong, or for rains to come to Ooagadougou—and not know where those places are located? It is exciting to pray with a map before you in order to pinpoint these and more familiar locations (e.g., Quito, Ecuador; Monrovia, Liberia; Lahore, Pakistan; Vienna, Austria).

Praying for a world of lost people becomes even more meaningful when you know exactly where and who those people are and how they live. Eventually your interest will concentrate on a particular area of concern, perhaps to a particular group. But in any event, as a foundation of a life in the cause of missions, be sure you have a good idea of the whole world in which you live.

WHAT BOARD SHOULD YOU CHOOSE?

If you are seriously thinking of missionary service, this is one of the most important questions. With the wonderful profusion of outstanding sending agencies seeking the services of qualified young men and women, it may be difficult to know how to choose the team with whom to serve. Pick up almost any major Christian magazine and you will note the overwhelming need for workers.

It would not necessarily be wrong to choose a name of a board by chance, hoping that filling out an application and having it reviewed would provide the answer to whether or not God has chosen that team for you. There may be missionaries on the field today who arrived there by just such uncertain means, although you are taking a chance on missing God's highest will, simply for lack of sufficient knowledge concerning those with whom you will be ministering. Mission Boards differ just as people differ. Matching people and Boards is a creative and complex matter. But just as it is imperative that there be agreement on major issues to ensure a lasting marriage, so it is with finding the right Board for you. Here is a check list of questions to ask of the people you would like to know about:

. . . What is their doctrinal stance?

. . . Are they denominational, nondenominational, interdenominational?

. . . Is their philosophy of Christian ministry compatible with yours?

. . . Is their method of support agreeable with your firm beliefs?

. . . Do they have sound financial management?

. . . Are they local, national, international, multinational?

. . . In what area(s) of the world do they serve?

. . . How much education do they require?

. . . What are their other requirements?

. . . Is formal Bible education a prerequisite to service?

. . . How long has the agency been operative?

. . . How many missionaries are already serving?

. . . How large was their last candidate class?

. . . Have you ever met anyone serving with this Board? What were your impressions?

. . . In what types of ministry are they involved?

. . . How strictly are missionary candidates screened?

The answers to most of these questions can be discerned by writing a letter to the General Director (by name if you know it) and asking for a copy of their most current periodical, a copy of their doctrinal statement, their latest financial report, promotional material, and a copy of their last annual report (which often appears in their periodical). You may wish to request an application and any materials pertinent to possible missionary candidacy. (With the possible exception of candidate materials, you should be able to obtain information on existing sending agencies in a Bible College/Seminary library, or from a missions instructor).

Is it wise to research more than one mission board? Do you buy the first new car you see? or the first home you find advertised? Do you marry the first individual who speaks to you? Few are the spur-of-the-moment decisions you will make in life where it concerns something as great as your finances, your focus, or your future. Comparisons are not always odious; in fact, when it affects the rest of your life (as well as that of your family and all who will be touched by your ministry), is it not appropriate to search out the matter with deep concern and wise choices? How else can you give yourself unreservedly to the teamwork of that group?

Many Mission Boards send representatives to Christian schools/ colleges/seminaries. They are available to answer your questions, to give you requested literature (or have it sent to you), to make you aware of their scope, their policies and procedures, and their requirements. Most of these representatives have served overseas, and are astute enough to size up your specific qualifications, match them with the known needs of their organization, and give you wise counsel and suggestions for furthering your call to missionary service. Many are honest enough to direct you toward another mission which may more meaningfully utilize your abilities, gifts and talents. (E.g., a board which has no medical work may suggest another board to a nurse who is seriously considering overseas service, rather than diverting her expertise to fit in with their own emphasis.)

A few letters, a few trips to the library, a few talks with missions professors—and a few chats with M.K.'s or foreign nationals who are your fellow students may prove extremely helpful in selecting a mission board.

A reference book which can aid you in getting acquainted with the many excellent mission agencies is **Mission Handbook**, published by MARC, a ministry of World Vision International. This hefty volume gives the names of all American Mission Boards, where they work, how many workers are presently members, what types of ministries they carry out and the name and address of their executive officer. (Available from MARC, 919 West Huntington Drive, Monrovia, California 91016)

One further consideration: If you are divorced, or divorced and remarried, you will need to let this be known to any Board to which you may consider applying. You will need to research mission boards to discover their regulations concerning divorced individuals. Such factors may exclude you from service with some Boards while it will be searched out very thoroughly by Boards which do accept divorced individuals for missionary service.

WHAT FIELD SHOULD YOU CHOOSE?

This question is an integral part of which board you should choose. You may feel a natural leaning toward a particular field and may have made plans toward a particular geographical area. After World War II, many servicemen and women wanted to return to Japan and Germany to preach the gospel. Many did just that. After the martyrdom of the five missionaries to the Auca Indians in Ecuador in 1956, thousands indicated an intention to serve among the Auca tribespeople. Few went. The slaughter of missionaries in Vietnam caused many to volunteer for service there. None were able to go.

Does God call to a particular field without reservation? Sometimes He does. And if He does, He will give you an immoveable assurance and peace as you pursue that calling.

But more typically, you will serve in a country which may be a complete surprise to you. For example, I was determined to serve in China. But China's doors remained closed to me. Through further waiting upon the Lord, the work among Muslims in India became my goal. For two years I waited for my visa. Three times it was refused. Then suddenly Pakistan opened its doors to missionaries—a whole new country consisting of Muslim Indians! And within three months I was in a country I had previously not considered for service.

A young couple planned for many months to go to the Philippines. Ten days before their departure the Indonesian government suddenly made visas available. The mission considered that a higher priority!

In my travels across Africa, and in attendance at missionary conferences in many locations, I have heard many, many missionaries give their testimony. Often they have stated, "When I gave my life to the Lord I said, "I'll go anywhere, Lord—but please, not Africa!"" How little we know of what God has planned for us and the lessons we can learn from following hard after Him through change and circumstance. And how pleasant it is to discover, as the years pass, that He chose the exact spot we would have chosen if we could have known all about it (as He does) right along—even to the place we least wanted to go.

Is it wrong to lean toward one particular geographical area? Of course not. But don't be set in marble. Be a good lump of clay in the Potter's masterful hands. Allow **Him** to direct you each step of the way. Missionary service is first a vocation and second a location. You may want to serve in the country; you may be placed in the city. You may want to serve in Kenya; He may place you in Paraguay. You may desire to work with the illiterate masses; He may give you the privilege of working with the educated elite. Trust Him fully to lead you aright. Your Shepherd knows where the best pasture is for you. Normally, once committed to a specific agency, that leading will come to you through the leadership of that consecrated group of people.

IN WHAT CAPACITY DO YOU WANT TO SERVE?

Missionary endeavor is not complete when you arrive at your place of service. You must **do** something. A hundred years ago, and in new fields generally, missionaries were sent out to evangelize the lost. That was their commitment; that is how they spent their time. But again, change has entered the picture. Today there are so many well-established fields that the missionary generalist is only one of many roles. We see a tremendous growth in the number of individuals going forth to serve in the fields of Medicine, Social Services, Business, Communications, Education, Support Ministries, Church Growth, and Administration. Most of these categories with their many-faceted endeavors are meant to enhance the follow-through evangelism efforts to which almost all older mission agencies are primarily committed. Whether a radio technician, a mechanic, an industrial engineer or a photographer is a missionary in the same sense as an evangelist or preacher might be debated. But the fact is that "we are workers together with God" in the tremendous responsibility of relaying the gospel message to the ends of the earth, first to new fields, and later through the further outreach of the new churches to their own people, and new fields further on. Today, as never before, we are understanding Paul's words in I Corinthians 9:22: "I am made all things to all men, that I might by all means save some," and in I Corinthians 3:6, "I have planted, Apollos watered; but God gave the increase."

God gives each individual at least one gift. Add to that all your natural talents and abilities. Now where and how can you serve Him most effectively? Remember, it is more blessed to give than to receive (Acts 20:35). It is not how much you will receive from your sacrificial service, but rather how much you can give in order to lead others into a personal knowledge of and steady walk with the Lord of life.

ABOUT WHAT PEOPLE GROUP ARE YOU MOST CONCERNED?

"People groups" and "hidden peoples" are terms which came into prominence at the International Congress on World Evangelization at Lausanne, Switzerland in 1974, and from that point on through the research, speaking, and writings of many mission thinkers, including Ralph D. Winter, Edward R. Dayton, and C. Peter Wagner. Previous to that time we tended to think simply of "countries" full of people without Christ (those who had never heard, and those who had heard and rejected the message). Other countries had many who were of an evangelical or solidly Christian persuasion.

In the growth of this new emphasis, charts, maps, and graphs appeared which distinguished people groups within people groups within people groups. We were now told not only that millions of individuals had not responded to the gospel, but that over two billion of them were sealed off in groups essentially out of reach of anyone from whom they could ever hope to hear the gospel understandably. We must not take this too far. It would be difficult always to discern precisely the boundaries of these groups within the world population. But the Bible does speak mostly of "nations", not "countries".

This type of "People Group" and "Hidden Peoples" thinking has heightened the awareness of Christians to the millions who are yet without Christ. Who will tell them of Him? It is the kind of reality that has stirred thousands to make a move toward missionary service in order to carry the banner of the cross to these unreached and hitherto unreachable peoples. Mission boards have been involved in gathering statistical evidence concerning unreached people groups in their own areas of ministry. Many of them are also recruiting workers to reach them.

With this in mind, do you have a particular population in which you have an interest? Or are you thinking only in vague terms such as Africans, Asians, or Latin Americans? Wherever the Lord may place you, refining your choice of people with whom to work (by gathering as much information as possible concerning the people of the world through reading and oral/written communication) will help you in your choice of a field and a mission.

So you are now ready to make some very difficult and life-molding choices. Your faith will be tested to its utmost. Your whole future is dependent upon your decisions at this point in your life. They ought not to be made lightly or prayerlessly.

QUESTIONS — CHAPTER 1

1. How does God call men and women into His service?

2. Name the types of professional education and experience which could **not** be utilized in missionary service.

3. Outline the initial steps you would take in seeking God's direction toward missionary service.

4. What types of considerations would cause you to decide to apply to certain mission boards?

5. What would make you **not** consider certain mission fields as viable options for ministry?

2
Facing the Challenge

For some of you, the excitement of being an ambassador for Christ through missionary service did not just begin. But there is no doubt that you have looked forward to the experience with keen anticipation, even in the face of certain questions and possible fears.

There was the initial step of acknowledging your personal relationship to God through Jesus Christ. There were the days — perhaps weeks, months or years—of considering what His will in Christ Jesus is concerning you. There has been the required training in Bible and other specialties. Another dilemma was solved when you decided to what country or area you would go and with whom you would serve. Perhaps one of the most difficult experiences you have faced thus far is that interminable wait between the day you applied for service and the moment you were approved. Of course, you fully expected to be accepted by the Board, but there was always the possibility of being turned down.

Through all of this, there was a certain aura of expectancy, of challenge, of hope. Always there was a reliance on the efficacy of prayer, and it was with joy and faith, as well as with a slight sense of uncertainty, that you spent many hours with the Lord, beseeching Him to show you His perfect will in these matters. The burden was shared with friends and loved ones who, because they cared, joined you at the throne of grace.

Some of you waited longer than others. In some cases, more education had to be obtained, medical matters had to be taken care of, debts had to be paid, or other specific requirements had to be met.

But it has been said, "all things come to those who wait," and the day came when you stood with a phone at your ear, or with a letter in your hand, and were assured, " . . . we are happy to inform you that you have been accepted for missionary service by unanimous vote of the Board." God had answered prayer. He had, once again, proven His faithfulness.

You knew it would come. You had waited rather impatiently for the exact moment of its arrival. And there you sat, having recovered from the immediate burst of elation and gratitude, and you began to ask yourself questions which you thought had long since been settled:

"Lord, I'm not worthy of such a calling."

"Are you sure I can do it, Lord?"

"Did I really make the right decision?"

"How can I possibly raise my support?"

"Am I adequately prepared for service?"

"Will I be able to learn the language?"

"What will it be like to give up my home and the stability of loved ones?"

"Is my love for Christ adequate for all I will be required to do in His name?"

"Is my faith strong enough to overcome **all** that will confront me in His service?"

"Am I sure, beyond a shadow of a doubt, that I am headed in the right direction?"

"Why am I questioning my position this far along the pathway?"

"Do I have enough to offer others to merit my going to them?"

Almost everyone faces these questions, or others like them. It is essential that they be considered right now before taking any more steps toward the mission field. The least doubt which comes to you on this side of the ocean can, and probably will, become a giant impasse to any kind of effective service "over there."

It is essential, then, that you consider the questions, Where Am I? and Why Am I Here? before you move forward.

WHERE AM I?

It is quite unlikely you would find yourself an accepted missionary candidate if you had not carefully considered the Great Commission which has been given in so many ways in so many places throughout such verses as John 4:35; Mark 16:15; Matthew 28:19,20; Isaiah 6:8; Romans 10:14,15; Acts 1:8; I Corinthians 9:16, and many, many others.

As you study the Word, and come to know God more intimately, you begin to understand something of His missionary heart. You also come to understand that He Who gave to man all He had in creation for man's satisfaction, knows something about stewardship. He Who gave Himself in the person of His Son, for man's salvation and sanctification knows something about sending and serving. He Who sustains you in every way throughout your earthly pilgrimage knows something about sacrifice and self-denial. And He Who created the angel, Lucifer, knows something about the snares of Satan.

Yes, God made you, understands you, loves you, and provides for your every need. It is very possible that out of gratitude to Him you have felt an urgency to give your life to missionary service, thus following in the steps of the Savior. You have now been accepted to do exactly that. That is where you are.

WHY AM I HERE?

This is another urgent question.

Assuredly, we are not in any way seeking to discourage you or bring unwarranted questions to your mind. In all fairness, however, we must seek to make the path before you as clear as possible, removing some of the thorns,stumbling blocks, and ruts which could so easily deter you from God's best for you later on in the ministry you have chosen for Him.

In order to accomplish our objective, we must be very frank in dealing with certain matters. It will be of great personal benefit if you are extremely honest in your consideration of these things.

1.   ON WHAT HAVE I BASED MY DECISION TO BECOME A MISSIONARY? To utilize certain natural talents and abilities? To lighten the load of an overworked missionary? To fulfill an inner need for adventure, challenge, and/or travel? To show a spirit of self-sacrifice? To please certain individuals who have prayed me to the mission field? To meet a specific need for a specific task in a specific area? Because the Word of God implies that is my duty? Because I was stirred by someone or something to devote my life to winning lost souls to Jesus Christ? Because I was pushed by my parents? None of these, of course, are dishonorable motives.

It is very important that you consider why you are presently an accepted missionary candidate. When you get to your field of service, there will be times when you will ask yourself why you are there. If you do no have an answer that is completely satisfying to you in your heart of hearts, you will be sorely tempted to return to the homeland.

What is a valid basis for missionary service? There is but one. It is your love and devotion to God Whom you serve which results in faithful obedience to His commands. Any other "call" is inadequate. No matter how much intelligence, education, training, or expertise you may have; no matter how desperate the plight of the people to whom you are sent; no matter how few workers are willing to go forth; no matter how ripe the harvest; no matter how willing you are to become involved—unless you can honestly go forth because of your love for and obedience to Jesus Christ, your efforts will be thwarted at every turn, and you will find yourself trying to fight spiritual battles in your own strength.

2. HAVE I THOROUGHLY CONSIDERED ALTERNA-TIVES TO MISSIONARY SERVICE? It seems illogical in the plan and purpose of God that every Christian should be a foreign missionary. (We tend to overlook this fact because the task is so great and the workers so few). But let's just consider to what this might lead if we went forth on such a premise. Every Christian in the United States would have to offer himself for service abroad. Every Christian in Kenya would need to offer himself for service in another area of the world. Christians in China would have to leave their homeland, as would those in Ecuador, Pakistan, Indonesia, etc., etc., **ad infinitum**. Meanwhile, those from other countries would be coming in to take the place of those who had left. It would become ridiculous if carried to its logical ends. And if missionaries were only to go to the neediest people, we might find our own State Department swamped with applications from Christians around the world who felt they should bring the gospel message to the needy and lost souls in America.

The Lord Jesus may have had this in mind when he said, "Many are called, but few are chosen" (Matthew 22:14). Isn't it possible that some missionary work has been mediocre or even meaningless because those who were "called" were not "chosen" of God for special ser-vice? Every Christian is called out of disobedience into a life of obedi-ence. Every Christian is called to be holy as He is holy; to follow His Word, His will, and His way; to do those things which will bring honor, praise and glory to the Lord of all the earth. Every Christian is called to be a witness concerning the gospel message. But—and this may come as a surprise—not every Christian is called to be a mission-ary overseas.

3. IS "TENTMAKING" A VIABLE CONSIDERATION? It has been said that in this life "only change is constant." And in the day in which we live, change is rampant. Whereas up to a few years ago it was considered that one who was "called and chosen" for missionary service should serve for a lifetime in the area and among the people to whom the Lord originally called, this is no longer thought to be necessary. Even secular employees today are said to be likely to change jobs seven times during their lifetime. While some countries are opening up, other countries and areas once open to the presentation of the gospel of Jesus Christ are presently going through inner turmoil, growing pains, and disillusionment. Some are seeking to outlaw freedom of religious expression by persecution. Many are promoting Islam as a "State Religion," in fact, frighteningly so. Many others are entrenched in the alarming spread of atheistic adherance. For these and other reasons, in many formerly "open" countries, visas and resident permits are being granted for only 5 to 10 years or are not being granted at all. In other areas, reentry permits/visas are not being granted to purely "religious workers." Some candidates have waited long periods of time seeking entrance to a country in the belief that God was leading them there, only to be refused repeatedly.

Because of the aforementioned difficulties which have been steadily rising as barriers to the "professional" missionary, a whole new concept has come into being. New? Not really. It is from the Apostle Paul, who worked as a maker of tents in order to provide the financial means for his missionary ministry, that we have coined a new word for Christian witness in closed countries, i.e., "Tentmaking." Although many books have been written about this alternative model for worldwide witness, perhaps the best known is, TODAY'S TENT-MAKERS by J. Christy Wilson, Jr.

Tentmaking is a means whereby individuals can move into a country to work at a secular job, attend a school or university, or be a government servant, and witness for Christ through a consistent life and testimony as time and rules of the land permit. Although this appears to be a way of circumventing laws prohibiting access to a country by "professional" missionaries, Wilson states that tentmaking also has several drawbacks.[1] Perhaps the greatest hindrance to gospel advance by this means is the restrictions agains religious proclamation placed upon those who go. Often papers must be signed in advance of

---

Wilson, Jr., J. Christy. TODAY'S TENTMAKERS, Wheaton, IL: Tyndale House Publishers, Inc., 1979, pp. 68-70

acceptance stating that no religious observances or beliefs will be openly practiced during one's tenure in the country. This could prohibit gospel witness of any formal kind, even in one's private home or office. Time limitations, lack of proper cultural adaptation, the tendency to be placed in a community with one's own countrymen, and the lack of spiritual fellowship or accountability to a reliable Christian sponsor are other major concerns related to this kind of ministry. Nevertheless, thousands of missionaries today, under regular boards, are working in partial or full "tentmaking" activities.

ARE YOU SURE?

Do you know assuredly that God has both called and chosen you for missionary service? Have you considered staying at home to be a mission-minded pastor, youth director, Christian education director, rescue mission worker? Have you decided in your own thinking and to your own satisfaction that working as a part-time witness in a secular job at home is not for you? Or, have you felt ill-at-ease seeking to put your witness to work in a homeland situation? Is it mere unrest in your spirit which seems to be an assurance of God's hand upon your life for specific service overseas?

Perhaps you have completely reckoned with these matters. But if not, be sure you do so right now. If you don't, you will, undoubtedly, find these questions haunting you on the field.

You are about to "launch out into the deep." Your feet are wet, and you're inching your way out from shore. It would be so easy if you could just take one flying leap into those waters and immediately be on the other side. But there is still a considerable distance to go before you are free, at last, to be in over your head, where the depth of the water makes it easier to swim. Meanwhile, each step forward produces cool shivers within you. Do you keep going, or run for shore?

This is a most important question for you to consider. And you must get it straight very soon now, or you'll be out too far to return, and unless you can swim against severe odds, you may drown. You do not have to know that overseas service is to be your life work, but you must know that this is the right step for you **now**.

Hopefully, each accepted candidate reading this book is absolutely certain of God's call to missionary service and has honestly considered alternatives to overseas work **before** getting this far. It is also hoped that some who may have earnestly desired to serve as missionaries have not been deterred along the way by well-meaning individuals who suggested that missionaries are second-class people—inadequately educated, intellectually dull, socially undesirable, unsuccessful in love, etc.—and thus you should really think about remaining a first-class Christian in the homeland.

WISE COUNSEL

Perhaps in some aspects we are becoming too sophisticated in our approach to missions with all the computerized testing, the long periods or orientation, and the hindrances that are made to seem formidable by those who should most encourage those who have set their hearts toward the mission field.

In recent years, many individuals have been held back from going to the foreign field because a pastor, or a church board has felt a growing responsibility toward the individual who has volunteered for missionary service. It may be that in the past we sent qualified people out to win the lost without asking their pastor or their fellow-believers in the local church if they felt this was a wise decision. Today, in some situations, those who are qualified, feel God calling them, have prepared by obtaining the best in biblical and secular training, and are applying to a mission board are stymied in their efforts since they must usually have their pastor give them a reference. And some pastors are delaying things by stating to the Mission Board that they feel this person needs some type of additional training, or more experience working in and with the local church, or must conquer some obnoxious habit in his life, needs to find himself or herself a spouse rather than going overseas single, couples ought to have a child before they leave to assist in adjustments, etc., etc.,etc.

It is good that churches are, more and more, taking an interest in their missionary candidates. When that interest becomes an overpowering and final decisive action contrary to the call of God in that life, however, it can be a very dangerous intrusion into a life (or lives) which can result in the missing of the will of God and a life without impact for the cause of Christ. The pastor or the church board may have very good reasons for withholding his/their blessing. If so, the whole matter should be discussed openly and honestly. If there is still disagreement on the outcome of such discussion, it is the better part of wisdom to get a second opinion by obtaining solid Christian counsel from another pastor friend, one of your Bible College/Seminary professors, or by speaking personally with the administrator or the Board of the mission to which you are applying. "Where no counsel is, the people fall: but in the multitude of counsellors there is safety" (Proverbs 11:14). But beware of spending months and years getting an opinion from everyone with whom you come in contact. This usually shows a lack of security stemming from immaturity, and ends by matching your own biased opinion with opinions which agree with yours. Counsel is important and beneficial, but only if the counselor does not impose his personal prejudices and ideas on the one being counseled — without due cause.

It should be made very clear that missionaries must be the finest and best that the Christian world can offer. The Father did not send us the least of all He had. He sent the very best. And we must do likewise. Being a missionary is a great privilege as well as a tremendous responsibility. Are you prepared for all that it involves? May God help you to be.

QUESTIONS — CHAPTER 2

1. What is **your** definition of a missionary?

2. What factors are involved in committing oneself to missionary service?

3. What are some questions which may arise when one has been accepted for missionary service?

4. What, in your opinion, is a valid basis for being a "full-time" missionary?

5. What, in your opinion, is a valid basis for **NOT** being a "full-time" missionary?

6. How do "tentmaking individuals" differ from "full-time" missionaries?

7. What do you consider the major advantages and drawbacks of "tentmaking" witness?

3
The Changing Missionary Image

What is the image reflected in the minds of those who hear the word "missionary?" Is it a vision of a plain-faced lady wearing a funereal expression, speaking strictly of "down-country" activities in the heart of Africa, so concerned about the needs of her tribe that she has forgotten the rest of the world? Is she speaking in a church which really has little concern for her and her people? Does she drone on endlessly without presenting needs and challenges? Or does she tell a few sad stories, especially about orphans and the awful state of womanhood, receive a good offering, and the meeting is termed a "success?"

There will, of course, always be a place on the field for the full-time missionary evangelist, winning souls to Christ, planting churches, building up the saved in their faith, training national leadership and "gossiping the gospel" to anyone and everyone with whom he comes into contact. In this day of specialization, however, it is as common for missionaries to use the title secretary, teacher, engineer, doctor, nurse, musician, printer, script writer, Christian education worker, administrator, lab technician, language specialist, pilot, announcer, technician, accountant, photographer or journalist, lumping them all together and calling them missionaries. They are Christian workers going about the Lord's work. Their first and foremost responsibility is to live the gospel of Jesus Christ as they serve in their specialized capacity.

In order to do this, missionaries and candidates have discovered that their person must be as attractive to those to whom they minister as the gospel itself. The day of the "dowdy" missionary has never been appropriate. We are beginning to realize that missionaries are human beings—men and women—and that they are in many ways no different than the dedicated Christian who longs to serve the Lord and give forth the gospel at home. Most women and men, although avoiding the extreme fashions of the day, wear clothing which is in good taste and carefully selected. A little color in the face has made a difference in the look of the female. Men have taken on a sportier look, have done away with the "funeral black" or "chocolate brown" suit and have chosen red, green, blue or orange ties. Remember, a well-groomed look is a credit to our Lord. And although casual clothing is "in," blue jeans, shorts, and cut-offs may best be left to teenagers.

The candidate no longer feels it imperative merely to lecture endlessly concerning his future experiences. He has learned that visual aids of many kinds are acceptable and appropriate in almost every church, and a presentation with quality pictures and attractive, colorful displays makes a far greater impression upon the listeners. He will be frank with the congregation. He will allow that there are problems to be met and overcome. He may even confess that he is human and has had to face some difficulties himself, and will, undoubtedly, face even more on the field.

Today's candidate will seem younger and more worldly-wise than those of other years. He may represent a specialized field of service which is difficult to describe. He will be well prepared in more than one specialty. He may be going to a country very few have heard mentioned, especially as new nations emerge, or change their names. He may have an electronic display with him, or a computerized project. He might use a beautifully prepared stereo presentation. His literature will be attractive and well designed.

The candidate will not look different from anyone else in the group. Yet, he will be a person of purpose, with goals to be reached and definite tasks to be done. He will be less structured in his thinking and more democratic in his decisions than many missionaries of previous generations. He will rebel somewhat at strict authority, but will be able to add good ideas to any group. He will demand the right to fail, and when given responsibility, he will expect to receive the authority to carry it through. He will have more psychological preparation than any generation before him. He will not be afraid of change. He will have greater resources at his disposal. He will be a conceptual thinker. He will not be afraid to ask questions. We are, undoubtedly, entering upon an era in which we will find the most dedicated, least self-conscious individual who will not require the luxuries of material possessions, but will work for the cause of Christ in the hardest of circumstances for the sole purpose of spreading love and peace throughout the earth. He will be allowed to contribute far more to the work than others who preceded him. He will be less visionary, more honest and practical in his Christian experience and what he will expect from the nationals. He will allow that he has something to offer the world, and will not hide behind the devastating cliche that "in me dwells no good thing." He will lose none of his evangelical theology and dedication to Jesus Christ, but his scope of ministry will be broadened. He may possibly have seen or experienced more of the world's pleasures and problems than those who have gone before him. He will, therefore, better understand his fellow-workers who have travelled the same road, and will be better able to reach out to needy souls who are facing the same problems.

We are coming to the place where the missionary profession is held in as high esteem as that of medicine or science. Thus mission boards are having to change in order to reach the people of the world with all available resources. Many candidates will go to the field as educators in their field for the specific purpose of teaching nationals how to do the work formerly done by the foreign missionary, e.g., building mission stations, manning radio and TV controls, preaching, teaching, pastoring, nursing, etc. Because candidates today will follow the advice of D. L. Moody that "it is better to get 10 men to do the work than to do the work of 10 men," there will be far more mobility and education in missionary work. The missionary will be willing to recognize the responsibility and authority of nationals and to assist in the training of leaders from among them. Trained administrators will allow decisions to be made on lower levels, thus conserving time and manpower in field operations. There will be better use made of available men and women. The candidate chosen will not as often be a jack-of-all-trades, but may be prepared for a particular role and be sent out for that specific task. And in some instances, when that job is completed, there will be little need for that particular missionary.

The people to whom the missionary is being sent are also in a state of change. They are becoming better educated and more sophisticated. They are being reached through literature, radio, television and education as well as through person-to-person evangelism. They are learning to think for themselves and no longer will appear satisfied to listen without questioning, or to believe without reasoning. Young people are caught up in the maelstrom of radical thinking. They are learning new methods. They are becoming acquainted with the outside world. Countries once dominated by Western countries and Western thinking are now independent and setting their own rules, regulations and standards—not always to the benefit of missionaries. Visas are seldom obtained automatically. Nationalism on the governmental level, if not on the grass-roots level, is becoming very strong. Although poverty and famine still keep many in the lowest socio-economic status, and there are still those who have attained wealth and prominence in the emerging nations of the world, a middle-class is also arising which did not exist previously. This, in itself, raises both new opportunities and problems for the missionary.

Because of all this, the missionary image must change. Missions, themselves, must rethink and plan for the future. Every man and resource must be used to highest capacity. Some of the old must make way for the new. Outmoded methods and operations must be updated. Candidates must be prepared to bridge the gap in this changeover. The extensive and exciting challenges and opportunities for creativity and innovation are before you. And YOU are a vital part of this new look in missions. Are you prepared for it?

The supporting church also has a part in the changing missionary image. In some instances, a Pastor of Missions has been appointed to establish a program which will keep missions constantly before the congregation. The Pastor of Missions may even provide a missionary candidate training program which works very closely with prospective candidates and prospective mission boards. This should strengthen the church-missionary bond which, in all too many cases, has been weak in recent years. It will also require missionaries to maintain better lines of communication with their home church.

Whereas missionaries—especially those serving with non-denominational or interdenominational mission agencies—have almost always had to travel hundreds or thousands of miles to speak in scores of churches to raise their necessary financial support, home churches are, today, feeling a greater responsibility in this regard. They are beginning to see the wisdom of providing more substantially for their "home-grown" missionaries. Therefore, the missionary image in the local church may not consist of a stranger arriving on the doorstep, but of a real person, known to all, who is accepted by the congregation as a friend and co-worker. In such churches, the missionary, in a very special and personal sense, becomes "our" missionary.

An attractive, new pattern of support is where a local congregation, with one of its own people to send out, deliberately seeks a working arrangement with, perhaps, five other relatively nearby congregations. The home church puts up half the missionary's support, and the other five churches put up 10% each. The home church then puts up 10% for missionaries sponsored by the other congregations. This, primarily, allows the missionary family (on furlough, as well as in the initial deputation period) to be spared the almost scandalously expensive and bone-wearying vagabond status of those missionaries whose supporting churches are scattered all over a continent.

QUESTIONS—CHAPTER 3

1. In your own mind, what image does the word "missionary" produce?

2. Does a person's outward appearance affect his ministry? How?

3. Consider a specific mission field and list five dramatic changes which have occurred there in the past 10 years.

4. How much education should today's missionary have? Why?

5. What part can the local supporting church have in the changing missionary image?

4
Personal Considerations

Although the newly accepted missionary candidate is thinking primarily in terms of "how can I raise my support, when can I leave for the field, where will I buy my equipment, what will I say in my meetings," etc., etc., there is one point that must always be kept in mind. There can be no suspension of the development of the personal life. The life of a missionary does not begin when one reaches the foreign field. The truth of the matter is, crossing an ocean or a continent has never yet changed a person overnight. It is true that surroundings, language, culture, clothing, food, shelter, and the whole way of life will be different. But the missionary candidate himself is basically the same when he walks up the ramp of the plane in the homeland and when he walks down the ramp on foreign soil.

For some, it is easy to adjust to a new pattern of living. Many find language study very tedious and difficult, or well nigh impossible. Others feel the whole adjustment is interesting and enjoyable. But one thing that does not radically change is YOU. And because YOU will have to live with YOU the rest of your life, it is well to consider some of the little things (and big things, too) in your personal life which can be or ought to be adapted, adjusted, deleted or enhanced. And it is never too early to begin! In fact, the earlier you start, the more you'll realize those things that need to be changed in your life to become an effective and stable witness on the field.

The first area to be considered is the PRAYER LIFE. Do you find it difficult to maintain a Quiet Time? Have you neglected this vital aspect of your spiritual life? Have you determined again and again that you would rise earlier or stay up later to have that time with the Lord? And have you been pressed from every side with work and worries and trials and problems so that you didn't have time for prayer? Have you been frustrated because you felt a need to pray but didn't make an opportunity for it? Have you realized a lack of fruitfulness in your life and through your life to others because you neglected fellowship with the Lord in prayer? Or have you simply taken time to pray for "me, my wife, my son John and his wife, amen"?

Lack of a personal prayer life may be the cause of more physical, mental, psychological and emotional breakdowns than we would dare to number. It keeps the individual from finding the working of the Holy Spirit in his life. Because of unconfessed sin, relationships are severed between friends and with co-workers. Then the missionary finds himself becoming self-centered, easily hurt, and gradually he becomes quite unmanageable for he is actually working out his own problems and getting himself into precarious situations when he should be seeking the Lord's help in all these matters. If any of you lack wisdom, let him ask . . . " [1] "If ye shall ask anything in my name . . . " [2] "Ask and it shall be given you, seek and ye shall find, knock and it shall be opened unto you . . . " [3] "Ye have not because ye ask not . . . " [4]

Just like any other part of your spiritual life, believing God can answer prayer does very little for you until, by faith, you step out and prove it. And if you do not have established prayer habits in the homeland, they will be far more difficult to organize and maintain on the mission field. Satan tries even harder to pull you away from such a ministry when you are in the thick of the battle and in his established territory.

It is a well-known fact that Amy Carmichael, that great missionary to South India, turned folks away from her door each morning—people whom we might say really needed the help she could have given, people who were hungry and sick and needed spiritual guidance—and yet Amy Carmichael felt that those morning hours spent in prayer before the Lord were worth far more than the feeble efforts she might have made to care for the needs of others when she had not spent time with her Lord.

The priority of prayer must be established and maintained. Yet it must not become a fanatical type of fetish. (Have you ever known people who had a whole day ruined if for some reason they were not able to spend two hours in prayer at the beginning of the day?) Prayer is not a charm. It is not something you have to do to maintain your salvation. It is not a matter of a short period of "Lord give me this, and Lord give

[1]James 1:5
[2]John 14:14
[3]Matthew 7:7
[4]James 4:2

me that." It should be the place of power. It should be a place of worship, praise and thanksgiving. It should be like getting your spiritual battery recharged. It should be a time of natural fellowship just as you would spend time talking to, sharing with, and listening to your dearest earthly friend. It should be a joyous time and not something to be dreaded or done away with.

If you do not enjoy prayer now, you will enjoy it less on the mission field. If you do not enter wholeheartedly into prayer with others now, you will not be especially keen on sharing others' burdens on the field. If you do not pray with your Christian brothers and sisters in the homeland, you will not find it easy to pray with your Christian brothers and sisters in the land to which you go.

Prayer is an essential part of your ministry. You cannot live or witness without it. Make a new beginning today, if necessary. It is hard work, the mind is prone to wander (praying aloud will help this), and time is at a premium, but prayer is a MUST.

Along with the prayer life must come DAILY BIBLE READING. God's Word is your message. It is a great part of the blessing you receive and the blessing you go to give. In it are the words of eternal life, and the rules for daily living. It is folly to think that the study of the Word of God in Bible School or Seminary was enough to last a lifetime except for following along in the Sunday services. No, the longer you live, the more time you should be spending with the Word. There are some who have chosen as their motto, "No Bible, no breakfast!"

You may not be going to the mission field as a preacher. You may not establish a church or churches, or be involved in a Christian education ministry. You may not be called upon to oversee a number of national pastors. And yet if your life is to be effective for Christ, and if you are to remain at peace within yourself, you cannot and must not neglect the Word of God.

Families find it more difficult to maintain a time for personal prayer and Bible reading or for FAMILY FELLOWSHIP than single folks. But it is something which must be established in the home, and it should be done NOW, or it will be doubly hard on the field—or may never be done at all.

Another matter which must be settled before you proceed to your service is that of GIFTS AND TITHING. Many missionary candidates have the impression that because their support comes from the gifts and tithes of others, there is no need to set part of this aside specifically for the work of the Lord. But what do we have in life that we have not received from others? No matter what comes into our hands, who it comes from, or how it gets there, we still owe it to the Lord to share it with Him and His work. If you find it difficult to give to the Lord at home, you will find it impossible to give to Him on the field. "But," you say, "isn't it enough that I have given my life to serve on the mission field?" No, it is not enough! Everything we are and have or ever hope to be must be committed entirely to Him. This includes our pocketbooks. "But when I receive such a little bit, how can I afford to tithe?" The question ought rather to be, "How can I afford NOT to tithe?" Have you discovered the glorious truth that you cannot outgive God? Have you found out for yourself that when you cast your bread upon the waters it comes back cake with icing? Be sure to give this aspect of your personal life a great deal of consideration now. The Old Testament insisted upon a tenth for the Lord. Should not our gifts and offerings far exceed the letter of the law? God has never been stingy with us. Is it right to be stingy with Him?

Then there are PERSONAL MATTERS to be settled. Have you ever stopped to ask yourself some of these questions:

Am I hard to get along with?

Do I have a temper?

Do I like to always have my own way?

Am I easily hurt?

Do I have feelings of instablity?

Do I basically like people and find worth in them?

Do I feel "at home" with people?

Am I concerned about people?

Can I get along with others?

Am I able to work well, even alone?

Have I had good results in witnessing?

Can I effectively deal with adults and children?

Do I love people for themselves, or only because of their spiritual condition?

Do I have a good sense of humor?

Can I laugh at myself, or only at the expense of others?

Is there anyone or anything in my life that takes precedence over God? Do I find it difficult to apologize?

Do I have a sense of perspective?

Do I stick to a job until it's finished?

Do I live a disciplined life?

Do I work well with others and share the credit with them?

Am I considerate of others?

Do I worry and fret over insignificant problems?

Do I make allowances for mistakes in others?

Is my way the only way a thing can be done?

Am I honest with myself and with others?

Am I generous?

Am I given to hospitality?

Am I jealous?

Am I a good listener?

How do I handle gossip?

Can I follow, or do I always have to be the leader?

Am I grateful or do I expect to receive more than I give?

How do I get along on a limited budget?

How do I react to sickness in myself and in others?

How do I handle stress?

What do I consider the necessities of life?

How do I see and accept myself and my abilities?

Am I forgiving?

Am I spiritually strong and stable in my faith?

Does my life genuinely show forth the fruit of the Spirit?

Although you cannot of and by yourself change your whole personality, there are areas which you can attempt to improve. But you must face the questions before you can answer them.

Perhaps even more to the point we might ask: What is my major motive for going to the mission field? Does my church expect it of me? Has my family pushed me into it? Am I trying to get away from an unpleasant situation at home? Is it an adventure? Do I have the feeling I can change the course of the universe? Do I feel it's my duty to go? Am I going because my life's partner feels called? Or am I going because of my deep love and concern for the people to whom I'm going, because God has unmistakably called me, personally, and because I am equipped to do something for the spiritual condition of those to whom I am going?

When you arrive on the field, Satan will try to question you over and over again why you are there, what you are accomplishing, and why you don't give up and go home. You must have an answer that will satisfy you and will turn away Satan at times like that. Therefore, you must carefully consider before you ever leave the homeland what your motives are for going, and then plan what your goals will be for staying.

You must never allow your mind to stagnate. Saturate it with good reading material. Keep posted concerning events in the country to which you will eventually go, and keep abreast of work in other fields. Find out what methods are being used and whether or not they are working. Seek out books which give the background and history of your people. Attend conferences and workshops which will keep you up-to-date on trends in the world of missions. If you are not interested in learning at home, you will not begin on the field.

COMMITMENT TO YOUR PASTOR AND HOME CHURCH. You may not have been fully aware of it, but individuals in the congregation of which you are a member may have a great interest in you. In some cases, they have watched you grow up in the church. In others, you have arrived on the scene more recently, but your presence has been felt—in the youth group, in the Sunday School, in the choir, in prayer meetings, or in the church as a whole. You are now receiving prayer and financial support from those who know you well. They feel a commitment to you. You must also feel a commitment to them—through your prayer ministry for them, by volunteering to serve, and by directing some of your tithes and offerings into the local church. (Being a missionary must never mean that you are no longer required to participate, financially, in the work of God.) For the spiritual benefit of all, it is essential that you maintain strong ties to your pastor and your home church.

YOU ARE A MISSIONARY TODAY. What you are today will determine largely what you will be tomorrow. And what you are as a person at home will determine mainly what you will be on the mission field. Are you content with your life as it is? Or are there some changes and improvements which you want to make to help smooth the pathway of your missionary career?

QUESTIONS—CHAPTER 4

1.   Make a list of your personal strengths and weaknesses
      a. in the spiritual realm,
      b. in the physical realm,

      c. in the psychological realm,

      d. in the educational realm, and

      e. in the moral realm.

2. How will your strengths affect your missionary service?

3. How will your weaknesses affect your missionary service?

4. Are all personal strengths good and personal weaknesses bad? Explain.

5. What specific personal considerations do you need to work on berfore going overseas?

6. Why should you be committed to your pastor and your home church? In what ways should this be done?

5
Preparation for Service Following Acceptance

Candidates who will be engaged primarily in church planting, teaching the Word, evangelizing, setting up Christian education programs and TEE among nationals, teaching in Bible Institutes and Short Term Bible Schools, coordinating the churches in one or more areas, supervising national pastors, and preaching ministries will, ordinarily, be required to obtain some Bible College and/or Seminary training in the homeland before acceptance (or are accepted with the proviso that such education be completed before the start of deputation ministry). Candidates who will engage in specific ministries associated with medicine, secretarial work, teaching, engineering, photography, administration, etc., should have a good background in Bible knowledge (formal and/or informal) as well as a degree in their particular specialty. Missionaries should be among the best trained individuals in the world. Your mission Board will, of course, set the educational standards for your ministry in accord with their own policies as well as those which may now be required by many Third World and other nations.

Apart from formal education, it should be the desire of those facing the field to become thoroughly acquainted with their Mission Board, its background, its history, its progress, where it works, who works under its auspices, its affiliation with other Christian groups, how it functions, what its policies and procedures are, what its requirements are, how much authority the leadership assumes, what part the missionary plays in the carrying forward of the administrative aspects of the work, what the support level is, what kind of schooling is available for children, benefits, retirement, insurance, health expenses. You cannot know your Mission Agency too well! Study it and be satisfied that you can work within its framework without stress, making a contribution, not criticizing, being proud of the work and the workers. Remember that no mission is entirely perfect, and even if it were, it would cease to be so when you join it!

THINGS TO DO PRIOR TO AND DURING DEPUTATION

Reading missionary biographies and literature is excellent preparation for what lies ahead. Much can be learned from the the work of others. This is what must be built upon. Knowing where others succeeded and failed can be of tremendous importance. The life stories of God's servants are stimulating, challenging, encouraging, and illuminating.

Bible and Missionary conferences should be attended, not just with the idea in mind that you may be asked to speak and thereby support might be raised. It is very possible that this may be the case, but first and foremost, attend seeking the Lord's blessing for your life, being fueled for the flight into an unknown sky, being strengthened in the inner man by the Word and power of God, and becoming excited about the opportunities for witness and the wide open doors for the Gospel to be preached in this day. You may listen to missionaries from the area to which you are assigned. You may also hear from those who are working in the homeland. It is good to hear these reports and to be reminded once again that the field is the world, and the work of a missionary is far more a vocation than a location.

You would benefit from availing yourself of the opportunity to take a correspondence course in Bible and/or in your specialty, just to keep your mind and knowledge up-to-date on these matters, to learn modern methods and procedures, and new ways of presenting old truths.

There are many short specialty courses available in most areas. A secretary may wish to brush up on shorthand, typing or bookkeeping at a local Business School; a nurse or doctor may have opportunity to attend workshops and seminars to increase knowledge and skills. Hospitals are sometimes willing to allow medical personnel the privilege of attending special courses to give them further ability and training in specific areas. It is vital that you take a day-long course in CPR (cardiopulmonary resuscitation) offered through your local hospital or the Red Cross.

Industrial experience or work in a secular setting may also be of help to some workers. Some missions require their engineers, for example, to work for a year or two in industry before going to the field, and other professional people have also benefited greatly from this type of training.

Learn about magazines which are available in your specialty and be sure these are ordered so you can keep in step with your profession while you are out of the homeland. You will be amazed at the rapidity with which things change! Stay in touch with the Christian world, too, through subscriptions to Christian magazines.

If you have children, get them started reading missionary books, or if they are younger, read missionary stories to them and try to explain about the location and probable living conditions of the country to which you are assigned.

Visit several organizations in the homeland to compare procedures and sources of information and methods of doing your particular job. If you are a doctor, visit several hospitals, ask questions, look at equipment; as a secretary, find out the latest and best office procedures, learn about machines available, do some cost analyses, learn something about computers (they are being used more and more on the field these days); make recommendations to your Board about equipment which you feel might make a contribution to the work (if it is not already available on the field). Be a detective! Always explain why you feel something should be available and how it will facilitate your particular work.

Develop a sense of mental alertness, keenness and observation. Learn some manual skills. You may have to be a fix-it man (even if you happen to be a single girl). Take up a satisfying hobby such as wood carving, sewing, stamp collecting, art, music, gardening, or any one of a hundred other things. Learn to play with people. Be a good sport. Take up sports. You will have times on the field when you will need the mental, physical and emotional recreation and stimulus which comes from play and laughter. Learn how to relax and how to help others to do so. It is good therapy. You may also discover that these types of activities can provide an "in" with the people to whom you go even though at this moment you can't imagine spending afternoons playing soccer with the fellows in the Philippines or badminton with the nurses from the hospital in Pakistan.

Learn to live with nervous tension and frustrations. How do you fare when your privacy is denied? How do you face loneliness? Find the answers. Be cheerful, patient. Humor is an essential part of your missionary life. The best humor is to laugh at yourself and your own mistakes. Learn now, before you get there, why humor should never be aimed against your fellow missionaries or nationals. That is not humor at all, and it often disguises unworthy attitudes. Develop vision. Don't live with blinders on. See your problems and your joys and your corner of the world as only one finite part of a gigantic whole. Give encouragement to those who are doing a hard job well. Develop gratitude and appreciation. Never forget Christian and common courtesy. Learn to give cheerfully of your time and of yourself. Don't take anyone for granted. Don't look down on people. Don't degrade yourself. Be strictly honest with yourself and others. You are, in truth, an Ambassador for the King of Kings. The more you learn at home, the easier it will be for you on the field.

One of the best means of learning how to witness more effectively to those in another culture is by reading books on or taking courses in cross-cultural communications, bi-culturalism, cultural anthropology and other missiological studies. A short course in linguistics might speed the learning of a new language or dialect. Several Christian colleges offer these subjects as well as other Christian organizations. Your Mission Board may direct you to such resources, or, on the other hand, request that you rely wholly upon the language study you will receive overseas.

Become acquainted with Church History, which is essentially the story of past mission work. Be sure you know your own Mission's policy regarding the establishment of churches and the way they are to be governed. You may be dealing with a church previously administered by another denominational group. Great care must be exercised in the areas of baptism, the Lord's supper, the place of women in the church, etc. Making a Church of England church into a Baptist church as soon as you arrive on the field can be confusing to the nationals and devastating to the work.

Seriously consider the advisability of taking further studies before you leave for the field, but don't use it as a delay tactic for putting off your departure. Many a nurse has realized, however, after being on the field for a few months, that she would have done well to get her Bachelor's or Master's degree in order to carry out her role properly. Other professional people may feel likewise. Even though it will delay your going to the field for another one or two years, it is far more practical to get your education now than to try to cram it into your furlough time, or have to ask for an extension of furlough or a leave of absence in order to obtain a higher degree. Inquire of your mission board as to where they expect you will be utilized in the overall sphere of your specialization. If it is in any type of supervisory or teaching capacity, question the possibility and feasibility of more training. Be sure you know any restrictions which will be placed upon you professionally in the country where you will serve. If you are in a licensed profession, maintain current, required licensure. If continuing education is a prerequisite for relicensure, be sure you know where and how to obtain it and what forms are required to report it. Do not go forth to serve without having and maintaining proper credentials.

On occasion, a mission board may request an individual to do a year of intensive internship in an established church or program. This may be under the supervision of a pastor and might consist of church visitation, working in the Sunday School, assisting the pastor in various ways, personal witnessing, etc. This is usually a prerequisite for those who have been Christians for a very short time, or those who have had very little experience in working with and witnessing to others.

If this internship can be carried out through your home church, under the direction of your pastor, it can be beneficial not only to you, but to those who will be supporting you on the field. It will allow you to spend time in a non-alien atmosphere rather than going as a stranger to an unknown community. In many ways, working among those who know you and whom you know is far more difficult than ministering to the world at large. Even Jesus stated what it would be like: "A prophet is not without honor, save in his own country, and in his own house" (Matthew 13:57). This is, of course, good training for your mission field experience.

QUESTIONS—CHAPTER 5

1. Apart from formal education, what kind(s) of experiences and/or training do you plan to become involved in before leaving for the mission field?

2. How would you plan to cope with a co-worker on the field who is unaccepting of you as a person? as a professional?

3. How do you plan to deal with individuals who have less education and experience than you do?
   a. Missionaries
   b. Nationals

4. You may be required to work with missionaries from other areas of the world who have education and experience equivalent to yours, but they have been trained to do things differently than the way you do them. How do you plan to work out those differences? (E.g., scrub room technique for doctors, spelling of words for literature workers, methods of teaching for instructors, discipline for children, forms of baptismal and wedding ceremonies for pastors).

6
Continuing Education and Life-Long Learning

When you finish high school and go out to get a job, you are a beginning practitioner. If you then go on to college and graduate **summa cum laude**, you become, again, a beginning practitioner. Then you go on for your Master's degree, and your Doctoral degree. After each step you are told at commencement, "You are now prepared to start becoming what you have been trained to be."

Life is full of beginnings, for life is ever changing and fluid. Time does not stand still for anyone. Neither does progress. So there is little hope that any person will have "attained" in one short lifetime.

Because you are ever beginning new things, new ministries, new methods of doing things, obtaining new equipment, even finding new diseases (if you are in the medical field), or finding new problems in other areas with government restrictions pressing in and legislation of one kind or another pushing down, it is absolutely imperative that the missionary of the cross of Jesus Christ be prepared at all times, not only to give a reason for the hope that lies within him, but to be the very best he can possibly be in the profession which he practices.

Today the cry we hear on every hand is for continuing education and a system of life-long learning. A Christian who becomes stagnant in his faith and practice is doomed to be left behind as he seeks to finish his course. A missionary who tries to reach today's developing countries with yesterday's means and methods is a hindrance to the onward movement of the Christian message and hope.

If you have prepared yourself as thoroughly as possible, or at least to the extent that your Mission Board has required, you are educationally ready for service overseas. But only for today. You must not end your education at this point. There is so much more to learn. And if you are to be all that you should be overseas, you must keep an open mind and heart to the whole area of learning, not only through living, but through study.

Already you are saying, but my work will keep me far too busy for any attempts at formal, or even informal, study. My responsibility is to the Christ I serve, the people who send me, and those to whom I am sent.

Exactly! That is why you must keep on top of what you are doing!

Suppose you are an engineer at a missionary radio station. You have only worked on 5,000 watt transmitters. You know your work well. You've passed every exam. You've even modified a couple of transmitters for better performance. You know what equipment is available and how it can be used. You've worked well with other engineers and technicians, and you feel professionally confident.

But now you are being sent to work overseas on 100,000 and 250,000 watt transmitters. And these will be powered by water. Will you just arrive on the scene and know what has to be done? Will you know the inner workings of those transmitters the moment you see them? Could you handle the engineering for the station if left to yourself your third day on the field? Would you know how to adapt this equipment for wider output and larger coverage? Could you modify them for specific conditions and situations? Could you repair them in a place where equipment and tools may not be readily available? Could you improvise until essential materials could arrive from the United States or Europe for repairs?

I suspect that you might have to spend some time studying to update your knowledge concerning transmitters if you are to do an effective job as an engineer.

Or suppose you are a nurse. You've had your 2, 3, 4, or 5 years course in nursing, and now you are ready to take your professional training to the mission field. Before you have finished language study, which is so essential to your ministry, you have been placed in a clinic situation. There are no lab or X-ray facilities, your medicines are limited, there is no doctor within 200 miles, and your only textbook is **Merck's Manual**. Will you be surprised when you discover your training did not include some of the information which you need right now if you are to save this mother, this child, this man? You find yourself without any of the sophisticated "tools" which were at your disposal in the homeland. Little did you dream how much you would need to know about tropical diseases, nutritional factors, the high-risk mother and infant, community health, communicable diseases, etc., etc. No one ever taught you how to tell the difference between malaria, typhoid, and typhus fever. Little did you dream that you would be called upon to do various forms of surgery if emergencies demanded it. It had never crossed your mind that you would be put constantly in a position of diagnosing and prescribing for your patients. No one taught you how to deal with 200 patients in your clinic every day, practically single-handed. You had no idea that much of your time would be spent trying to figure out improvisations for treatments and therapy which were cut and dried in the homeland. You probably never saw a patient at your home hospital lying in bed in tractions, utilizing pieces of pipe and wood from which ropes and makeshift pulleys held oil tins filled with sand or water to the desired weight of traction needed. You were not used to treating patients out in the open air where dust, flies, and other sources of germs were inevitable. Nor did you ever assist a doctor in an Operating Room where the sole responsibility of one person in that room was to "swoosh" the flies away from the operating site.

Yes, you have your certificate from an accredited School of Nursing. You have that piece of paper stating you are a Registered Nurse. Thus you are prepared for your work as a medical missionary!

Now these, of course, are illustrations which may seem to be stretching a point by taking the worst of mission field experiences and bringing it to bear upon a missionary candidate who is eagerly awaiting that day when his work will actually commence on foreign soil. Rather than argue that what has been described is more often the rule than missionaries care to admit, let this word suffice. When you arrive on your station and find these conditions, just remember: I told you so!

Now what can be done to help you—not only in orienting you to things as you'll find them, but what you can do in the midst of them? There are many resources available to you. We can only mention a few of them here, but perhaps this will encourage you to seek help before you are overwhelmed on the field.

If you will be working in the area of communications, why not consider the Program in Communications, Communications Dept., Wheaton Graduate School, Wheaton, Illinois 60187.

If you need a year of solid Bible study under competent leadership amidst refreshing Christian fellowship, consider studies in a one-year certificate Bible course offered by many Christian institutions.

If you will be utilizing your musical abilities overseas, consider a refresher week (or more) at a school offering short workshops or courses. Others may want to take a summer course in missionary radio technology, communications, missionary aviation, or in Bible or a Bible-related subject.

Some Christian colleges have a short term summer Missions program. These institutes are designed especially for missionary candidates and missionaries on furlough. Check with your denominational institutions, or with any of the many evangelical liberal arts colleges or Bible Colleges. A winter interim course may also be available to you.

Schools such as Columbia Graduate School of Bible and Missions (P.O. Box 3122, Columbia, SC 29230) offer short quarter courses in June and December each year. Though only three weeks in length, a semester's study is completed. Graduate or undergraduate credits may be earned, or courses may be audited. Subjects in cross-cultural communication skills, counseling techniques, creative writing, missions, music, Christian education, and a number of biblical studies are offered.

Columbia Graduate School also offers a program for college graduates who have no Bible training. This includes advanced study in the Scriptures, mission strategies and methods, doctrine, and other related subjects. A certificate in Bible is earned at the completion of the one-year program. (An M.A. in Bible, M.S. in Bible and M.Div. degree are also offered for those who wish to study longer than a year).

CGS also offers credit for a single, four-unit course entitled, "Perspectives on the World Christian Movement," through the Institute of International Studies (1605 Elizabeth, Pasadena, CA 91104). In 1985, this course was offered in 59 locations with thousands of students enrolled. While it is not exclusively for missionary candidates, it is an excellent foundation of understanding of the world of missions today.

For an even shorter "shot-in-the-arm" experience of Bible review, contact Walk Through the Bible (5293 N.E. 53rd, Portland, Oregon 97218). They hold one-day seminars in all areas of the country. Or if you are interested in working with young people, you might inquire into the ministry of Bill Gothard's "Basic Youth Conflicts" courses.

For those who may wish to continue their theological training, there are fine correspondence courses available from most accredited schools. Moody Bible Institute, Back to the Bible Broadcast, and other institutions offer home study courses. The Scofield Bible Study Course from Moody takes the student through the complete Bible in approximately one year. A Doctor of Ministry degree can now be earned through many seminaries. This involves short visits to the institution in most cases, while most of the work is done through correspondence and written papers.

If you are a nurse, it is essential that you keep informed about legislation which affects you. Laws have been passed in a number of states requiring every nurse to obtain a certain number of continuing education credits (the number varies with each state). In those states where continuing education is mandatory, a nurse cannot be relicensed unless she has proof of accredited continuing education credits. Since each state's laws vary, and changes are coming quickly, it is essential that every nurse be kept informed of legislation which affects her. Otherwise she may be forced home from the field because of lack of proper credentials to obtain a valid license to practice. Nurses should maintain constant contact with their Board of Nursing or State Nurses' Association concerning requirements. (When you are overseas, be sure you ask them to send any forms or information to you via airmail.)

Doctors, dentists, and allied health workers should keep in touch with their professional agencies so that they, too, will be constantly aware of legislative rulings which affect their ministries.

There may be some of you who feel the need of practical experience in Christian witness before you go on to the mission field to which you have been appointed. That type of training and many other programs are offered by Missionary Internship, Inc. (P.O. Box 457, Farmington, Michigan 48024).

For those interested in theological education by extension (TEE), contact Fuller Theological Seminary School of World Mission (135 No. Oakland Avenue Pasadena CA 91101). For courses available through Biblical Education by Extension (BEE) contact Columbia Bible College (P.O. Box 3122, Columbia, SC 29230).

If you feel learning the language of the country to which you are assigned will be one of your biggest hurdles, you might want to consider taking a program in Language Acquisition Techniques. This will not teach you the language you must learn. But it will sharpen your language learning abilities. You will practice phonetic drills which will help you recognize and produce non-English sounds. You will learn how to get the most out of language school, or to program your own language learning course. Many universities offer such programs. The Toronto Institute of Linguistics is excellent for this. Write the Institute at 25 Ballyconner Ct., Willowdale, ON, Canada M2M 4B3.

For those who would like to obtain information concerning a Christian college, contact your denominational headquarters and ask for information concerning all Christian colleges within your denomination. Or write to **Moody Monthly Magazine** requesting a copy of their issue listing the major Bible Schools, colleges, and Seminaries in the United States and Canada. You may also wish to contact the American

Association of Bible Colleges (P.O. Box 1523, Fayetteville, AR 72702). They can put you in contact with over 100 accredited Bible Schools and Colleges.

The Alliance School of Theology and Missions (Nyack, New York 10960) offers a 2-year course leading to the Master of Professional Studies degree. This is a post-baccalaureate program consisting of 10 months of full-time resident study on campus, with a second year of experience in Christian ministry, concluding with a ministry-centered research project. Missionary candidates are encouraged to apply. Trinity Evangelical Divinity School, Wheaton College, and Fuller School of World Mission also offer postgraduate courses leading to an M.A. in Missiology or Applied Ministries.

One of the most widely felt needs on the mission field is the desire of nationals to learn English. The ability to teach English to people for whom it is a foreign tongue is not automatic just because your mother tongue is English. TESOL (Teaching English to Speakers of Other Languages) is a needed field of study. At this writing, an excellent program, offering a Certificate in TESOL and also an M.A. degree (often essential, especially for tentmakers) is the William Carey International University, currently the only Christian school offering the M.A. degree in TESOL. (Contact the Institute of International Studies, 1605 Elizabeth St., Pasadena, CA 91104).

These are just a few of hundreds of opportunities for you to obtain further and/or continuing education, as well as keeping up in your profession. And we have only made mention of a few of our Christian resources. Let's not forget to take advantage of that which is offered to us by the community. Fire and police departments often offer excellent courses in CPR; the Red Cross offers courses and refreshers in First Aid and Life Saving; professional organizations offer workshops/seminars/retreats conferences in your specific field of interest; colleges and universities offer evening sessions,continuing education, and course offerings in your area of professional concern.

But knowing such programs exist will be of no benefit to you unless you become involved in them. Adult and continuing education programs are available. Their content differs. Their prices vary, as do their requirements. But there is something for you if you look for it. (And there are often grants or scholarships available to those who need them).

As a servant of Christ, you must be prepared to the very highest of your capabilities. The governments of the developing countries of the world are now looking for leaders, supervisors, managers, administrators, and teachers who can pass their expertise on to national leadership. It is very possible that the extent of your previous and continuing education will determine the amount of time you will have to minister in the country to which you are dedicating your life. Never stop learning, for when you do, you will stop growing. Without growth there can be little satisfaction in one's own life, or much of significance to offer others. And, unfortunately, when growth ceases, atrophy sets in.

When you get to the field, it will not be easy to keep updated in your field of practice. But don't forget to subscribe to professional journals, ask for textbooks to be sent out, keep in touch through correspondence courses, ask your mission leaders to arrange for a management seminar, nurses' workshop, Christian education conference—at least once every two years, when those with expertise in their field are invited from the homeland to update their colleagues overseas. If you are in an urban setting, it might be possible and a fine learning experience to take a course, or sharpen a skill by attending a local university. For those in rural settings, you must make time to read literature and journals, or listen to cassette tapes related to your avenue of service.

Two journals of particular value to evangelical missionaries are **Evangelical Missions Quarterly** ($11.95, EMIS, Box 794, Wheaton, IL 60187) and the **International Journal of Frontier Missions** ($15.00, Frontier Missions, P.O. Box 40638, Pasadena, CA 91104).

No matter where you are, who you are, or what your age, there will be an area of service where you will be a beginning practitioner. Learn your lesson well, and keep on learning until there is nothing more to learn. This is the responsibility of each one who wants to be a witness in the world in which he lives. Professional guesswork and staunch Christian faith cannot abide under the same banner.

QUESTIONS—CHAPTER 6

1. How do you plan to keep up-to-date in your profession while you serve overseas?

2. What is your understanding of the term, "continuing education?"

3. What is your understanding of the term, "life-long-learning?"

4. Is it necessary to study the Bible formally after obtaining a Bible College education? Why?

5. Are continuing education and life-long-learning important in whatever ministry you undertake? List those ministries which are excluded.

7
Developing Financial and Prayer Support

In what follows, we are especially focusing upon the deputation ministry of those missionaries who will not be salaried (as are many who serve with denominational mission boards) but who face the prospect and challenge of "raising their own support." Don't be confused, however. All missionaries must be diligent in deputation or the cause of missions will suffer.

Immediately following your acceptance, with the approval of your Board or Agency, you will want to begin lining up friends and meetings in order to present your testimony and the work in which you will be engaged. Even though you may have another year of Bible School, work experience, professional training, college, or Graduate School to complete, it is best to get started with deputation work immediately. This not only gives you a longer time to make yourself known to friends and churches, but as funds come into your account, it helps with the outgoing expenses which, of necessity, cause a heavy drain on your account at the time you leave for your field of service. It also helps you to get involved in the work of being a missionary right where you are, and keeps you enthusiastic about your future ministry as you share it with others.

The most important place to begin asking for deputation meetings and speaking engagements is in your home church, in the churches of your closest friends, and where you are known best. Although in many ways, your home church area is the hardest place you will ever have to speak, it is a place where you will often find folks most sympathetic to your calling and ambition. It is at least a starting place to get your feet off the ground in this difficult, yet joyous and rewarding task of deputation.

But where do you go from your home church? Or perhaps your home church does not favor your decision. Or perhaps, as a member of a "Faith Mission Board" you cannot be supported by your denominational church. Or having been saved through a non-congregational ministry, you have never become a member of a local congregation. How do you find opportunities to present your work?

Let's list a few possible areas where meetings may be obtained:

1. Your pastor may have friends in the ministry who would be willing to give you a hearing in their congregations.

2. If there is an Evangelical Ministers' Association in your area, contact the pastors within this group.

3. Your Bible College Alumni Association will have a list of pastors which they will share with you, by area.

4. Friends in other areas may invite you to their church or school.

5. Never overlook the possibility of interviews on radio, television,newspaper, and other media.

6. Daily Vacation Bible Schools may be willing to present you as their missionary project.

7. Rotary Clubs, Girl Scouts, Boy Scouts, Lions Clubs and other civic, social and community groups may ask you to speak. Additional contacts are usually made through these channels.

8. You may be invited to present a class in a public/ private/ Christian school on the history, geography, or culture of the country to which you are going.

9. Meetings are often held in homes where interested folks gather in small groups to hear you. Or you could invite them to **your** home, or suggest having a meeting in theirs.

10. Many camps and conferences utilize missionary speakers during the summer, and are willing to make a project of giving to a missionary candidate. (In some areas of the country there are also winter and/or year-round conferences which might be available to you.)

11. Become aware of missionary conferences to be held in churches in your area. Present yourself to these churches. Many times they are seeking those whom they can support. And if they do not pledge financial support, often much prayer support is gained.

12. If your mission has deputation/regional representatives, be sure to contact them for meetings when you are to be in their area. (Be sure to give them as much lead time as possible.)

13. Even if your Board does not have representatives appointed to help with deputational contacts, it is very possible they will share with you the names of churches from their mailing and donor lists.

14. Obtain telephone directories from your local phone company for cities and towns you wish to visit. The yellow pages will list the churches in the area.

15. Seek out possible opportunities to speak at Home Bible Study classes and/or prayer groups.

16. City and large town newspapers usually carry a church page once each week, and smaller town papers will carry this in their weekly issue. Churches in the area are almost always listed.

17. Contact the Chamber of Commerce in areas where you plan to travel, and ask that they send you a list of churches in their area.

18. Denominational groups often support candidates and missionaries who serve with other mission societies. Request a copy of their denominational yearbook. This will give you the name and address and pastor of each church within that denominational group.

19. Speak at mission prayer group meetings at your Bible College or Seminary.

20. Seek out those who are involved in setting up youth rallies, or who teach Child Evangelism Good News Clubs or Week-day Bible Clubs, and ask for an opportunity to present yourself and your field.

21. If you are involved in a secular job, be sure to enthusiastically proclaim your plans to fellow-workers.

After obtaining the names of churches and groups that might be interested in utilizing you in a meeting, write a personal letter to each one asking if there is a possibility that you could present your testimony and your work at their convenience, or when it would be mutually convenient. If you must send a form letter, be sure to include at least a short personal note at the close.

This letter should include the following:

1. Your full name and where you can be reached.

2. Give complete details concerning what you plan to present in your meeting.

3. Mention the types of meetings at which you are prepared to speak (morning service, evening service, mid-week prayer meeting, ladies' meeting, men's club, Sunday school, children's churches, Junior or Senior High young people, Pioneer Ministries, special meetings, etc.)

4. If you have slides, tapes, films, visual aids, literature, posters, displays, curios, or other "props," be sure to mention what is available and ask what they might like for you to arrange to use.

5. Offer at least two dates when you would be available to speak.

6. Be sure to give adequate information concerning the Mission of which you are a member, where you expect to serve, and what type of work you will be doing. (Some work has more appeal to one church or group or area than another.)

7. Enclose a piece of general literature from your mission.

8. If you have prayer cards, enclose one.

Always enclose a stamped self-addressed envelope with your letter of request. Use Mission letterhead stationery if it is available to you. (This makes your request more "official.")

It is often true that you receive surprisingly few responses. Don't become discouraged with this. No matter how few places you may speak, or how few people may attend the meeting, BE ENTHUSIASTIC. And keep contacting other groups. You will be encouraged, too, when you receive requests from various groups. Some candidates are requested by so many that outgoing support and expenses are raised with very little correspondence being necessary. A few are fully supported by their home church. Most face the challenge of extended efforts, working long and hard at deputation with infrequent results. Do not, however, just sit back and expect invitations to come to you. Diligently seek them out.

After you have received word from a church, group or individual concerning a meeting date, be sure to acknowledge this promptly in writing and reveal definite plans.

As a basic matter of faith, you cannot succeed if you are merely out for money. A basic purpose in your deputation is to minister to people. Unless absolutely essential, never turn away an opportunity to present the challenge of Christian missions and the work of your ministry to a group of people interested enough to invite you. You will be amazed and thrilled to see where God has placed His people. YOUR SUPPORT WILL USUALLY COME FROM THE MOST UNEXPECTED PLACES. Friends and churches you had depended upon may not be the source of God's supply for you. A meeting with one person has often been rewarded by substantial prayer and/or financial support.

On the other hand, as much as possible, work in one geographical area at a time. Cross-country hops are both time and money consuming. Unless especially invited by those who offer support beforehand, pray earnestly before traveling great distances (over 200 miles) for a single meeting.

As you build up a list of interested friends, they will, normally form four distinct categories:

1. An inner circle of prayer supporters (those with whom you will share problems and joys in a personal way).

2. Financial supporters (those who will pledge monthly or annual support).

3. Those who have a general interest in you.

4. Those who have a general interest in your Mission Board.

Some of these categories may overlap, of course.

There is a possibility that you could volunteer your services in local churches, helping organize a visitation program, visiting the sick, teaching a home Bible study group, or assisting the pastor. In this way you will become known by these people and you will be able to minister to their spiritual needs. But, again, do not offer such assistance to a body of believers with the sole hope of gaining financial support from them.

Some of you may be in an internship program and have already been promised your support by a church. Or your home church may have promised to supply all or most of your needs. It is still essential for you to speak to other groups and gain their interest in you and your work. Again, consider it a ministry to them and a privilege to have them share your prayer burdens. Don't deny them the possibility of having a part in your work. Also, if you are supported by individuals in a church, there is a possibility that you may need help from others in the future. An additional child in the family, the death of a supporter, or an increase in the field allowance will mean more funds will be required. The more widely you are known and prayed for, the more concern they will have for you when you face additional needs.

You may not be a member of an organized church, but have been deeply involved in one or more para-church organization(s), (e.g., Campus Crusade, Inter-Varsity, Navigators, home Bible study groups). It is highly desirable (and often a requirement by a Mission Board) that you become involved as a member of a local church. Although you are a member of **the** Church in the broad sense of the word, having the fellowship, concern, and personal interest of a specific local congregation upon whom you can call for counsel and support is appropriate. An organized church often provides more long-term stability and discipline for an individual than other types of Christian communities. In congregational life there may be more continuity and indepth teaching on major Bible themes. People may be more in focus with the world as a whole and maintain a vigilance over the candidate, to a degree not available through either very large or very small para-church organizations. Ideally authority and accountability will be maintained, and the discipline of the church practiced, to back up the candidates's lifestyle and vision.

It is difficult to be a church planter, for example, if one does not, himself, have roots in a local church. It may be difficult to convince believers overseas to become involved in an organized church if you do not feel a need for such affiliation. All of this may be difficult for the candidate to understand until he has worked overseas and has had to consider all factors concerned with witnessing, church growth, and training leaders for the national church. But it is important to give such things serious consideration before you leave for the field. Furthermore in many instances you may not be invited to speak in a church if you are not in some official way related to a local church.

QUESTIONS—CHAPTER 7

1. What steps would you take in order to obtain your necessary support, equipment, and outgoing expenses?

2. Write a sample letter to be used when requesting an invitation to speak concerning your missionary future in a church where you are not known.

3. If an individual from a church you are visiting invites you to be his dinner guest, what 10 major topics will you mention to him concerning your calling, your present ministry, and your future missionary service?

4. Why is it important for you, as a missionary candidate, to be a member of a local church?

5. How should you, as an accepted candidate, handle the situation if you are a member of a very liberal, non-mission minded church and can expect neither prayer nor financial support from this group?

8
Preparing For and Presenting your Meetings

There will come a day when you receive an invitation to speak at your first deputational meeting. You may have mixed emotions. You will be glad for the opportunity, and you will be wondering what to say and do. Let's glance at some guidelines:

There are several things you should NOT do:

. . . Do not give a Bible Study

. . . Do not preach

. . . Do not try to be something you are not

. . . Do not run down other missions or missionaries

. . . Do not try to tell everything you know

. . . Do not give the impression you have given up everything worthwhile in life in order to become a missionary

. . . Do not be apologetic in your approach

. . . Do not plan to speak for more than 20-30 minutes (unless specifically requested to do so)

A presentation may be far more difficult in your home church than in one where you are not known. Those in your home church know you! This has advantages and disadvantages! Usually, however, you can be much less formal and explain your plans in more intimate detail as you speak to those who are your friends, relatives, and close acquaintances.

If you are speaking in a church that knows you well and has been following the Lord's leading in your life, it may not be necessary to give your experience concerning your "call" to missionary service. But in places where you are not so well known, the best way to acquaint people with you and your work is by way of your personal testimony. (Be sure to prepare as carefully to give your testimony as you will to present in other ways.)

Since, in most cases, you have not visited your field of service, you will not be able to give detailed reports of that which is happening on the field. You cannot show your personal slides of your work. You can merely quote facts and stories which have come down to you from someone else. Although these can be used very effectively by some, others are not at all good along this line. On the other hand, you may have been raised on the mission field, or served as a "short-termer" and this, of course, will provide you with greater knowledge and ability to share your future ministry.

A personal testimony is your very own. No one can give or take this from you. It is a way of sharing the Lord with others, and giving an opportunity to folks to see that the Lord has led you step by step. It allows you the privilege of communicating your salvation experience to English-speaking people before you have to do the more difficult task of giving this witness to people of a different language.

Perhaps your mission board has loaned you a set of slides, or a film depicting the work to which you will be going. A friend in the mission may have loaned you pictures. Or you may have been a short-term worker on the field and have your own slides. Be sure, at any rate, that you understand the work which is presented in this way. Make sure you can answer questions which may be raised from such a presentation. Know the names of the missionary personnel with whom you will be serving. Be sure you view and review the slides several times before presenting them in public. If you have questions, write or call your mission for answers.

Preparation is your key to success. It is easy to think that giving your testimony requires no prior consideration. This is not true. Although a testimony belongs to you, and you alone, it is not merely a recital of "I did this, I did that, I went here, I went there, and all of a sudden here I am going to the mission field." A testimony is far more than a life history. It is, in fact, a Psalm of praise and a witness to the fact of God's working in your life. It is not YOU at all, but HIM. It is not a false pretense of attributing to Him what you have done, but a life lived so completely in harmony with Him that unknowingly it has been His life lived through you. Your testimony must never leave people feeling sorry for you, or stir people in such a way that they remember only an emotion. Their emotions will be involved, of course, if you have been saved out of the drug culture, or out of deep moral degradation. But your words must always direct the hearer to the Lord Jesus Christ and what He is able to do in a life that is committed to Him. People WILL remember you, but they should always be pointed to the Savior. A word of warning here, too. Never add to your testimony details which are not pertinent, not true, or not revelatory of God's leading in your life.

Many missionary candidates miss out on opportunities for soul winning in their deputation meetings because they focus attention on themselves rather than on the Lord. A true testimony not only shares what Christ has done for you, but what He can do for each one who is present in the meeting. Missionary work begins in your very first meeting. Don't miss out on these occasions by presenting yourself instead of the Lord. And yet remember—DON'T PREACH UNLESS YOU'VE BEEN REQUESTED TO DO SO! Pray that God will help in this delicately balanced presentation.

With these things in mind, be sure to plan for every minute of your first meeting. If you are given 30 minutes, plan for 29 and be through in 29! This will please both pastor and people and may provide an opportunity for a return visit. NEVER RUN OVER THE TIME ALLOTTED TO YOU. Have a goal when you speak. Don't cover everything in one meeting.

Preparing for a 30-minute presentation is not nearly so difficult as preparing for a 5-minute spot. Never despise the little time given to you. But be sure you have in mind exactly what you want to give and how you are going to present it. To be sure, you cannot give your testimony, a history of your mission, tell what you will be doing on the field, and be assured that people will take in all that you say. But dwell on one fact. Make sure this one aspect is clearly in the minds of your listeners when you are through.

If you have planned on a 15-minute film or slide presentation in the 30 minutes available to you, be absolutely certain that you have an alternate 15-minute presentation to fill this spot in the event the lights should fail, the projector jams, or your bulb burns out. Such situations can be disastrous if you do not have an alternate plan!

Humor is not out of place on the platform. Illustrations have their place, also. It is true, however, that people will sometimes leave a service remembering only a joke that was told, or a cute story which illustrated your main point, and for the very life of them they can remember little else of what you have tried to get across to them.

Be spontaneous in your presentation. NEVER READ YOUR TESTIMONY. If you have notes, be sure to refer to them sparingly, and do be careful not to spill them on the floor!

Each time you speak you should say things in a different way. Don't become stereotyped. Don't speak by rote. Be enthusiastic. Your own enthusiasm will, many times, determine the response of your congregation. We hear much about the "enthusiasm of youth." Older folks warm up to this type of presentation. It takes them back to the days when they, too, were "on fire" for the Lord and His work. Many of them may have cooled off through the years, and your presence may well be the spark that ignites them to once again serve the Lord with vigor. (And what pastor wouldn't be pleased to have ten people become enthusiastic about teaching Sunday School, or providing transportation for DVBS, or praying, or volunteering for work in Pioneer Ministries, Awana Club or the Church Library?) Just make sure your enthusiasm is based on reality, and not just something you have manufactured along the way. If the work to which you have been called does not thrill you, perhaps you need to reconsider your call, or at least your attitude toward it.

There are other things which you may want to take into consideration as you prepare for those first meetings. Are you musical? Perhaps you will want to provide a musical selection during the time allotted to you. Are you a chalk artist? It might be good to illustrate your talk, or provide a short example of what you expect to be doing on the field.

Of course you will take into consideration the group of people to whom you are speaking. Your presentation to a Junior Church group should differ considerably from that given to an adult prayer meeting.

For some of you, the very thought of deputation meetings will be almost more than you can bear. Being shy by nature, introverted, not used to speaking in public, insecure—the task looks gigantic and impossible. Perhaps you are going to the field as an engineer, secretary, or mechanic. You may think that people will not be as interested in you as they are in those who are going to work in a hospital, an orphanage, or in "down-country" village evangelism. But YOU ARE THE ONE WHO CAN MAKE THE DIFFERENCE. Be yourself. Exalt the Lord. And "with God, nothing is impossible." (And if it is any encouragement to you, sometimes the poorest platform personnel are really the best missionaries). Don't despair. Don't give up before you begin. Don't let your enthusiasm wane. God has given you a job to do which cannot be done by anyone else. Is this not sufficient cause for sharing it, even if the words come haltingly?

Along with a very thorough preparation for your first meeting is the most important ingredient for your presentation. We are speaking of PRAYERparation. Time spent in prayer is never wasted. Dependence upon Him and gratefulness to Him can tremendously magnify the effectiveness of your presentation. Commit your way unto Him, and He WILL bring it to pass. He WILL guide you with His eye as you look "full in His wonderful face." Prayer not only makes your presentation effective, but it can pave the way for the working of the Spirit of God in your meetings.

In the case of married couples and those with families, it must be decided whether both you and your wife will speak during the time allotted to you, or if one of you will do the speaking for the family. It will depend upon whether you are to have one meeting at a given group or church, or if there will be other opportunities. Some folks have found it effective to introduce their children in the meeting, and if a musical team can be formed, a song sung in the language of the people to whom you are going can be most effective. But NEVER FORCE YOUR CHILDREN TO PERFORM IN PUBLIC.

Be prepared for the unexpected. You must always have a backup program for your services. And you must have a few extra messages up your sleeve, for you will often be asked to speak at several meetings rather than just the one for which you were requested. Or perhaps there are several speakers and when they get to you, your time has diminished from 15 minutes to 2 minutes! You will surely panic in such a situation if you have never thought of the possibility of it.

Preparation should take into consideration this important fact: Not only should you tell people what YOU want them to know. Be sure you tell them what THEY want to know.

In many churches you will be "competing" with other missionaries for a hearing, either those already supported by the church, or other candidates passing through. Only by "being yourself" and presenting an honest picture can you hope that the group will remember you.

It is best to have your own projection equipment available in the event the church is not prepared for you. Plan to arrive at least 15 minutes before meeting time. If your family will be with you, be sure to inform the church in the event they want to provide meals and/or accomodations. (Always indicate the ages and sex of the children.) Plan how you will set up your display table and request this facility in your correspondence. If you will need an electrical outlet available for your display, be sure to mention that before you arrive.

Occasionally you will run into a church which has split or is having inner disputes. Stay absolutely neutral in these situations. Do not side with factions. Do not talk about other members of the congregation. Do not become involved in church difficulties.

Some Mission Boards request, and/or candidates believe, that financial needs should NOT be mentioned in public. This is understandable, and the candidates should stand by their board and their own conscience in this matter. You will, however, find that people will ask you specific questions. What is your total monthly support need? How much do you presently need? How much will be needed for your outgoing expenses? Are there special items or equipment or machinery which you still need? These questions, and others directed to you, should be answered as thoroughly and candidly as the person desires. Money cannot be ignored or rejected. Outright advertising of specific needs, however, may be against the policies of your Board. Be sure to clarify this point with your Home Office before you begin your deputation ministry.

Always be courteous and considerate in the homes where you are entertained. Don't impose on your host or hostess. Offer to help with their work. Send a note of appreciation to all who have provided hospitality or help for you.

The prayer support obtained during your ministry is essential. Some groups will pray; others will give financially. Both are necessary.

Deputation work is not merely a matter of speaking in a great number of churches to try to raise funds to build up your account. Each individual contact is important. Be interested in the people and their outreach and ministry. Never act as though you have come to give sacrificial service just to obtain an offering. If this is your goal, you will not be blessed or be a blessing in your ministry.

Some of you may be very outspoken and opinionated. You will have to learn how to express yourself and to present your needs in such a way that you will not offend those to whom you speak.

If you have been called to missionary service in middle-age, or even in retirement, you may find it difficult to fulfill your deputational requirements. You may have worked for many years and been fully self-supporting and independent all your life. Now you will be dependent upon others. Remember always that what we have comes from the Lord. We may earn it as a farmer, storekeeper, businessperson, or secretary. But it comes from the Lord. And now, even though your salary will be provided by individuals who may or may not know you, it comes from the Lord as His provision for you. There is only one financial resource for Christians. Your supporters will need to trust the Lord for His provision, and you, too, must trust Him to provide for you—and not be unduly concerned about the source of that supply on the human level.

QUESTIONS—CHAPTER 8

1. You have just been accepted for missionary service among the Kew Tee people of Lower Watta with the Upward and Onward Mission. You will be involved in team evangelistic efforts. Write an outline for a 15-minute deputational presentation for a prayer meeting in your home church.

2. Describe six ways you could present your future service to a group of teenaged young people. (Do not include the straight lecture method).

3. What facts should be kept in mind when utilizing humor in your presentations?

4. In what ways is your deputation ministry good training for your years of ministry overseas?

9
Form Letters

The term "prayer letter" was apparently coined to designate form letters sent out by missionaries in which various facts were mentioned as prayer items on the part of those who received this correspondence. Perhaps the broader term, "newsletter" would be more appropriate today since most missionaries try to give items of interest about their field, their work and their family along with definite requests for prayer and praise. This does not take away from the importance of prayer, but rather gives those on your mailing list a more "in-depth" look at your work so they might catch a bit of the flavor of your ministry, and thus be able to pray even more effectively for the requests that you will bring before them. Your first letter will probably be sent at the time of your acceptance for missionary service or immediately thereafter.

The simplest, and LEAST personal way of keeping in touch with folks is by means of the periodic printed letter. Even so, it is a necessity to get this word into the hands of those who are interested in you. It should be as personal as you can make it, for in many cases, it will take the place of the personal letter you do not or cannot write.

The following matters should be determined before you sit down to write your prayer letters:

1. What should be included in the letter?

2. How often should it be sent?

3. To whom should it be sent?

4. What should it accomplish?

5. Why is it important?

6. What format should I use?

7. Should pictures be included?

Set goals for your letters. Aim for a unity throughout. Make your letters unique. Make them attractive. Make them meaningful. Avoid vague and general statements and the use of foreign words unless pertinent and interpreted. Make them concise. Be careful of grammar and spelling. Use pictures, maps, illustrations and/or line drawings where feasible. Determine whether or not you will send them to unsaved friends.

Your letter should be something that your friends, supporters and acquaintances will look forward to receiving. People are far too busy to wade through two or three pages of material which is so full of meat that it hardly contains paragraphs. Condense your material into bite-size pieces. Line drawings can often produce more of an impact than a full page of solid print. A photograph in print gives impact to what you write. (This is more true if YOU are in the picture.) Be sure to leave plenty of "white space" on your letter. Use word pictures so that reader can "see" where you are and what you are doing. Try to avoid typographical errors. If at all possible, have your letters printed (offset press) or mimeographed. You might also have them photocopied or run off as a computer print-out. To be read, they must be neat, attractive, and clearly printed.

Avoid beginning your letter with a verse of Scripture. The unsaved are not interested. The saved pass over it, assuming they know it already. Scripture verses may be utilized in the body of the letter as necessary and meaningful—and are far more effective in the natural flow of the letter.

Rather than a normal letter-like circular, you might want to use a newspaper style with various headings, or a journal, or a diary. In some cases a letter within an outline is very effective. (The map of Africa or South America, for example, is excellent for this type of presentation). Or for special letters you may want to write in the shape of a Christmas tree, cross, wedding bell, or heart. If you have time and a way with words, try a poetic letter now and again—rhymed or in free verse.

Remember that before any of the material you have labored long hours to produce has been read, the appearance of your letter will determine its ultimate effectiveness.

You are not limited to black print on white paper. Colored stock makes a better impression with people than white even though the cost may be slightly higher. Use a good quality of paper. If you are mimeographing both sides of a single sheet, use a heavy enough paper so that the print doesn't show through. Printed letters should never be on less than 20# paper. Because of weight limitations, if you are sending them from overseas, you will not want to use a weight heavier than 24#.

Your letters are not for the purpose of preaching a sermon. This can be done in personal letters if you feel led to do so. But the prayer or newsletter should contain information concerning you, your mission, your work, and the part that those who receive your letters can have in your ministry by prayer.

When you mention prayer requests, especially specific prayer for meetings or special campaigns, exams, or definite events, be sure that those dates are still pertinent by the time your people receive the letters. There is nothing more frustrating that being asked to pray for a meeting that was held the previous month. Always follow up your prayer requests in later letters by giving answers which have been given to specific requests.

Don't let your letters sound like a form letter! Make them personal and intimate, as though each one of your readers were the only one receiving the letter. To make them even more personal, add a handwritten note to each one, or at least sign them personally (unless an individual or a church has volunteered to send them out for you). Occasionally give information as to where changes of address can be sent. Whenever it is humanly possible, it is best for you to send your letters personally. Even when you are on the field this is a good practice if the regulations of the country in which you find yourself allow you to do so. In letters sent from overseas, you will, of course, omit any reference to politically or religiously sensitive subjects. Censorship still exists, and the very presence of missionaries in that country may be at stake according to the information which is sent to the homeland.

For those who feel they need special help in the area of writing readable and meaningful letters, be sure to purchase one or more of the books on writing listed in the bibliography at the end of this book. Let a friend read your letter and ask for helpful comments.

As a point of interest, if you plan to send your prayer letters from the field, be sure to use a stamp or stamps from your country on the envelope. There is nothing more devastating than to receive a letter from a foreign country that has been run through a stamp machine, especially if the individual is an avid stamp collector. A real stamp on the envelope sets your letter apart from others and makes it unique. It is a curiosity arouser, and thus it stands to reason that the addressee will be more apt to open the flap and pull out the letter. If he's gotten that far, it's a cinch he will open the letter and at least glance through it.

And if you have made your letter attractive and readable—and included a picture or two, he will take the time to enjoy it, and, in fact, will look forward to receiving the next one. This is true of letters mailed in the homeland, also. Use commemorative stamps rather than ordinary postage or machine stamps.

A family picture should be included at least once a year. You know how quickly the children change, and how anxious everyone is to see that the mission field has not drawn away every ounce of physical beauty and stamina from you! For single folks, it is always well to include a picture of yourself in some aspect of your work—at least once a year.

Less than three or four prayer letters sent each year cannot keep the interest of people focused on you. Keep in mind for future reference that a small token souvenir enclosed in your letter sent from the field will produce far more interest than you can imagine. Send a snapshot, postcard, bookmark, clipping from your local newspaper in the national language, a few cancelled stamps. Inexpensive, but thoughtful.

How do you build up your letter list? This will vary with individual preference. Some missionaries send a newsletter to every friend, relative, and acquaintance with whom they come into contact. Others send only a few letters, just to supporting churches and individuals. There are several ways of building your list:

1. Close family friends and relatives.

2. Obtain lists of individuals in your home church who want to receive your news.

3. When in new churches, leave mimeographed request sheets on the display or literature table, mention them, and allow people to sign up to receive your letters.

4. Announce in your meetings that if people want your letter, they should speak to you personally.

5. In supporting churches, ask the pastor how many copies he feels can be prayerfully utilized. (Some will want permission to copy your letter, or have you send enough letters so they can be placed in each Sunday bulletin—others will simply want one to tack on a bulletin board).

6. Prayer groups at your Bible College or Seminary.

7. Home Bible study and prayer groups you have visited.

8.   Professional colleagues, neighbors, and other acquaintances who specifically request that you send them.

At least once every two years, send a card asking people to return it if they want to be taken off your mailing list. DON'T OBLIGATE PEOPLE TO CONTINUE RECEIVING YOUR LETTERS. Give them this opportunity to be removed from your mailing list.

Be sure to put your FULL name and address and your mission name and address on the bottom of each letter. Not everyone on your list will know these facts, and this is especially important if you marry on the field.

If a friend or organization in the homeland is going to send out your letters for you, be sure they keep you informed of address changes. You should have an up-to-date list in your possession at all times. It is preferable to send letters by first class mail, but this will depend upon the size of your mailing list and the amount of financial burden you can underwrite for this project. Bulk mailings will be less expensive, but if this method of distribution is chosen, your letters will be demoted to the category of "junk" mail.

Always send a copy of your finished letter to the Home Office. Some Boards will require you to have your letter o.k.'d by them before you are allowed to mail it. The Home Director or Field Director is responsible for this detail in most instances. Check with your Home Office concerning specific regulations in this regard.

Usually your Home Office is not equipped to handle the mailing of your newsletters. They would, however, be appreciative of names and addresses of those from your list who might like to receive general mailings from the mission.

Try to confine your letter to one page. Long letters lose readers.

Newsletters are usually a personal expense or work support item. There is a great deal of work involved in getting out a mailing. Unless you are paying an organization to do this for you, be sure to send a word of special appreciation to the church or friend(s) who may be carrying on this ministry for you each time a letter goes out. If you are mailing your own, don't hold up letters for a month or two thinking you will have time to write a personal note on them. Send the form letters and try to follow up with special friends or supporters with a note or postcard at your earliest convenience. But be courteous enough to write "Thanks for your support" on every letter you send to a financial or prayer supporter. Many a missionary has lost his support because of an oversight in expressing gratitude.

QUESTIONS—CHAPTER 9

1. What types of format can be utilized for your prayer/newsletters?

2. What are the advantages and disadvantages of each type?

3. Write out a sample prayer letter you might write a month before you leave for your specific service in Lima, Peru.

4. Why is it important to write personal letters to friends and supporters even if they receive your regular prayer/newsletters?

5. How will you build up a list of those who receive YOUR prayer/newsletter?

6. Why is it important that your full name and address, and the name and address of your Mission Board be printed on every prayer/newsletter you send out?

10
Prayer Cards

A picture is worth far more than words. Those who have met you recently, those who may have been impressed during your one meeting in their church, those who are most apt to forget you because they know you the least—these are the ones who will appreciate having a reminder of the one for whom they are praying and in whom they are interested. (Of course your friends and relatives will want to tack you to a world map or put you on the refrigerator door with a magnet.)

Although some missionary candidates feel that much money is wasted on prayer cards, it would seem that this is not an accurate assessment. It is true that many prayer cards are disposed of in various ways, either immediately upon arrival in a strange home, or shortly thereafter. But if only one in ten, or one in twenty produces a more sincere prayer burden for you, it is an inexpensive piece of literature.

How do you go about preparing the prayer card? First of all, let's consider the essential items that MUST be included on it:

1. Your picture
2. Your name
3. Your address (either home or field—or both)
4. The Mission's name
5. The Mission's address
6. Where you will be serving

Other factors are entirely up to you. For example:

1. Do you want a family picture?
2. Do you want to include the names of the children?
3. Do you want to include a map?
4. Do you want to use a line sketch drawing which will indicate at a glance the type of ministry in which you will be engaged?

5. Do you want the card printed in one color, two colors, full color?

6. Would you prefer to use colored stock with black ink?

7. Do you want white stock with black or colored ink?

8. Do you want heavy stock, light stock, coated stock?

9. Do you want a wallet size, bookmark type, folder (2-or 3-fold), special cut (e.g., nurse's cap, praying hands), formal invitation type, flat type with no flaps, printed on one side or both?

10. Do you want to include a Scripture verse?

11. How much can you plan to spend for these cards?

12. Where will they be printed?

13. How many will you need?

Your prayer card should identify YOU and YOUR ministry. It should not be so large that it will not fit in a Bible, or on a map of the world. It should not be so small that it will become easily misplaced. It should not be gaudy, but in good taste, and colorful enough and attractive enough to be a true prayer reminder. It should be distinct. It must be printed well.

Before designing your layout, art work and color, set down on paper or in your mind the goals you want to reach by distribution of these reminders. Once you have decided these basic factors, locate a printer who is willing to help you choose the card which will be best suited to your particular needs. After you have outlined to the printer (or the artist, if you have opportunity to work through a professional) just what you want your card to communicate, be sure to determine approximately how many cards you will want printed. (Once set up for printing, large quantities may not be as expensive as you had anticipated.) Always insist on the highest quality of work.

The next question is the matter of distributing these cards.

Again, this is a personal choice and there is no "right" way of distribution. There are many ways, however, in which these cards may be used:

1. You may want to enclose one in a letter telling of your acceptance for missionary service.

2. You may wish to put them on a literature table at your deputation meetings and let individuals take one if they desire.

3. You may want to wait until your second or third newsletter before sending a card to your mailing list.

4. You may want to enclose a card with each letter you send to churches requesting meetings.

5. You may choose to enclose one with each thank you letter to those who contribute to your account at meetings, or those who provide hospitality for you along the way.

6. Churches where you have spoken may request a quantity for distribution.

7. You may have a sign-up sheet at the back of the churches where you speak so that if a prayer card is wanted, you will have the opportunity of sending one in the mail at a later date. (This, of course, serves the purpose of renewing a contact with a very casual acquaintance.)

8. You may decide to give them only to your supporters.

9. You might ask your pastor if you could enclose them in each bulletin on a given Sunday.

10. You might want to send them to arrive with a letter telling of your departure date.

The old saying, "out of sight, out of mind" can be very true in missionary life. As you travel from church to church and home to home, people will appear to be very interested in you and your work and your field. But a year later, when several others like you have passed through, there will come a numbness of memory concerning you. A pictorial reminder which has been slipped into a Bible, tacked on a wall, or placed on the mantel will, in a moment, bring back clear memories of you and your visit. It is a silent, yet forceful reminder of you and your ministry.

Some mission boards may supply candidates with prayer cards since they may prefer a specific format and feel uniformity can identify you in the minds of church members as belonging to that particular mission board. Be sure to check with your Home Office concerning this matter.

For some candidates, the prayer card will be a personal expense item. Others will be able to charge it to their mission account as a legitimate outgoing expense. In some cases, a friend will volunteer payment for them. Sometimes a printer will donate his services as a personal or tax-deductible ministry. But whatever the case, it is important that you put into the hands of those who are interested in you the information which will help them remember you. And perhaps the most vital and personal reminder is your prayer card.

You will change through the years, so be prepared to have new prayer cards made during each furlough period. Some folks use the original card—or at least the original picture—for two or three terms of service. This completely destroys the effectiveness of this prayer reminder.

Be sure to send a number of your prayer cards to your Home Office. Churches and individuals will often request copies of these to be used for missionary conferences, or to give to new supporters, or to be used in their missionary scrapbooks or on their missionary bulletin boards. Ask your Home Office how many prayer cards they will be willing to file in your folder to accommodate those who may write requesting one or more of them.

QUESTIONS—CHAPTER 10

1. Why is it important to have prayer cards printed?

2. List the essential items which MUST be included on prayer cards.

3. Sketch out a mock-up of a prayer card you feel would be appropriate for you to distribute to friends and supporters. (If you have not been assigned to a specific field or ministry, choose these at this point, simply for the purpose of providing information to complete this project.)

4. How do you plan to distribute your prayer cards?

11
Preparing a Display

Many times, especially if you are invited to a missionary conference, the inviting church will request that you set up a display depicting your field of service or area of work. In a day when people are used to high quality and technical work, it is imperative that your display be both exceedingly attractive and tell exactly what you want it to say about whatever point(s) you want to emphasize.

Displays should be portable enough to carry on planes, trains, buses and small cars, and durable enough to withstand a great amount of wear and tear. It may be possible (but expensive and inconvenient) to send your display ahead of you. But often you will have to carry it yourself, so be sure to take this into consideration.

In some instances, your Board will have had some excellent displays prepared by professionals. These may be available at your request. Be sure to notify your Board well in advance of a meeting or conference of your need for this material, and give complete details concerning the place and date of your meeting and when and how you want the display to arrive.

Unfortunately, not all missionaries have the Home Office on which to fall back. Most Boards feel that displays are expensive, difficult to keep updated and in circulation, and unwieldly to store and manage. Thus you will be forced to use your own creativity or obtain the help of a friend in planning your own.

Try to remember that you may be speaking at a large conference for a week with 60 other missionaries who have set up 25 or 30 displays. You are competing for attention. Make your display say something, do something and be something very special.

Perhaps you can get ideas from TV ads. You may attend a convention where professionals are displaying their goods. You may get ideas directly from a newspaper, or from your local grocery store, or from a window while you are shopping. Displays are more common today than ever before. Everywhere you look you can pick up ideas for an effective visual presentation.

Lettering on a display should look professional. The space available to you should not appear to be cluttered.

Be sure you include some items which can be picked up and handled, even by children. (This would exclude expensive, breakable objects.) It is best not to display some items (such as jewelry made of gold or silver, snakes in jars of formaldahyde, or full-face pictures of naked people).

Perhaps you will want to use a continuous film or slide series as your main focus. Or you may wish to use pictures (5" x 7" or 8" x 10"—in color, if at all possible) as your background. Captions should be short, meaningful, and easy to read. Mission literature can be placed in the foreground. Always have literature available, but NEVER call a literature table a display!

A pad and pencil may be necessary so passersby can sign up for your prayer card, prayer letter, or to be put on your mission mailing list.

Some of today's displays may even include a computer which will answer questions asked of it, or display pertinent information and give printouts of that information to those who are interested. But this is an expensive proposition, and should not be coveted for use by all.

You may want to use a map of your country as a backdrop. Large maps can be readily obtained quite inexpensively at local map stores. If it is a map of a continent, be sure to outline your country of service in a color which will stand out—and if you know your exact location of service, indicate it by means of an arrow.

Curios may be utilized to good advantage in your display. A Japanese lantern, national newspaper, stamps, flags—you will think of dozens of items which can lend color and meaning to your display.

Books concerning your country of service may be displayed. It is also possible to obtain a tape or record which can be played so that people will come to understand how difficult it may be for you to learn the language of the country. It will also give them an idea of the language you will be speaking and listening to for the next few years.

A display is a unique program geared to telling a complete story. It will probably be manned by you or a member of your family or mission board—but in the event it is not, it should speak for itself and answer questions through visual presentations.

When you are asked to provide a display, be sure to ask the following questions:

1.   How much space will be available?

2.   Will a table be provided?

3.   Will there be space at the rear and sides?

4.   Will backing wood or cardboard be provided?

5.   Will cloth or corrugated paper be available?

6.   Will I need to carry my own cloth, nails, hammer, ruler, and other tools?

7.   Is an electrical outlet available at the site of my display?

8.   Will extension cords be needed?

9.   Will anyone be sharing this area with me?

10. Will someone be available to help at the particular time I will be setting up my display?

11. At what times will the display be open to the public?

12. Does the church have any regulations in regard to what can or cannot be utilized in a display?

A good display will not only be attractive and informative. It should raise questions in the minds of those who pass by. This stirs conversation and gives you a greater opportunity to minister to those who want to learn about you, your mission, and your work.

If the display is to be in place for several days, it will produce more interest if you change some of your pictures, have a second or third set of slides for continuous showing, add new pieces of literature each day, and display different curios from time to time.

Your display is another extension of you and your Board. Strangely enough, people will be far more attracted to both if they appreciate your display. Your efforts will be well rewarded, and at each conference you will probably pick up good ideas from others to incorporate in your future displays. It is not so much how expensive your display is, but rather the results it produces which are important to consider. An unprofessional, sloppily-put-together, uninteresting display will hinder rather than help your candidacy!

QUESTIONS—CHAPTER 11

1.   What are the essentials of a "good display"?

2. You will be working under the Lost Sheep Mission Board in Papua New Guinea. You will be assigned to responsibilities at their radio station. Sketch out how you would prepare an attractive and effective display to feature your mission as well as your anticipated work.

3. What types of questions should you be prepared to answer as you "man" your display booth at a missionary conference where 20 mission boards are represented?

4. When a church requests that you provide a display when you speak there, what questions will you ask before sending/taking your display?

12
Outfit and Equipment

From the time you receive word of your acceptance for missionary service until the day you actually leave for the field, you will be faced with the question of what to take with you.

At one time it was necessary to take not only those things that would make life normally comfortable, but also the bare necessities. Although there may be some remote corners of the earth where essentials are still not available, for the most part you will not need to load yourself down with food items, toilet tissue, soap, tin bathtubs, and other such niceties.

Normal questions are posed by the candidate:

. . . Are there items which the government of the country to which I am going prohibits my taking with me?

. . . On what items are customs duty excessive?

. . . How much clothing do I need to take?

. . . Should I take appliances?

. . . What about our wedding gifts, i.e., good china, sterling, crystal?

. . . Will they have shoes to fit me?

. . . How much will it cost me to ship my unaccompanied baggage?

. . . If I don't take everything with me, are packages allowed to be sent to me later?

. . . What about a car or truck?

. . . Should I take a gun?

. . . Will I need special permits for any items?

. . . Will I need to take professional tools/equipment?

There are no uniform answers to these questions. Your Mission will provide a general listing of items which you may wish to take with you. This may be broken down into two or three categories which list essentials, those things which are optional, and those things which are handy to have but would be considered "luxuries."

It is always a good idea to correspond with one or more folks who have been stationed on your field for a number of years. They will know the things which are now available in the country, whether these will serve your purpose, whether it would be less expensive to buy them in the homeland and ship them rather than purchasing them at a higher price on your station, those things which should definitely be included in your equipment, types of clothing which are most practical, or taboo. You will find out what the temperature and weather is like in your assigned field. It makes a world of difference whether it will be cold or hot, damp or dry, urban or rural. You may be on the equator, but if you are 10,000 feet above sea level, the weather will be cool!

The matter of customs duty on items going into the country with you, as unaccompanied baggage, or sent in by packages during your term on the field is unpredictable. It must be taken into consideration as you plan your outfit and the funds to provide it. Someone leaving the field may be selling an item you have considered buying. This would solve the problem of having to pay customs.

Although once considered luxuries, a stove and refrigerator are generally thought of as necessities today. It may be possible for you to purchase these on the field. Or you may need to take them with you. Ask your Home Office or friends on the field. Some feel a dishwasher, a freezer, an air conditioner, and/or a computer are essentials. It really depends on how much you want to appear like a poor national or like a rich expatriate. Remember, the missionary goes forth as a soldier of Jesus Christ. The amount of gear he takes with him can help or hinder the battle.

When you decide to take appliances with you, be sure to check on the power supply and voltage in the country to which you are going. Electric razors, toasters, mixers, blenders, electric blankets, as well as stoves, refrigerators, freezers or dishwashers won't take 220 volts of power if they are made for 110. You may have to take a transformer, or more than one, with you. Or you might consider taking gas-powered appliances if gas is readily available and not exorbitantly expensive in the area to which you are assigned.

It is a good idea to take a pretty set of plastic dishes. Certainly many an unhappy situation can be avoided by using plastic. In fact, one can even smile when a servant heads toward the kitchen with a load of dishes and that all-too-familiar clatter of a dropped tray filters back to the dining room! Certainly, however, if one has good china, sterling, crystal, and other such items on hand when preparing to leave for the field, they should be wrapped and packed with extreme care and taken along. There is little merit in storing such items in an attic in the homeland if you intend to spend most of the rest of your life on the field. It is better that they be used on the field with the possibility that they may be damaged, stolen, or destroyed, than that they go untouched and unneeded at home.

For everyday use, stainless steel is adequate. It does not get "lost" or "misplaced" so readily. But today, many missionaries have the privilege of entertaining local and national officials, as well as prominent guests passing through, at teas, meals and social functions. Although not trying to be ostentatious, it is always in good taste to provide the very best on such occasions by setting a beautiful table with lace cloth, fine china, crystal and sterling.

Probably of all the comforts of home, an individual's bed is the most appreciated. Rope beds, stone beds, or lumpy cotton mattresses and bed rolls can prove to be intolerable—especially when sickness comes. For this reason, you may want to take a comfortable rollaway bed or a box spring and mattress for each family member. Again this decision must ever be based on information received from the mission, the field, and according to your own budget limits. There are nations which do not allow the importation of goods made of wood, so be sure to check on that before sending furniture to the field.

Don't forget a raincoat, footwear and an umbrella. Be sure to take a typewriter. Some missions require secretaries to take an office typewriter, but every missionary or missionary family should have a portable typewriter in his possession. In some cases it can be arranged to have special characters on your machine which will allow you to type in both English and Spanish, Japanese, Arabic, German, Portuguese, French, or other languages. Take a good camera and a supply of film. Usually a 35mm is best, although some will want a movie camera as well. Camping equipment and light nylon bedrolls are useful. A car, Jeep, truck, Land Rover, trailer, or other conveyance should be carefully considered. In most areas, a four-wheel drive vehicle is the best choice. Luxury vehicles are impractical.

When you arrive on the field, there is nothing more pleasant than making your house a familiar home. No matter of what material this house may be constructed—mud, stucco, wood, brick, mortar, grass—having a few favorite items from the homeland is essential. Perhaps it will be a picture which has long been a part of your life, or a piece of furniture. For the children it could be a stuffed animal or a worn toy. It might be a small rug at the entryway, or ruffled curtains in the living room. But this will be your home, so remember to take a few things to help produce a real home atmosphere.

On most mission fields there are a few items which are not readily available, but which, if taken with you, are a great joy to you and your fellow workers as time goes by. Along this line we might include such things as paper napkins, birthday candles and decorations, note paper, ball point pens, inexpensive games, birthday, get-well and anniversary cards, Christmas cards and ornaments, coat hangers, curtain rods, tacks, pins, towel racks, soap dishes, etc. These are not essentials, but can be very useful.

If you play a musical instrument, take it with you. An item as large as a piano or organ would need to be given approval by your Board, but accordians, wind instruments, stringed instruments, and music books should be taken along for your relaxation, and for the entertainment of others. They will, of course, be of help in your ministry as well.

A tape recorder, record player and/or short-wave radio may be included on your list. Many Boards require that a tape recorder be taken for language study, and thus the inclusion of a few musical tapes will not add appreciably to the weight or worth of the equipment. (Be sure to take a good supply of extra blank tapes, as well). If you do not want an expensive short-wave radio, do take a small transistor radio to listen to the daily news of your nation. It will help you to hear the language, too. It is not wise, however, to take a four-year supply of batteries!

An equipment list would not be complete without including some very necessary items. At least one good reference Bible in easy-to-read print; a Bible commentary; a Bible dictionary; Bible study books. Spiritual material is essential and most missionaries utilize "Daily Light on the Daily Path" or other familiar books for personal and family devotions. Flannelgraph stories, backgrounds and easel should be taken. Good fiction and biographies for adults and children are needed. Subscriptions to religious and secular/professional magazines should be ordered as soon as you can give them your overseas address.

Do not feel obliged to purchase every item on your equipment list. Some items will not be necessary for YOU. Candidates have actually gone into debt to buy things they think their mission feels are essential. One should keep in mind the effect that a very large and expensive equipment shipment will have on both the nationals and your fellow missionaries who may have very little of this world's goods even though they have served many terms. Although people in the homeland are more lenient toward missionaries having modern conveniences than previously, not every first-term missionary should take what he thinks he will need for a life-time of service. Most Boards will set a weight and financial limit on the amount of goods that a first-termer is allowed to take to the field. This limit has been carefully considered for your station and you should tenaciously and faithfully abide by the rules.

In most countries heretofore unobtainable items are now sold in the stores of the larger towns and cities. Even if some items are more expensive than at home, you avoid high duty charges on some items as well as the cost of transporting it to the field. This must be taken into consideration. Other items will be more practical and less expensive than those available in the homeland.

WHERE TO OBTAIN AND PURCHASE EQUIPMENT

Now that you have an idea of the items which you feel you will need to take with you to the field, let's consider where these things can be obtained.

1. You may have clothing and household goods which you will take with you from your own home.

2. Friends will give you various items, either things they have that you might be able to use, or things you need that they are willing to supply for you.

3. Churches and friends will often give a going-away shower to missionary ladies. Many useful clothing and household items are obtained in this way. (If you have been told that a shower is going to be given, and you have opportunity to request it, do urge folks to carry this out at least six weeks in advance of your leaving for the field. A shower the day before you are leaving produces some terrible packing headaches and plays havoc with those lists of outfit items you have had to fill out in sextuplicate!)

4. You will have funds set apart for outgoing equipment expenditures. You are free to purchase items which you feel you will need from these funds. (Make sure to stay within the limits established by your Board concerning this.)

Much consideration needs to be given to the quality and price of items to be taken or purchased. As a matter of fact, you may not feel every item donated to you personally or through a shower will be of enough value to you to take it halfway around the world.

Although some will be taking a washer from the homeland, many missionaries still must rely on the dhobi or washerman to do the laundry. This is always an interesting event since their soap usually consists of lye and grease mixed into a soap compound. Their washing board is a rock in the middle of a small stream, canal, river, or gutter; their dryer is the parched ground or bushes in the hot sun. Starch comes from potato or rice water (and don't be surprised when your underwear and pajamas are as stiff as a board and your dresses and shirts are as limp as a dishrag . These folks are not acquainted with the various parts of Western clothing!) Because of the hard wear your clothes will be getting, it is usually pennywise and pound foolish to buy the cheapest quality clothing. Neither will you spend a fortune on fancy, elegant apparel. But the best quality and the best price need to be considered. Clothes guaranteed "colorfast" will not hold their color forever under the above-described circumstances. But they will hold up longer than clothing which will "run."

Your ironing may need to be done with a kerosene or charcoal iron and the heat cannot be easily regulated. Therefore, unless you like scorched clothes, it is good to purchase either a fabric that can be ironed with a fairly hot iron, or one that needs no ironing at all. (REMEMBER again that those who may do your ironing do not usually have a knowledge of various types of materials and settings on an iron.)

Of course, you may be planning to do your own washing and ironing to preserve your clothing and linens. But on the field, in the heat, where 16-hour days are common, or when you're down with an attack of malaria or dysentery, or you are dealing with an individual who is on the verge of accepting Christ, your plans for family washing and ironing may run amuck. So do not set your compass on plans of this type.

In many cases, store owners will give a discount to "religious workers." It is never out of place to ask if a store has such a policy. But NEVER BEG FOR DISCOUNTS. Do not expect that a businessman should lose his profit on merchandise or services just because you happen to be a missionary candidate.

There are organizations which are subsidized by gifts from Christian groups and individuals so they can offer regulation items of all kinds at greatly reduced prices. Discount houses, and wholesale outlets, and companies specializing in overseas shipments may offer extremely favorable prices. Some Mission Offices have supplies of drugs and other items at greatly reduced prices readily available for their personnel. Check with your Home Office concerning the names and addresses of suppliers.

Keep in mind how your equipment items will be shipped to you. If they are to go by air, weight is a serious factor. If you purchase on the West Coast and expect to fly from the East Coast (or vice versa) you should keep in mind that it will be far less expensive to purchase the needed articles near the place from which they will be shipped. In some cases this is not possible. But, for example, those living in Minneapolis who will be going to Latin America would do well to purchase large articles of equipment and appliances in Miami, thus saving the overland shipping costs. When practical, missions located in such port cities are willing to help even those from other boards.

Be sure to consider known government regulations concerning the import of items into the country in which you will be serving. Some countries will not allow the import of articles made of wood. Others will not allow certain food items. Still others prohibit new shoes. You may pay 100 to 200% duty on a car or truck in some lands and this is a definite consideration in purchasing items of this magnitude. Some items may require permits or detailed information from you. Either you or your Board would do well to contact the Embassy of the country to which you are going to obtain information concerning questionable outfit items and special requirements concerning them.

In most countries of the world today, you are able to purchase the normal commodities of life. If at all possible, consult before purchasing articles in these lands. It is possible that ready-made items are much more expensive and not as nicely made as those that are custom-made to your specifications. It is also possible that items can be obtained from others who are leaving the country (government workers, other missionaries, embassy personnel, etc.).

If you are handy with a needle and thread, you may prefer to make your own articles of clothing. Financially, this makes sense. Remember, it may be necessary to take several sizes of children's clothing and shoes if these are unavailable or difficult to obtain at your place of service. Children grow, and it is hard to know if they will grow up, out, or both! So ask the Lord to guide you as to the sizes and quantity you should take with you—whether you make it yourself, or purchase it.

PREPARATION AND SHIPMENT OF OUTFIT AND EQUIPMENT

Although there are a number of companies that specialize in crating and shipping, unless you are thoroughly familiar with the organization, it is usually better to pack your own baggage as much as possible. If baggage is to be sent by surface means (ship or truck), steel drums can be utilized and are good for storage purposes on the field. Before shipping, make certain they are packed solidly, are spot welded on top to inhibit pilfering and are securely padlocked. In this day of air travel, however, there will be less need for the steel drum. Fiber drums are now utilized since they are both light-weight and sturdy. They can be secured properly, and they, too, make fine storage areas on the field.

Your baggage can be packed in foot lockers or sturdy cartons and banded with steel. (A more practical method, however, is to utilize containerized shipping.) If items are being sent via air freight, cumbersome wooden crates are not necessary. You will, of course, have hand baggage and odd items (guitar or other musical instrument, tennis racket, baby carriage, tape recorder, etc.) which may be handcarried.

In every case, be sure your baggage is clearly and distinctly identified. With barrels, it is wise to stencil your full name, port of debarkation and field address on both the top and side of each piece. Foot lockers should also contain this information on top and bottom. Other luggage should contain your full name and address inside each case as well as on a tag on the handle. All these items will have the company shipping tag on them, but these do not include your name. Be sure to number each piece, and as you pack, make a list of items in each box or package, making sure the number on your list corresponds to the appropriately numbered container. It is a good idea to have at least six copies of this list with you. You must have it when going through customs. One list should give the approximate RESALE value of each item. Another list (for insurance purposes) should give the REPLACEMENT value of each item.

Clothing and shoes should be worn at least once, and linens should be laundered before packing. These, then, will be listed as USED items.

Appliances should be used before packing so (1) they can be declared used, and (2) you will know they are in working condition before taking them with you. Some countries require that appliances be used a certain number of months in order to meet the requirement for "used" goods. Check with your Field Director concerning this matter, or with the Consulate for the country to which you are going. Then be sure to carry with you the sales slip for each appliance you are taking with you to prove that you are meeting the demands set forth.

Always check with your Field Director or a missionary friend on the field before taking large items of equipment. Special permit papers may be required. Or certain items may be prohibited by law.

In some cases, your Board will handle the arrangements for shipping. In others, the Mission's official shipping agent will handle these matters. And in yet others, the missionary is responsible to locate his own agent, airline or freight company. This should be done with care and upon the advice of an experienced person. If crates are needed, it is usually less expensive to make them yourself than to have them made. (Yes, you can do it ladies!) If large items are purchased, they can usually be ordered packed for overseas delivery. Some stores have special offices that handle only overseas shipments.

If you have permission to send your baggage ahead to your Home Office, or another location at the port of embarkation, be sure to put your name and the mission address indicating clearly that this is to be trans-shipped to your field address.

If items are sent to an airfreight or other company, be sure they do not arrive more than 30 days before they are to be shipped. Storage charges turn into money. As soon as items are shipped to your forwarder send a letter to the company specifying in detail the number of pieces, kinds, when and how they were sent, and a copy of the waybill, if possible. Ask them to expect these and request that they be held for shipment on a certain date and give complete shipping instructions. Also indicate whether or not more pieces will be added to the shipment from companies, and if so, which ones. Also identify further pieces you may bring to them personally at the time of your departure. Usually if the same agents are used by a Board for all new and returning missionaries, the company is most helpful and careful in handling your outfit.

Some foreign countries require a person to have arrived in the country before any baggage can be received in his name. In such a situation, it is important to make sure your things are sent AFTER you have left the homeland. Usually this is set for from one to three days following your departure, depending on the loads the line will be handling during that period and the number of flights they make to that country. Some countries don't allow you to receive things as part of your outfit if they arrive more than 30 days after you arrive in the country.

For those who will spend six months to a year in Language School, other problems arise. Since it is not wise, and in many cases it is illegal, to ship goods into a country before your arrival, you have to plan on sending only what is absolutely necessary to your Language School address if it is not in the same field as your country of work (which is true with many missionaries to Latin America who study language in Costa Rica, Mexico or Bolivia). A friend in the homeland would then have to be appointed to keep your goods for you, sending them at the time you indicate, making sure they contact the agent at the point of departure from the homeland. In some cases where a mission has storage room or a warehouse, they can handle receipt of baggage at the time you leave for Language School and then ship it when you arrive on the field. Or you may find it necessary to put your things in storage with a warehouse at the point of future shipment. This is the most awkward course of action, and most expensive, but sometimes necessary.

When making your list of items for customs purposes, it is not necessary to list each pair of socks and each piece of underwear, or each pot and pan. Generalize your categories, i.e., personal effects, household items, books, clothing, etc. You should be specific on items such as a typewriter, tape recorder, radio, or other small appliances. Also be sure to keep a record of the serial numbers of all such goods, including cameras. You should get a stamped paper from the customs department before you board your plane which shows proof that you have a camera with you—what type, what brand, etc.—so when you return home you will not have to pay customs on the camera as though you had purchased it while out of the country (unless, of course, you did).

Be sure to check on insurance coverage for your baggage. You may want to take out extra insurance to cover your shipment both within the homeland and overseas.

Check with your Mission Board concerning the agent who will be handling your baggage on the receiving end. It may be a company, or it may be an agent appointed by your mission for this express purpose. Many times a national affiliated with your mission is appointed to this position and does an excellent job.

When you, personally, depart the country, be sure to state to the airline or shipping agent how many pieces of unaccompanied luggage you are having sent. Keep the original bill of lading with your important documents. You will need it when going through customs. Also inform the customs officials the exact number of items being sent to you as unaccompanied baggage.

New missionaries are often asked by missionaries on the field or by the mission itself to take items for other people on the field. Customs usually looks down upon this practice. If, however, you care to be troubled with such items, make sure you have given permission in writing, and then keep a record of whose articles you are taking, weight involved and customs duty paid to be reimbursed by the missionary involved if you care to do so. If your shipment has been completed and you do not wish to add other items to yours, it is in order to write a letter of apology to this missionary stating you find it impossible to carry out his request. Items should never become part of your outgoing equipment unless o.k.'d by you beforehand. (Remember, however, you may want someone to do you such a favor in the future and it is difficult to expect others will do for you what you have not been willing to do for them.)

After you have notified the proper authorities concerning the exact number of unaccompanied items you have sent, do not expect to be able to have other items added as an afterthought. Unless initially listed upon your entry, equipment comes to you through the usual channels, and may have a high duty rate assessed. In some countries such parcels would be financially prohibitive. In others, they would be completely disallowed.

When packing, be sure to utilize your space to the best possible advantage. Stuff shoes with small, soft items. Pack breakables in soft towels or linens. Put appliances in the midst of clothing. If packed correctly, your baggage should need very little if any extra padding. It is wise to note that you should not pack soap in the same container with dry food-stuffs—nor moth balls with candy (unless extensively and securely wrapped in heavy aluminum foil). You should guard against putting any items together which will be ruined by the association. Plastic bags can be utilized to great advantage and will come in extremely handy on the field. Remember that newsprint rubs off on everything it touches!

If you have ever watched freight being loaded or unloaded, you will die a thousand deaths when you think of what can happen to your baggage. But if it is packed well, banded securely, locked insofar as possible and prayed over concernedly, you will usually make out better than anticipated.

You may also be wondering how you get your shipment from

your home to the port of embarkation. There are many ways of transporting this. It can be sent by truck, by car, by bus, by plane, or with friends. Many times moving vans will be happy for your small additional weight to complete a shipment they are making. Be sure to discover the approximate arrival date at the destination, and also find out what provision, if any, is made for transporting it to your shipping agent. Those missions which are located in the area of embarkation may be willing to pick up and transfer your shipment. In other cases, you will have to make other arrangements. If you are traveling by car, you may want to hire a small rental trailer to carry your freight. For smaller shipments you may wish to consider using United Parcel Service (UPS), an air express company, or the U.S. Postal Service.

An additional note needs to be included here to short-term workers. If you are to be in the foreign country for only a few weeks or months, it is very possible you will not be allowed to take excess baggage. You will probably not be obtaining residence papers and without a change of residence, only personal baggage can be taken with you. Be prepared for the possibility of heavy duty charges on excess luggage.

When shipping to some countries, the bags and boxes should be marked to include the names of all in the family since exemption allowance in customs is granted on an individual basis. If they are sent in the name of only one person, all goods above the allowable amount for that individual may be dutiable.

One last reminder. Your outfit and equipment have been obtained through the gifts of others or from personal funds. You have spent a great deal of time getting just the things you felt you wanted and needed. You are looking forward to setting up housekeeping with the things you are sending to the field. For some married couples, it is the first time you have had brand new things to put in your home. For single folks, it may be your first attempt at setting up your own home situation. Thus it is natural to prize highly your outfit and equipment.

Keep in mind, however, that material things can be quickly taken from you. Barrels can be lost in transit. China can be broken. Items may be stolen. Customs may hold up delivery of your good for several weeks or months and then you may find that the children have already outgrown some of the new clothes you had purchased or made for them. Occasionally an airline or shipping strike will delay your possessions for several weeks. Remember always to keep your values in the proper perspective. Always "set your affection on things above, not on things on the earth." [1] Material goods are another of God's gifts to you on loan. And if they should be taken from you by one means or another, don't let it ruin your whole ministry. How you take the "spoiling of your goods" [2] will certainly set the climate for how you will react in other stress situations. Can you commit this to the Lord in quietness and confidence? Do consider your relationship to material possessions very carefully and don't be bound by them. It is amazing to see how simplified your life will become when it is not encumbered with the care and concern for "things." In truth, one can get by with very little, and do so very happily.

QUESTIONS—CHAPTER 12

1. How will you go about finding out what essential household items you will need to take to your appointed field?

2. What do you feel are the advantages and disadvantages of taking a vehicle to the field as part of your equipment for your first term of service? (Be sure to state where you are going. If you have not been assigned, choose a geographical location before answering this question).

3. List the items you will plan to take with you to help maintain a healthy spiritual life during your first term overseas.

4. What kinds of consideration should be given to the obtaining of the necessary items on your outfit/equipment list? (Where to purchase, what needs to make known to those who ask, cost, etc.).

5. List the steps necessary to get your outfit to the field from the time you purchase it until the day it arrives at your mission station. (For this exercise, you will not be going to Language school before reaching your field of service.)

---

[1] Colossians 3:2
[2] Hebrews 10:34

13
Financial Matters

One of the first questions an accepted candidate is going to raise is "what do I live on while I'm engaged in deputation work?"

In Faith Mission Board practice, there is no guarantee of salary from the Mission Board for living expenses from the moment of acceptance. In most cases, the candidate will continue in a full-time job and take weekend and evening meetings close to his home. Many are able to obtain their full support in this way, and thus work until the time they leave for the field. Most employers are also sympathetic in allowing time off from work for special meetings if the privilege is not misused.

Some Boards allow the candidate certain travel allowance money from his own account, from the funds received at meetings, or from the Mission's General account. He is not allowed to use more funds than he has in one of these accounts.

Those who serve with most denominational boards are supported from the time of their acceptance, their outgoing passage and equipment is paid for, and unless sent as a special representative to meetings by the Board, they do not have to engage in deputation ministry before leaving for the field.

Those with other than denominational boards may feel led to terminate their employment and enter full-time deputation. They may receive special personal gifts from friends to cover expenses, be given lodging and food at no expense to them, or they may choose to use money previously saved.

In most cases it would seem best for a candidate not to quit his job the day his acceptance letter arrives. You should at least plan your meeting schedule before giving up your visible means of support. This is especially true in the case of married couples. The Lord will supply all your needs in unusual ways, but common sense also has to be exercised,

Some Boards allow candidates to set a target date for leaving for the field, and 3 to 6 months previously, if funds are available in their account, support is given each month on the same rate as Home Mission workers.

The usual financial matters which must be cared for before the candidate can leave for the field are:

1. Missionary support. (In the case of those planning to be married shortly after arrival on the field, or expecting an addition to their family in the near future, it is necessary to take this into account when seeking to raise support.)

2. Travel funds sufficient to cover transportation, shipment of baggage to the field, and estimated customs duty.

3. Outfit and equipment. The range of needs will be great in this category. Some folks can get by with very little. Others feel they must have a great deal. Many missions set a limit on the value of outfits an individual is allowed. In this case, set your priorities carefully.

4. Language School expenses if the Candidate is to attend.

When offerings are received from a church or individuals, they should be sent to the Home Office with full details concerning the donor and address so an official tax-deductible receipt may be issued. These funds are then put into the candidate's designated fund. If personal gifts are received, no mission receipt needs to be sent unless requested by the donor. The candidate, however, may elect to put this money into his travel or outfit fund.

Your mission will probably request monthly or quarterly financial reports from you, indicating the name and full address of each donor, amount received, purpose for which it was specified, whether it was sent to the Home Office, and if not, how it was utilized. Forms for this accounting will usually be supplied by your Board. If not, it should be carefully typed or written on a sheet (or sheets) of paper. Do not send bits and scraps of paper with various notations on them. Always keep a copy of the information you send to the Home Office. Be sure you keep a record of the checks you send, too.

Remember that you will need to plan on at least one-third to one-half of the declared value of your outfit and equipment to ship it to your field and pay customs on it. The duty on a car or truck may be as high as 100% or more of the cost of the item. Many times the customs expense is not as high as you had figured it to be. In that case, the funds will be retained in your account either for furlough travel or to be used as required and approved for the purchase of equipment/outfit items while you are on the field.

Be certain your supporters understand the financial setup of your particular Board. Explain Work Support, Missionary Support, Project Support, Passage and Equipment, Personal Gifts, etc. Ask them to contact the Home Office at any time they have questions. Also ask them to check their receipts each time they send a gift. If you are listed with your mission as a code number, a set of initials, or a Project, be sure to confide this to your supporters. This is the only way they can tell if their gift has actually been credited to YOUR account. A receipt which gives their support to #51 or Project X will not be meaningful if they aren't aware that you are listed that way with your mission. Then if they get a receipt marked differently, they can question the Accounting Office. (Believe it or not, no matter how careful, there have been mixups in the number, initial and project systems even when fed into computers.)

Do not hold funds received from meetings for more than a week or two. Some candidates insist on holding funds to send with their monthly or quarterly reports. This may save time and postage for you, but it produces hard feelings with donors who expect rapid expediting of their gifts, and also wish to balance their check book at the end of the month—and rightly so. If you receive cash gifts, convert them to a check or Money Order before sending it to your Board. Never send cash through the mail.

Most missions set the support figures needed for each adult and for each child 0-5 years, 6-11 years, 12 years through High School, and High School graduates through college or age 21. These amounts will be discussed with you thoroughly upon your acceptance. Other missions have established a salary scale, and you will be apprised of the details of that plan by those Boards which utilize it.

Most Boards will allow a candidate to obtain over-support of between 10 and 20% of the annual support figure. This is not a requirement, and will not hold the candidate back from the field if he does not get it, but in the event extra support is pledged, it is allowed to this extent since it is used to build up the account. If your financial needs change during your term of service, it may come in especially handy. If your Mission pools all support incomes, this over-support can be of help to others who may have had difficulty raising needed funds. In Boards where a monthly salary is received, the extra funds will build up the individual's account to be used for travel or other **bona fide** expenses which normally come from the support account.

Each candidate should feel a sincere responsibility in the matter of raising support. Even in the case where a Board may allow the candidate to leave for the field without full support, every effort should be made to raise at least the minimum amounts required.

If your mission sets a financial limit on the value of equipment you are allowed to take to the field, it is essential that you make a fair declaration of the items you are taking. It must also be kept in mind that included in the total amount will be those funds which you will set aside to purchase necessary equipment items on the field. For some fields, this can be a sizeable amount. Be honest in your estimation of these expenses added to those items which you will take with you or send from the homeland.

The financial aspect of our lives may be the most difficult of all to dedicate wholly to the Lord. And yet money is only a commodity loaned to us by Him for our use. It is certainly not the most important thing in our lives. It cannot buy happiness, peace, security, or health. It cannot love or respect us. It is a fine servant but a despotic master. And it is true that "the love of money is the root of all evil" (I Timothy 6:10).

Before entering the future, be sure to seek answers to some of these questions:

. . . Am I happy about the prospect of living on a substandard salary?

. . . Am I, a doctor or engineer, satisfied to receive the same monthly support as a teacher, secretary, nurse, or Bible teacher?

. . . Will the lack of financial remuneration become a stumbling block to my ministry?

. . . Am I able to prepare a budget and stay within it?

. . . Can I trust God concerning finances when I long for better things for my children and nicer things for my home?

. . . Is it in my nature to be envious if my co-workers receive large personal gifts and I receive none?

. . . Suppose my co-worker insists on food items which I feel are unnecessary, but for which I have to pay my share?

. . . Who owns my purse?

At this moment you will slough off these questions. But there will come a good many times in the days ahead when this will be a very serious matter.

Men and women have left the mission field by the scores over the simple matter of finances. When they left the homeland, they completely understood the financial policies of the Mission. They knew exactly how much they would receive, where it would come from, and how often they would receive it. They knew of the possibility of the support scale being raised during their term of service. They realized folks at home might have to drop their support or lessen it for one reason or another. They knew additional children would bring additional expenses and additional support needs. But in the midst of the battle, it was not easy to struggle with financial matters. They never went to bed hungry and they had the necessities of life—but others seemed to have more, or they looked back and thought of what they could have had in the way of material things back in the homeland. And they've left the field discouraged and lacking fruit. Oh, candidate, before you leave for your service, get this matter of finances settled in your own heart and mind. God is not a pauper. Where He guides, He supplies. Trust Him fully in this matter today and in the days ahead. If you honestly cannot do so, determine right now that you will not go to the field—at least not until such time as you can handle this matter of finances.

If a candidate withdraws from his Mission prior to his going to the field, there should be an accurate accounting of all funds received. Unless there is a request from the donor for redesignation, all such funds are turned over to be used in the Mission work as the Director or Board deems fitting and proper—unless the donor requests that the funds be returned. Personal salary, gifts and deputation expenses are not usually reimbursed, although some candidates feel responsible to return these funds to the mission or the donor from their personal finances. This is an individual matter of conscience.

If friends want to give you money for a particular part of your outfit, send all such gifts to the Home Office designated for that purpose so that proper receipts may be issued. Remind all donors that if they designate a gift for your work through their church (i.e., they give an offering or check to the church designated for your Mission or your ministry) the church will send it to the Mission for processing, but it will be the church that gets the receipt from the Mission. At the end of the year, the individual donor will find that the church will acknowledge that the gift or offering(s) were received. For income tax purposes, however, the gifts will be accounted for as gifts to the church and not to the Mission Board. In other words, they cannot receive a receipt from the Mission and then also receive a receipt for the same gift from their church. Some churches request that the mission issue their receipt directly to the individual donor. In those cases, no receipt would be available from the church for those gifts.

Any bills for equipment purchases you send to the Home Office for payment must have a letter of authorization from you, indicating that you did, indeed, make this purchase, and funds are to be released from your account for payment of the invoice.

For regular payments you wish to have made on Mutual Funds, insurance premiums, home mortgage, etc., be sure to give clear instructions to your Home Office and a source of personal funds to pay for these. This can often be accomplished through setting up a checking account where checks can be signed either by you or by a trusted person in the Business Department of your Mission's Home Office.

The candidate should make arrangements to carry sufficient monies with him in the form of Travelers Checks when leaving for the field to cover baggage costs, first month's living expenses and incidentals. A full accounting of such funds should be given to the Home Office. A complete record should be kept concerning the expenditure of all monies and Travelers' Checks. Many countries require you to fill out a financial form when arriving in their land, specifying how much cash and how much in travelers checks you have with you. Then upon departure from the country, you must give an accounting of what funds you are taking with you, and how you spent the rest of what you took in with you.

QUESTIONS—CHAPTER 13

1. What financial matters are of primary importance when raising funds for missionary service?

2. Why should funds received be sent to your Mission Board rather than being utilized for current living expenses?

3. According to the Scriptures, what is God's perspective of money?

4. Should funds designated for a specific purpose by the donor be utilized for any other purpose? When? Why?

5. Is it necessary to budget your money when you are serving overseas? Why?

14
Medical, Dental and Legal Matters

Although most Boards are very careful concerning medical and dental matters, some do not require a thorough medical and dental examination before the candidate is accepted for service. Other Boards do not check through on questionable items contained in these reports (e.g., history of nervous breakdown, allergies, heart disease as a child, susceptibility to certain diseases, diabetes, degenerative diseases, etc.). In other cases, an examination is required during the application process, but the candidate may not actually leave for the field for a period of two or three years, with no further examination requested. During the intervening time, there may have been a serious problem, an operation, the birth of a child, or several other matters which will have caused, or are causing, physical concern to the candidate.

Some Mission Boards require their appointed mission doctor or his/her recommended colleagues, to perform all psychological, physical and dental exams on accepted candidates. Other Boards send you forms to be filled out by the physician of your choice. In either case, be sure the examinations are thorough. If you have any question about any matter, get it settled before leaving for the field. Good health is important for effective service.

Although we find that medical and dental facilities on the various mission fields of the world today are improving, there are still many areas where good professional help is not immediately available. Some missions operate their own clinics and hospitals and have their own doctors and nurses; many do not. Some governments operate efficient, well-kept facilities that are perfectly acceptable to expatriates. But in the out-of-the-way places, it is still possible to have to travel 500 or 1,000 miles in order to obtain good medical treatment. Emergencies do arise on the mission field. But if there is a tendency toward illness in a special realm, it is good to have this cared for at home, or at a time when it may not take your life or ruin the effectiveness of your ministry.

Dental care is probably less adequate in most places than medical care. Therefore, insofar as possible, it is imperative that all needs be cared for in the homeland. For those who wear artificial dentures or bridgework, it would be wise, if possible, to take an extra set with you. It is amazing what stripping sugar cane can do to false teeth! (Or, for that matter, teeth have been broken on less dangerous items such as a slice of toast or a piece of camel meat.)

If a hearing aid is prescribed, ask questions before purchasing. Be especially concerned about any adjustments which might need to be made. Ask what kind of batteries should be used, and how long those batteries can be expected to last. This could be a critical concern in some areas of the world where batteries are difficult or impossible to obtain.

It is also important to have a good eye examination before you leave the homeland. Glasses are not obtainable for your prescription except in the larger cities. (Be sure to carry a prescription for your lenses.) Carry at least one extra pair of glasses. For all practical purposes, contact lenses are less available to you and may prove troublesome in extremely hot, dusty or other unfavorable climates. You would do well to have at least one pair of prescription sunglasses as well. It is true with many people that they have had perfectly normal vision when leaving for the field only to find that constant language study, reading up and down or from right to left rather than in the normal pattern, has taken its toll and once strong eyesight begins to weaken. If trouble occurs, be sure to have it checked the first opportunity you have to be near an eye doctor on the field, but be sure he is reputable, for poorly-fitted or wrongly-prescribed glasses can cause as much or more trouble than no glasses at all. Most lenses today are made of plastic. You might wish to consider glass lenses for at least one pair of glasses, especially if you are in a very dusty country. Plastic lenses are known to scratch far more easily than glass ones—but many prefer plastic, nevertheless, since they are less heavy.

If you should find yourself in a mission which does not require a thorough medical or dental examination each year, for your own sake, be sure to get a check-up before you leave the homeland, including chest X-rays. If any medication is required, take a sufficient quantity with you. If treatment is recommended, have this cared for. Sick missionaries are not an asset to the work, and although the unexpected illnesses will come to most all in the course of events, some of the major problems can be cared for by a simple but thorough examination before departure.

Before you leave for a tropical field, ask your doctor for a prescription for two medicines: (1) an anti-malarial medicine, and (2) an anti-diarrheal medicine. Start taking your malaria medicine three weeks before arrival on the field, and be sure each member of your family continues to take this medicine until you have been back in the homeland at least three weeks after your term of service.

During the last two months before leaving for the field, it is essential to obtain all shots required for the area where you will be serving. A smallpox vaccination may not be necessary. Be sure you know when booster shots are needed and obtain them. Many folks get no reaction to any of their shots. Others will have some discomfort from them. Unless there is a real allergy to the vaccine, a couple of aspirin (if you are not allergic to them) and good use of the affected arm will help reduce the pain and fever which sometimes accompanies polio, typhoid, para-typhoid, tetanus, yellow fever, and other shots. Be sure to set up a schedule to receive your shots so they will be completed at least two weeks before your anticipated departure date. Check with the Home Office of your Mission concerning the immunizations required for your field of service. These will vary. You will need to find the best possible sources of vaccine for each shot required. Yellow fever is usually given only by a Government Office or by an agency authorized by them. You may wish to receive your other shots from your family doctor. In some areas, free, or relatively inexpensive immunizations may be obtained from your local Public Health Department. Check with them on this possibility and be sure to find out what days the various immunizations are given. If, on the other hand, you are acquainted with a nurse, she may be able to work with a doctor on this. She would administer the shots and the doctor would sign the certificate. This could save the family money. In all events, be sure your health card is duly signed, authorized and notarized with appropriate notations by the covering doctor, Public Health Officer and other legal stamps, seals and signatures.

Be sure to find out if your Mission Board has a medical plan. Understand what benefits you receive from such a plan and what responsibilities fall to you if you require medical or hospital treatment. As one who may not yet be considered an "employee" or "salaried member" of your mission, be sure to have medical coverage of your own until your insurance becomes effective with your Board. There is often a time limit stipulation as to when an "appointee" may be included in the overall program of the Mission.

A word should be mentioned concerning medical matters pertaining to members of your family who will remain in the homeland. Often a missionary will leave for the field knowing a mother and/or father is ill and in need of medical attention. This is a matter which must be entrusted to the Lord, and plans must be made for the care of those for whom you are responsible. In some cases it may mean making arrangements to admit the sick relative to a Rest Home or Nursing Center. For others it may mean having someone stay in the home during your absence. It might even require you to delay your going to the field for several months or indefinitely. Such situations are very difficult, but they must be settled before you leave. In a day when missionaries can fly around the world very quickly, it is a temptation to leave a medical matter hanging in mid-air, assuming that if the situation worsens, a flight home can readily and easily be arranged. But we must give some thought to what happens in Language School or on the field when a person is suddenly removed from the scene. We need also to consider the extra expense involved in this additional travel. Of course, emergencies do arise, but if there is a situation which can be handled before you leave, be sure to take care of it now.

Missionaries do not go to the field with the feeling that they will give their lives for the cause of Christ, although they are willing to do so, if necessary. With this in mind, there are several legal matters which should be taken into consideration before the candidate leaves the homeland. One of the most important documents in anyone's life is a WILL. Even though you may feel you have nothing of importance to leave to posterity, it is still important that you have a will properly executed and filed. In the case of missionary parents, it is essential that your will contain an indication as to who the guardian of your children will be in the event that you should both be killed, or die of natural causes. The exact designation of property, personal belongings, bank account, jewelry, etc., should be indicated. An executor must be named for your estate.

Be sure your will is written in conformity with the specific laws of the state in which you claim your legal residence. Some states will not consider a will valid unless it has been executed in that state with the named executor of the will living in that state. Other legalities may also be in force. Call a lawyer or your State Bar Association for specifics of writing your will. Along with a copy of your will, a letter should be filed with your Board in which those whom you have appointed to care for your children in case of your death(s) have signed an affadavit saying they are willing to take on this responsibility.

INSURANCE may be carried on your life by the mission, or by

yourself. Be sure that this clearly indicates who your beneficiary(ies) will be in the event of your death.

Your complete POWER OF ATTORNEY should be given to a close friend, relative, or lawyer in the homeland in the event legal papers need to be signed during your absence on the field. This is a very highly important power and therefore should be entrusted only to one who is well-known and trusted by you.

A PASSPORT must be obtained if you are leaving the country. The occupation listed on your application should be your profession or status. If you are going strictly for evangelical preaching, it might be listed as "missionary." For many, however, this occupation will rightly be stated as secretary, administrator, printer, engineer, doctor, nurse, housewife, pilot, teacher, musician, teacher, etc. Check with your mission concerning its preference for you in this matter. Take special note of the renewal date for your passport. Do not let it lapse.

An individual passport must be obtained for each member of your family.

If you have never previously been issued a passport, you must apply in person to (1) a passport agency; (2) a clerk or judge of any federal court, state court of record, or probate court where applications are accepted; (3) a main Post Office; (4) a consular or diplomatic office overseas. You will need to show your birth certificate (or a previous passport) proving your citizenship. The certificate must show your given name and surname, your date and place of birth and the date the birth record was filed. If no birth certificate exists, a baptismal certificate or a hospital birth record is sometimes acceptable.

If you have had a passport within the past eight years, you may obtain a new one by signing and sending a passport by mail application, two recent photos (signed on the reverse side), your previous passport, and the required fee to your nearest Passport Agency office, or to Passport Services in Washington, D.C.

Naturalized citizens, those claiming citizenship by virtue of being born of citizens abroad, a child of naturalized parents, and aliens, must comply with other specific requirements.

The loss or theft of a valid passport is a serious matter. It should be reported, in writing, to the Department of State, Passport Services, Washington, D.C. 20524, or to your nearest passport agency. If the loss occurs overseas, it must be reported to your nearest U.S. consular office immediately.

Various countries require VISAS and ENTRANCE PAPERS. In

some cases someone on the field must obtain RESIDENCE PAPERS for you before your arrival. A visa is usually rubber stamped in your passport by a representative of the country to which you are going (and other countries you may visit on the way). It certifies you have permission to enter that country for a certain length of time and for a specific purpose. Some visas have a limit of one entrance. Others are multiple entrance visas.

Be sure you are aware of the government regulations concerning the country to which you are going as well as the requirements of your own government in this matter. Your Home Office will probably handle these matters for you. In some cases, if you attend Language School in a country other than the one to which you have been assigned, entrance papers for your field of service cannot be obtained from the homeland. In such an event, the Field Director will handle the details for you. Be sure to give him complete information by the quickest possible means when it is requested from you. If you are the first from your mission to enter a new field, some of this work may be done by an older, well-established board already at work there. Such rapport and helpfulness between missions is usually the rule on the field. In filling out your visa application, it will be necessary to state the purpose of your visit/stay. Check with your Mission Board concerning its advice in this regard.

It would be well to check with your local SOCIAL SECURITY office concerning various aspects of the Social Security program so that you might better understand your relationship to it. Your Home Office will also be able to give you information concerning this matter.

Although you may not have to pay INCOME TAX during your term of service because of your residence outside the homeland, it is possible that you have other income (rent, stocks and bonds, bank accounts, trust funds, interest and the like) which would make it necessary for you to file a form each year. At any rate, an income tax statement needs to be considered. Be sure to check with your Mission Accounting Office concerning this vital matter. If there are further questions, contact your nearest office of the Internal Revenue Service. A few large U.S. Embassies overseas have a special department for IRS help and filing. If such is not the case where you serve, contact the regional office for the area of your permanent U.S. address. Some Boards file income tax forms for their missionaries, but you must provide them with required information.

It might be advisable to use the facilities of a SAFE DEPOSIT BOX to store important legal documents in the homeland. Some missions have facilities for storage of important papers in their office safe. Your Board can tell you what their policy is concerning these matters.

Be sure to keep LICENSES renewed. (Nurse's registration, Doctor's registration, Engineers license, Electrician's license, Driver's license, etc.). It may be difficult and/or time consuming to renew these if they have been allowed to lapse. Remember, you cannot legally practice a licensed profession without a current license. An INTERNATIONAL DRIVERS LICENSE may be useful to you. It is inexpensive and easy to obtain if you have a current driver's license.

Many countries require you to take with you an AFFIDAVIT FROM YOUR LOCAL POLICE DEPARTMENT showing that you have no police record. Check with your Home Office concerning the need you may have for such a paper. Your HEALTH CARD, showing innoculations and immunizations received, should be kept with your passport at all times. It should be kept up-to-date and be duly signed and sealed.

You may want to keep an open BANK ACCOUNT in the homeland. Deposit and withdrawal slips should be left with the Home Office in the event you want them to transact business for you. In this case, the signature of a mission officer should appear on your account. This is often essential when candidates attend Language School in a country to which funds cannot be transmitted. The Mission will deposit funds in this account and the missionary will draw against this to receive his monthly allotment and to pay his Language School expenses. A friend or relative might be able to cosign your account if you would prefer it.

Although your passport should serve the same purpose, it would be good to carry a copy of the BIRTH CERTIFICATE for each member of your family. For couples, it might be well to have a copy of your MARRIAGE CERTIFICATE.

A copy of your ORDINATION PAPERS and DEDICATION and/or COMMISSIONING SERVICE is required in some countries.

Be sure to REGISTER your camera(s) with the proper officials in the homeland and carry your registration paper with you in your passport. Without such registration, your camera may be confiscated, or high duty charged.

If you are a registered voter and want to vote by absentee ballot while serving overseas, be sure to carry a VOTER'S REGISTRATION CARD with the address to which you must write for absentee ballots.

An American married to a non-American may require additional legal papers.

Always check with your Home Office to determine the various legal matters which must be cared for before you leave the homeland.

QUESTIONS—CHAPTER 14

1. How important are medical and dental examinations for those about to leave the homeland? Why?

2. Are psychological examinations useful? Why?

3. What difficulties can you foresee overseas if you have difficulty with hearing?

4. Should an individual with an obvious physical handicap apply for missionary service (e.g., blind, deaf, partially paralyzed, etc.)?

5. What kinds of legal papers should be in order before you leave the homeland?

6. How do you plan to keep your legal papers secure in the place to which you are going?

7. How do you plan to keep your professional license(s) renewed while you are overseas?

8. What are the difficulties associated with voting while you are overseas?

15
Ordination, Dedication and/or Commissioning Service

Many candidates with the proper educational background and credentials will want to become ordained ministers of the Gospel before going to the field. This is most appropriate, even though your main ministry may not be as pastor of a church. On out-of-the-way stations and in situations where there are few missionaries involved in the work, there is need for an ordained missionary with the legal right of marrying and burying, and performing other pastoral functions. (Being ordained does not mean that you must, of necessity, use the title "pastor" or "missionary" on your legal entrance papers.) Upon arrival on the field, be sure to find out what specific government restrictions may apply if you are to engage in a pastoral ministry.

Dedication and/or commissioning services are usually sponsored by your home church or Bible School. On some fields today, it is essential that such a service be held, and a copy of the cerificate received at that service must be turned over to the proper authorities on the field to establish the fact that you are, indeed, in that land for specific Christian work.

The pastor of your home church, supporting church, or the leaders of the Bible School you attended will usually perform this service. It is your prerogative to have an official from your mission present and to take part in it. If furlough folks from your mission are in the area, or other candidates, invite them and perhaps allow them to take part in the service. This is a time of publicly being set apart for service on the field. It can be very meaningful to the candidate and very challenging to those who attend—more so, perhaps, if you are going out from your home church.

If the service is conducted at your Bible College or Seminary, it may very well be the means of others volunteering for service. It will provide prayer support for you as your friends become more personally involved in your ministry. And it will encourage you in your service as you look back upon your commissioning.

If you are responsible for the plans for this service, be sure to prepare well in advance and send word to your mission office concerning it. They must make plans to be in attendance, so the date and time must be cleared with those who will take part and/or attend.

Some Home Offices have commissioning certificates available for your use. Or they may be obtained from a Bible Book Store.

In some cases, a commissioning service cannot be held until your preparation for the field is complete and the Board of Directors votes for your commission of appointment as a missionary. Other Boards view all candidates as having been commissioned and appointed before the official service takes place.

The service may be brief and informal, or may take the place of a regularly scheduled meeting, or may be a special meeting called for this purpose. At a Bible College, it may take the place of a Chapel service. Missionary hymns may be sung. The candidate should be allowed an opportunity to give his testimony. There should then be a challenge for prayer support with a time of dedication and prayer following, led by the pastor of your home church, a representative from your Board, the Chairman of the Missionary Committee of the host church, and/or specially invited guests. If your parents are Christians, or in the ministry as a pastor or missionary, you will surely want them to have a part in the service. At any rate, it would be well for parents to stand with their child/children during the actual commissioning.

This is a time of serious commitment on the part of the candidate as well as for those in the church to uphold the missionary with prayer and financial support.

Programs may be printed outlining the service, or if it is a part of a longer service, a special announcement in the bulletin will suffice. Often there is a reception at the church or in the home of one of the members following the service so friends can greet the candidate in an informal setting and assure him of support during the days and years to follow.

QUESTIONS—CHAPTER 15

1. What are the pros and cons of a missionary being ordained?

2. What steps would you consider necessary to prepare for your commissioning service in your home church?

3. Design a sample program which might be appropriate for your commissioning service.

16
Relationships to Your Mission Board, Your Home Church and Your Other Supporters

From the time your application is submitted to the Board you have chosen, you are committed to them and responsible to supply any and all information they request, as much as possible to speak at services arranged by them for you, and to notify them of your itinerary and where you can be reached at all times (address and phone number).

A copy of each prayer letter should be sent to both the Home Office and the Central Field Headquarters (if the two are in different locations). As mentioned previously, your Board may require you to send a copy of each form letter to them for approval even before you send it out. There may be situations, also, where a copy should not be sent to your Field Headquarters. If the country is especially tense and sensitive, it may be best not to send any letters which contain information concerning specific work, people, and national involvement.

Prayer cards should be on file with the mission in the event there are requests for them from churches or individuals.

Funds received in meetings should be sent in regularly with reports. These may be directed to the Finance Department or to the Home Director. Your Board will fully inform you concerning the details.

The Board should be kept well-informed as to how much support you have, what is lacking, your goal date for reaching the field (or Language School).

Nearer the time of your departure, an equipment list should be sent for approval.

If your Board has to prepare papers or provide for the shipment of equipment, they must know the details, values, insurance requested, date to expect the shipment and other pertinent details.

When your Board asks questions, answer them immediately. They would not request information without having a good reason for doing so. Even when you don't understand why certain details are being requested from you, TRUST YOUR BOARD, and supply the answers they need. (It could mean the difference between obtaining your entrance visa or not, of having an opportunity to speak in a church which could provide your full support or not, or just maintaining a good relationship with your Board or not).

If you ever have questions concerning policies or procedures, contact your Board at once. Keep the lines clear on such matters.

In all of your meetings, defend your Board with 100% faithfulness. At this stage, of course, you may not understand all the reasons for your board's policies, etc. But deputation is no place to express any contrary ideas. Your leaders will listen to your ideas and help you to better understand them. You must possess full confidence in your board whether or not you "see" everything the same way on a given point. If you lack confidence in your Board, either change your attitude or choose another Board. Even though there is room for improvement in all human institutions, it is neither logical nor meaningful to destroy the confidence others place in your Board. There is no reason to think you are going to change the entire trend of a Board which has been functioning and doing a commendable job for the past 30, 50 or 100 years. Nor will you gain any merit for yourself or the work of the Lord by sharing inner-mission problems with "outsiders." Remember, too, as a candidate you are not able to view the total picture accurately. Therefore, withhold your judgment of anything or anyone until you are able to provide an answer that will solve the matter in question. It doesn't take brilliance to criticize and condemn. It may take a great degree of patience and spiritual strength to wait for the answers to be worked out in a manner which is biblically sound and personally acceptable. Again, trust your Board and its leadership. They are trusting you.

Be thoroughly conversant with the Constitution, By-Laws, and Principles and Practices of your Board. Make yourself familiar with all provisions and demands of the Board.

Know assuredly what the doctrinal stand of your Mission is. While there may be room for individual opinion and expression on minor doctrinal interpretations, it is foolhardy to serve with a Board with whose theological stand you totally disagree. Even one major point of difference can bring disastrous results to your own spiritual walk and will bring confusion to those with whom and to whom you minister overseas. You and your Board cannot walk together unless you are agreed.

When you are transacting business with the Home Office, be sure to include a separate note concerning each item you want handled. For example, monthly reports may not go to the same individual as requests for items to be purchased, or information concerning equipment lists. Do not send a general letter to the Director which includes items of business which need to be handled by several individuals. Your Board will be careful to tell you to whom each category of business should be sent. Although to conserve postage you may wish to send only one envelope, be sure each item is on a separate sheet of paper, and the name of the individual or department which is concerned is clearly printed at the top of each sheet.

A decision to become engaged to be married will be best reached in consultation with leadership in your mission. Unless your fiancee is also a candidate or a missionary under your Board, your engagement will change your status with respect to your candidacy. Until the one to whom you have become engaged is also accepted by the Board, your candidacy will be held in abeyance in most instances. If children are added to your family, give your Mission full details immediately. This, again, changes the amount of support you will need, the outfit allowance you may be able to take, and the housing which may be needed for you on the field.

You must maintain effective communications with your Board at all times. They are your closest friend and ally as pertains to questions needing answers, policies needing clarification and work which needs to be accomplished. Get to know your Home Office staff and Mission leaders personally, if possible.

Don't forget to send your prayer requests to your Mission Board. They are your friends, and in their staff prayer meetings, they will want to pray for you. The more specifically they know your needs, the more specifically you will get your answers. Otherwise you will be included in a general list of individuals with little personal involvement.

You ARE your Mission to all who come in contact with you. What you are now determines what your Board is. And you will also determine in the minds of Christian friends what the future of your Board will be. You are a member of a team and must function as such. Decisions made without official approval can affect the entire structure and outreach of your Board. Work in conjunction with the other members of your team. You cannot do the job by yourself, and neither can they!

Know who is on the Advisory Council and Board of Trustees of your Mission. Know them by name and occupation. Learn the full names of the administrative personnel and their positions. Acquaint yourself with as many of the staff members as possible, and find out their functions. (You will want to pray for them as specifically as they pray for you.)

WHAT YOU MAY EXPECT FROM YOUR HOME OFFICE

Your Home Office is a vital segment of your missionary experience. Its dedicated Christian workers are your friends. They desire God's highest and best for you and are willing to help you in every way to attain to it. They follow your deputation ministry with interest. They rejoice when your support and outgoing expenses are provided. They eagerly await the day when you are on your way to the field. They share your prayer burdens all along the way.

If you have any questions concerning finances, mission policies, requirements, equipment, or any other of a thousand things, they stand ready to give a prompt response in person, by letter, or by telephone.

If you need Mission letterhead stationery, envelopes, literature, or other supplies, it is available through the office. When you need report forms, they'll be happy to send them.

You should expect to receive periodic statements concerning your financial standing, and the various donors who have sent in funds (which is, of course, an indication that thank-you letters should be sent to each one).

The Home Office should be able to supply you with a definite equipment list, a complete and personal financial sheet showing your actual requirements for the field. They should notify you when it is time to apply for your passport. They should either apply for, or give you information concerning applying for your visa and/or entrance papers and work permits. They should give you a list of required immunizations and when they should be received.

If your mission has area representatives, be sure to check with your Director to understand what business, if any, should be handled through this representative.

You should receive news items from your field through the Home Office. You should be on their mailing list to receive regular mailings unless your Board sends packets of these materials to each candidate.

You may be able to obtain a film, curios, slide-tape series and/or displays from the office. They may also be able to give you requests for speakers they have received from your area. (Do not, however, expect the home office to obtain your support for you if you are expected to secure it for yourself. Do not expect the office to do your work for you.

It is there to assist you to do your work more efficiently and effectively.)

Check to see if your important papers can be left in the mission safe, or what alternate plan they may have available for this purpose. If you have questions to ask of missionaries on the field and do not know them personally, the Home Office may send your questions by ham radio contact or in official correspondence. Or they may give you the name(s) of individuals who could best answer your request.

You will be amazed at the many details the Home Office cares for on your behalf. The longer you serve with the Mission, the more you will appreciate the many services available to you—from receipting your support funds, to purchasing equipment at discount; from answering questions, to transporting you to the airport when the day of departure arrives. Be grateful for these faithful workers and avail yourself freely of the services they offer you.

You will need Mission literature for use at literature tables, and in contacting individuals. Request as much as you can assuredly use. Printing of literature is expensive, so never order surplus quantities and then throw it away. (In this regard, when you leave a church, leave only a few pieces of literature for their use. The rest should be carefully gathered and used in future meetings).

Again, remember that office staffs spend definite segments of time each week in united prayer on your behalf. And there have been occasions when an office person has felt led of the Lord to take on some support for a candidate. Send your prayer requests regularly.

Because your Home Office is set up to serve you in so many different ways, sometimes some will try to take advantage of this. Unless an individual specifically volunteers to do it, do not expect that one of the staff members will house you and your family for a week or two before you leave for the field, or that someone will be kind enough to purchase various personal supplies, or that one will be willing to accept responsibility to see that your car or trailer is sold. Unless your Board is exceedingly small, the office staff just cannot do the things which you, with a little forethought and planning, can do for yourself.

YOUR RELATIONSHIP TO YOUR SUPPORTERS

It seems hardly necessary to remind you that it is imperative for you to keep in contact with those who are supporting you by their gifts and prayers. As soon as the Mission notifies you of gifts sent to your account, write a note of thanks to each donor. Even a postcard will do. A friendly word genuine gratitude and the certain knowledge that you appreciate their gift (in some cases, a sacrifice) will establish true Christian fellowship and friendship with those who will make it possible for you to serve. In a very real sense, you are co-laborers together with Christ. Your supporters are not under obligation to continue your support indefinitely, but the more you can do to show your sincere appreciation for their ministry, the more interested they will be in caring for your needs.

Don't ever give in to the thought that it is the duty of your friends and relatives to send funds to your account because you are in full-time Christian service. Remember that they work for THEIR money, too. And what do any of us have which we have not received from Him?

Your friends support you because they have confidence in your ability not to let them down. They feel they are making a wise investment of their money. But you must cause them to continue to feel you are worthy of this interest. A laborer is worthy of his hire. Are you giving a full measure of work as a candidate? And do you give your supporters an indication of what you are accomplishing so that their funds will produce eternal dividends? Are you sending them prayer requests and answers to prayer? Are you thoughtfully keeping in touch? Are you concerned about them and their needs? If not, you will suffer loss, for support will drop; and your mission will lose out because friends will judge it by you.

Newsletter will never take the place of a personal note from you—even if it is just an added note at the bottom of the page.

Be sure to pray for your supporters. And if, as often happens, a child or teenager pledges toward your support, be especially careful to write to him/her. Although these gifts may be small in comparison to those received from adults, it can change a young person's entire attitude toward Christianity in general, and missions in particular, if you will take the time to correspond with him and thank him for his dime or quarter. There are no little gifts when they are given at the urging of the Lord on your behalf. Always send your letters directly to the child and not to or in care of his parents. Make your message personal and informative. You have the opportunity of paving the pathway for a future missionary or dedicated Christian layperson.

Never hint to your supporters that you have special financial needs in the hope that they will feel sorry for you and send you extra gifts. If you feel you should mention a need, do so very straightforwardly. Some may ask you from time to time if you need anything. In this case, be prepared to give an honest answer.

If your children receive personal gifts from individuals, or specified support gifts, and they are old enough to write, be sure they send a note of thanks. Don't do it for them. Contributors appreciate the uninhibited expression of gratitude they receive from children.

Never put your security in your supporters or their money. Your confidence must always and ever be in the God Who is enough. HE supplies your needs—through people, yes—but through people who give their money to the Lord, even though it may be designated for you. And thus it is a loan to you from Him. You are serving Him—not your supporters. This, of course, makes your responsibility great. Your supporters usually realize this, and thus they will pray for you and have a special interest in your ministry along with giving their financial gifts. Don't ever disappoint them by ignoring them. They are, after all, your line of supply. Without them you could not serve. You may think you lead a full and busy life. You will get tired, discouraged, and feel that busyness is going to cause burnout before you ever reach the field. Always remember that your supporters are going through this same rat race, and yet they are willing to do so to support themselves, their family—and YOU! So contact your supporters and show gratitude to them for their giving. This is a priority matter. Be sure to treat it as such.

As happens so many times within the family circle, it seems easy to neglect those who are the nearest and best-known to us. If relatives, or close friends pledge to your support, be sure to thank them just as often, sincerely, and appreciatively as you do those who are strangers to you. Even though you may write more often and openly to these folks, it is easy to forget to say "thank you." Priorities like this are often especially difficult for missionaries.

As a missionary, you may have the occupational hazard of having to manage an extraordinarily large proportion of your time. Normally, this means you will have a terrific problem maintaining even your own perceived priorities. In some of these areas, you may need to "post" with your spouse (or better, someone less sympathetic) what you are planning to do and ask him/her to check with you later about your achievement. Otherwise, "pressing needs" may outrate your priorities far too often.

QUESTIONS—CHAPTER 16

1. Why are you important to your Board?

2. Why is your Board important to you?

3. How much authority should a Board exercise over its missionaries?

4. To whom should you go if a minor problem arises between you and your Board? A major problem?

5. What may you expect in services and supplies from the Home Office of your Mission Board?

6. What types of services should you not expect your Home Office to provide for you?

7. What can you expect from your supporters?

8. What can your supporters expect from you?

9. Why is it imperative to write letters of gratitude to you supporters?

10. List five things you must keep in mind when setting priorities as regards to your time limitations.

17
Home Missionaries and Workers in Mission Offices

Human beings form two categories. They are either ministering, or being ministered unto. They are either saved or lost.

It is a common fallacy among some to think of a missionary more highly than they ought to think. It is also a tendency to make heroes of "foreign" missionaries merely because they have gone to a lonely ministry "out there," wherever that might be. And the farther away a missionary goes, the more "pity" he receives, and more prayer support. (Nothing is ever ALL bad!)

But what about Home Missionaries and those faithful few who are serving in Mission Offices or as regional representatives across the homeland? Is their ministry of less importance than that of those serving on the borders of Nepal, amidst thronging crowds in Hong Kong, or amongst hardened hearts in Europe? NO, NO. A thousand times NO!

Is there a need for Home Missionaries?" Consider for example, these facts:

There are about a million native Indians in the United States, and even more in Canada.

There are several million Asians in our country.

The second largest group of people in the U.S. are Spanish-speaking.

At least 50% of the population of almost all our major cities is comprised of black Americans.

Approximately sixty million Americans live in rural areas, and it is estimated that ⅓ of these are totally unchurched.

Then consider the large populations of other ethnic groups within our borders—Puerto Ricans, Italians, Irish, Haitians, Cubans, Vietnamese. Public schools in Los Angeles record 127 different languages are spoken in the homes they serve!

There are missions to migrant workers, Jewish missions—even a mobile ministry to the truck drivers of America. There are countless needs for workers and opportunities open here in the homeland for those workers who see a potential in this type of work all around them.

If you have chosen to serve your Lord in this way, be sure to keep your supporters informed about your work, because we are all too prone to think of and pray for our missionaries overseas, while those of you who serve at home are neglected, and sometimes forgotten.

You may have all the conveniences of home, fresh bread on the table, Engish-speaking people surrounding you, clothes that are in style, even a barber or a hairdresser on the corner to help with the beautification procedure. But you are true soldiers of the cross of Jesus Christ. You have sought God's will and found it. You are His love slaves. And whatever else it may entail, you are ready to do it.

For many, it will mean learning a new language. It is said that Navajo is one of the world's most difficult languages to learn, for example. Or you may need to learn Yiddish, Spanish, Creole, Italian, French, or Vietnamese. You usually do not have the privilege of attending Language School, so you learn it tutorially, or from those among whom you work.

You will usually be responsible for maintaining your own living quarters. Although your standard of living may be higher than for those overseas, your daily work hours are no less. Yet you will not have the privilege of having servants do your shopping, prepare your meals and clean your house and care for your yard.

Perhaps in many senses yours is the harder missionary life. The temptations which face you are certainly as strong as those Satan presents to God's workers in a secluded and demon-worshipping area in the heart of Africa. Testimony is sustained only by dwelling in Christ, and by the prayers of those who undertake to participate in this Specialized ministry.

It takes no less devotion and dedication to work for Him at home than it does to trust Him on foreign soil. A Home Missionary should never minimize his ministry as he speaks in meetings. He should never apologize for God's choice of his place of service. He should not feel inferior to other missionaries. On the other hand, he should never forget that there is a WORLD in need, and converts should be thoroughly taught concerning giving and supporting ALL God's appointed ministries—including those at home as well as those abroad.

MISSIONARIES BEHIND THE LINES

There is a growing awareness of the crucial importance of people serving the mission cause but who are necessarily "behind the lines" in their home country. We must remember that the essence of missions is not travelling, but of reaching the unreached. The latter part of the 1980's will see massive, new mobilization taking place as missions such as SIM International believe God is calling them to double their force in seven years. TEAM is actually assigning new recruits to extended home service to assist in recruiting. Young people in the Caleb Project are serving many missions as their recruiting vans criss-cross the country to reach InterVarsity groups and Campus Crusade meetings with their challenge to field service.

There are good reasons for people who are absolutely sold out for the global mission cause to work for long or short periods in their home country. Even the writing of this book is a part of helping the cause of mission, I have been told. And there are other examples.

Many serve at Christian radio stations in the U.S.A. which broadcast the gospel message into Mexico, French Quebec, Navajoland, and other areas. There are others who once served overseas who are now assigned to the U.S. for the purpose of making radio tapes to be used on stations which broadcast worldwide. Others have served overseas and have been requested by their Mission's governing body to serve as Home Director or Project Director or Personnel Director in the homeland. You feel something has been taken away from you because you are no longer bodily on the "foreign" field. Yet you are carrying out the purposes of God for this time in your life, and you are still a missionary, assisting other missionaries or reaching out with literature, tapes, or music to a world dying without Jesus Christ.

For those of you who are headed for the foreign field, consider carefully those of His men and women who are serving at home. You may envy them for not having to leave loved ones and face the struggles of adjustments in a foreign land. Yet while you may dwell securely in a mission compound in a fairly large and lovely capital of the world with few discomforts and lacks, that one whom you envied, or looked down upon, may be struggling with a difficult new language, or may be working in a dangerous area where his life means nothing to those who kill for the sheer pleasure of it. Or he may be preaching his heart out, telling the Good News of Christ to dispassionate men and women who seek the Messiah but who will not accept Him. He will be lonely, weary, discouraged. Then, too, he will be encouraged, joyful and heartened, even as you will be in your ministry. He is simply laboring in a different part of the vineyard. Your mud hut may appear like a palace to him, depending upon the circumstances.

For you who work as full-time missionaries in the homeland, you have not chosen an easy road. At the end of life's journey, you may have fewer souls for your hire than the one who has found fruit among the tribal Indians in Brazil, or amongst the elite in Paris, not because you have not been faithful in your labors, but because God gave you a more difficult task to do. It is good to remember that no souls are converted apart from the ministry of the Holy Spirit and His convicting power. Being faithful in living and preaching the Gospel is the greatest calling of all, wherever you are and whatever you're doing.

Just because your mission field is in the homeland does not mean that you should not carefully guard a specific time for holiday/vacation each year. And be sure to take full advantage of your furlough time. Yes—you, too, must take time to visit your supporters, report on your ministry, raise new support, and show slides/films of your work. Those who give that you may go are as much in need of faithful reporting as those who give to workers who go overseas.

You must be careful in the kind of life you live as a missionary in the homeland. It is easier to spend too much money on material things, recreational endeavors, and food which is too rich and fattening. You are accountable to the Lord for the way you utilize the funds committed to you for carrying out your work.

We may think of the powers of Satan being especially strong overseas where there may be few Christians, no churches, and an inadequate supply of Bibles—perhaps none in the language of the people. But be aware that Satan is very interested in disrupting God's work, no matter where it occurs or who is involved. His attacks may be more subtle and thus more unrecognizable. Be on the alert for anyone or anything that would lead you away from God's will and God's way. Remain strong in your faith. You have every possible means at your disposal to strengthen you in spiritual matters. Pastors are available to counsel and help, Christian friends are only a telephone call or short walk away, churches are available where you can worship and fellowship, Christian literature is found in bookstores in most towns and cities, radio programs and TV programs proclaim the truth of the Word of God, the Bible is available, Bible courses may be pursued . . . Be grateful for every opportunity you have of strengthening your own faith as you seek to win others to the Lord and cause them to be built up in Him.

If it were not for the Home Office workers of sending agencies, the work on every field of the world would come to a startling halt. Yet this whole category of dedicated workers are often forgotten, neglected, or ignored. The ropes must be held on the home end, and those who respond to God's call for the ministry work hand in hand with those out on the front battle lines. The work of receipting funds, making purchases, providing travel and hospitality arrangements for those passing through; writing churches, arranging meetings, keeping missionaries on furlough informed of field events and vice versa; providing ideas, missionaries, literature, slides, tapes and programs for missionary conferences across the country; answering questions, using a typewriter, speaking a friendly word on the phone, giving a tract to a delivery man, operating a computer, keeping in contact with the field by means of ham radio contacts, and a thousand other details are part of the work of a Home Office worker.

It is true that according to many people, workers in Mission offices are not missionaries. Yet the activities they perform and the services they provide are an essential element in the total program of world-wide missions. Prayer support for the entire missionary family is also a vital part of the home worker's responsibility.

Even though you have not experienced precisely the same kind of call to missionary service that others have, you are a significant factor in their success or failure. And, as has happened in many instances, it is possible that through your involvement in missions through work in the Home Office, you may feel the Lord tugging at your heartstrings to offer yourself for full-time ministry in missionary service.

QUESTIONS—CHAPTER 17

1. What are some of the major problems faced by missionaries in the homeland?

2. Is there a distinction between what we term "home" missionaries and what we term "foreign" missionaries? Explain.

3. Is there a distinction between a Home Missionary and a Home Office Worker? Explain.

4. What kind of job openings might be found in the Home Office of a Mission Board?

5. Should all workers, whether supported or salaried, who are under the authority of a Mission Board, be Christians? Explain.

18
Short Term and Summer Workers

In today's world of instant breakfasts, instant success, short hops around the world by plane and fast, accurate journeys to the moon and back, it is not surprising that we are faced with situations which demand quick action, temporary employment, and specialized services. The United States Government saw the need for this type of individual and was able to challenge thousands of young people (and many older folks, too) with the work of the Peace Corps, VISTA, USAID, and similar programs, providing low pay and hard work for a period of one to two years.

Missions also began to think in terms of meeting urgent needs by utilizing men and women in their specialized fields on mission stations which lacked personnel—perhaps because there were too few missionaries to fill the posts, or furloughs took essential workers away from their stations, or there were no trained persons in a particular position. Short term missionaries, in most fields, have provided a very necessary service and met crises with courage on many mission stations. Some have even given their lives while serving, and become martyrs for the sake of Christ.

Often a short-termer is a young person who is not yet ready to commit his entire life to missionary work, but who is anxious to see just what missionary life is all about, and therefore applies for from three months to two years of service. Middle-aged people are also applying for this type of ministry. Perhaps they had planned on becoming involved in missionary ministry, but circumstances or personal choices had deterred them from applying and being accepted by a Board. Now they want to give, as it were, a tithe from the middle of their lifetime to help in a specific project. Retired folks are also becoming involved in this endeavor, many going at their own expense to help build buildings, work in the financial office, tune pianos, counsel missionaries, become houseparents in missionary schools, care for the hospitality in a large mission headquarters, provide medical or dental services, teach in a school for missionary children, dig wells, plant crops, etc.

Some short-termers are supported in full by their home church. Others raise support from interested friends and churches just as full-time workers do. Some go at their own expense. Some boards may help in support through General Funds (especially if they urgently need the type of expertise which the short-termer can give). Some Bible Colleges ṣend workers with money raised through gifts from fellow-students. Many are sent with full support under the auspices of their denomination or local church.

Many missions are also willing to accept a limited number of young people (usually those of college-age) for a period of six weeks to three months, if they can fill a need on the field. Language may be a significant barrier on some fields, but there are many jobs for a summer worker even without the language, e.g., musicians, lab technicians, secretaries, engineers, nurses, construction workers, and any and all who have the gift of helps and want to use this gift to give a hand to missions.

For those who serve for short terms in a "secular" capacity, it is probably better to refer to them as "Workers on the mission field" rather than "missionaries." Being a missionary does, after all, involve active participation in expanding the church through teaching and preaching the gospel of Jesus Christ. But many short-termers become heavily involved in witnessing and teaching and should be considered missionaries of the cross of Jesus Christ.

There are disadvantages for short-term workers. They usually do not have a broad background concerning the people to whom they are going. Most do not speak the language or dialect of the nationals (unless they were raised of missionary parents in that locale). Many young workers have had no real experience yet in their field of specialized service. Most have not had to attend Orientation Sessions in the homeland and thus may be very uninformed or misinformed concerning health matters, mission policies and practices, social amenities as they concern nationals, nor are they acquainted with their exact responsibilities on the field. And those on the field are not always prepared to receive these short-term workers, do not know how to assimilate them into their lives and ministry, and are unprepared to give them responsibilities or to guide them in their early days on the field. In some cases, workers are immediately thrown into very difficult situations, or are asked to intervene in very "sticky" problems. For some, experiences of this kind have turned the short-termer against missions completely.

To the Mission Board there can be certain advantages, however, although one would wish that ALL workers were full-time. Often it takes a full-time worker a year to be processed for service, another year to obtain support and outgoing expenses, and possibly another year in Language School. Short-term workers are processed in a much shorter period and usually take no language study. They are young, eager to learn, full of new ideas, and ready to fill a vital role.

Full-time workers are required to have formal Bible training as a prerequisite for service. Short-termers must have an acceptable Christian testimony, but formal training may not be required.

Full-time personnel are often delayed because support is not forthcoming. Many short-termers provide their own support, or have been promised support by their family or home church, and therefore are ready to go to the field immediately upon acceptance.

Full-timers often have tons of equipment with them! Short-termers usually live with folks already established on the field, and this, of course, eliminates the need for taking any and all household items so that the short-term worker often arrives with a foot locker and a suitcase, can settle in the first day, get acquainted the next, and then plunge into the ministry for which he has offered himself. Summer workers usually are not allowed to take more than a visitor's amount of luggage into the country. Be sure to check with your Board concerning items which you CANNOT take with you.

It usually takes a lot more time to obtain the kind of entrance visas and residence papers long-term, full-time workers need. Depending on the length of anticipated service, short-termers can often travel on a tourist visa or temporary papers with a minimum of red tape and no long delays involved.

Yet, short-termers and summer workers are filling large gaps in the missionary ranks all over the world. And many are later applying to the same Board, or another, for full-time missionary service. At that time, they must normally follow the required pattern established for all missionary candidates.

For those who may be considering short-term service, or for who may be counseling young people (and older ones as well) concerning this matter, you may want to check into some of the following opportunities.

Contact the mission board of your choice to see if they utilize short-term workers, what requirements are placed upon volunteers, and what types of ministries are available to those who apply.

Contact your denominational headquarters. They, through their Missions Department, will know what kinds of workers are needed and what types of ministry are available.

INTERCRISTO (P.O. Box 9323, Seattle, WA 98109). This organization publishes an Opportunities Directory. Openings at home and abroad are listed. For a fee, you may place your name in their computer to have your abilities, gifts and talents matched to hundreds of openings available in any of hundreds of sending agencies.

OPERATION MOBILIZATION (244 Godwin Avenue, Ridgewood, NJ 07450). This service of personal witnessing has widespread openings. By means of missionary ships, O.M. distributes Christian literature, holds conferences for pastors and Christian leaders worldwide, and sells the best in Christian books.

YOUTH WITH A MISSION (Box YWAM, Tyler, TX 75710). This sending agency is international and interdenominational. It is primarily engaged in evangelism and training for evangelism with an emphasis on short term service for youth.

TEEN MISSIONS, INC. (P.O. Box 1056, Merritt Island, FL 32952). This ministry utilizes young people from ages 13-29 in both work teams and evangelistic teams in the homeland and overseas. Some serve as team leaders. All serve in groups.

Your home church, your pastor, your Bible College missions professor, or agencies in your local area may be able to advise you of individual programs in which you can take part on a short-term basis. Seek out the one where you feel you can best use your talents to their fullest in service to your Lord and to those who need Him so desperately in the world around us.

Short-term service should not be considered for the wrong reasons. Some may wish to get away from home, some may look forward to travel, others may wish to boast that they have been overseas, some may be trying to avoid a bad home situation, some may feel they will find a life partner. Missionary work is serious business, and those who pursue it, whether full-time or short-term, must be concerned that they are fulfilling God's will for their life, must be willing to put forth their best efforts in the work committed to them, must have a burden for lost souls, must be willing to cooperate with their fellow-workers, and must be willing to give up worldly pleasures and monetary gain to give themselves to the task at hand. Short-term work can be beneficial or detrimental to the work of the Lord. It should, therefore, not be entered into lightly by the Mission Board or by the worker himself.

QUESTIONS—CHAPTER 18

1. What advantages does a short-termer have over those who plan on life-long service on the mission field?

2. What disadvantages does a short-termer have over those who plan on a lifetime of service on the field?

3. What are several reasons for short-termers deciding to become full-fledged missionaries?

4. What are several reasons for short-termers becoming disinterested in long-term service?

5. Should short-termers be called "missionaries"? Explain

19
Women and Missions

These are days when women's lib, equal rights, male chauvinism, and other kinds of "feminist" thinking have assumed a prominent place in the minds of the American public. As one who will be representing the Lord Jesus Christ, it is essential that you discover what your personal views are concerning the place of women in missionary work—whether you are a male or a female. It is important that you deal with matters pertaining to the role of woman in the plan and purpose of God. You will inevitably find it coming into play in your relationships with mission administrators on the field, fellow missionaries, and knowledgeable nationals.

At the same time, you must take into consideration that much of your own perspective will pertain only to **your** particular culture— that of the West in general, and that of America in particular. And never should you seek to impose your cultural biases upon others. Missionaries have already done this far too often . . . so much so that those to whom you go may already find it most difficult to separate certain purely western cultural elements from universal Christian teachings.

The Bible makes it clear that God loves women. It shows that He does for them exactly what He does for men. He provides salvation, answers prayers, gives comfort and direction, bestows His blessings, etc., etc. He also requires faithfulness, obedience, love for one's neighbor, personal integrity, etc., etc. Promises, blessings, commands, and guidance are given to both men and women. Where God has a specific function for either sex to fulfill, or a specific command for man or woman, He is careful to state this in His Word.

Solomon knew something about women! In Proverbs 31:10-31, he gives what he feels are the crowning qualities of womanhood, namely: a devotional spirit, modesty, liberality, given to hospitality, wise, and virtuous.

Women had a ministry in the life of Jesus here on earth. We think of Elizabeth; of Mary, His mother; of His close friends, Mary and Martha; of Mary Magdalene; of Joanna, Susanna, and others who ministered to Him of their substance. We see Him going out of His way to talk with the Samaritan woman, to help the woman with the issue of blood, to heal Peter's wife's mother.

When Paul speaks of the spiritual gifts which are given to the church, and the spiritual fruit which should be an integral part of witnessing, he in no wise excludes women.

There has, of course, been a great deal of controversy over the interpretation of Paul's words concerning the role of women in the church. He implied that women were not to be teachers in the church; in fact, they were to keep silence in the church (I Timothy 2:12; I Corinthians 14:34). He suggested that if the women wanted to know the truths of the Word, they should ask their husbands at home. Why? Because women are/were inferior to men? NO! Because in Paul's day, the church was just becoming established and the gospel had not yet had extensive effect upon the surrounding culture. The church often met in homes (Acts 12:12; Romans 16:5,23; Colossians 4:15; Philemon, vs. 2); the temple (Acts 5:12); public school auditoriums (Acts 19:9), or synagogues (Acts 14:1,3; 17:1; 18:4). The Lord's Day morning service consisted of the reading of Scripture (Old Testament, of course), exhortation by the leading elder, prayers, and singing. The evening session was a celebration of communion. Because it was the custom of the times in that area, men and women were seated in separate areas during worship (as is still the rule in many places of the East). Whenever, during the services, the women would whisper or talk to one another, it was very disruptive (and still is)! Paul urged that women, under the circumstances, could best learn and worship if they would keep silent in church services, and if they didn't understand, ask their husbands in the quietness of the home.

But even in Paul's day, the women performed many services in the church. Phoebe was a deaconess (Romans 16:1). Philip's daughters served the Lord, and historical references lead us to believe they fulfilled the functions of a prophet (Acts 21:9). Priscilla was a staunch supporter of Paul and a mature Christian leader in the early church at Ephesus (Acts 18:18). Syntyche and Euodia were prominent in the church at Philippi and served with Paul (but, unfortunately, did not get along with one another, thus threatening to split the Philippian Church) (Philippians 4:2,3). The women helped in providing welfare services to the needy (Acts 9:36-41). Women, at the dawn of the Christian era, made a deep impression upon the Roman world around them because of their love for others, and their pure and happy home life.

It is not our purpose to delve into church history at this point. But it is interesting to follow the role of women in the church through the centuries. We remember, for example, that some of the reformers' wives were eminent scholars in their own right, as was Susannah Wesley, mother of John and Charles. Then women began to take leadership in the prayer meetings and Sunday Schools which came into being in the late 1700's. After seminaries were founded and missionary work at home and abroad became activated, some women began to take training in biblical studies, and a far more active part in both church and social activities (which, at that time, were fully inter-related). The colleges were still all-male, but by the middle of the 1800's, there was a demand for missionary women to be trained. Women's colleges like Wellesley, Vassar, Bryn Mawr, Radcliffe, etc., all sprang into being to fill this need.

Even so, something which must still be reckoned with is the universal need for orderly family structure and authority. The Word of God gives several imperatives to married women:

Women were to be in subjection to their husbands (Genesis 3:16; I Peter 3:1).

Women were to submit to their husbands (Ephesians 5:22).

Women were to have the man as their head (I Corinthians 11:3).

Women were to learn in silence with all subjection (I Timothy 2:11).

Women were not to usurp authority over the man (I Timothy 2:12).

In all this, however, Paul was careful to point out that the husband also IS TO BE IN SUBJECTION TO CHRIST (I Corinthians 11:3).

Yet women must go one step further than that of a husband's authority, for they, too, are under the authority and mandate of God. God deals with individuals—man, woman, boy, girl. He asks us to be faithful followers of Him and obedient to His commands. And in the world in which we live, there is a need for both men and women, married and single, to proclaim His gospel to the ends of the earth.

You will have to settle your own scriptural position concerning these matters, keeping in mind the policy of your board. You will have to relate your conclusions to your own call and choosing. But never forget that women are not inferior beings. God does not intend that they should be unthinkingly moved about like pawns by male leadership into slots that men have been unwilling to fill through the years. Their efforts are not less necessary and expedient than those put forth by men. And if women can help meet the need for intensified missionary and other Christian outreach in this day and generation, more power to them! We need all the help we can get! Many women are doing the job. Until Third World mission agencies began sending forth workers, far more women were willing to go forth than men. Of course, women should maintain a proper sense of balance, willing to relinquish their places to more qualified men as they become available or as national leadership is trained. And in all of this, they will want to keep themselves guiltless as concerns doing to men what they feel men have been doing to them through the years, i.e., putting them down and minimizing their efforts.

What can women in missions do? They can do all that their spiritual gift(s) allow(s) them to do. This includes:.

1.   THE MINISTRY OF THE WORD

    a.   **Prophecy**—proclaiming the Word of God

    b.   **Evangelism**—leading others to Christ

    c.   **Teaching**—nourishing others in truth by interpreting and communicating it clearly and systematically

    d.   **Exhortation**—motivating people to action, using God's Word as their authority

    e.   **Wisdom**—applying God's truth to real-life situations

    f.   **Knowledge**—understanding what God teaches

    g.   **Discernment**—knowing truth from error

    h.   **Music**—expressing relationship to God in song

2.   THE MINISTRY OF DIRECTING OTHERS

    a.   **Leadership** (administration)—leading others

    b.   **Faith**—trusting God beyond the probable, and raising the vision of others

3.   THE MINISTRY OF HELPING

    a.   **Serving**—assisting and aiding in ways that give strength and encouragement to others

    b.   **Giving**—making and distributing money for God's work

c. **Showing mercy**—working joyfully with those whom the majority ignores

d. **Craftmanship**—working with the hands for the benefit of others

e. **Healings**—making others feel better physically, spiritually, and emotionally

Since women are recipients of spiritual gifts as well as men, it is imperative that these gifts be utilized. Paul says, "stir up the gift" (II Timothy 1:7; I Timothy 4:14). He also says that our gifts should edify the church (I Corinthians 14:12). Gifts are given for service (Ecclesiastes 9:10), "Whatsoever thy hand findeth to do, do it with all thy might." And women, as well as men, will be held accountable for the use of their gift(s). We must assume that the impressive role of women in the Chinese house church movement, and at the Cell level in Korea is something with which God has been pleased and which He has abundantly blessed.

Many women do not feel capable of assuming the role of apostle, prophet, evangelist, pastor, healer, administrator. Or if confident of success in one of these roles, they are reticent to accept such a position. But even some of these positions must be considered by women whom God has chosen for a life of missionary activity. Isn't it logical that a woman who is an enormously influential nursing administrator in a mission hospital will also function effectively as a member of the Field Council? Is it something else for her to be the administrative head of a station? If a woman can safely assume the position of Prayer Chairman in the entire area in which she serves, why can't she also assume the title of Chairman for Outreach and Development? In the homeland, before getting into missions, many single women who were shocked at the very thought of women pastors, have arrived on the field to find themselves involved in church planting and pastoral ministries in areas where no men are present and no national leadership is available. Or they may end up in areas where the male missionaries do not feel that type of ministry to be their calling, and therefore refuse to assume it. Interestingly enough, in a poll taken among some 150 individuals at a Christian Bible College recently, when students were asked questions such as, should a woman be a pastor? a Sunday School Superintendent? a Christian education director? a mission administrator? a teacher? an evangelist? it was the men who overwhelmingly gave approval for such positions. It was the women who answered in the negative. Perhaps we need to consider whether or not women are afraid to assume creative roles and added responsibilities!

Here we do not present unalterable conclusions concerning the role of women in missions, but perhaps your appetite has been whetted to look into the matter further through research and study. (The excellent—and only—comprehensive study of the amazing role of American women in missions is Beaver's **All Loves Excelling**, a real must for all women in missions. It is out of print at Eerdmans, but still available from the Church Growth Book Club, 1705 North Sierra Bonita, Pasadena, CA 91104).

Some of the questions you will want to consider, whether you are male or female, single or married, are:.

Is it right for a mission board to send single women to a field where, in the national culture, women are downtrodden, and men are excessively authoritative?

Where do family responsibilities end and missionary responsibilities begin? How much should a missionary wife seek to do? Does your Mission require full-time service for the wife as it does for the husband?

How much does competence have to do with women's role in missions? How would you react if your mission were to appoint a woman to its Board of Directors?

What should the attitude of women be toward the men in the mission? And how should the men view women—married and/or single?

Is it God's ideal that men should be the spiritual leaders of Christian work and ministry?

Are men associated with strength and women with weakness, thus accounting to the fact that men are usually chosen for missionary leadership positions?

Must the unmarried woman missionary submit willingly to every move to another station, every change of co-worker, and every area of responsibility submitted to her by her Field Director?

Because for so long women have played an overtly submissive role in Western society and even to some extent on the mission field, what is the best way for them to develop their spiritual gifts for the edification of the church?

On the other hand, how can women best assume the many administrative and supervisory positions which are open to them in the mission world?

What are some of the major considerations in appointing a

woman to run a station, be in charge of a hospital, dispensary or clinic, head up a mission school, be responsible for whole blocks of Christian education, etc.?

Do women have the knowledge, stamina, decisiveness, patience, wisdom, tolerance, understanding, emotional stability, and whatever else is needed, to become counselors, leaders, supervisors, administrators?

How would you, as a male administrator, deal with a woman or women under your authority who are unwilling to be submissive to your decisions?

Women play a very vital role in missionary work. They've done a tremendous job through the years, and it is to their credit that often, without adequate recognition of their administrative gifts, they have, nevertheless, been willing to devote their lives behind the scenes.

Today, however, doors of opportunity for women in missions are wider open than ever before, for those who want something more . . . those who seek expanded roles and more far-reaching ministries . . . those who are capable of leading as well as of following. For some it will mean having a desire to become involved not only with a program of life-long learning, but also in continuing education— updating their knowledge and skills as preparation for a more vital role in their field of missionary endeavor. For others it may mean entering a new sphere of activity which will meet the needs of the people to whom they have gone to minister far more effectively than through their former profession or training.

There are many areas of supervision and administration which are open to women in missions:

EVANGELISM AND CHURCH GROWTH: Teaching, counseling, music, youth work, women's groups and committees, area councils

EDUCATION: Schools, libraries, continuing education, educational counseling, adult education, extension education (correspondence courses)

COMMUNICATIONS: Record librarian, letter writing, broadcasting, TV, layout work, bookstore management, writing/editing, art, statistical data and research, proof reading, translation, computer operation

MEDICINE: Doctors, nurses, medical technicians, public health and community health workers midwives medical librarians, X-ray

technicians, laboratory technicians, nutritionists/dieticians, physiother-
apists, occupational therapists

SOCIAL SERVICES: Sociology, counseling, child care, family
planning

BUSINESS: Bookkeeper, public relations, secretary, administrative assistant

SUPPORT MINISTRIES: Housemother, linguist, ham radio
operator, literacy worker, hostess/hospitality

MUSIC: Vocal, instrumental, choir director, hymn writer/
translator

Having said all this, it may often seem that women in missions
are needed only when they are fully qualified with expertise in a particular discipline, and they can fulfill that ministry best only when there is
no man available for the position.

In any case, it is true that missions must have the finest, best,
most qualified women available from the Christian world if they are to
accomplish all they want on the mission field. But we have come to a
point where a woman ought not to be sent overseas simply because she
is a Christian, has Bible School training, and feels "called" to go. In
most longstanding fields we are no longer living in the era of the "general missionary," when the principle task was to teach the Word and
begin the work. It is not primarily because Americans have become
more sophisticated in their choice of a profession that makes it needful
for women to have a definite place of service on the field, but because
of the growth and progress of the churches overseas and the educational
advancement, nationalism, and the rapid rise of the newly developing
world which is demanding ever more and more of those who would
seek to serve within the borders of their jurisdiction, sometimes almost
beyond reason. Those who once went forth as missionary nurses, for
example, are being replaced by national nurses. American nurses now
more often assume supervisory teaching, and other leadership
positions—or are leaving nursing for another perhaps lesser, role. The
developing countries no longer want us to assume their obligations.
They are willing, however, to let us train their own people for increasing responsibilities and effectiveness.

A few countries are placing a moratorium on the number of missionaries allowed into their country. This puts a burden upon mission
leadership as to what work is most essential and who is most qualified
to do it.

On the other hand women in missions are finding that some lands, long closed to missionary work, are now open to teachers, nurses, and other professional personnel. Again, you must decide whether or not this is the kind of situation where, by your life and by your faithfulness in doing the best job you possibly can, you can best witness for Jesus Christ in a dark land. Many women are willingly volunteering for just such service today.

Moreover, there are some areas of ministry on the field that are best carried out by women. In Muslim areas of the world, women work with women and children while men work with the male segment of the population. In many lands women have been able to deal with the problems of mothers in a way that could not have been adequately handled by men. There are areas of the world where women are so depressed and downtrodden that they have no way to earn a living in the event of the death of their husband, or an unexpected divorce. Women missionaries have had an opportunity to teach such women how to sew and work with their hands in order to make goods which are saleable and from which they can earn sufficient funds to care for themselves. As the work is done in small groups, there is much opportunity for gospel witness during the work hours—a real missionary outreach.

Married women play an extremely important role on the mission field. They are almost always extremely capable and fully involved in the work, but often far less recognized than single women because they are the "shadow". Married women often run clinics in their home, teach English classes, counsel those with problems, entertain guests . . . while others take on even more far-reaching pursuits such as adult primary education (by extension) programs, correcting Bible correspondence courses or providing nursery or elementary school facilities from their own home. (The book, **By Ones & By Twos**, written by missionary Jeannie Lockerbie, should be read by every woman—single or married—anticipating service on the mission field. Order it from William Carey Library, P.O. Box 40129, Pasadena, CA 91104).

In considering the place of women in missions today it is essential that you be very sure you have something vital to offer those to whom you are sent. More than that, be absolutely certain that you have set those priorities for your life and ministry which will bring praise and honor and glory to Him Whom you serve.

Finally, remember this, and go forth in its truth: God always chooses the best man for the job—even if it's a woman!

QUESTIONS—CHAPTER 19

1. What do the Scriptures say concerning the work and ministry of women?

2. What types of ministries can women perform overseas?

3. What are some questions you would like to raise concerning women in mission leadership roles?

4. How can women be best used in church planting ministries?

5. If a Mission is engaged in team ministry overseas, what roles should women be allowed to play in those teams?

6. Should women missionaries be placed in positions of authority in Muslim countries of the world? Why?

7. How do you feel the priorities of married women with children differ from the priorities of single women on the field?

20
The Single Candidate

In the absence of the usual family-arranged wedding pattern known all over the world, American society has allotted the marriage initiative to the men. Thus, proportionately, there are far more single women candidates on the mission field than single men candidates. Perhaps some in-depth research should be done to pursue this phenomenon further.

Of those who go out to the field single, fewer men stay single than do women. (Perhaps this is because there are so few men to share with so many women!)

Sometimes the attitude toward single missionaries, both on the part of people in the churches at home, and of married couples on the field, is that because you couldn't find a mate in the homeland, you are now going to try the mission field. This, however, is true in very few instances. Most single workers have turned down proposals of marriage or have not asked for a hand in marriage in order to give full devotion and attention to the service of Christ. Many tasks can only be done by single people. And although we hear more often of those single women who are serving, we must remember there are also many single men doing an effective work in very difficult places.

If single workers could share the most difficult part of their work, they would probably agree that it is loneliness. Married folks have each other and their children. Single folks have their work and a busy life among multitudes of people, but they can face loneliness at the end of a busy day and be far away from any with whom they can share their joys and burdens meaningfully.

But there are also advantages. During your days of deputation, you are free to go and come as you please. You are free from your parents, and you can put your full strength into your deputation work. You have only one mouth to feed, and although you may have to exercise faith for the next meal, there is not the responsibility and the constant burden of feeding your spouse and children. You can go to the field with far less equipment and you need to raise less support than a couple or a family. This means you may be able to leave for the field sooner than your married fellow-workers in some cases. You should not listen to those who feel sorry for you. You are entering a full and satisfying life.

Once you are sure of the Lord's call and after you have been accepted by your Mission Board, you must be careful that your calling is not changed by falling in love with one who does not share your missionary vision. It can be a very real temptation. It has ruined many a missionary career and has often ended in a second-rate marriage because of the guilt which can develop from not continuing in the Lord's best will.

Many times the Lord honors a stand to follow Him to the ends of the earth by allowing a life partner to enter your life at Candidate School, Orientation, Language School, or on the field. But there are far worse things that could happen to you than being single. It is true that as a single person, you will face various temptations and must meet these in the strength of the Lord. Among these will be loneliness, stubbornness, impatience with married couples (especially if you are expected to be a babysitter), the feeling that you will be pushed from one station or area of service to another whenever a need for a worker arises, the awful anticipation of being accommodated with a family or married couple with little opportunity for privacy, and that strong, overpowering desire for marriage and a home. All of these feelings come occasionally to most single people. But compensations come from the liberty you will have of entering fully into His service, available at anytime to anyone without reservation.

Single candidates should be stable people. You must know how to bear responsibility. You must be able to use authority, for if you are not in an official administrative position during the course of your years with the Mission, you will surely find yourself in situations which demand from you some kind of administrative ability, supervision and/ or leadership role. You may have a way of being either too dogmatic and authoritative, or lacking in these qualities entirely. It is especially important for you to become aware of others and their feelings, and the great complexities of the daily life of your married fellow workers.

Discretion should be used in your platform presentation. Personal references should not be an advertisement. A single girl who said publicly from the platform, "I'm praying that God will give me a man before I go to the mission field," found a gentleman, twice her age and with one marriage already behind him, proposing to her after the service. When she refused, he followed her to several churches where she was scheduled to speak, and eventually travelled several hundred miles to her home to propose again. She learned her lesson and thereafter made her concern known only to God!

You must be careful to keep yourself from unsuitable friendships involving those who do not seek to give God glory in their lives. Strong attachments of this type have resulted in loss of effective Christian witness. We are, after all, in the world, but not of the world.

You should guard yourself against volunteering for more than you can effectively accomplish. You may even accept too heavy a deputation schedule, or assume too many responsibilities for the Mission. Normally you will not be able to carry as strenuous a load on the field as you can in the homeland. Learn your limitations.

Don't envy your married colleagues. Don't make fun of marriage. Don't expect always to be included in groups of couples. Don't be discouraged when you can't brag about your children. Throughout your deputation meetings, always be sure you have an answer that fully satisfies your own heart when you are asked the question, "Why aren't you married?" If you can't give a good answer, think about it for a while. It will be asked a good many times at home, and will surely be asked on the field by the nationals who often cannot understand such a status since it is in opposition to their whole way of life in a culture where marriages are arranged for children by their parents.

The mission field may provide a mate for you. But make absolutely certain that this is God's will for you. Don't spend time and energy seeking a wife when you should be searching for lost souls, or hunting a husband when you could be heralding His grace. "Seek ye first the kingdom of God and His righteousness; and all these things shall be added unto you" (Matthew 6:33)—as much as you need for the work to which you are dedicating your life. "No good thing will He withhold from them that walk uprightly" (Psalm 84:11).

A word of caution should be given at this point. It has not been an unknown thing on the mission field that a single girl has flirted with and won the affection of a married man; an older, married missionary man has fallen prey to a young national woman; single men and women have become involved with homosexual/lesbian practices. Obviously, such actions are not in accord with the will of God, and should certainly not be condoned by fellow-workers nor be allowed to become an example to those whom you have gone forth to reach with the gospel of the Lord of your life. Just as with other sins which can so easily beset us, all temptations must be placed at the foot of the cross. It might mean speaking very frankly to your Field/Regional Director, or your Home Director to ask for an immediate transfer to another station or area. It will always involve your own ability to discipline your thought-life and actions stemming therefrom. Never allow Satan to lead you astray. He is an expert in striking at your weakest point(s). Rebuke him and run to the Lord for shelter from his wiles. In the midst of every circumstance with which you may be faced, remember that God has given you His Holy Spirit Who will keep you from defeat in every area of your life. Giving in to sin is destructive—to you, to others involved, and to your ministry.

Not only should your relationships with your fellow-workers be beyond reproach but great care must be taken in your relationship with your national students national language teacher(s) and the nationals among whom you work in other capacities. Single missionaries have been strongly attracted to their language teacher. In a few instances, comparatively speaking, love has grown and marriage has followed quite successfully. But in all too many cases, love being "blind", the missionary has discovered after engagement or marriage that the man has wanted to marry a Western woman for the prestige and honor it will bring him among his own people, or because it provides easy access for him to move permanently to the United States or Canada. Often there is no desire to stay in his own country for gospel ministry among his own people. And, unfortunately, the truth does not surface until after the marriage has taken place.

On the other hand, there are many fine examples of national/ missionary marriages which have been much used of the Lord. But deep consideration must be given to this type of relationship in areas such as God's call, your ministry, your relationship to those in the homeland (including your own family), the rules of your Mission Board, the probability of children, citizenship, lifestyle, retirement plans, living conditions, customs, in-laws, food, language—and much more. It is difficult for first-termers overseas to realize how profound (and very nearly permanent) such differences can be. Many counselors should be consulted, and all questions should receive answers which are satisfactory to you before going ahead with a step of this kind.

If you are single, thank God for it and rejoice with others whom the Lord has joined together. If you are married, befriend the single folks. They need your loving concern. And may you be completely content in whatever state you find yourself. God can and will use you in

His service—even as a single person. Again, the book **By Ones & By Twos** by Jeannie Lockerbie is a refreshing study of this whole area.

QUESTIONS—CHAPTER 20

1. What advantages do single candidates have over married couples?

2. With what disadvantages do single candidates have to contend?

3. What personal characteristics should the single candidate seek to develop?

4. List at least 10 "cures" for loneliness.

5. What should the attitude of the single missionary be toward those on the field who are married?

21
Marriage and the Mission Field

In those wonderful days just before the knot was tied, you probably thought within yourself that nothing would ever tarnish the beautiful relationship which had been established between you and the one whom you loved dearer than life itself. The Lord had provided you with a mate whose desires and goals were the same as yours; who complemented you in every possible way; who seemed to understand your moods; who entered completely and gladly into your joys and disappointments. How wonderful that the Lord had led you separately, and then together, to this place of missionary service. Others, looking on, were grateful for the Lord's provision on your behalf.

No matter how long you have been married, you will agree on at least one thing. Living 24 hours a day, 7 days a week, 365 days of the year with someone—no matter how much love is involved—is difficult. It is a rare pair, indeed, whose background, tastes, decision-making processes, personalities, moods, fears, etc., etc., concide and mesh so perfectly with each other that all discord is forever banished and bliss is attained. You have discovered this already! When one can say of his partner, however, "She's (he's) not only my wife (husband), but also my best friend," you have come a long way down the path of togetherness and blessing.

If you have found that problems have arisen, questions have been raised, tempers have flared, and discussions have turned into arguments in your marriage at home, you should know that in your missionary lives together, the stresses and strains upon your marriage will possibly be even magnified and multiplied.

It is important to be aware of potential difficulties before you ever set foot on foreign soil. Ask your close friends at home to remember your needs as a married couple serving the Lord in strange surroundings. You will need all the prayer support you can find.

What are some of the problems which arise so inconspicuously and yet build themselves into such stone walls of resistance not only to each other, but to the work and will of God?

Perhaps the wife learns the language quickly and well while the husband struggles to understand and to be understood with seemingly little success.

The husband may be away from home often and/or for long periods of time.

There are so many demands upon your time that there is little effort given to a daily devotional time together.

Being away from loved ones, family, friends, the home church, the niceties of life, the privilege of solitude, can place severe strains upon relationships.

If both husband and wife are engaged in a number of totally different activities, time for sharing is far too limited. Neither fully understands or enters into the burdens the other is bearing.

It is possible that the wife is a far better administrator than the husband, and nationals may come to her for counsel rather than to him. If a man becomes known as Mrs. So-and-so's husband, it is cause for friction.

Jealousy and envy raise their ugly heads when you least expect them.

There can be an unnatural and/or inordinate physical attraction to a language teacher, a national co-worker, or a fellow missionary.

Isolation produces its own set of stresses in marriage. Loneliness in an isolated situation is often not allowed or understood by one mate while the other cannot seem to live above it.

Spending more time with the nationals than with the family can be devastating to a marriage. Priorities in this regard must be set and maintained after being mutually agreed upon.

The very busyness and exhaustion of a day's work can destroy any form of leisure fellowship and worship within the family circle.

The wife may find a rich and rewarding ministry while her husband is placed in a situation in which he is extremely unhappy—and vice versa.

Few men are at their emotional best when laboring in the desert where the daily temperature hovers around 120°, or after a ten-day trek by mule, or after an all-day ride on an overcrowded bus, or after a particularly difficult session with an inquirer. And few women feel romantic after supervising the antics of the sweeper and the cook, entertaining a group of village women who do not have the same concepts of time or convenience, or after staying up all night with your child who has just come down with what appears to be typhoid fever.

You will almost always be pressed for time. There is so much to do. There are so few to help. Your responsibility is great. Souls may enter eternity without Christ if you do not do all in your power to get the gospel message to them. So you spend more time in the work and less with your family and with your Heavenly Father.

Often there isn't even time to ask forgiveness on the field. So, little wrongs grow into bigger wrongs. And as the hurts and sins and wrongs become larger, the oneness of your relationship is severed.

There is separation within the mission field experience. One of the hardest to bear is when children have to leave home to attend the school for missionary children (often scores of miles away), or when young people must be sent home for further education.

Excess fears and concern about sickness can develop when you know there is no doctor nearby. Concern about sanitation and cleanliness and the possibility of catching serious diseases has finally broken many a missionary and ended his/her ministry, especially if the concern centers on your children.

There may be abnormal uncertainties in the situation in which you find yourself. The political pressures upon missionary activities as a whole, or upon your work in particular, may be of such a nature that "normal" living conditions are difficult to maintain. You may be placed under "house arrest" and not allowed to leave your home or compound for days or weeks at a time. Or there may be the constant threat of covert activities, riots, war, expulsion—and you may be on 24-hour alert, knowing you might at any moment have to leave the country with, at the most, two suitcases and your lives. There may be tribal uprisings surrounding you, or an imminent government takeover, or the arrest of expatriates. There may be times when your government officials do not force you to leave your country of service, and your Mission Board gives you the option of staying or leaving because they feel you know the situation better than they do in the homeland. These are times when there must be agreement in the family. Yet they are also stressful times when problems can easily arise, tempers may flare, and family life is disrupted.

There will be changes to which you will need to readily and successfully adjust, sometimes tumbling over each other so rapidly that you will find it difficult to enter fully into so many non-static conditions. You may have to face one set of circumstances and conditions at Language School, others as you are placed on a station, and yet others as you may be moved to a new field, station, people, or language. Each move will provide some trepidation as you face the seemingly unknown, and each change will cause you to have to make adjustments within your personal relationships within the family unit.

Pressures may also build simply because of a lack of communication with the outside world. This, too, may lead to impatience, frustration. and undue concern, adding to an already tense situation.

The disruptions of planning for furlough, going on furlough, and returning from furlough produce their own peculiar frustration levels.

Disease factors and psychological problems are a constant factor in the life of a couple on the field. Many a missionary has had to return home because of an inability to accept dirt, germs, boiled water/milk, threat of disease and fear of known or unknown factors within a given situation. Suppose the wife is unable to adjust adequately to so many new conditions. Perhaps she will seek to avoid confessing this to her mate until the problems mount to an obsession. She has tried to keep it to herself because her husband has found a satisfying ministry and has none of the fears that his wife is experiencing. There is less and less communication concerning these adverse factors, and all of a sudden, the woman's health breaks, and they are forced home. It takes a spiritual giant of a man to accept this kind of situation, and it can adversely affect a marriage to such a degree that there may seem little hope of continuing satisfaction within it. You must always, however, claim Romans 8:28 in every trying situation, including one as devastating as this.

Satanic attacks will be both more subtle and more frequent in most areas of service overseas than they were in the homeland. Be aware of this, but do not dwell on it to the extent that you cannot find victory in the Lord.

Oftentimes a couple will be placed alone on a station. How longingly you may recall how at home you could run down to the corner store, visit a neighbor, go play golf, call a friend, read a book, go to church. But out there you are by yourselves. And no matter how much you love a person, there seems to be something within each individual that craves companionship and communion with others. And that which you find with the nationals doesn't always take the place of your friends back home.

You may have several younger single missionaries stationed with you. They will have their own special needs, and you may not wish to be "bothered" with their problems and concerns because it takes time away from your own family needs. There must come to every missionary the acceptance of his co-workers, and you must function as a group in accordance with all that God's will has led you to accomplish in the place where you are stationed. The fruit of the Spirit will be needed to fulfill His commission.

Here in the homeland, your mate may have certain annoying habits which you try to overlook. They may be just little things (e.g., squeezing the toothpaste tube from the top, throwing dirty socks on the floor, or cracking knuckles). Little things like this, however, can wear on your nerves over there, so be very careful to commit even the little things to the Lord every day of your life.

One of the lovely parts of marriage is the fact that there is a listening ear, a shoulder to cry on, and a companion to laugh with available to you. But often there won't even be time for this. Or you may both need to cry at once!

With so many stresses placed upon a couple on the field, even sexual relations may grow merely out of your need for physical release rather than from a fullness of love for your mate.

Stress is not uncommon in any close relationship, and certainly not unknown in marriage. It can, in fact, be a very healthy situation whereby growth to fuller maturity is attained. If two people see an accident they will have each seen it from a different perspective. When both give their testimony, much more is known about what really happened than if only one gave a report. From this we understand that no one person can see an entire situation perfectly. We must give room for another opinion, and seek to learn more than is already known.

Unfortunately, under strained conditions, a couple is very apt to turn against each other rather than seek a satisfactory solution to the actual problem which is the source of the stress. Thus fellowship and companionship is broken and the problem remains unresolved.

Each partner in a marriage must plead with God to give him a tender heart, a gentle spirit, an understanding mind, the ability not only to forgive when wronged, but to seek never to wrong the other.

The word "stress" indicates tension, fatigue and/or exhaustion. It has to do with emotional or physical factors to which a person has failed to adapt satisfactorily. It can cause physiological and psychological tensions. Stress (the amount of force exerted within or upon someone), subjects one to hardship, affliction, depression, and/or distress.

Stress can result in strengthening. It can also produce breakdowns. A certain amount of tension is essential for normalcy. But individuals must learn to cope with it—adapting, changing, growing. If one cannot successfully adjust to minor strains and stresses, it will come to a point where every simple marital or work problem will turn into an all-important family crisis.

The foregoing remarks are, by no means, intended to imply that going to the mission field is going to adversely affect your marriage, anymore than pressures and difficulties will necessarily tear down, rather than build up, marriages back home. Generally missionary families confronting problems together are wonderfully strengthened. But you should be well aware of some of the unusual and unexpected causes of tension and friction which may disrupt your personal satisfaction as well as the effectiveness of your ministry.

The period of candidacy can be a good test of how well you will adjust as a family overseas. Seek to learn as much as possible about coping with change and exercising faith in these pre-field days.

Unfortunately, divorce is not unknown among missionaries. This is a fairly new phenomenon. It can devastate not only those personally involved in the family itself, but supporters, home churches, co-workers, and especially the nationals among whom you will labor.

Divorce should not be considered a viable option for getting out of a situation about which you no longer agree as a couple. Through prayer and wise counsel, virtually all marriages can be saved if those contemplating divorce will be willing to work out the problems. Don't ever believe the lie that going overseas will change you sufficiently to discourage a contemplated divorce. Any marital problems of such a serious nature must be settled before considering missionary service. If they arise during your candidacy, they must be solved before leaving for the field.

A marriage works best, both at home and overseas, when each partner is willing to go, not half-way, but 100% of the way toward making it the constant joyous experience of sharing and caring that God intended it to be. It is, perhaps, a little more difficult to go that distance on the mission field.

QUESTIONS—CHAPTER 21

1. What are several stress situations which may be placed on families during their deputation ministry?

2. What are some of the best ways to cope with change?

3. Is stress dangerous? Explain.

4.   What kinds of stress situations will a married couple usually face on the mission field?

5.   What kind of relationship should married couples maintain with their single co-workers on the field?

6.   Are there areas in your life which need to be reckoned with if you are to cope with adaptation to change overseas? If so, explain.

7.   What types of "rippling effects" can result when a missionary couple separates or divorces?

22
Children of Accepted Candidates

Mission Boards have sometimes received letters of inquiry stating, "My wife is opposed to my decision to be a missionary, but I'm going ahead with it anyway." One lady, with no qualms, appeared in a mission office stating, "My husband didn't want to go so I left him home with the children, but I am ready for you to send me to the field immediately."

We smile at those who actually believe they are following the Lord by cutting off a mate who doesn't have a "call" to the mission field, or those who volunteer to serve in order to get out of a situation which cannot be solved.

But what about the children in your family? Are they considered in your decision?

"Oh," but you say, "they are too young to know" or "they can't make this decision for us." In many cases this is, and ought to be true. No one on earth has the authority to dictate the will of God to another, and therefore a decision to become a missionary family has rested entirely with you.

Before you even applied to a Mission, you should have prayerfully considered the pros and cons of raising a family on the field. If you are only now planning your family, or if your children are very young, they would, of course, abide by your decision. (Even so, you will do well to consider the health factors that will be involved, any disability your child may have, psychological problems which may be developing, and your own reaction to bringing up these little ones in a land which may be less sanitary than your own, with children of a different culture, language and thought pattern and the long separations which may be involved if, under certain circumstances, you conclude that your children must be sent away to school.

But for children who are aware of the world around them, those who have already begun to choose their friends, their likes and dislikes, and more especially, those teenagers who have already found it difficult to adjust to the various physical and psychological changes in their growth without the further problem of adjusting to a completely new way of living, it is logical to follow the command of the Word which directs us to "do all things decently and in order" (I Corinthians 14:40).

Your call to the mission field, backed by the Word of God and the assurance of His Spirit must dominate the entire life of the family. Children ought to be subject to the decisions of their parents. But a rebellious child at home could be obnoxious and troublesome on the field. If you cannot discipline your child in the home, it is not really fair to expect that a missionary teacher can make him docile and satisfied. (It has and can be done, but it should raise serious questions in your mind.) If there is any tendency toward unnatural dependence and instability or other psychological disturbances, professional help should be obtained in determining the child's ability to cope with the drastic changes which will come to him as an M.K. The Mission Board must be informed of any physical or psychological problems or tendencies discovered in your child or children. The Board will need to make the decision as to whether or not you will be accepted for service under such conditions. In some instances, God's will may allow you to go forth as planned; in other instances, it may be God's way of placing you in another ministry which will bring greater glory to Him.

One of the main factors in a child's adjustment to life itself and the possibility of being raised on the mission field is the parents' attitude toward the call and service of God. Despondent, discouraged, unstable, critical, complaining parents will find that their children will not readily adjust to change. Those who go about their work optimistically, zealously, lovingly, purposefully, and with a sense of humor without the constant negative aura that you are making a tremendous sacrifice to serve, will find your children enjoying this new open door of their lives.

Children should be helped to understand the importance and urgency of missionary work. They should have a share in the family life. They must never be left out to such an extent that they feel mother and dad always have time for supporting churches, nationals, other missionaries, and mission problems, but never have time to be concerned for them. (Your deputation ministry will help you to work out the problem of spending quality time with the family.)

Children are sometimes forced to speak or sing in public during days of deputation. Some children thrive on this, but others are embarrassed by it. Forcing the children to participate can have severely adverse effects on them. Other children will feel left out if they do not have a part in the program. A son and daughter of a missionary couple felt so much a part of the total missionary effort that when the annual Mission I.D. cards were sent to the parents, the teenagers questioned why they didn't receive cards, too. What a joy to a family to see their children considering themselves not as children of missionaries, but as an actual, vital part of the Mission.

Your children should be taught discipline and they should be disciplined, both because it is biblical, and because it can save you from many awkward and unhappy situations with co-workers on the field in the days ahead. And they will have many aunties and uncles to contend with in the years to come! When they travel with you to deputation meetings, you will have unusual difficulties keeping them completely under your control. When you are invited to stay in homes along the way, it will take extra pains to maintain them well behaved and grateful. Allowing them to use crayon on the walls, pulling the cat's tail, interrupting you when you are talking, refusing to eat the food offered to them, indulging in temper tantrums, etc., etc., will greatly hinder your effectiveness as a deputationist, and may greatly diminish the amount of support you will raise!

In some instances, missionary children develop the idea that they must always wear the worn out or grown out clothing left over from more well-to-do children in the homeland. (Unfortunately, this has sometimes been true.) There are times when there may be too much frugality on the part of parents when it comes to clothing their children and providing those few little extras that mean so much to all children (and adults) everywhere.

Your youngsters need to be allowed as much as possible, to live a normal, happy life. They are no different than other children their age and should not be made to feel that they must abide by altogether different principles. Commit them daily to the Lord. Instruct them and teach them in the Word of God. Love them and don't be afraid to express your love for them. Show by your own life that Christianity means something to you and is, in fact, the most important thing in your life. You may be able to fool the nationals or your co-workers, but you will never deceive your children. They know what you are before coffee in the morning, after the ninth interruption during your message preparation, when you come home exhausted trying to determine why the antenna switching system didn't work well, when you are frustrated and discouraged at how slowly you are learning the language, and when they see and hear your reactions to mission plans and policies. Your life is the greatest influence in the lives of your children. Your actions and reactions will mold their thinking.

Then, too, do you really feel you can trust your children to the Lord's keeping when an epidemic of typhoid sweeps through your area, when they are 500 miles away from you in Boarding School, or 10,000 miles away in college? Do you have the patience to teach your children if there is no opportunity to send them to school? Can you help them adjust to a new situation to which you, yourself, are not fully acclimated?

Perhaps your children are excited about the prospects of moving to a foreign land. It may sound like a thrilling adventure. But they must understand, if they are old enough, that this adventure is going to last a good many years. They should study about the country to which they are going. They should read good missionary books. You should encourage them and lead them in enthusiasm.

People often ask if there aren't too many disadvantages to consider taking children to the field. Some newlyweds even question the advisability of having a family at all if they are to serve the Lord in a foreign country.

Actually, there are far more advantages than disadvantages to the well-adjusted M.K. The educational level of most schools for missionary children is very high; the additional culture, customs, history and language of the adopted country are broadening; friendships with young people from other lands is stimulating; the knowledge that mother and dad are "serving the Lord" is spiritually invigorating; seeing the changed lives of those who believe is encouraging; having a part in tract distribution and other vital witness is rewarding; proving the promises of God from day to day is strengthening.

You will not be able to determine accurately your child's endurance level before you are actually in a mission field situation. But do not neglect the consideration of these young lives committed to you as you prepare for service. They are your first responsibility. And then, having found His will in the matter, go forth in His strength. There will be many trials and discouragements along the way, but what greater thrill could come to a missionary mother and father than to see a son or daughter return to the mission field for service, or to serve the Lord as a dedicated Christian in the homeland? To a large extent, it all depends upon YOU.

To help you further in the area of missionary children, be sure to read **The Missionary Family**, by Betty Jo Kenney, **The Life & Times of an MK**, by C. John Buffam, and **Missionary Kid—MK**, by Edward Danielson. (These books are available from William Carey Library, P.O. Box 40129, Pasadena, CA 91104.)

QUESTIONS—CHAPTER 22

1. What basic factors should be considered when children are involved in your missionary plans?

2. What advantages do missionary children have over their peers in the homeland?

3. What disadvantages do missionary children face?

4. Should missionaries plan to have few children, or many? Why?

5. How can children be utilized in deputation ministry?

6. Is it necessary to spend quality time with your children during your deputation ministry and when you go overseas? Why?

7   What is your attitude concerning disciplining your children? Explain.

23
Bon Voyage

The final step before leaving for service entails the very difficult matter of fond farewells to friends and relatives. In some instance, this will not be accomplished without a very large quantity of the grace of God. For others, parting, although never easy, is the threshold to greater joys than have ever before been anticipated ore experienced, and in the expectation of all that lies ahead, the temporary parting is made peacefully and swiftly.

Among the most difficult departures are those who must leave a very ill family member, a loved one who will not join you on the field for another year or two even though you are engaged, those who have depended heavily upon their circle of friends and loved ones and do not find it easy to adjust to new friends, and those who leave without the blessing of their family upon them (many being callous and indifferent to the gospel and thoroughly opposed to the step you are now taking).

Send-offs can be quiet and quick, or they can result in a large delegation of well-wishers waiting to say a "God bless you." These moments will long be remembered and cherished by all concerned. In some there will be that last quiet question of what has left and what may lie ahead. In others it will be complete resignation to the will of God by which even the most painful separation becomes a song of praise.

When the kisses are over, and the hand waving is no longer visible, the missionary candidate speeds forth to that wide open door which God has chosen for him to pass through. It's joys, sorrows, challenges, victories, hardships, fun times, hard work—all await.

May God's highest and best blessings be yours as you enter, with Him and with your fellow-laborers, His field of service for you.

PART II
RUNNING THE RACE
Field Experience

24
Arrival at Last

You have looked forward to this moment for a long time, and the day has finally arrived. You are stepping upon the soil to which you feel God has called you. It will become home to you. You will make friends here. Your life will be changed because of this moment.

You are exhilarated. Your eyes see in depth, for the first time, the people among whom you will work. Your ears hear the languages(s) which will become so much a part of your life. Your nose will pick up the odors which, just now, are new and strange, but which will become so commonplace in a few weeks.

In almost every instance you will be met at the airport by a senior member of your missionary staff or by a designated representative. Your first hour(s) will be spent being cleared through customs, signing endless reams of papers, showing your passport, visa, and other required papers to those in authority, and exchanging some money into the currency of the country to which you have gone.

Then you can take a deep breath and look around to see where you are. Things will happen so quickly, you will not be able to take it all in. Unless you have visited or been a short-term worker in the country previously, everything will be unique to you. You thought traffic was bad in the homeland? You've seen crowds before? Just think—you are a stranger in a foreign land, and there is so much to learn.

Perhaps the mission activities are not far from where your plane landed. On the other hand, you may have a day's ride by bus, train, or a small plane before landing at your place of ministry. You will learn a thousand things about culture before you reach "home,", even if you have only a ten minute ride in a horse-drawn carriage to get you there.

As you arrive, you will probably be greeted warmly by your expatriate co-workers as well as some of the nationals in the area. If you are in the more developed urban areas of the world, your arrival may not be noticed; in a rural area you will be watched in every move you make. You are the one who is different! You will be tired from the excitement, but you must be on your best behavior. After all, this is the start of a new life, and you want to make a good impression. This is the most exhausting experience of all, for you are dying to be **you**!

You may be acquainted with those with whom you will now live and work or they may only be names you have prayed for. They will be more knowledgeable than you in many things. Although adjustments are imperative, it is almost always easier to be stationed with those who have served some time in the area rather than with those who are also new to the field. Senior missionaries know the language, the customs, the people, the needs, what is available to eat, and how to deal with servants. They have been through and survived all that you will be facing, especially during your first term of service.

You will need a great deal of wisdom and discernment from the Lord if you are placed in an area by yourself and rather remote from other missionaries upon your arrival. This sometimes happens—but most mission boards protect their new workers by allowing them to live with, or close to, other missionaries during the first crucial months on the field. If you are assigned to open a new field for your board, it is usually possible to team up with missionaries from other boards in an urban location until you feel you know the people and the language well enough to go out on your own.

If you will be part of a large mission station, you will be welcomed, but after the greeting you will discover everyone has gone off to his/her assigned tasks in the hospital, clinic, school, radio station, or village. You will be invited out for your first meals, but before long you will be expected to fend for yourself. You are an intruder in a circle of friends and it may take some time to become "one of the gang." It is easier, in some ways, if several new workers arrive at the same time, but this can cause problems in that they will tend to "stick together" and not become a part of the established whole. If one single missionary arrives, there will have to be innumerable adjustments. You will not find your co-workers giving you the time and attention you really desire and need at this point. It will be, for the most part, your responsibility to fit into their circle. This can be a real problem for shy, introverted types. It can be especially embarrassing for a single fellow arriving on the field. There may be a dozen single girls in the area, and several families seeking to match you up. Single folks—be your own person!

Even though you have been to Language School, you probably will not be able to converse in your new language for long periods of time. If you have not yet begun to study the language, you will be almost completely dependent upon others. It can be very traumatic to hear only a language you do not speak or understand. It is frustrating, but perhaps the best motivation for studying the language immediately.

You may find the food of the country is tasty and agreeable. Or you may find it intolerable. When you visited that Japanese Steak House in Chicago, the food was delicious. But now you are in Japan. The pigs, chickens, and cattle eat a diet of fish. So besides the seemingly always present raw fish, fish stew, fried fish, broiled fish, boiled fish and baked fish which you will eat, you may discover that your eggs taste like fish, your bacon tastes like fish and your roast beef tastes like fish. And you have never liked fish!

Or you may be used to a bland diet, and now you are served hot, spicy curries, or injera and wat, or tamales. You may enjoy the change, but a constant diet of these foods may not be enjoyed by your tummy! Care must be taken in becoming acclimated to this new diet. Never stuff yourself the first week. Take it a little at a time to build up your tolerance.

You will need to learn some basic customs which will stand you in good stead with the nationals. Stories have been told in some lands where a missionary has complimented an individual on a beautiful baby, and has been given the baby! In some countries you do not openly admire things. If you do; it is yours. But you are also expected to give things which are admired. Use of some colors of clothing and styles must be carefully avoided in certain lands because of taboos and non-Western meanings. In most Eastern countries, especially among Muslims, the left hand is considered dirty and is never used for normal activities. (This is sometimes difficult for southpaw missionaries!) Customs are learned in time, but you can become involved in very embarrassing situations in the learning process.

You must try to fit into the action around you as quickly as possible. Ask how you may be able to help. But don't start out by implying you know how to do some things better and more efficiently than those who have lived overseas for a long time. If you have patience—and you know patience involves tribulation—you will come to understand why things are done the way they are. When you have been accepted as a full member of the staff, you will then be able to suggest changes which may be helpful. It is always best for a missionary to be seen and not heard for at least his first year on the field if he is stationed with senior missionaries. You must **earn** the right to contribute your expertise and/or knowledge. If you are a trained professional, you will be asked to contribute extensively and far earlier in your career than one who is assigned to itinerant evangelism or the program department of a radio station. In every instance, however, your opportunities will be given to communicate your knowledge and feelings. Be wise and patient in your beginning days. You have much to learn. There will be a day when you are respected and loved. Then you will be able to give your greatest contributions. Those who arrive on the field and bulldoze into a situation without knowing the facts surrounding it will find themselves in difficult circumstances before they ever start their ministry. You may become irked and irritated by what you see and hear. You may have real questions about the effectiveness of a missionary or a ministry. But this has to be a team effort, and you must play the part of a junior member of that team until you prove your capabilities.

You may need to become accustomed to a shortage or absence of electricity. Your water may have to be brought to you in tins or animal skins, or pumped from your own well. You may have to get used to political turmoil and threats to yourself and to your work. You may well have to learn to barter for everything you buy and to resist the temptation to give a "buksheesh" to every beggar you see. It may take a while to understand what it means to see dire poverty as well as exceeding wealth.

If you are one whose moods are affected by weather, you will need some further fine tuning in this matter. Little dries and most things mold in a prolonged rainy season. The dry heat of the desert or wet heat of the jungle may disagree with your constitution. If you lived at sea level at home and are now stationed at 9500 feet, you will notice a marked difference in your ability to breathe normally when exercising. You will wonder why boiling water never seems to be hot. And the first angel food cake you bake, using sea level measurements, will look like a flapjack! You'll be surprised how lightly you need to hit a tennis ball or shuttlecock in the thinner air before it goes sailing over the mountainside. Some find it more difficult to sleep soundly at higher elevations. Those who have lived in the mountains in the homeland will have to cope with the opposite circumstances if they now live in a low-lying area.

Many of you will have more subtle adjustments to make. You may be stationed in the heart of a city housing development among upper- or middle-class nationals whose lifestyle is not that different from that from which you have come. But language can still be a barrier—although normally you will find more people able to speak English. You may have more responsibilities placed upon you more quickly. You may even be more isolated from fellow missionaries than in an outstation where all live together on a single compound. Many such missionaries live in homes or apartments in the area of the city that seems logical for language school or ministry, so you may be very much alone in your strange new home. You will find the cost of living is exceedingly high in large urban areas, and because there are more resources available, you may be prone to overspend your monthly allotment (for utility bills, transportation, available foodstuffs, and/or luxury items which are available, though expensive).

You will see many unusual souvenirs in your adopted land, and you may wish to purchase a number of them. Always keep in mind the cost. Never purchase items without the help of knowledgeable people with you at first. They can bargain, they will know what the item is worth, and usually know what offer the seller will accept. You will always face the possibility of your "pure ivory" being "real cow bone" or your "jade" being a polished piece of glass or your "ebony" being painted pine. But these are tricks of the trade of which you must always be aware and over which you cannot become too disappointed. Remember, too, that you will not have safe storage areas for items which may be of some value, so it may be well to wait until furlough time to buy those pieces of silver, those beautiful paintings, or those alpaca rugs.

In tropical areas, particularly, you will become acquainted with certain creatures you never met before. Lizards, snakes, scorpions, spiders; rabid dogs, bats, wild wolves, hyenas or jackals; monkeys, baboons or gorillas; pet leopards and jaguars; lions, tigers, rhinoceri, hippopottami, giraffes, zebras, camels, elephants . . . some countries are a zoo! Goats, sheep, water buffalos, chickens, cattle, camels— all walking down Main Street with hordes of people surrounding them. Even in suburban areas, animals may be omnipresent. Sitting next to a pig, goat, or chicken on a long bus trip can become quite distracting!

You may have to get used to reporting to the police every time you leave your town or village. Rules are very strict in many countries concerning where you go and for what purpose. You may be stopped on the highway to show your police papers. Signing in and out at the police station can take most of a day. Buying stamps at the Post Office or picking up or mailing a package may also take much valuable time.

In the homeland, everything goes by a clock. Unless you are a teacher, radio station operator, nurse, or other such professional, your clock may be the sun in many Third-World nations. Although many countries do operate by hours, seldom do they consider minutes. Invitations for a seven o'clock dinner will probably mean an eight o'clock arrival time, so don't despair as the food grows cold. Simply plan on an extra hour or two of lead time. And when you are invited out, never arrive early. It can be bad taste and very impolite. On the other hand, if the custom is to be on time, or even early, plan accordingly. Time is a commodity which is useful. In the homeland we tend to make a fetish of it.

On the other side of laxness in time is the fact that you may consider you are wasting hours of precious time in idle chatter over a cup of tea. But this is what your ministry will involve from now on. No longer are you confined to the hours of 9:00 a.m. to 5:00 p.m. You may need to arise at 4:00 a.m., rest in the heat of the day, and counsel or teach until 10:00 p.m. Time will come to include different dimensions than you've known before. But you will almost never have to make sure your watch is precisely attuned to Greenwich Mean Time!

You will probably find you are using more physical strength than you have formerly. You will be walking and exercising more than you did at home. You may have a desk job in some situations, but you will almost always be involved in other activities which require physical exertion. A good night's sleep of 8 hours is essential for all.

When you arrive on the field, you may feel physically well and strong. But it takes only a tiny germ, bacterium, or amoeba to put you on your back in pain, disease, or distress. Illness is never a pleasant experience. It is especially discouraging on the mission field, especially if it is of prolonged duration. You will be aware that others must spend precious time caring for you. You feel helpless and useless—too sick even to study the Word or learn the language. You become restless which produces stress, which often prolongs the sickness. A very few missionaries have never experienced a day of illness in 45 years on the field. So don't assume you will become a victim of a germ or parasite. But if you do, relax as much as possible, work at getting well, and take care not to get the same illness again. A healthy mental attitude during times of illness is vital toward making you whole. Constantly remind your friends at home to pray for your physical well-being.

In the homeland, you may have been a big frog in a little pool. Now you are a little frog in a big pool. Hardly anyone is aware of your personal needs and desires. You may have to learn to cope with your problems as well as you can without the help of a close companion. Your constant resource must be the Lord your God. If you do not lean heavily upon Him, you will begin to be swallowed up by circumstances. He must always be your controlling factor.

The temptation for a newly-arrived missionary is to start attacking the beliefs of the people among whom he is assigned to minister. Many a missionary has made this mistake to the detriment of his future ministry. You are among these people to learn from them and to share with them. You are a guest in their country. Your argument must always be from the Word of God and from the experience you have had in relationship with Him. Attacking a creed, a tenet of belief, a lifestyle, or an individual will not prove effective. But your Christian testimony cannot be disputed. You have lived through it and can share what the Lord means to you. Later you will have opportunity to teach the Word—but early in your ministry your life and your testimony will be the most meaningful forms of witness.

You will be homesick when you arrive on the field. After the first blush of newness has faded, you will miss your family, your friends, your hometown, your job, your car, your AM/FM/stereo, your TV, your telephone . . . you may become very confused as you seek to speak a language you do not understand. (It may be consoling that a basic knowledge of approximately 1800 words will allow you freedom in most of the world's languages.) Although you will have to endure bouts of homesickness in times of sickness or trouble, it should not be an overwhelming emotional factor in the life of a mature individual.

As "the new kid on the block," you may be asked to assume tasks which you feel are beneath your knowledge and experience. Remember, you are first and foremost a servant of Jesus Christ and wherever you can assist His cause by service to others, He will give you grace and strength to perform it. You are a beginning practitioner, and it is excellent discipline to start at the bottom and work your way up. On the other hand, you are a worthwhile worker, and there may be times when you will need to refuse to be "used" by older missionaries (e.g., single girls always being asked to babysit for the children of senior missionaries, or single fellows always being asked to trek downcountry to try to solve disputes).

Your arrival on the field will be noted only on **your** calendar. It will not, in most cases, drastically affect anyone else. In a short time you will feel like a part of the group. You will probably best understand the arrival of a missionary on the field when you are the one who welcomes the next new staff member from the homeland. You will see many things in a different light once you have adapted somewhat to life on your station. You will always be learning and adjusting—but it is no longer overwhelming to you. You will always remember the thrill of that entrance to your field of ministry. You'll have hundreds of slides and pictures to recapture those first days and weeks. But now it is a matter of getting involved in the work to which you have been assigned—not looking back to what has transpired, nor ahead to furlough time, but dealing with each hour as it is given to you by Him, the Giver of all good and perfect gifts. May your life show forth His praise throughout your missionary career, beginning with your wide-eyed moment of arrival.

QUESTIONS—CHAPTER 24

1. How much time should a missionary be allowed to utilize in settling in and becoming adapted to his new culture before he is asked to participate in some type of ministry?

2. What adjustments do you expect will need to be made in your lifestyle if you are assigned to an urban area?

3. What adjustments may be needed if you are to be in a rural area?

4. If you are invited to a national home for dinner and find you cannot tolerate the food, how will you cope with the situation?

5. If you are alone in your room studying for a language exam and you see a scorpion crawl under your dresser, what will you do? A cobra?

6. In what ways can you become involved in missionary activity before you can speak the language fluently?

7. When should you begin to feel free to share your ideas for the ministry with your senior missionaries?

8. How soon should you confide in another person as to how you **really** feel about yourself?

25
Language Study

Many committed Christians are panic-stricken when they consider the fact that being a missionary almost always means learning a new language—and sometimes more than one. This is not nearly so traumatic to Europeans because most of these people have a working knowledge of two or more languages. The American school system, however, has fallen behind the rest of the world by not requiring students to study a foreign language in many high schools and colleges. Perhaps because of this, language study has become something of a psychological impossibility until a student actually begins to work on it and finds it quite enjoyable. It certainly should not be the deciding factor as to whether or not an individual becomes a missionary. Of course, there is always a possibility you have grown up in the country to which you are now returning as a missionary—and you will already know the language.

Mission Boards have differing requirements for language study, depending on where you will be stationed and what language you will learn. For example, those who will work in the so-called Francophone area of Africa will be required, by some boards, to spend a year in France to study French, the franca-lingua of these countries. Then upon arrival in the country, you will be required to learn a national or tribal language as well. Missionaries to Latin America often spend a year of intensive study in language school in Costa Rica, Mexico, or Texas. Some Boards feel it is better to send you directly to your field of service to learn the language the way your people speak it. As you know, there is a great deal of difference in the way Spanish is spoken in Ecuador, Mexico, Costa Rica, and Spain.

If you have had no background in language study, your board may ask you to take some linguistic studies at a university, or to enroll in a program such as Wycliffe or Missionary Internship offers. You will not learn a language, but will be able to study the mechanics of how languages are put together, which will help you understand how to learn whatever language you are assigned to study.

In some cases, missions recommend that their personnel study a home course (e.g., Berlitz) in basic languages such as Spanish, or French, or Italian, or German. Learning by means of records, tapes, and workbooks can be meaningful so that when you arrive on the field you will simply have to refine and strengthen what you have learned and add theological expressions to your knowledge. If you are a professional person, you will always need to study further on the field to learn how to express yourself in your designated professional field.

There are few missions today who send their people to the field and expect them to "pick up" the language on their own by living among the people to whom they have been sent. Provision for language school and/or private language tutoring is almost always the norm for all first-term missionaries.

The ideal situation is to arrive on your field and go immediately to language school—or obtain the services of qualified language tutors. This gives you the feeling of being in the place where God has led you. It puts you in a semi-isolated situation where you can fall back on the language of your homeland with fellow students. Yet it allows you ample opportunity to utilize what you are learning with nationals living in the area where you are studying. National teachers are usually utilized for teaching since very few expatriates "speak the language like a native." There are situations where no national teachers can be used because (1) they do not know English, or (2) they have no teaching ability. Many languages have no textbooks and must be learned by means of oral communication. Your field leadership should be careful in the choice of those who teach language. In Pakistan, for example, many tutors or Language School teachers actually teach more Punjabi than Urdu. The two languages are similar in many ways, but sufficiently different that you could easily be misunderstood or not understand by learning and speaking a mixed language (especially in areas which speak Pushtu, Multani, or other languages).

On some fields, missionaries are assigned to live in the home of nationals during their language study. This helps them to utilize what they are learning and have opportunity to hear the language spoken. Such interaction is extremely important since hearing and understanding is certainly as important as being able to speak. This type of situation is also helpful in learning customs, dealing with marketing, and getting along with those with whom you will be working.

To some, language comes readily. To others it can be a nightmare. Some missionaries never learn the language to the point that they feel comfortable with it. Others begin to think, reason, and dream in their new language after just a few months of study.

One of the basic qualities a language student must have is the ability to laugh at himself. We are told that outgoing, talkative individuals have less trouble learning a language than shy, introverted people. This is probably true because extroverts will utilize the language they are learning, mingle with people from whom they can learn and to whom they can speak, and are not as fearful of making mistakes. And if they do have a slip of the tongue, they can laugh it off and go on.

And language learners do make mistakes! Some must learn tonal languages in which one word has many meanings depending on the tone in which it is spoken. One missionary, studying Chinese, thought he was saying, "Our Father, Who art in heaven . . . " until he discovered he had said, "My pants are in the field." Some words sound somewhat alike but have entirely different meanings. I had meant to tell my language teacher that "Some American farmers have horses." What I actually said was, "Most American farmers are horses." A friend, in the conversation section of a language lesson was telling the story of Christ's betrayal and arrest. She meant to say, "Jesus was taken into custody," but what she actually said was, "Jesus had diarrhea." A co-worker was giving a message on God's law—the Ten Commandments. But each time she thought she was saying "God's law," she was actually saying "God's water pipe." The gathered group began to giggle and finally burst into full laughter. These are devastating experiences unless you can see the funny side of it, too.

Perhaps you have thought you could never learn a language from a book. Although some languages have textbooks, you will learn most from spending time with the people. If you no longer hear your own language (except on your own mission compound) and constantly hear conversation in the language of your adopted country, you will discover it is far easier to learn than you had expected. Then, too, if you are speaking and cannot find the word you want to say, almost always your audience will chime in with the correct noun or verb. (I don't think I ever completed a sentence by myself during my first year on the field!) Even in an English-speaking country (e.g., Liberia), it may take some time with the people to understand what they are saying.

If you have children, you will be amazed at how quickly they will learn to speak the language. They may not always have the right form of a verb on the tip of their tongue, but they will make themselves understood to both children and adults. They have far fewer inhibitions, are not afraid to use the words they know, and are not beyond playing charades to act out something for which they do not have a word. They will, at first, mix their own language with their new-found language, which can be quite amusing. But left to themselves, they will be speaking and understanding as well, if not better, than you in a few short months. Do not become discouraged by this. The young usually learn faster, and language is no exception.

It is important that your Mission allow you to study language immediately prior to or upon arrival on your field. Language and cultural acquisition are closely related and it is imperative that both be well in hand before you engage in full-time ministry among those to whom you have been sent, even if it takes the greater part of two to three years to accomplish. Pressure is often put on doctors, nurses, teachers, and other professionals whose services are acutely needed, to put off language study or to take an abbreviated or accelerated course of study. This often ends in regrets—and may lead to an early end to a missionary career.

Don't become discouraged, after learning a new language, when you discover for a more effective ministry you will need to learn yet another new language—or perhaps more than one. Some missionaries have been moved to other countries for various reasons and have to start all over again. Flexibility must be part of a missionary's personality!

Obviously, the best solution to a language barrier is to remove it by learning the language. Services of an interpreter may be utilized, but you will never have the "in" with your people by this means that you will have by communicating directly with them. Even a poor knowledge of the language utilized with care, concern and love will provide you with an effective outreach. It is important to learn the language to the very best of your ability, but actions will forever speak louder than words. Character is the greatest communication tool.

Just as we never stop learning English, we ought never to become stagnant in our acquisition of another language. You will be learning idiomatic-expressions as long as you live.

Even though you will come to many plateaus in the acquisition of language knowledge, you will find real joy in finally being able to speak and understand—to think in the language of your people—to give the plan of salvation and receive a response. Don't become discouraged by comparing yourself to others who learned quickly and well. Don't become overconfident in your own ability if you have been successful in acquiring this essential communication tool.

As an encouragement, I would suggest that if God calls you to the mission field, He is perfectly capable of meeting **all** your needs. Language study may seem formidable because (1) you've never done it before, or (2) you've tried before and failed. He does not give us dying grace until we need it. And He may not give us the ability to learn a language until we need it. Many missionaries who found studies difficult in high school and Bible College have learned a new language with a minimum of effort. Folks back home will be praying for you. You must study with concentrated effort. And God will give you the language skills you need for the work He has called you to do. Never doubt Him!

QUESTIONS—CHAPTER 25

1. What is your personal attitude toward having to learn a "foreign" language?

2. How do you feel a new language can best be acquired?

3. In what areas does the utilization of a translator limit you?

4. How will you cope with the situation if you feel you have not obtained enough language preparation for the work to which you are assigned?

5. How important is the acquisition of the language to your ministry as a missionary?

6. How important is it for you to communicate with your national friends in their language concerning matters other than the Gospel?

7. What advantages are there to having to learn a language such as Spanish compared to a language such as Japanese?

26
Spiritual Food/Worship

A missionary is responsible to the Lord to be a witness. He goes forth to preach and teach the gospel, to win the lost and to strengthen the believers by the Word of God.

Before going overseas, you will probably think primarily of the ways in which you can and will be able to minister to others . And this, of course, is very important.

You will find, however, that no matter how dedicated you are to the task assigned, and how much you desire to give forth the Word of truth, there must be times of building yourself up in the area of spiritual food. A dry sponge does little but scratch whatever it touches.

If you are assigned to an urban area, there may be established churches you can attend on occasion. There will be Christians with whom you can have fellowship and fellow missionaries from whom you can obtain counsel.

If, on the other hand, you are assigned to a rural area without an established church, where there are few or no Christians, and where your family or you and your co-worker are the only Christian workers within a hundred mile radius, you will discover your spiritual resources are quickly depleted.

The basic source of spiritual help is, of course, your daily devotional time with the Lord. This cannot be a "rush in—rush out" portion of the day. No matter how busy you are, how many problems must be cared for, how joyful or desperate your situation, you must never lessen the time you spend in quietness before the Lord in reading His Word and in prayer. It is more necessary than your daily food. Without it you will begin to falter, fail and fall.

In the homeland you were carried along with the momentum of Christian friends, caring and helpful pastors, willing supporters, worship and prayer services, Christian magazines, radio and TV programs, Bible conferences. The Holy Spirit's presence was available. It was there and you seldom acknowledged it because it was so commonplace.

Now you have been placed in a situation where there are very few, if any, believers. You are **the** Christian in your area of town. There is no church you can attend because you are the pastor/teacher of the people. The lack of the Holy Spirit's presence will be felt, and satanic influences may come into play, especially in areas where Satan worship is popular and demonic pressures are powerful. Until you discover the darkness yourself, it is difficult to explain it to others, and they, too, must experience it for themselves. Watching intelligent, well-dressed individuals bowing to gods of wood and stone, burning incense to the dead, lighting candles to pay for purging their sins, seeing men stripped to the waist, beating their own backs with chains, knives and razor blades, hearing the mourning of those who have lost loved ones to the unknown beyond, noting the burning bodies at the edge of a "holy" river, watching the incantations of a witch doctor . . . and so much more. And almost all of it in the name of religion. You realize as never before the sinfulness of sin, the darkness of the world without Christ, and the inherent need of mankind to bow to a superior creature.

As you live in a territory Satan has controlled for centuries, you realize how imperative it is that your personal faith be stronger than it's ever been before. You must, amidst all other circumstances, allow for time with your Lord. His Word must be your daily portion. Communication with Him must be a constant.

If you live alone, you will find a thousand things you "ought to be doing" which will try to draw you away from your devotional times with the Lord. If you live with others, you may find it difficult to find the time and space to be alone. If you are a family without servants, you will find it extremely difficult to find time to be quiet before the Lord, and you will discover you cannot **find** time; you must **make** it. And it must become your pattern for life.

If you are able to attend worship services or prayer meetings in your area, be sure to do so. If you are attending Language School, there will, undoubtedly, be planned chapel services which you ought to attend faithfully.

One of the responsibilities of your home church should be to send you a taped message as often as possible. Other organizations are also happy to send Gospel messages free of charge to missionaries. In some remote mission stations, these messages are utilized for expatriate worship services. They can be a great encouragement to you, personally.

Be sure you take several devotional books to the field with you. You will be amazed at the way God will use these to meet your specific needs on many occasions.

If possible, order Christian magazines to be sent to you, or ask folks in the homeland to send theirs on to you after they read them. (Books and magazines are free of duty.)

You will want to have several tapes of Christian music with you (and a tape player). And if you play an instrument, you will want to have one available on the field to use in your personal worship as well as in the ministry to which God has called you.

But I've been called to Europe, you say. There's a church on every corner! You will be absolutely amazed at the fallacy of that statement. There are thousands of towns and villages in Europe without a church and even more without a gospel witness. You will find it extremely difficult to find a place to worship and be strengthened in the things of the Lord.

Your spiritual diet is your most important consideration as a missionary. Your entire life and ministry, including your physical, emotional and psychological well-being are affected by it. Your ability with the language is far less important than your relationship to the Lord. If you live and work in the strength of the flesh, your ministry will be of the flesh. If you live and work in the strength of the Lord, your ministry will be of the Lord. It is your choice, and a more important one will never be made. It will be a battle all the way as you fight against the wiles of the Devil and the powers of darkness. It is not enough to be able to argue a point of view and win your point. You must have a living, loving relationship with Him Whom you claim to love more than life itself—without Whom you are nothing. You will fool no one, including yourself, if you become the least bit lax in a disciplined devotional life.

Does it happen to missionaries? It certainly can and does—to the detriment of the Lord, the work, the supporting churches, the nationals, your fellow-workers, yourself—and the Church as a whole.

Perhaps medical workers need to be more alert to this problem than others. Although called upon at any hour of the day or night to attend to the physical needs of individuals, they are seldom shielded to the extent that they obtain compensatory time to spend with the Lord, in study, or with their families. The highest attrition rate of missionaries is among medical workers. There is a correlation!

When your spiritual life is not properly fed and exercised, you will become a weak link in the gospel chain. Eventually you may break, leaving those on the other end of the chain to fall and suffer loss. It happens far too often. Don't let it happen to you!

Teaching your children the importance of maintaining a close relationship to and short accounts with the Lord may be difficult. You must teach by your own example in family devotional times. But children also need to realize they must search the Word of God and depend upon the Lord for their own needs. Remember, they have not been to Bible College. Some may not yet be a child of His. They cannot lean upon **your** spiritual encounter to meet **their** needs. Often they will have no Sunday School they can attend. If there is a worship service, it will probably be in the language of the people and "over the head" of your 5-year old child. It's unlikely that there will be a Child Evangelism worker to provide meetings. You will be not only his parent. You will be his teacher, his pastor, his spiritual example. It is a tremendous responsibility, and certainly every bit as important as the ministry to which you have been called. Don't save the world and lose your own children!

You may also be in a ministry of nurturing new believers. There is no greater privilege than teaching new converts the importance of a devotional life You may have to consider new ways for them to worship if you are in an area where illiteracy is rampant. But you will be their greatest example. Keep in mind that you cannot come back from a place to which you have not been. Nor can you be the guide you ought to be if you have not been to the place to which you are directing others. You are being followed—far more than you realize. Where are you taking those who are tracing your steps? Does it really matter to you? What kind of role model are you to your family . . . your co-workers . . . the nationals?

If you have any theological doubts whatsoever, you must work them out before the Lord. If you are not sure of what you believe, you cannot with assurance lead others into the paths of righteousness.

All of this is true in the homeland, although you probably gave little thought to it. On the mission field, it is of utmost importance because of the lack of spiritual crutches which you used in the homeland. The health of your spiritual life will determine the results you can expect in ministry, whether at home or overseas. It is a continuous, uphill battle. But you have access to spiritual weapons to fight it through. And as you are being watched and followed, one may well ask what Isaiah asked Hezekiah as recorded in Isaiah 39:4, "What have they seen in thine house?" And you may, with confidence answer, "All that is in mine house have they seen: there is nothing among my treasures that I have not shown them." And may it include a faithful, disciplined devotional life which provides the grace, peace and strength He promises to those Who follow Him in **all** things.

QUESTIONS—CHAPTER 26

1. What do you believe is the most important, continual, and urgent responsibility of every missionary?

2. How would you deal with a situation where you are determined to focus on personal spiritual growth through disciplined devotional times while your co-worker (or spouse) feels little need for time alone with the Lord?

3. What spiritual temptations would you expect to encounter overseas which may not have been a problem in the homeland?

4. How can missionary children be taught in the things of the Lord in a place where there is no church, no Sunday School, and few or no Christians?

5. Make a list of 10 specific items you have taken with you overseas to help you have a more effective personal devotional life, or items you will request that others send to you.

6. How would you teach a new, illiterate believer how to have a meaningful and strengthening devotional life? Give details.

27
The Work of the Ministry

You are now at your assigned station. You have completed the initial stages of your required language study. You have been provided with an apartment, a duplex, a home, or at least a room where you have settled in and made your living arrangements as comfortable as possible. Whether you are part of a large mission compound, alone in a rural outpost, or part of a team effort in a modern world capital—the time has come to begin your active ministry among those to whom you have been called.

Prior to this time, you have only dreamed of what it would be like to share the Word of God with these people who have been in your prayers for so long, about whom you spoke during your days of deputation, and among whom you now live.

Whether you have had a personal relationship with Jesus Christ for many years or few, whether you know a great deal about the Bible or little (it is strongly suggested that formal Bible training be obtained before you go to the field), whether you are ready or not—the time has come when you have the opportunity to share your faith through meaningful dialogue and a consistent Christian life as a MISSIONARY!

Remember however, even though you have become a supported worker who is involved in the expansion of the church in a culture other than your own—a full-fledged missionary, if you will—you are a beginning practitioner. You don't know all the answers; you don't even know all the questions! You **must** remember this as you go forth. You **cannot** do the work of the ministry in your own strength. You must have the help of the Lord. You must also seek counsel and assistance from those who are older, wiser, and more knowledgeable about the field than you are. In so doing, you will avoid some serious problems which could easily arise. For example, you may be in a land which prohibits baptismal services which are performed by other than nationals. You are unaware of this policy, and in the excitement of finding several believers who want to be baptized, you arrange for a service. You did not feel you needed permission from your Field Director, or from your nearest missionary neighbor who lives 60 miles up the rail line.

News spreads rapidly, and you find scores of people have come to view the baptismal service. Among the spectators is a policeman, or a CIA agent, or a friend of the witchdoctor in that area. Before the day is over, you are picked up by the police and put in jail. Within a week you are expelled from the country. You are forbidden to return. Your missionary career is over!

During at least your first year of ministry on the field, it is wise to request counsel from missionaries who have been on the field longer than you concerning protocol, customs, procedures,policies, rules and regulations. Seek help from both nationals and expatriates. Ask questions constantly. This may seem to be difficult if you have no experienced co-workers nearby. But it is worth inviting your Field Director to your station from time to time, or visiting him periodically to ask questions and receive answers.

If you are part of a mission compound which has several ministries—a Bible Training Center, a hospital, a clinic, a grammer school, an evangelistic team, a radio station, a national church, a youth camp—you will be assigned to a specific ministry of preaching, teaching, evangelism, leading prayer groups—or you will become involved in your professional responsibilities as a doctor, nurse, engineer, teacher, children's worker . . .   You will, undoubtedly, work with or under a more experienced individual until you are fully able to carry the responsibility by yourself. Your co-worker(s) may be expatriates or nationals. A missionary colony, of course, is a more ideal situation for new missionaries than being placed alone on a station.

Many times, however, because of lack of workers, furloughs, emergencies, or growth of the ministry, you may be thrust into a ministry by yourself and will be expected to fulfill your obligations without constant supervision or help. Be prepared for the possibility of this. Don't panic when put on your own—to preach a sermon or to perform surgery very early in your missionary career. Yes, you may speak falteringly and you may need help from others in the operating room. You may feel you have failed in your first attempts to witness or teach. But give yourself the right to fail. If you are a perfectionist, you will be terribly discouraged and may contemplate leaving for home. But all beginning practitioners have to learn. A baby does not leave the delivery room walking and talking. Learning is part of normal growth.Be patient during the process. Bathe your ministry in prayer. Trust God to speak through your life and words. Lean on the strength God will give you because of the prayers of faithful friends back home, as well as your own.

Your greatest ministry in these first days will grow out of your love and respect for the people to whom you minister. Good looks, perfect pronunciation of the language, solid theology, material possessions . . . will be almost meaningless to those to whom you minister. Your people will, first of all, know if you have a sincere interest in them as individuals. As an unbeliever in South America once stated, "If the missionary had cared half as much about me as he did about my soul, I might have been convinced by his message."

Too many young missionaries feel so burdened to convince men/women/children concerning Christ that they do not allow themselves time to come to know individuals. You may feel that spending time talking to or doing this with unsaved nationals is a waste of time. You have gone forth as a witness, an ambassador of Christ—and your message is extremely urgent, at least in **your** thinking. And it is definitely true that time is short and there are multitudes to be reached.

But there are two sides to every coin. The people among whom you now find yourself did not beg you to come to them. They may be completely content with their way of life, their customs, their religion. You, in their understanding, are a disruptive element. You don't agree with their standard of living (as borne out by your own lifestyle). You are an outsider who is trying to get on the inside, but your motives are not clear. You may look strange to them in your western-style clothing, if you are in a developing country. You are trying to change or modify their religion which may be far more a part of the life of these people than Christianity is a part of American life.

Just being among people is no assurance of acceptance by them. Love and respect must be earned, and this cannot be accomplished in chance greetings or intermittent meetings. How did **you** feel when Swami Rajneev from India moved to your town back home? He purchased an expensive home and decorated it with silver, gold and crystal. He brought together others who believed as he did. These believers stopped you in the airport, approached you on the beach, met you on the streets and sought entrance to your home to give you literature or to tell you the virtues of being a follower of the Swami, or to ask for money for their cause. Did you accept them and their message? What did you think and what were your inner feelings about these people? How did you react to them? What was your response to their invitations to accept literature, attend meetings, or to become involved in their way of life?

In the homeland, it was difficult enough to try to sort out various denominations and sects and deal with them. Completely alien religious beliefs could be overlooked or ignored, and those who propagated them did not have to be accepted or invited into your home, or encouraged in any way to have further contact with you.

Should you expect the situation to be so much different in the area to which you have been assigned? Of course, if you join a missionary community which has been present in an area for a number of years, where a witness has been established, or where a church, or churches, are active, you will find far greater acceptance among the people.

But suppose you are a missionary to Holland. You are part of a six-member team. One member does scheduling and office work. A second is responsible for all music and musical programs. A third manages a Christian bookstore. Two are involved in door-to-door evangelism. The sixth is responsible to work with Christians and new believers, to train them in the things of the Lord. All six work among a population of 50,000 people in a town near Rotterdam. No one from your Mission has worked there previously, although one of the evangelists and the musician labored in Amsterdam during their first term of service.

You are one of the evangelists. Your assignment is to knock on doors and present the Gospel of Jesus Christ in a knowledgeable and acceptable way. For the most part, Europeans are not rude. You may be turned away, as politely as possible. But you may also be invited into the home for a cup of hot chocolate and some home-made bread with cheese. Will you take this as an opportunity to "cram the Gospel down their throats," leave a tract and go on to the next home? Would it not be well to spend some time building a relationship with this family? They will surely ask why you are in their town. You will have many opportunities to speak of Christ, and show Him to them by your life and actions. As you leave, you might ask about the possibility of returning to discuss the Truth further with them. You may or may not be invited to return. You may be invited many times. But the point is, you will have to be accepted by those to whom you go—and acceptance takes time . . . time you may feel is wasted in socializing, or playing games, or being involved in sports activities, or in idle chatter. Remember the example of our Lord. True, He preached to the multitudes and spoke to individuals along the highways and byways—but the major portion of His 3-year ministry was spent in the training of 12 individuals. He lived before them, He loved them, He did things with them, He talked with them, He walked with them, He ate with them, He went fishing with them—but He was always teaching them the Truth.

You may feel forced to reach out to the thousands in order to send out glowing reports in your prayer/newsletters, indicating the many who have believed and who are growing in their faith. You may be working in an area where such reports are based upon reality, because you have been blessed with seeing God at work in mighty, saving power. Or you may be ministering to Muslims or others, and converts are few and far between. Your responsibility is to be faithfully obedient to your Lord. Your business is to sow the seed; it is His business to yield the fruit. Only as a co-laborer with Him can that fruit be harvested. You will have to trust that your supporters understand.

In some cultures of the world; forthright ministry for missionary women will be confined to the women and children, while men will work only with men. In other countries, Christian witness and training will be possible among the entire population, whether the missionary is male or female.

You may not be on the field as a full-time preacher or evangelist. You may be an auto mechanic, assigned to keep all mission vehicles in good operating condition, which may involve periodic travel to all stations in your district or country. But you are a missionary as well as a mechanic. You will take every possible opportunity to live the life and speak the message to represent Jesus Christ. Whether you are teaching nationals the basics of being a mechanic, travelling by bus or train to an outlying mission station, or becoming involved in gospel witness in your own home or mission compound, you are His ambassador.

Travel can provide open doors for witness, or for strengthening believers. If you are a pilot, transporting a sick patient to a hospital; if you are on a train, headed for holiday; if you are on a bus, going to the other side of the city; if you are in a horse-drawn carriage with other passengers; if you are going some distance by car and offer to carry a national friend or family with you—there will be ample opportunity to share your testimony, and give forth a Christian witness.

You may own, or have access to a vehicle which will provide your transportation as you minister. In some areas, it is absolutely essential to have your own means of transport. Actually, if you really want to get to know people, use your newly acquired language, learn the customs of the country, and become better acquainted with the area to which you have been assigned, utilize public transportation as much as possible and feasible. It does not matter where you work, travelling will almost always play a large part in your ministry.

In some countries, you will discover you are more accepted if you wear national clothing as you live among the people. In other countries you will gain and maintain more respect by dressing in your usual attire. Western clothing is almost always the norm in an urban setting. In rural areas, you may want to become as much like the nationals as possible. There are no strict rules in regard to your dress except that it be modest, comfortable, attractive, and acceptable to those among whom you work. Obviously, you will need to fit in with what is appropriate for Paris or Kathmandu. You will not "go native" among the all-but-naked tribes in the jungle. You will not flaunt the latest fashions. Women will not wear shorts or designer jeans. You may discover that the clothing in the country you now live is far more practical and comfortable than what you brought from the homeland. (Sitting cross-legged on the ground for a two hour service in Pakistan can become unbearable if you are wearing a knee-length skirt or a Sunday suit!)

You may be ministering by means of radio. It is all too easy, when you are alone with a microphone in a tiny studio, to think no one is listening to the broadcast. But you can be sure multitudes have tuned in—people whom you will, in all probability, never meet. Your message must be geared to the individual—not to the crowd. It must be personal, purposeful and persuasive. The message must be clearly and caringly presented. It should communicate with the individual listener. It should provide food for thought, and an opportunity for response. It must build up believers; it must also touch those who have never entered into a personal relationship with the one, true, living God. Radio ministry is difficult. You may never know who or how many have been reached through your ministry. You will be encouraged by a few letter responses, but you can be sure God is using your life and ministry to influence others.

Many nurses and doctors become frustrated in their lack of opportunity to witness personally to each and every patient who comes under their care. Because of the crowds lined up for treatment each day, it is often necessary to stop seeing patients before all are cared for. Asking a patient what his/her symptoms are, where it hurts, how long this has been occurring, etc., etc., does not take the place of sharing Christ with each individual. On the other hand, the very attitude of the doctor or nurse, his/her knowledge, caring, and treatment can go a long way toward paving the way for a national worker or expatriate evangelist to witness to the patient. A word here and there can be given by a doctor as he speaks with the patient. A nurse may have longer periods of time with patients, especially in a hospital setting where she may witness while giving a medication, or sing a hymn while taking temperatures. Some workers may wish to follow up patients in the ward or in their home. But the pressures of time may preclude this as a regular ministry.

If you are such a worker, you must be satisfied in knowing you are part of a team effort, allowing others to spend time with these patients to make the Word of God clear to them. You should not work in the hospital or clinic 24-hours a day. You must have time off. You must make opportunities to give a personal witness to your neighbors and those with whom you come in contact. You will need to work out your hangups and frustrations concerning lack of time for forthright witnessing, and allow the Lord to use your abilities, and your loving kindness to attract men and women to the Savior Whom you serve.

Perhaps you are a teacher in a school for missionary children. Never assume that each child in your class is a Christian because he/she comes from a missionary home. Your responsibility is to represent the Lord in such a way that each child will welcome the opportunity to become a child of God and grow in grace and knowledge of Him. You may also be teaching national children, embassy children, and those from surrounding countries. What an opportunity to teach Christ along with your assigned subjects. You may also want to become involved in a witnessing ministry apart from your school responsibilities. There are countless opportunities to do so. Personal witness is not limited to specific times and places.!

There may be times when your ministry is hindered, not by a lack of those who will listen, but by having too many people present at one time. As a newcomer to an outlying area, you may be a novelty! Word of your approach to a settlement or village may have preceded you. (News has a way of getting through to the multitudes without sophisticated technological communication systems.) You may have expected to go from home to home to speak with the people. But you feel like the Pied Piper. The whole village is following you wherever you go! There is no opportunity to speak personally with people. As time passes, your newness will wear off, of course, and you will be better able to speak face-to-face with individuals. It will take time and patience. Meanwhile, you will get to know these people, learn to listen to them, answer their questions, and establish a rapport with them which will aid in future ministry.

If you labor in a populous, international city (e.g., Hong Kong, Singapore, West Berlin or Rome), you will hardly be noticed as you move about. Most will probably assume you are a tourist, albeit you may speak their language. Only as you reach out to individuals will they understand the purpose for your presence in their midst. Even if those around you are seemingly unaware of your being there, never be more than God's servant, and never less than His Ambassador. Your kinship to Jesus Christ must always be revealed through what you are, what you say, and what you do.

You will be amazed at some of the things you will be expected to become involved in on the field, for which you have no background or training. Many a missionary has had to deliver babies, pull teeth, organize a church, teach literacy classes, teach English, take over as Field Director, or become a ham radio operator. If you are in an urban church ministry, you may have to become an audio-visual expert. You may be asked to find housing for newly-arrived missionaries. You may be in charge of the bookkeeping for your station or field. You will learn as you go and grow as you learn.

At no time should you allow your ministry to hinder the work of other missionaries in your area, or on your station. On most fields, mission comity has been established so that organizations do not overlap in their ministries. Large cities are usually open to all agencies. But suppose that a church has been established by missionaries from a specific Mission Board. They have requested your Mission to assume responsibility for that church for a year because they have no one to cover during a furlough period. The church was set up to function as a Presbyterian entity. You are a Baptist and decide to do away with infant baptism, and you insist upon immersing adults. That's a good way to create havoc. Never should such a thing occur. Adjustments will need to be made so that the ministry will continue and the people will not be divided. Denominatiònal barriers are far less emphasized overseas than they are in the homeland. Nevertheless, harming or disrupting the work of other missionaries can produce only divisiveness and cause detriment to the total plan and program of God.

God has called you to be His minister. It is not always possible for you to serve only within the parameters of your specific field of training. You must be pliable and willing to assume those tasks which are necessary for the overall "success" of the work. And this is especially true in your first term of service. You may be asked to do many different things so that you, and your field administrators can discover where your greatest contribution(s) can be made. You will be both stretched and strengthened in these beginning days.

Remember that God does not hold you responsible for the salvation of every person in Peru or Papua New Guinea, or the Philippines. He does require that you be faithful to Him in your daily walk and talk, in your witness, in your professional life, and in the honest accounting you give to your supporters. He will reward according to faithfulness. "He that is faithful in that which is least is faithful also in much" (Luke 16:10a). "Moreover it is required in stewards, that a man be found faithful" (I Corinthians 4:2). " . . . Be thou faithful unto death, and I will give thee a crown of life" (Revelation 2:10). Don't allow anyone or anything to make you unfaithful in any way to Him Who called you to serve Him where you now are.

Even if you were a pastor in the homeland before leaving for missionary service, you will run into situations in the church overseas that you never previously had to face (e.g., a new convert is legally married to four wives. How will you deal with this?) You were a teacher in the homeland, but were never a housemother. You were an engineer at home, but never worked on a steerable antenna system. You were a builder, but had never constructed homes from a mixture of mud, straw and cow dung. You were a knowledgeable surgeon but had never removed a ruptured uterus. You were a nurse, but had never removed a cataract. You had done personal work, but had never been beaten or stoned.

Missionary ministry will involve, in many cases, a reaching out to individuals in personal ministry. Seeing individuals come into a relationship with God through Jesus Christ must never be the ultimate aim of missions, however, Believers must be brought together as a group, no matter how small the group may be, for fellowship and worship. Establishing churches must be a vital concern of your missionary thrust. Some of you will be committed to a ministry of evangelism. But when souls come to Christ, they need to feel a part of a body which is made up of others who are like-minded. Although important for all, it is especially imperative when you are working among those who are illiterate, if you expect new Christians to grow in their faith and knowledge of Him. Establishing groups of believers and providing for their spiritual growth is the responsibility of the missionary until such time as a national can undertake the responsibilities of the pastorate.

For those working in areas where churches are already established, it is important that new believers become involved in a church situation immediately. Perhaps in a day when groups are meeting in Bible studies while avoiding church attendance in the homeland, it will be difficult for some missionaries to expect new believers overseas to become part of a church body. Yet, if you expect to establish a strong and nurtured body of believers in your overseas setting, you must be responsible to see that they are given the opportunity to join with others of like precious faith in the unity of a church setting. And you must be an example to others by your faithfulness in attendance and involvement.

Yes, missionary ministry is a challenge. It takes the very best you can offer. It produces its share of frustrations and discouragements. But it is the will of God for you. And though varied and tiring and many times thankless, you will be thrilled at the privilege of having a part in the fulfillment of the Great Commission. You will receive far more than you give. You will joy in the many victories, the answers to prayer, the encouraging events along the way. And you will affirm with Timothy, "I thank Christ Jesus our Lord, who hath enabled me, for that he counted me faithful, putting me into the ministry" (I Timothy 1:12).

You were chosen by God "for the perfecting of the saints, for the work of the ministry, for the edifying of the body of Christ" (Ephesians 4:12). Are you willing to fulfill that calling today—and throughout the days to come?

QUESTIONS—CHAPTER 27

1. As a beginning practitioner, what are some of the immediate problems you may face in your ministry in a rural area of a developing country? In an urban area of a developing country? In a developed country?

2. Do you expect to find you are immediately accepted by the people to whom you will minister? Why?

3. List some ways in which you may earn the love and respect of your co-workers. Those to whom you minister.

4. You are the record librarian at a missionary radio station. In what ways can you be a witness for Jesus Christ?

5. If your Field Director asks you to take over a ministry or task for which you have had no background, training, or experience, how will you respond? Why?"

6. Have you chosen a life's verse from the Word of God? If so, what is it? Why did you choose it? If not, what kind of verse do you feel might be appropriate to select?

7. Is it important to establish churches for new believers? Why?

8. Where churches have already been established, what is your responsibility to those churches? Why?

28
A Wife's Involvement in Missionary Work

When a couple is accepted by a Board for missionary service, the husband and wife are accepted on their individual qualifications, education, abilities and Christian experience. It is assumed by almost every Mission that the wife is as much a missionary as the husband.

As to actual field experience, Boards differ in their requirements for missionary wives. Some feel that a woman without children should make her husband her first responsibility and only as it will not interfere with her home life should she consider openly witnessing to and ministering among the people. If there are children, these Boards consider the husband and children to be the woman's chief concern, and other than providing hospitality or visiting homes and attending services, she is under no obligation to be engaged in ministry.

Other Boards feel that a married couple, supported as two individuals, are equally responsible to provide a ministry among the people to whom they have been sent. Thus a church planter, or an engineer, or a doctor may be married to a school teacher, nurse or secretary. Each will be engaged in his/her specialty, much as would be the case if they were in the homeland and each of them worked. Care of the children may fall to an amah, ayah, or other trained household worker.

Every missionary—single or married—must be convinced of the call of God to service. Not only should there be a willingness to go overseas; there should also be a strong desire to serve Jesus Christ as an ambassador. A wife should never consider herself merely as going along for the trip, or volunteering because her husband feels so strongly about going. Do not marry a man, they say, unless you can't live without him! A wife should commit herself to the work which lies before her and intend to fulfill a place of usefulness.

In obscure cases, it may be possible for a wife to stay at home and care for all the Missionary Kids in the area, which would free other wives to become involved in work among the nationals.

If the wife opts to stay at home, with or without children, she may find herself in an extremely lonely situation which could destroy not only her, but her husband's missionary career. Satan loves to tempt idle hearts and hands.

Both husband and wife must study the language of the country to which they are assigned. Sometimes the wife learns the language more quickly and better than her husband. It is important that this tool be put to use.

There must be some consideration given to those who faithfully provide financial support from the homeland. It is all too easy to forget how hard supporters, for the most part, must work for their money. They could just as easily spend the portion of their money which they have designated for you, on themselves on their home, on their children or grandchildren, or on other Christian workers. They have chosen to give that portion to **you**. Admittedly, their funds are given to the Lord for your use. But most supporters feel a laborer is worthy of his/her hire. Glowing reports concerning others on the field will never take the place of becoming involved in the action yourself.

After language study is completed, if there are no children when the couple arrives on the field, the wife may find herself taking on increasing responsibilities in the area of women's and children's work. Once having been involved in a satisfying ministry, she will find it difficult to give it up while raising a family. She may, however, be able to contemplate a ministry of home visitation, and personal witness to women in the area. One of the privileges of missionary mothers is the "in" her children give her to homes and hearts. Women seem to have a universal interest in children and they often provide an open door of witnessing opportunity. Wives may have opportunities to do literacy work with both children and adults. Or classes in English may be provided. The Taiwanese, for example, are intensely keen on learning to speak and read English. Even when their reading is done from the Bible, and when conversations turn to matters related to religion and Christianity, they are apt pupils, eager to learn—men, women, and young people.

Missionary wives may be placed in a rural area, and their time will be spent in evangelistic endeavor mainly with women and children in Eastern countries, but including men in areas such as Latin America or the Philippines. She may travel to more remote areas as a team worker with her husband, to train new Christians, or to reach the unsaved. Her responsibility may be manning a ham radio while her husband flies down country or to outlying stations.

A wife in a large mission focal point may be a nurse, teacher, secretary, pianist, broadcaster, Sunday School worker, personal worker among hospital patients, bookkeeper . . . the list could go on and on.

Many missionary wives opt for a middle path of service. They are willing to devote two or three days a week to actual involvement in missionary work. The rest of the time is spent on the responsibilities of home and family. In this way she can care for her home, plan special meals, spend time with the children, and provide prayer support for her husband and his co-workers. She can also become involved in activities of ministry which are well-suited to her and which can produce job satisfaction. She can feel she has met the responsibilities and privileges placed upon her by her supporters, her family, and herself. It may also meet the demands of the society in which she lives. Obviously, schedule changes must be permitted in this option so that freedom is allowed to give more time to the family when indicated (sickness, guests, etc.) and more to the ministry when essential (conferences, special Bible class instruction, etc.).

Part of a woman's ministry ought always to be that of prayer and intercession as her husband labors for the Lord and as nationals struggle against unbelievable temptations and problems. Of course, husbands must pray, too, but the wife ought to have a special ministry in this regard. Working with her husband in prayer will accomplish more than spending her full time in effort while neglecting their devotional and prayer life.

A missionary wife will find a ministry among her own family. Her husband will need her encouragement, love, patience and humor to help him through difficult decisions. Time with her preschool children can be the foundation upon which their lives are moulded into the image of Christ, resulting in their desire to follow Him.

In most areas, school-age children will be sent to a Boarding School, perhaps hundreds of miles away from your station. If a wife has not entered into a missionary ministry previous to that time, she will surely want to become involved when the children leave home. If she has already had a part-time ministry, she may be able to give more time to the work of the Lord by adding to her own schedule those forms of witness she has prayed for, or by picking up the responsibilities being left by a woman going on furlough.

The life of a missionary wife has no reason to be lonely, or without sufficient duties to make life full of excitement and blessing. Unfortunately, some women are perfectly willing to drive to the city twice a week for groceries, to pick up workers, to show visitors the sights of the country, to find a restaurant where good meals are served, or an inn with a swimming pool which is available to expatriates at low cost. But she is unwilling to accept a ministry which brings her into direct contact, and face-to-face encounters with the nationals to whom she avowed God was calling her. Once on the field, she decides to be her own person and do her own thing. She gets money every month whether she works or not. Her home is provided for her. She knows the language well enough to get around and do what she wants to do, and thus ends her commitment to missionary work.

Fortunately, most wives thoroughly enjoy the mission field with its changes and challenges. They long to do more and more to advance the gospel of Christ. And they are eternally grateful for churches, family and friends at home who stand behind them in prayer and financial partnership. With these the Lord must be well pleased. And surely it is a joy to a husband to find his wife entering upon her duties with a sense of God's calling.

A wife must take special care in the way she behaves before national men as well as before expatriates and co-workers. In many lands, men are tempted to moral degradation by the most unobtrusive manners of women. In a land of veiled women, for example, only prostitutes show their faces openly. Enter the female missionary! She must be exceedingly discreet in her speech and actions to avoid embarrassing and sometimes dangerous confrontations. It is said that in Japan a woman will show the nape of her neck as a come-on to a male. In Pakistan it may be an ankle or wrist. A wife should dress in all modesty and behave at all times in such a manner that she is not thought of as a seducer of men—even of her own husband. She must take great care when studying the language with a male tutor. Touching, winking at, or being alone with those of the opposite sex should be avoided whenever possible. Missionary marriages have been broken up when undue attention has been shared between the wife and a man other than her husband. Avoiding even the appearance of evil may be difficult under field conditions, but insofar as humanly possible, it must be achieved.

The missionary wife may have more problems in adjusting to life overseas than her husband. She may be more concerned with the lack of bathroom facilities, the necessity for drinking water out of earthen vessels, and the endless task of trying to make a house a home, than her husband is. It may be up to her to deal daily, in patience, with the servants. It will usually fall to her to care for those in the family who are ill. She may miss the conveniences of a telephone, TV, stereo, or automobile. She may long for a day in a department store where she could purchase a new outfit just her size! A husband readily becomes involved in his work and is too tired and too busy to worry about the comforts afforded him in the homeland.

A problem may arise in a household if the wife is a professional person and the husband is a master-of-all-trades. Missions do have need for women doctors, for example. Although the husband may have a fine Christian testimony, a Bible school education, and a desire for missionary service, he was accepted by the Board in part because of the need for his wife's professional abilities. In the homeland it takes a strong man to be known as Mrs. Smith's husband. It is no different overseas. Men need to feel they are the breadwinner, the leader, the strength of the family. In such instances, there is a reversal of roles, and perhaps the husband feels more like most missionary wives feel! But there is much for him to do and he will find his niche. Perhaps this type of situation will result in not having a family, or planning to have children during furlough periods. On the other hand, a woman doctor needs to be allowed the privilege of being a wife and mother just as any other missionary wife. These must be personal decisions and not demands made by a Mission Board. A call to missionary service ought not to violate any part of the plan and purpose of God, revealed in His Word, regarding marriage and family responsibilities.

It would seem, then, that there are opportunities on every hand that the missionary wife may take advantage of. How involved she becomes, in actuality, is a decision to be made by her, her husband, her family, her Mission Board, and her commitment to the Lord. There may be no easy choices, but there are open doors for all who are willing and able to walk through them.

QUESTIONS—CHAPTER 28

1. What are several stances various mission boards take in regard to the type and amount of work a missionary wife should do?

2. What pitfalls can a missionary wife fall into if she has volunteered for overseas service because her husband is so eager to serve the Lord in a specific area?

3. What happens when a marriage takes place because both individuals have been called to the same country, but they are not really in love?

4. What types of obligations should a missionary wife feel toward her financial partners in the homeland?

5. How do children affect the ministry of a missionary wife?

6. What are some of the reasons a missionary wife might be overcome with a sense of utter loneliness?

7. What should a missionary wife keep in mind as she works with, studies under, or has contact with national or expatriate men?

8. What are some of the adjustments a missionary wife must make which are more severe for her than for her husband?

9. What problems are apt to arise if the missionary wife is more readily accepted than her husband by the people among whom they work?

29
Cross-Cultural Communications and Relationships With Nationals

It is not easy to go to a land which is foreign to us, and immediately find close friendships among the nationals among whom we live and work. Making ourselves understood by the people to whom God has called us is a slow and ever ongoing process as well.

Even when one has studied hard and obtained a fairly decent working knowledge of the language, communication can be difficult. Getting a message across to another person, or to a group of people, involves far more than simple oral presentation. In the homeland, we may take for granted that people accept us or reject us because of what we say, the way we say it, or to whom it is said. Yet when we think of it, our words are really not what make us acceptable to others. It is our character with which individuals are drawn to or turned away from us. It is what we are, not so much what we say, which communicates with others. We grow up in a certain milieu and become accustomed to acting in certain ways, saying certain things, and responding in a learned fashion.

But when we enter an entirely new environment, we are forced to change our communicative apparatus, if we are to survive, make ourselves understood, and be able to understand and interpret the words and actions of those around us. Cross-cultural communications are not readily learned, but it is **imperative** that we communicate with understanding and with acceptance for our survival.

Oral communication is important. Yet many missionaries who have been least able to express themselves in their acquired language have made the greatest impression upon those among whom they have worked. Every effort should be made to speak correctly. But placement of a verb, or the wrong gender of a noun will matter little if there is a recognizable love and respect for those among whom you live and move and have your being.

Years ago, when China was wide open to missionaries, hundreds went forth to serve. Each was given a Chinese name very soon after arrival on the field. This name signified to the Chinese what their first impression of the missionary had been. An appellation such as "face with a smile" or "gentle one" or "truthful friend" would be a cause for rejoicing. But what of the ones named "one with a temper," "cruel master," or "impatient sister"? Perhaps in a moment when the missionary thought no one was listening or observing, he/she let down the guard and let human nature take control. And in that moment, a name was placed upon him/her which lasted for many years or even a lifetime. Care must be taken to avoid thoughtless, careless, moments of sinful behavior to control one's actions, since things are not judged in the same light.

How you treat your national friends, new acquaintances, coworkers, spouse, children, servants, expatriate friends, storekeepers, those in positions of leadership, those serving under you, those to whom you witness . . . is noticed by those to whom you have taken the Gospel. This will be taken into account as you speak, preach and teach.

One must learn the customs of those to whom he ministers. Breaking custom is a sin in their eyes. Never be surprised at "strange" happenings. You may be at a banquet in Japan. Because they see you as an honored guest, they may bring you a fish head and allow you the privilege of eating the eyes by carefully removing them with your chopsticks. The eye of the fish is a delicacy in Japan and you must be grateful that you have been chosen to receive the very best.

You may be in a Muslim land. You are in a well-to-do home in the city of Jakarta. You are served tea in a beautiful china cup and saucer. When you finish your repast, the cup is smashed before your eyes. (Your saliva is considered to be unclean and thus the cup cannot be salvaged.)

Or you, being left-handed, eat your chapati and rice using your left hand in a village home in India. You disgrace yourself before all who are gathered. (The left hand is considered unclean).

You may admire a baby, a picture, an article of clothing, or a piece of furniture in a home in which you are visiting. If you express your admiration in many lands, you will find yourself forced, not only to take the admired baby or material possession, but also to reciprocate with something of equal or better value.

Learn the customs of your country as early in your career as possible in order to avoid untold numbers of communication problems.

Communicating theological concepts may be far more difficult than you imagined they could be when you were in the homeland. How do you explain your sins becoming white as snow in a desert country which has never had snow fall on its land? How do you explain the love of God to those who have no concept of a Supernatural Being who expresses such emotion? How do you answer a Muslim who believes if God, indeed, had a Son, then God must have a wife? How do you defend against reincarnation? How do you explain to a Hindu why you eat beef? How can you explain to a Zoroastrian that earth, air, fire and water are not the ultimate of man's existence?

You see, in the homeland you dealt mainly with individuals who, even if they didn't believe them, at least were acquainted with Christian concepts and beliefs. And overseas you may find a general knowledge base of Christianity in Catholic countries and lands where foreign domination has been a factor for long periods of time. But much of the world is under the influence of Mohammedanism, Shintoism, Confucianism, Buddhism, Hinduism, Zoroastrianism, Animism, Satanism, and other isms. Communism resists the message of Christ. Atheism and agnosticism are prevalent. And the messenger of Christ must be prepared to communicate meaningfully with those who have no knowledge of Christian truth, starting from the most basic fact, namely that God exists! No easy task, indeed!

The way one dresses, sits, eats, walks, conducts business; the way one responds to danger, disaster, death; works with nationals, expatriates, protagonists, antagonists; all have much to do with the way you are regarded by those who are watching very carefully and listening very intently.

It is important to understand the hierarchical establishment of the family in the country where you serve. Is the man the leader of the home or clan, or is the woman? It will make a difference as you approach a family with the message of the Gospel.

Are initiation rites part of the experience of the people among whom you labor? Can you respect them for what they do, even though you do not understand?

Are you in a country where people spend a great deal of their time philosophizing rather than coming directly to the point? You may need to learn how to speak on many subjects other than the message of Christ, if you are to make an impact.

Your communication may be that time is a top priority and actions must be quick and responses immediate. Your actions and attitudes in the area of time management can make or break your ministry. You should allow yourself ample time to make a point, bring up a subject, or terminate a conversation.

Your attitude toward those to whom you speak and among whom you work will indicate whether you consider them your equals, below you, or above you. Speaking down to people can be a fatal flaw in your ministry whether overseas or in the homeland.

Everything you are, say, or do is communicating a message to those around you. It is a high and holy calling to which our Lord calls. But as Jim Elliot wrote, "He is no fool who gives what he cannot keep to gain what he cannot lose."

It is sometimes difficult to form close relationships with nationals. In Muslim countries and other male-dominated areas, male missionaries must take extreme care in any contact with the women of the land. Women must also avoid frequent or unhealthy relationship with male nationals—whether they be language teachers, co-workers, or just those whom you meet in the homes and shops you visit.

But as you minister, you will form friendly relationships with many who may become prayer partners and co-ministers of the Gospel. Beware of jealousy in any such relationships. Be sure you do not play favorites or extend privileges to a certain few—whether nationals or your own countrymen.

One of the things of which missionaries are accused is that they prefer fellowship with other expatriates rather than with nationals. This is often true, to the detriment of an otherwise "successful" ministry. Nationals may not understand the intimate problems of your complex life, but sharing with them in meaningful encounters about your needs and goals is very important. You are human, after all, and they should realize you face the same problems, temptations, discouragements and joys that they do.

Hospitality provides a means of communication which may win more souls than preaching! Ignoring the pleas of the **truly** needy, boasting of one's homeland, acting superior, barking orders, impatience—all will speak volumes. One burst of temper can destroy years of ministry.

Relationships with nationals will determine the whole trend of your gospel witness. You must earn their love and respect. You must work **with** them. You must allow them to submit their ideas and plans, and utilize them. You must trust them. You must realize they know their fellow-countrymen far better than you do. Give them responsibility with authority. Assure them of your help, support and prayers. Go with them rather than expecting them to go always with you. Invite them into your home and treat them as equals.

Another area of cross-cultural communications and relationships which must be considered is that having to do with working with several expatriate nationalities. A missionary from the United States may work with missionaries from Canada, England, Scotland, Wales, Ireland, Denmark, Holland, Germany, Australia, New Zealand, South Africa and others, as well as nationals from the country in which you serve. Communicating with other expatriates may be more difficult than imagined. Again, culture and customs play a part in these relationships. Language may be a problem. Ways of doing things may vary. Education, background, training, and social status will differ. Even the thought processes will seem incompatible with yours. Professional workers, especially in medicine and technology, will find it difficult to understand why and how things are done. It is one thing to not be able to borrow a spool of thread until you realize your co-worker knows it only as "a reel of cotton." But communications become more widely separated as you work with one another in ministry.

One thing must always be kept in mind. **Your** way is not the universally **right** way! There is much room for understanding others. Much can be learned from expatriates and nationals which will make you become a better individual and will assist in making your missionary work more profitable to all.

Being a missionary will mean giving up many rights to yourself and to your opinions. But it will strengthen your faith and broaden your outlook, and thereby be a blessing to you and to those who sit under your ministry.

Those who take a position of superiority, who refuse to listen to others, who make themselves obnoxious by their opinions and attitudes, will find their ministry is fruitless and unsatisfying. Paul felt it was worth his while to be made "all things to all people, that by all means I might win some" (I Corinthians 9:22). The servant of God—the missionary—must have the same purpose.

QUESTIONS—CHAPTER 29

1. What factors make up your communication to others in a foreign setting?

2. How can you best learn about the customs in the country where you serve?

3. What must be considered when forming close relationships with nationals?

4. What problems might arise in working with English-speaking expatriates from countries other than your own?

5. Why do you think many feel missionaries from the United States try to make "little Americans" out of those among whom they work and live overseas? Is is a true appraisal? Why?

6. If your medical training and background is different from that of those from other countries, how can communications decrease interpersonal, interprofessional barriers?

30
Schooling for Missionary Children

Although much progress has been made through the years in providing adequate schooling for missionary children on or near the fields in which their parents serve, there are still many areas where the nearest school is far away.

In some remote areas, on jungle stations where travel is extremely difficult, or in situations where a child might have to be sent to the homeland at a very early age for schooling, missionary parents may have to teach their children themselves. This has been made easier through the preparation and distribution of properly graded materials from either Christian or secular sources. Although somewhat expensive and, at times, frustrating because of the unreliability of mail arriving and departing on schedule, some parents opt for this method of education. It may mean a full-time responsibility for the missionary wife. If several families from an area are forced to this option, because of their remote location, a "school" may become feasible where the children have classes and interaction—an important part of the educative process. If children vary widely in ages, however, it may fall to each family to teach his/her own children. It is time-consuming and it may be difficult to obtain sufficient resource materials for children to dig into for their homework. Yet, exams must be passed, and often children who have studied privately at home do very well overall.

Blessed are those who have a school for missionary children close enough to home that they can walk, bike, be bussed, driven by family or friends, take a train or another form of transportation to classes each day. In Tokyo or Quito, this is a very real possibility; in Shikarpur or Lae, it is not.

In some countries, there is one school for missionary children. Many families will live hundreds, even thousands of miles from the school. Therefore, children must be sent and boarded at the school for approximately nine months each year. (In some countries, even those who live nearby are required to board in order to have a unity among the student body). Parents may be able to make a limited number of visits during the year because of distance and costs. Children may be able to be at home with their parents at Christmas and Spring breaks as well as in the summer. In some areas, the school is located in the hill region where most parents take their holiday. This is true in Murree, Pakistan and in Mussoorie, India, for example. Because of this, many of the children are able to stay with their family during the warmer days of the summer while they commute by school bus or private car to classes. Then in the colder snowy winter, they have their usual three-month vacation. At that time they are with their family on their mission station. In some instances, this can mean that the children are actually with their parents from 4-6 months each year.

This schedule may, of course, present problems when furlough time is due because of the odd sequence of school attendance, depending on whether the school is U.S., Canadian, English, Australian, or other country-oriented. But such problems are usually worked out in the homeland.

Many children who attend a school for missionary children are often further advanced academically than their counterparts in the homeland. This is caused in part by the fact that some of the schools are more closely allied to the British system of education than to the American. Often, then, when a child is enrolled in school during furlough time, he may find himself advanced one grade to avoid having to repeat material already learned. Upon return to the field, he/she then enters the normal sequence of study (as if he had taken the year in the next class on the field) and he is in step with his classmates.

Being placed in a boarding school has both advantages and disadvantages. A child may miss out on a great deal of family life with his parents and siblings. He may be very lonely, shy, and uncomfortable with strangers. He may not feel free to share with his houseparents, teachers, or the principal of the school. He may need or want more love and attention at certain periods of his life than can be given by those to whom he does not belong. He may have questions as to why he has been placed in a position which he did not choose and why his parents seem to put far more time and effort into their work than they do into him. To counteract feelings of insecurity, parents must give their children a great deal of love and attention when they are together. They must also convey confidenced by their attitudes that God has directed toward the boarding school education option. Therefore it is best for the child in God's plan for him.

For the most part, however, missionary children enjoy life overseas. They have opportunities never afforded their friends and relatives in the homeland. Their studies are interesting. Their classes are small. Their teachers are knowledgeable, patient, loving, and understanding. They make strong friendships with other M.K.'s, not only from their own homeland, but from several others as well. They learn the customs and the language of the country in which they live. They begin to understand why their parents felt so strongly about the need of the Gospel in that land.

Those who are administrators, teachers, and staff members at missionary schools are chosen carefully and, for the most part, are the best in their fields. They provide not only an educational atmosphere, but also plan fun times, travel experiences, camp-outs, and contact with the nationals. Moral values, spiritual values, and eternal values are taught and modeled. Proper punishment is provided. The children become part of a larger family, and seem to respond well to being surrounded by aunts and uncles who deeply care about them. Many have married the "childhood sweetheart" they came to know in the M.K. school.

There are fields which have no provision for M.K.'s and the nearest school is thousands of miles distant (such as Kijabe, Kenya, which cares for students from several East African countries as well as some from West Africa). Passports and visas must be put in order, and children do not have as much opportunity to be with their parents as they would like. But such schooling is certainly an option which ought to be considered by missionary parents. In almost every instance, the children are far more excited about the prospect of attending boarding school than the parents. It may be very difficult, and seem almost cruel, to have to send young children away. But the Lord has His own ways of making up this loss to both parents and children. Children, especially, quickly find compensation for their losses. And unless there are severe political problems to complicate the situation, a sudden tragedy in the family, or an instability in either a child or a parent, adjustments will be made. The child will be happy, and the parents will be content with the situation. Looking forward to flying or travelling by bus or train to be reunited with the family is half the fun of being away. So keep your emotions under control insofar as possible, and trust your children to the care of those who are adequately trained and who find it a privilege to provide the best possible learning situation for your children.

Some schools for missionary children are able to provide education only through grade school. This means that when young people are ready for high school, a decision must be made. Teaching high school at home is difficult at best. Correspondence courses can prove to be inadequate and students are left without competition, companionship, or interaction. There is the possibility of sending them to a high school in a nearby country, or one which is at least on the same continent. In some situations it has proven profitable for students to be enrolled in local government schools. This is especially popular in European countries where the high school student continues his education entirely in the French, Italian, Spanish, German, Swedish, or other European language. If he has been in the country any length of time, he will have a working knowledge of the language. It may take time to adjust, but it is an alternative which might be considered.

Even very young children may be placed in national schools which have high academic and moral standards in some countries of the world. Perhaps a trial period in such a setting will prove the worth (or lack of it) of putting your children into local situations.

If national schooling is given serious consideration, however, you must keep in mind that learning is by "rote" in many countries. Supplemental studies in U.S. History, for example, will be required through home study or personal research. Parents must also consider whether or not they would be at ease if their child should marry a national because of their close alliance through such an educational program. Carefully weigh the obvious advantages and disadvantages of national schools before committing your children to them.

When a young person is about to enter high school, he should be consulted regarding the school of his choice. Some opt to go back to the homeland for these final three or four years of high school. They may want to become reacquainted with their homeland. They may want to become involved in sports and social activities which may not be available to them on the field. They may look forward to living with relatives who are willing to make a home for them. They may want to study in English rather than in a foreign language. They may feel more grown up if they are further away from their parents. They may have seen on furlough some of the material benefits and sinful attractions available in the homeland, and being teenagers, they "want to be where the action is."

A boarding school in the homeland is another alternative, especially if children have been used to this on the field, or when there are no relatives willing or able to take full responsibility. Finances will be a factor in decisions of this kind.

If a child is sent home, it must be decided whether he will attend a public, private, or Christian school. Finances must be considered. There must be a place where he can go during the summer vacation period. (Many young people visit their parents on the field during that time). And if problems develop which cannot be handled by mail or telephone, a parent may have to fly home to solve it.

It is never easy for a parent to send a child away for school, whether it is 100 or 10,000 miles away. This is a heartache which must be bravely borne by parents and children alike, whether the child is preschool, or entering college. Yet perhaps out of such experiences, the Lord places on the mind and heart of your son(s) and/or daughter(s) a desire to follow in your missionary steps.

Missionary children are human and are prone to the same temptations, problems and joys as all children. There may come a day in the life of one or more of your children when personal pressures or the stresses of the mission field seem to be more than can be safely borne. Discipline problems may arise which are more than the M.K. school can handle. Rebellion may rear its head, seeking to destroy all that has been learned of Christianity. In some cases, young people will work hard to fail in order to gain the attention of parents or those in authority. Sometimes young people are just no longer able to cope with their overseas experience. Stress can affect any person at any age. The sooner it is dealt with, the better life will be for the individual(s) involved.

As much as missionary parents desire to continue their ministry and finish the tasks which they have begun, it may be necessary to take an extended leave of absence to care for the needs of your children. They are your primary responsibility before God at home or on the field. Trust the entire situation to the Lord. And then look forward to what He has for you to do until the time you may be able to return to the field. A girl who refuses to eat, a boy who rapes a national or missionary child, a child who attempts suicide, a child who cannot sleep, a child who is a real "loner," these and other problems must not be ignored, nor should parents make a boarding school responsible for those with such abnormal behavior. Treatment must be found as soon as possible in the homeland. Your children are **your** responsibility. You will not find it easy to explain the situation to others. But because of the possible serious ramifications involved, you must seek counsel away from the field. Mission Boards are understanding concerning such necessary actions. Supporters, too, will understand the seriousness of a situation which would draw you away from your ministry. Never be ashamed when such a situation arises. God will help you weather the storm. It is one of His "all things."

It is possible that a year at home will solve the situation. It may be necessary for you to stay at home until your teenage children are settled into college, vocational school, or a work situation. But 4-6 years at home will not be wasted time. It may save your children. It will strengthen your faith. It may prepare you for years of service later on. It will not be a futile experience. God will see to that. There will be lessons you, personally, need to learn in order to be the ambassador of Christ you have volunteered to be. Your children must learn how to become mature and stable in their faith and actions. Even your home church and supporting friends need to learn that missionaries are not exempt from trials, tribulations and temptations. Such an experience ought to increase their desire to pray more regularly and give more faithfully to those who serve **in their stead** on the mission fields of the world.

If a child attends high school on the mission field, it is important, if he plans to attend college/university, that he send for information concerning several institutions as early as his freshman or sophomore year. Mail is slow. Competition is great. Scholarships are limited. Therefore it is wise to choose an institution of higher learning as early as possible. Arriving in the homeland, expecting to choose a school, meeting the requirements, filling out the forms, taking the tests and getting enrolled within a period of a month or two is almost always impossible. Preliminary work must begin at least a year (two years is better) in advance. Even young people with a high grade-point average will find it difficult to get into a school at the last minute. Plan ahead. You may wish to apply to more than one institution to be sure of acceptance at the required time.

Whether a child is at home or a school, a missionary parent has a tremendous responsibility of education. The way you act and react to your missionary service; the way you treat your family; the way you deal with the nationals; the amount of respect you have for your fellow-missionaries; your personal walk and talk with the Lord; your assessment of your mission board; the way you handle stress; the way you speak, your utilizing of His money; your love for your children; your care and concern about your supporters, prayer partners, family and friends in the homeland—all reflect the Christ whom you serve—or detract from Him. Your children should know who is the head of your household. And no matter what ministry you are in, the father should be the godly family leader. Your child will learn his lessons in reading, writing and arithmetic. These are important. But when he is with you, and through your communications to him when he is away, he will be attracted to or dissuaded from coming into a personal relationship with Jesus Christ.

Another responsibility of the missionary parent concerns your relationship to the local church in the area where you serve. As well as your relationship to your home church. If you are in an area where there is no established church, it is important that you provide a worship service for your child(ren) once a week as well as allowing them to take part in daily family devotions. If there is a church, whether in its infancy, or well-established, your children should be made to realize the importance of their attendance upon its services. Church attendance should not be considered a habitual routine. It should be meaningful. This will mean children must be educated in the importance of a church affiliation.

If your children attend a school for missionary children, you can be certain they will be required to attend chapel services, and provision will be made for worship services. If, on the other hand, they are enrolled in secular situations, you must make it possible for them to enter into fellowship with other believers in meaningful encounters in a church situation.

By the time your young people leave you for high school or college in the homeland, they should be able and willing to enter into a local church situation where they can both share their experiences and be strengthened in the things of the Lord. Apart from a church family, a young person can too easily turn aside from Christian principles. A love for Christ and His church must be taught from a child's earliest remembrance—not just by your words, but by your example.

Children are a gift from God. They are the means by which the Gospel will reach the next generation. How important it is to provide for their schooling in the best possible circumstances so they will be trained and educated for learning and for life.

Be sure to read **The Life & Times of an MK**, by C. John Buffam, and **Missionary Kid—MK**, by Edward Danielson, for extremely helpful material concerning children and the mission field.

QUESTIONS—CHAPTER 30

1. What are several schooling alternatives for children overseas?

2. What are the advantages and disadvantages of teaching your own children?

3. Name several advantages and disadvantages to placing your children in a boarding school for M.K.''s.

4. Under what circumstances and at what age might a child be sent back to the homeland for schooling?

5. You have received word from the Principal of the M.K. school that your child is disrupting the classroom and the dormitory with chronic, unruly behavior which responds neither to love or discipline. What will be your course of action?

6. List at least 10 things that play an important role in the education of your child.

7. What plans should be made for enrolling your child in a Bible school, college, vocational school, or university? When?

31
Servants

Many of us have never had the experience of being waited on by servants in the homeland. Yet few could manage on the mission field without those who are available to help with some of the tasks which are so daily.

Missionaries seldom tell about the joys and sorrows of having maids, cooks, sweepers, bearers, ayahs, translators, and others who help them in their household and work responsibilities. It may seem a bit presumptuous to speak of having servants, and you may be afraid of being misunderstood by those who are supporting you. You think they will feel you are living on a much higher plane than they can afford; yet they are giving their money to keep you on the field. It does cause a dilemma. Little do people back home realize that they are employing literally thousands of people, out of sight, who are "waiting on" them every time they pick up partially prepared foods in a supermarket, push the button on their automatic furnace, start their dishwasher, turn on their garbage disposal, etc., etc.

Accordingly, missionaries, through the years, have found that they had no time to minister if they were constantly tied down to the more complicated cooking, housekeeping, and marketing tasks required by their field situation—especially if they labor in a desert area where the temperature rises to 120° most of the year, or in a mountainous area where strength is limited because of the 10-12,000 foot altitude, or in a tropical coastal area where 100% humidity is debilitating. Few desert stations are air-conditioned, nor are dehumidifiers readily available. You can't plug these into the sand—and electricity may be at a premium, if available at all. How grateful missionaries are to be able to find a servant (or servants) whom they can train and pay to do the shopping, cooking, and cleaning up. Sweeping brick floors which are laid in loose sand can be a daily chore which takes precious time. All kinds of cleaning take time: In other words, what is wise in the use of time and money is a different kind of problem in the drastically different situation.

How good it is to find a faithful servant who is willing to take on the cleaning chores. And if yours is a large family, or several people eat at your table, it is good to have one who can set the table, bring the food to the table (since many kitchens are separate rooms some distance from the rest of the home), and clear up afterwards. If only one or two live together, one servant may be found who will do all the household work. On the other hand, there are countries where more than one servant must be utilized since individuals know how to do only one thing, or they refuse to learn more than one responsibility because a "caste" system still exists in practice, though not in law.

Unless you find someone who lives close by to work for you, you will need to provide living accommodations for your primary servant(s). He then lives on the property, either alone or with his wife (wives) and children. You may also need to hire a watchman, who may request living accommodations. In most cases, servants live very simply, needing only beds and an area where they can make a small fire to do their own cooking. Pay is usually small for these who work for you. If you can find a faithful and honest servant, you will want to reward him with periodic pay increases as well as supplying him with foodstuffs, cloth, and other necessities of life. Not all servants are of the caliber you would desire. Stealing goods can be a problem for these who have so little and who see you with so much. A cook may assume that if he can bargain in the marketplace and get national prices on goods, he can then charge you expatriate prices, thus making a bit of extra spending money without your knowledge. (He cannot produce computer cash register receipts for his purchases, so you must take his word for what he paid for a given article.) Even so, you will usually pay less than as though you had purchased the items yourself.

Many servants will be untrained. They will not have worked for foreigners previously. They have no idea what you eat or how you prepare it. But they are almost always willing to learn. Some learn quickly. Others never learn: Someone has to teach these folks how to do things. They may be illiterate, so they must remember everything they are told without taking notes. Because of this, it is usually not wise to expect to have fancy foods prepared for your table. It may be necessary to start with national foods which, fortunately, usually includes fried or boiled eggs and dry toast: You will need much patience to teach your cook how to make doughnuts, bread, roast chicken (without feathers) or mashed potatoes. Even the best of training does not always prove as effective as you thought it would. A new cook knew my missionary friend loved baked potatoes. To be sure he had one ready for her noon meal, he cooked it at 6:00 a.m. and then refrigerated it. This way he was sure it was something she would like, and it would be ready anytime she wanted to eat it!

Not only will you have to teach the basics of cooking in many cases, but you must also teach respect for cleanliness. There is often the necessity to be sure all milk is boiled and cooled before using. All drinking water may also need to be boiled. Teaching a servant to boil water for ten minutes may sound like a simple task. It is not: Many foods (especially salad ingredients and fresh fruit) must be soaked in permanganate, Clorox, or other disinfecting material to destroy harmful bacteria, and then rinsed in **boiled** water before serving. Ice cubes must be made from **boiled** water. How can you be sure this has been done? Only by constant teaching, checking, teaching, checking, teaching . . . Explaining why these things must be done is a difficult task in itself. Blessed are the missionaries who have safe sources of food and water.

It is often the lady of the house who has the responsibility of training the servants. She will be frustrated often both because of her lack of full ability in her new language to explain what she wants done, and by the misunderstandings which can occur between master and servant. It may be even more difficult in a male-dominated society when a group of lady missionaries acquire a male servant. It takes time for the man to respect women—it is a wholly new experience to be endured. Yet in those same areas, except for widows and prostitutes, all women are married and must care for their own family. Women are not free to go out to take a position—even as a servant—to help out with family finances in many areas of the world.

It is important to accept your servants as individuals with worth. It is also your responsibility to witness to them, or to build them up in the faith (if you are fortunate enough to obtain the services of a Christian). I believe a missionary's testimony can be ruined in an area because of servants. After all, they see the missionary morning, noon, and night. They see how he treats his family, how he responds to disappointments, how angry he becomes when things don't go his way. Every act of impatience, unconcern, and dishonesty is noted. And servants talk with those in the streets, in the marketplace, in the city/town, and in the neighborhood. Your life is an open book to the whole world. What you say and do is repeated to anyone who will listen. And if your servant doesn't see Jesus shining in and through your life, no amount of striving will convince others that your Christian cliches are worth heeding. How desperately important it is to have a clear and strong faith which can be seen and heard at home as well as in your formal and informal meetings with nationals.

There have been instances where servants have brought trouble to their masters. Some have been involved in heinous sins; some are gamblers, drunkards, wife stealers. It has not been unknown for a servant to rape or otherwise sexually molest a missionary wife or child.

Great care must be taken in the selection of those who will aid you in the things of your life which are so daily. You may be fortunate enough to utilize the trained servant(s) of missionaries who have gone on furlough. In such a case, you may find they are fully able to make out their own shopping lists and menus, thus relieving you of endless hours of kitchen labor. On the other hand, you may wish to hire a new convert from your town or village, or one to whom you want to be a witness. Such individuals must be taught patiently, both to become skillful in their trade, and in the Word of God.

You may wish to do away with helpers in the home. But you will find it difficult to fit the work of the household in along with caring for the children, studying the language, and being involved in a ministry.It will have to be your decision, of course. And utilizing workers to clean, wash and cook may be a better decision for you than utilizing a national to care for your children. This is a far more personal matter and the greatest of care must be taken in your choice of a helper in this area of your life.

Many a national has come to know the Lord because of the witness he/she has received by working in the missionary's home. Yet great care must be taken in living before these servants. They see you at your worst as well as at your best. Some have even been known to be connected with the police or government, and reports are given on your activities as interpreted by your servants. So there must be some caution exercised and control maintained.

Servants can be a tremendous help to missionaries. Keep in mind, however, that they are not your slaves. They are to minister to you in areas of your greatest needs in the areas of household or other chores assigned to them. There are many ways in which you can also minister to them.

QUESTIONS—CHAPTER 31

1. Should missionaries utilize the services of paid workers for household duties?

2.   List at least five characteristics you must develop to deal effectively with your servants.

3.   In what ways can you witness to a non-believing servant?

4.   In what ways can your believing servants be strengthened in the things of the Lord by you?

5.   What problems are apt to arise if your children are put in the care of a servant from an early age? What benefits can be derived?

6.   What differentiates a servant from a slave?

32
Medical Concerns

Few missionaries spend a lifetime overseas without experiencing episodes of physical impairment. Diseases, accidents, birth of children, dental problems, slight loss of normal sight or hearing, psychological hangups, emotional disturbances . . . any of these, or other physical needs, may arise to hinder the ministry of God's ambassador.

On the other hand, just because you are a missionary, do not feel you will fall victim to certain sicknesses or diseases just because "every missionary comes down with them sooner of later." If you are assigned to Europe, Singapore, Tokyo or Rio, you will probably not be endangered by amoebic dysentery, typhoid, or malaria! Not everyone succombs to hepatitis! Not everyone undergoes an appendectomy. Missionaries often stay healthy throughout their entire career.

Many illnesses are short-lived and easily overcome. Stomach upsets from strange foods or unclean preparation of meals are among the most common ailments. Headaches resulting from altitude, stress, perseverance with the language, or change of diet are also common. But other sicknesses are prevalent in the tropics, and missionaries are not immune to any of them—even though the proper shots have been administered, anti-malarial pills are ingested faithfully, and great care is taken in the handling, serving, and eating of foods and liquids. Innoculations, even when booster shots are received according to precise schedules, may not guarantee that the disease will not be contracted. It should mean, however, that the disease will have less severe consequences if you acquire it. Therefore, it is very possible for you to come down with typhoid fever. And almost always, when a disease is taking its course in the body, other physical ailments will be stirred up, aggravated, or increased.

There are many who are carriers of disease, even though they may not have outward manifestations of it. Amoebic dysentery is often present within those living in the tropics. Yet it may never be a problem unless aggravated by another disease which debilitates the strength of the individual. It should not be surprising if you have an attack of malaria as well as suffering symptoms from a flu virus.

If food has been carelessly handled or improperly cooked, the result from eating it can be bacillary dysentery. It is possible to get a severe case of diarrhea—which may or may not actually be dysentery—from a change of drinking water, eating highly spiced foods, or overindulging in eating after exercising, recovering from an illness, or stressful work.

If there is a doctor nearby, it is best to be seen by him/her as soon as symptoms of any disease or sickness appear. This may not be difficult for a team worker in Austria, or a missionary working on a large medical compound in Zaire. But if you are stationed in an isolated area with no medical personnel or facilities nearby, you may have to call for help on your ham radio, and be taken by plane or helicopter to the nearest medical facility where proper diagnosis may be given and treatment undertaken.

If it is impossible to get word to those who can help in such a situation, it may be necessary to be cared for, or to take care of yourself at your station. No matter how strenuous the set schedule, or how committed you are to the task at hand, it is foolhardy not to give in to your disease. You absolutely must rest. That does not mean doing everything from your bed that you would ordinarly do if you were not sick! It means complete, total, undisturbed rest. You must drink sufficient liquids to keep your body from dehydration (which can happen all too easily if, for example, you are running a high fever and have severe diarrhea). Aspirin (or an aspirin-substitute) should be administered if you are not allergic to aspirin. If you are in the tropics, even during periods of sickness, you should continue to take your anti-malarial medicine. Anti-diarrhea medicine may be useful in some cases. If surgery is indicated, the best possible means must be found to transport you to a hospital.

If the sickness continues, the body is weakened, or there is little or no change in the condition, plans **must** be made to reach a medical base where the disease can be identified properly and care can be given.

Because of primitive conditions which may prevail in outlying areas, reinfection as well as spread of the disease(s) is a constant concern to the missionary family. Servants, if any, should be carefully taught proper sanitary principles and techniques. The boiling of milk and water, foregoing the eating of raw foods, protection from flies, mosquitoes and other germ-carrying insects, screening of all windows and doors, and care in washing the body (particularly the hands) will provide some protection against disease. More special concern needs to be taken if polio is prevalent, hepatitis seems to be spreading, or rabid animals are known to be in your area.

Perhaps of greatest concern to families are the sicknesses and diseases which come to children. Measles, mumps and chicken pox can be handled without too much panic in the homeland. But when a child is lying limp, with a fever of 106°, and has a severe headache which does not respond to medication, parents have every right to be concerned and fearful. Prayer will sustain you in such times. But it is urgent that medical help be found as quickly as possible. Children—especially very young ones, will not have the stamina of an adult and therefore strength will be drained far more dramatically and quickly. Constant care may be demanded, day and night. It will be disruptive to normal eating and sleeping habits, and could be the cause of making you susceptible to illnesses. Again, care must be given as adequately as possible, and medical or surgical intervention should be sought in whatever way feasible. Missionary children have died on the field as well as missionaries . . . just as individuals die in the homeland. God allows the rain to fall on the just and the unjust. You live by faith, both at home and overseas. Even with the most modern medical facilities and finest of professionally trained doctors in the homeland, God allows death to come to households. One day He will make it fully known why His will was fulfilled in any and all of our circumstances.

If a child is born prior to your going overseas, it is imperative that he receive his routine shots.

There are, of course, individuals who are not as susceptible to pain and disease as others are. Such people should not be condemnatory of those prone to sickness, but should willingly "hold the fort" and fill in as much as possible and necessary for those who are laid aside. They should also be grateful for the measure of health the Lord has bestowed upon them.

On the other hand, there are certain individuals who seem to delight in being ill. A hangnail or a blister is excuse enough to cancel meetings, go to bed, or indulge one's self in things unrelated to the ministry to which he/she has been called. Such folks can be detrimental to the work of the Lord, causing others to work an overload while they free themselves for personal endeavors and self-pity. It is difficult to accept a co-worker who uses such "weak" excuses for not fulfilling obligations. Perhaps confronting the situation in a face-to-face encounter, sharing how difficult the work becomes when there is a missing link in the chain of duty, is possible. It may be necessary to report the situation to your Field Director and ask that he look into the matter and deal with it. Interpersonal relationships are difficult under the best of circumstances, and such stress should not be endured interminably. When little things are not brought out into the open, they will cause rifts, guilt, and occasionally missionaries will give up and go home over such seemingly insignificant situations.

Dental problems on the mission field may be even more difficult to handle than medical ones. Many areas have few, if any, well-trained, qualified dentists available to the expatriate. Rural people in developing countries may have to depend upon the local barber, druggist, or witchdoctor to remove a tooth. A missionary in Vienna, Tokyo, or London will, undoubtedly, have access to the best in dental care. But a missionary on an isolated station may have to travel a long distance to get a tooth filled, replace a lost or broken denture, or have a dead nerve removed. Some missionaries are knowledgeable about pulling teeth, but would do so only as a last resort for a fellow missionary!

It is a good policy to have a dental checkup at least once a year. This can usually be arranged during your vacation time when you are more apt to be in an urban area where dentists are available.

Accidents happen on the mission field. Therefore each missionary should have some knowledge of how to stop bleeding, make a temporary splint, do CPR, transport victims, and snakebites. Reviewing a good First Aid book twice a year should be a priority responsibility of each individual.

Missionaries have access to swimming areas in some situations. Cardiopulmonary resuscitation must be known by all. It can, has, and will save lives.

A national may be brought to you after a bus, car, or motorcycle accident; being severely gored by a wild animal; having a leg almost cut off by the undisciplined swing of a machete; badly burned by falling into a fire. A fellow-missionary can also suffer from these as well as other accidents. It is wise to consider before an accident occurs what you should do, where you can obtain help, who should be notified, and how to get the victim to the nearest available doctor and/or medical facility. It is not just doctors and nurses who must deal with such difficult situations!

If you are expecting a baby, you must decide whether it will be born at home with the help of your husband, a midwife, or a co-worker who has had medical training, or if you will go to a hospital. There are many M.K.'s who have been born at home, not by choice, but by necessity! Babies do not always wait for sterile conditions or white-robed doctors! Most mothers-to-be, however, plan to deliver in a Mission Hospital, or at a local government hospital. If any problems develop during the pregnancy, a doctor should be consulted. It may be necessary for the wife to make arrangements to stay with friends closer to the town or city where the hospital is located. Sometimes it is possible to live at the mission hospital compound for several weeks or months until the baby is born, if it is a difficult pregnancy. It is important to consider several options for the pregnant mother in the event problems arise or the baby is delivered sooner than expected. All due care should be taken to avoid serious illness or prolonged periods of stress—as well as emphasizing good dietary habits—during pregnancy.

Babies must be exposed to the least possible amount of germs and contamination. On the other hand, you cannot keep a baby in isolation. Normal precautions should be observed, but abnormal fears should be subservient to faith in God's protecting power and His ability to sustain little children in the midst of conditions which might not need to be endured in the homeland.

If there comes a time when you feel your hearing has become less than normal, it is important that as soon as possible, an otolaryngologist (ear doctor) be consulted. In many cases it will be necessary to be tested repeatedly. If furlough time is nearly due, it will be best to have this problem cared for almost immediately upon arrival in the homeland. A hearing aid may be recommended. If so, take into consideration its feasibility on the mission field. Will it be practical? Will it be useable for an entire term of service? What happens if it breaks, is lost, or needs repairs? Will batteries be available overseas, or can they be sent to you? Getting the correct aid for your particular hearing loss is essential. It just may not be available on your field of service.

If visual acuity is a problem, you should seek out one who can carefully screen your need for glasses. There may be a doctor in your mission on your field who can care for this matter. Nationals may also be qualified in this responsibility. (Do beware of those who simply ask you to read an eyechart and then sell you a pair of magnifying lenses!) Be sure your glasses are well-fitting with the proper lens strength for the problem of your individual eyes. Poorly fitted glasses will only further harm your ability to see properly and increase the danger of permanent damage.

Much thought should be given before purchasing contact lenses. They may not be available overseas and, of course, special testing is needed before acquiring them. If you work in desert areas, contacts may not be adviseable because of the constantly blowing sand. (Plastic lenses are not recommended in such areas either, because they will soon become scratched—leaving you with the need for glass lenses). Contacts should be backed up by at least a second pair, or with conventional, framed glasses. You must be able to have a supply of cleansing and soaking fluids on hand for use with your contacts, too. Although seemingly costly, it is imperative to have two pairs of glasses available if you are dependent upon them for writing, driving, working, etc. Prescription sunglasses may also be required.

Occasionally a missionary will experience psychological, mental, or emotional disturbances or dysfunction. Although one should not be overly hasty in reporting such matters to those in the place of leadership, it could preserve a missionary's ability to function if immediate attention can be given to any such problem. Those who live and work under stressful circumstances, those who may have lost a child or spouse through a recent accident or illness, those who have found it difficult to adjust to field living, and those who would choose to go home but who stay on the field because the spouse or co-worker has a meaningful ministry which would be disrupted or hindered through treatment of their infirmity— these and others may develop severe psychoses or neuroses that can be dealt with only by a professional psychiatrist and departure from the field. After adequate treatment, a return to the field may be possible. If the psychiatrist feels the field will again bring on abnormal behavior and adverse reactions, he will insist on a ministry in the homeland after adequate treatment. Children may be affected with emotional and psychological problems sufficiently severe that a return to the homeland will be indicated for the entire family.

Having to leave the field for medical reasons is not a happy prospect. In many instances, return to the field is appropriate after treatment. But it is at times like these that faith will be fully tested and revealed. Whatever the outcome, it must be remembered that God has His own way of dealing with each one of His children. Trust Him, no matter what the circumstance. He will bring glory out of chaos and rejoicing out of the most critical changes in life. Trust in the Heavenly Father, full dependence in prayer, and carefulness in daily living is our part in keeping healthy. It is then up to God to do what He will for our highest good and His greatest glory.

QUESTIONS—CHAPTER 32

1. List several diseases which might be contracted by a missionary working in a tropical country.

.2. List several physical problems which might be experienced by a missionary working in a European country.

3. List several possible causes of prolonged headaches suffered by a missionary in Japan.

4. If your co-worker is laid aside because of nausea, stomach cramps, diarrhea and a fever of 102° F., what would your plan of action be to best help him/her?

5. Your child is very ill with typhoid fever. The nearest doctor is 50 miles away. Your spouse is away for meetings with the nationals and cannot be reached. How will you handle this situation?

6. What factors need to be considered when a serious dental problem arises?

7. What factors must be decided upon when it is known the wife is pregnant?

8. What factors need to be considered if your hearing is becoming impaired? Your eyesight?

9. What course of action should be considered if your co-worker (or spouse) is showing signs of bizarre behavior and/or irrational speech?

10 If an illness is severe enough to return you to the homeland, what factors need to be considered if you opt to return overseas for further missionary service?

33
Rest and Recreation

A flood of material has been published concerning how to avoid stress and burn-out. In their rush to gain fame, power, and finances, men and women have been burning the candle at both ends, striving to outdo others in their field, and pushing themselves all out of proportion to the job assigned to them.

If you have held a secular position, you will know something of the competition, paper work, social agenda, conferences and daily load you are expected to carry in today's business world. Many individuals have seen their families fragmented and their marriages dissolved because of the intensity with which they have sought to maintain their position in the company. Sunday School, Sunday evening services, prayer services and all forms of ministry have been forsaken. If couples work, they may not even take vacations at the same time. Those in sales are often away from home for several days at a time at frequent intervals. The same is true with bus or truck drivers, pilots, executives and others. Those in Real Estate are almost always busiest during evenings and on weekends. Even pastors find themselves attending meetings five nights a week, visiting the sick, visiting newcomers, preparing messages, counseling, administrating . . .

As a student, you may have had a job and a family as well as trying to maintain an acceptable grade average in your courses and learn all you could from each class. Then you were accepted for missionary service. You probably held down a job as well as speaking at various churches and made plans and purchases for your field experience.

Now you are a missionary. You are involved in learning the language, getting to know the people, teaching Bible classes, and working at your profession. You may have a family which needs your time and attention. You may have slight or severe physical problems due to changes in food and climate. There is always so much to do and so few to do it. There are constant demands upon you. You feel tired. But you continue full steam ahead.

Missionaries ought not to appear to be sluggish or lazy. They need to do their share of work and not leave it for others to do. But you must also be sensible in caring for your body—for the body is the temple of the Holy Spirit. You should learn from the fact that God took a full six days to create the heavens and the earth when He could have done it in one day—or less!

It makes sense to take one day in seven as a day of rest. Unfortunately, most Christian workers are unable to take Sundays off. In fact, it is almost always the busiest day of the week. But it is entirely possible to take one day off each week. Many prefer Monday. But the exact day will need to be determined in consultation with others on your station. Those who have defined hours in a classroom, office, radio station, hospital, or clinic will usually be allowed two days off each week. No matter how heavy your schedule, or how many responsibilities you would like to take on (manning the Bible Bookstore, doing home visitation, preaching, teaching, being involved in the national church activities, instructing women in handcrafts, or showing men how to build better houses) be sure you allow yourself one day a week for rest (God did!) and recreation. If you refuse to do so, you will weaken your ability to serve the Lord with vigor, and "water down" each of your ministries. Learn to do a few things well!

No matter where you are stationed, a picnic can be arranged. Play Scrabble. Write letters to friends at home. Read a book or some magazines. Go for a walk and smell the flowers. This is a day to look forward to when you can do the things you truly **want** to do—not the things you have to do. Except in a case of **extreme** emergency, it should be made known to national friends, co-workers, and servants that you are not to be disturbed. (Remember to allow them the same privilege.) You'll be amazed at how much more clearly you will think, study, and minister after a day away from the books and the work. Too few missionaries in the past have given themselves this opportunity for physical renewal.

Not only should you plan a day off every week; you must plan for an annual period for a longer holiday. Your mission board probably has rules and regulations regarding the length of your holiday time, depending on the climate in which you labor, whether or not you plan to take further language study, or if you are going apart to rest a while.

You will find there are many restful vacation spots in the country to which you have been called, or countries nearby. Your mission may even have "rest homes" in the hills or at the seashore, or by a lake, where you (and your family) may hire an apartment or a home for a month or six weeks. Usually the cost is minimal. You are free to go and come at will. It will be a time of renewal for body, soul and spirit. Take advantage of this opportunity and truly rest. Some folks think to rest, one must sleep for a month. This is probably the worst kind of refreshment! Two or three leisurely days is almost always long enough to get weariness out of your bones. After that, you will want to take short trips, go fishing, go into town, cook some special treats, get to know other expatriates, talk with nationals in a neighborly fashion, answer letters . . . and after two or three weeks, try assessing what you have been doing in your ministry and how much you are accomplishing. Make plans for the year ahead. There will be hours when you can pray without interruption. You should return to your station with new zeal and vigor to carry out the ministry to which you are assigned. Of course, if you live on an extremely busy mission station, and are constantly with other people, you may want to be completely by yourself (or with your family) during your holiday time.

Some countries have one or two holiday sites where most expatriates gather. You will come to know missionaries working with other boards. They will be working in other parts of the country with different types of people and a different language. Spend time with them and learn from them. You will find your problems and joys are similar. Attend Inter-Mission prayer meetings which may be available to you. If there isn't one established, start one. If a great number of individuals are gathered in one spot, there may be special church services and weeks of meetings with spiritual leaders invited from various parts of the world to minister to you. Although you will want to have national friends and co-workers, you will also be encouraged by fellowship with other expatriates—not only from your homeland, but from many lands.

Because air travel is so quick, some missionaries are tempted to use their vacation time for a trip to the homeland—especially if they are stationed in Central America, northern South America, or the Islands of the Caribbean. It is important to seek council from administration if a member of your immediate family is gravely ill in the homeland. Permission is often asked to fly home for a graduation, birth, wedding, anniversary or other special occasion. A mission administrator who can give a wise response to such requests from those under his authority is much to be desired.

There are several reasons why trips to the homeland must be considered very carefully:

1. Many of your supporters have not seen loved ones for years, and even though they live only a thousand miles away, they cannot affort to visit. They may question the need for you (or your family) to head home every year.

2. If you go home for vacation, you will be compelled to speak and minister to individuals, groups, and churches.

3. You will spend funds which might be more wisely utilized on the field.

4. You will be separated from the culture, people, and language in your first years of service.

5. You will be tempted to stay in the homeland.

6. You will want to return to the field with material goods which may be unnecessary.

7. You may appear to show a lack of dedication to your work on the field.

8. You silently indicate to national friends that you do not consider their country a place where you can enjoy yourself.

9. You will find it difficult to change gears when you return to the field after your vacation.

10. You will never get to know your fellow-workers or other missionaries in an informal setting.

11. Your fellow missionaries may question your need to fly home between furloughs.

12. Your board may be brought into question for allowing you this privilege, especially if it seems to be overused or abused.

13. Don't take a long vacation in the homeland, or to some distant country, and then send a prayer/newletter to supporters immediately upon your return in which you "beg" for money. Your support may be dropped since it may appear you have more money than those who are providing for you, or that you are poorly utilizing "tithes."

Of course there are exceptions when you feel God is speaking to you about taking your holiday time in the homeland because of the serious illness of a loved one, or receipt of a special gift designated for you to go home for a very special occasion (parents' 50th wedding anniversary, birth of your first grandchild, or wedding of one of your children). If you are seriously ill and medical help is unavailable on your field, it is also imperative that you return home to seek specialized care.

Serious consideration needs to be given to any thoughts of flying home before your regularly scheduled furlough. Even if money is not a problem with you, you may find relations with fellow-missionaries becoming strained, and nationals may not understand what or to whom your commitment is.

In most instances, vacationing in the field of your service, or in an adjacent country is more restful, less expensive, and is in line with your mission policies. Jealousy is not unknown on the mission field and trips home are a luxury most cannot afford. So consider well what you feel God would have you do. If you work in Mexico and can drive to your home in Texas in the matter of a day or two, you might well consider going home for vacation. But for those who labor in distant lands, it is usually impractical and financially impossible to return home every year.

If you are not in the habit of taking vacations, you may need to learn how to relax and enjoy time that is not spent in work. If you have labored hard and long for several months, you may find it difficult to relax and recreate your strength. The harder it is for you to do it, the more you really need to get away.

Some missions allow only one vacation time per year for a generous period of time. Others request that you take several separate weeks throughout the year in order to find those who can take over your responsibilities during your absence. When you think of getting away, it makes good sense to be away for at least a month. Arrangements will need to be made for your accommodations while you are gone. It takes time and money to get there, and it will take you a week to unwind before you begin to settle down to enjoying this time. Weekends away are not long enough to fully refresh you. You need quiet time for reflection, prayer, and planning. You need fellowship with others. You will want to spend time with your family (and therefore you will do your best to plan your vacation when your children are out of school and able to be with you).

You can go a full term on the field without proper rest and recreation. But you and the people with whom you live and work will suffer for it. Don't feel guilty about taking time off. On the other hand, not only when you play should you play hard, but when you work, you must also work hard. Missionary life is not one big vacation. But certainly the times of rest and recreation are the times that can and will strengthen you spiritually and physically. And when you have been strengthened, you will be able to strengthen those to, with, and among whom you minister.

QUESTIONS—CHAPTER 33

1. What did God teach us by taking six days for creation instead of one?

2. Why do individuals need a time of rest and recreation periodically?

3. For what reason(s) would you consider flying or driving to your homeland for vacation?

4. What are the advantages to spending your vacation in your country of service?

5. How would you cope in a situation where you are expected to be available for ministry 7 days a week, 24-hours a day?

7. What types of activities should you pursue on your weekly day(s) off?

8. How often do you stay home and work because you feel no one can "fill your shoes?"

34
Loneliness and Loss

Loneliness is a universal emotional reaction. Whether we are rich or poor, male or female, young or old, married or single—all of us feel lonely at times. Sometimes it is when we are alone; sometimes when we are in a crowd; sometimes when we have nothing to do; sometimes when we have too much to do; sometimes when our ministry seems at an impasse; sometimes in the midst of rich blessings.

Loneliness is like a fog which arrives out of nowhere to envelop the soul and cause it to feel lost or wayward.

Often we do not share our feelings with others, so they have no knowledge of our situation. Sometimes it is those among us who seem the strongest who, in actuality, are overtaken by their aloneness and loneliness.

Occasional bouts of loneliness will be easily overcome by fellowship with others, a game of badminton, baking a cake, writing a letter, reading a book, or playing a musical instrument.

If loneliness lasts for a long period of time, it erodes the ability to work well, and produces a number of problems, both in relation to personal matters as well as in the area of ministry.·

Loneliness often turns to self pity. In and of itself it is not a sin. But self-centeredness can result and this will lead to all kinds of temptation to sin.

There are many causes of loneliness, among which are bereavement, sickness, being out of a familiar environment, aloneness, the physiological process of aging, lack of security, need for attention, failure, lack of trust, perfectionism, rejection, longings and unfilled desires, withdrawal, lack of someone to trust and with whom to share, being released after being dominated by another's authority, thwarted communication, jealousy . . . you will be able to list many more.

Loneliness usually reaches its highest point when the child of God is walking farthest from his/her Lord. It is important, therefore, to maintain a close walk with the Lord at all times. Those who are characteristically happy and optimistic can more easily find the joy of the

Lord in every situation. Unhappy people are usually more prone to lonely feelings. An unhappy individual is often self-centered, envious, jealous, discouraged, not motivated, apathetic, easily hurt, selfish, has a poor self image, feels sorry for himself, insecure, finds tragedy in every situation, or is deeply troubled. Troubled people have difficulty getting along with others, feel threatened, are discontented, make light of serious matters or are overly serious, are disorganized, dreary, or don't enjoy what they do. Any of all of these characteristics may lead to loneliness.

What are some of the prinicples which if followed, will help those who suffer severely from loneliness?

Basically, you must maintain close fellowship with your Heavenly Father; then discover the joy of giving of yourself, as well as of what you possess, to others, live with an attitude of gratitude; live in the assurance of God's unchanging, abiding love; share your heart concerns with a trusted friend; try new things, or new ways of doing old things; reach out a helping hand to a needy world; live with an openhand policy; try to live in harmony with all people; be forgiving; learn to laugh; discover that failure is not final, but often is a stepping stone to greater ministry; squelch criticism and a critical attitude; maintain a healthy body, soul and spirit. Look at things in their proper perspective; resist the temptation to look to others for your living standards; enjoy the fellowship and companionship of those whom God sends into your life; be thankful for fulfilled desires and do not grieve over the unfulfilled; think about things which edify.

Single missionaries must never marry out of loneliness. As much as you may long for a life partner, be certain to recognize that marriage is not a cure-all for loneliness. Too late, many couples have discovered they are more lonely married than they were single.

Loneliness can be good for an individual, if kept within normal limits. It can bring out creative genius which would otherwise never be discovered. It can be the motivation for deep personal worship and effective public ministry. It can help you understand those around you who are alone and lonely.

There is help, hope, health and happiness for those who are lonely. Or there can be bitterness, discouragement, defeat or despair. Loneliness will come at one time or another to every missionary. How you deal with it will make or break your effectiveness as an ambassador for Christ.

Not only is loneliness a very real factor in the life of a missionary, but loss can become reality as well. You receive a call, a letter, a cable, or a ham contact indicating that a beloved parent, relative, or close friend has died. You may not even get word until after the funeral, depending upon your field location. Are you needed in the homeland? Should you pack up and leave? Or is it the better part of wisdom to remain with your hand on the plow in the field where God has placed you? No decision should be made without conferring with your Station Head and/or your Field Director, of course. In most situations, unless you are due for furlough, you may not wish to return immediately to the homeland. It will, perhaps, be more difficult as you get ready to return for furlough because one you loved dearly will not be there to meet you. But fortunately, much of the grieving process will be past, and the Lord will have proven Himself sufficient in comfort to ease your pain and loss.

But death may not always occur in the homeland. Many a missionary has lost a spouse on the field through accident, disease, martyrdom, terrorist attack, murder, or war. How does one cope with this type of loss?

It is imperative that a child of God have a firm faith in the sovereignty of God, acknowledging His right to do with us what will eventuate to our good and His glory. At the time of loss, it is difficult not to ask "why". It is far more difficult to overcome your own grief, accept God's will, and continue in the ministry to which you have been called. Only the grace, love, and peace of God will bring you into sure victory within yourself and among those with whom you labor.

You may want to get away to a quiet place by yourself, or you may prefer to be with people you care about. Never be ashamed of tears. Don't try to play the martyr's part by staying in your place of service if you find it impossible to overcome your anguish within a reasonable time period. If children are involved, they should be taken into consideration before any hasty decision is made.

Many widows and widowers have returned to the homeland upon the death of a spouse, but the call of God was to the mission field, and most return either to their original field of service or to another. Many have found God providing them with another mate, and long, useful years of ministry have ensued. God will never give a trial too heavy to bear.

Many a family has lost a precious baby or child on the field. Disease and accidents are no respecters of persons. They touch the very young and the very old . . . and those in between. There is certainly not an unusually high toll of missionary children, and a child is as safe overseas as he is in the homeland. A missionary child is no more "sacred" in the will of God than a national child, however. When death comes to your home, it will always bring more far-reaching agony than when it comes to a neighbor down the street. Trusting God with the lives He has created is difficult even for the strongest Christian.

In the event of the loss of a spouse or child, arrangements must be made for a Christ-honoring service and interment. Only in rare situations will it be possible to have a body embalmed and sent to the homeland for burial. In most areas of the world, a death in the morning necessitates burial before sunset and a death in the evening necessitates burial shortly after dawn. Americans may find this difficult to accept. (In some instances, a child has had to be buried while a father was away from home and unreachable. This is exceptionally hard on the family, of course). Simple coffins are sometimes made from pieces of pine wood, or packing crates from the homeland are hewn into a box. Some are simply placed in a clean white sheet for burial. Grave diggers may be available if you reside near a cemetary. Family and national friends have often had to provide their own manpower to dig a grave on the mission compound. A simple wooden cross may be the only monument on earth to the one God has, for His own reasons, taken to Himself.

Additional trauma is brought to a family when there is no body to bury as is the case with some who drown and whose bodies are never found, or those who are killed in remote areas in fiery plane crashes where no one can reach the remains of the loved one. In our society, a body always adds to the realization and finality that the dear one has passed from death to life. Otherwise there may always be a slight hope, or an unhealthy concern, that the individual may still be alive.

In the loss of a child, parents must accept God's will in the matter. Some have been known to close off the child's room, leaving everything intact as it was when the child died, refusing admittance to anyone, and unwilling to leave the home lest the room be disturbed. Others have been unable to accept that a loving God could be so "cruel". They have given up their service and returned to the homeland, becoming bitter, resentful, and unable to assume Christian ministries. Sometimes counseling is imperative.

Most individuals know that dying is a part of living. Although a healthy attitude toward death will never make up for the deep loss you have suffered, you will realize that your own life must go on, and you are still committed to the Lord and His plan for your life.

There are, of course, other types of loss you might experience overseas. Occasionally, material possessions have a way of getting broken, lost, or stolen. Fires, floods, earthquakes, landslides, and local uprisings have resulted in a missionary escaping with nothing but his life and the clothes on his back. This is extremely difficult, for although much can, in time, be replaced, there is a possibility that the only extant manuscript of the New Testament in your tribal language, on which you have worked tirelessly for a dozen years, is forever lost to the elements; or the well-stocked clinic for which supporters gave sacrificially is destroyed just a day before it was to be dedicated; or your Christian bookstore has disintegrated and your books and tracts have been carried away in flood waters, without a trace. But God is not unaware of what you are going through. And although you will need the patience of Job at times like these, He will sustain you, and use your testimony as a witness to those whom you have prayed would trust the Heavenly Father as **you** do. You see, a missionary is not a witness only in word—but in all of living. You must show to all that God is either Lord of all, or not Lord at all!

Loss may also be the result of the birth of a physically or mentally handicapped baby, a paralyzing accident or illness, backsliding national Christians, new believers reverting to their former religious beliefs, sin amidst the missionary community, divorce—or something much more common such as your best friend leaving for furlough, retiring, or resigning from the work.

Each missionary will have a different reaction to loneliness and loss on the mission field. Fellow-workers and national friends will be a source of support when difficult days come along. In every circumstance of life, it is absolutely imperative that your faith in the love and goodness of God does not waver. God gives us so much of good, and gratitude must be given for every situation He allows to touch our lives. In His eyes, **all** He sends is good. He is not in the business of being unkind to those whom He loves enough to have allowed His Son to give His life for them. He must never be accused of testing us beyond what we are able to bear. One day He will provide us with a full explanation of all the way He has led. Until He does, we must accept by faith all He sends into our lives.

QUESTIONS—CHAPTER 34

1.   What are some of the causes of loneliness in your life?

2. How do you cope with feelings of loneliness?

3. What are some of the outcomes of unhappiness?

4. List 10 principles which may, if followed, help you conquer loneliness.?

5. What good can come from feelings of loneliness?

6. What major types of losses may you have to face overseas?

7. What other kinds of losses may you experience?

8. What is the responsibility of the missionary to those with or among whom he works when they suffer loneliness or loss?

PART III
CONTINUING THE RACE
Furlough

35
Reasons for and Length of a Furlough

Most of us have heard of missionaries who have "gone national", decided furloughs were not vital, and have, therefore, stayed on the field for exceptionally long periods of time. This used to be more popular when travel was not only expensive but extremely difficult; when men determined they would probably give their lives for the sake of the gospel; when full-time service was a 24-hour day, 7-day week, with no time for rest, family, and the homeland.

In some cases, missionaries still have these basic principles which they intend to follow. But things are vastly different today; Mission Boards have been set up to see that the needs of their missionaries are met in every way: one cannot get away from such niceties of life as the retirement fund, life insurance, health insurance, Social Security, and along with this comes the Board policy that furloughs must be taken every so many years. Why have they come to this conclusion? Why should you take a furlough?

1. To become renewed physically through medical attention and obtain rest and a change of environment in order to preserve or restore health and energy.

2. To be refreshed spiritually through Christian fellowship.

3. To be strengthened emotionally through contact with friends, family, and supporters.

4. To seek a place of fellowship where you can be nourished by the Word of God and be supported through prayer.

5. To evaluate what has been accomplished during your term of service.

6. To set realistic goals for your next term of service.

7. To bring personal reports to your supporters.

8. To maintain and add support to your account.

9. To make your Mission, your field, and your work known as widely as possible.

10. To obtain a change of environment.

11. To obtain intellectual refreshment (through special work at college, university, seminary, radio or technical school, secular work, etc.).

12. To keep in touch with trends in your specialty.

13. To keep you current of happenings in the homeland .

14. To allow your children opportunity to become acquainted with their relatives and their homeland.

15. To renew acquaintance with casual supporters.

16. To interest others in joining you on the field under your Board.

17. To encourage churches and individuals in their responsibility to missions.

18. To discuss lingering problems with your mission leadership.

Some feel it would save money, confusion and time if furloughs were eliminated. This is true. On the other hand, as we look at the intensity of the service performed on the field and the drain on you, a furlough is essential for your best spiritual, physical, mental, social, psychological and emotional health to be maintained properly. Without this balance, missionary service will become fruitless and discouraging.

It is interesting that soldiers and missionaries are both given furloughs. And as good soldiers of Jesus Christ, His servants need this departure from the things which are so daily on the field, and the problems and heartaches which are faced, in order to return to the battle and "fight the good fight of faith" (I Timothy 6:12). You owe it to your Lord, yourself, your supporters, and your Mission Board to take advantage of this time to renew your mind, strength, soul and body.

You'll be amazed at how problems become smaller when seen from a distance and in a right perspective. You become prepared to return to those servants, those unbelievers, those troublemakers, those difficult co-workers—with a new slant on the situation. You may discover things will be better if you learn to take orders, to give orders; to discipline, to be disciplined; to organize; to get the job done with less tension; to give credit where credit is due; to allow the nationals their rightful place, etc.

Having returned to your homeland, you may see that the problems and seeming disadvantages of the mission field are not nearly so great as you had thought them to be. Trying to fit into the home situation will often make your call to the field even more pronounced. When you weigh both sides of the matter, you will discover how wonderfully God has prepared you for your place of service.

A furlough is a time for evaluating your entire missionary calling and work, and seeking it in its proper perspective. If you had your life to live over again, what would you do with it? May God impress upon you the fact that you became a missionary because of your love for Him.

If you were once assured of His calling, be sure you are certain of His continued leading. Without a sure knowledge of His directing, missionary work will be fruitless, discouraging and a total loss to you and those to whom you go. So settle this fact with Him during your furlough. Then commit yourself to Him more fully than ever before for the work to which He will lead you for your coming term of service.

There may be questions as to the appropriate length of your furlough period. For most missionaries, we have seen the demise of the 6-year term of service. Most Boards now give their missionaries alternatives such as:

2 years on the field and 3-4 months of furlough

3 years on the field and 8-9 months of furlough

4 years on the field and 1 year of furlough

For varying reasons, missionaries are wisely choosing the plan which is most convenient for them, although the Board usually sets the time limit for the first term missionary.

There are advantages and disadvantages to your choice of furlough length. Let's consider some of these:

1. Two years on the field and 3-4 months at home.

ADVANTAGES

No need for missionaries to be moved to your station to take over your work, and perhaps continue on, forcing you to move to a new station upon return.

DISADVANTAGES

Often a missionary takes over your work as well as doing his own. Thus the work drags along until your return. Or a short-term replacement, whose heart is not with your people, may be sent.

ADVANTAGES

For parents with children, there may not have to be a transfer to a school in the homeland, if furlough is summer-long.

Children may have to be left in school while parents take a brief furlough.

Air travel makes every country close to the homeland.

It keeps your supporters updated on your activities.

You can get away from your work, evaluate it, and plan goals for your return.

Supporters and relatives can be visited, and since short furloughs usually occur during the summer, there is opportunity to attend Bible Conferences.

DISADVANTAGES

Some colder countries have school vacation in mid-winter, the hardest time for parents to leave their work.

Children will want to go to the homeland with their parents, and should be encouraged to do so.

Travel home every two years will become a heavy financial burden to you, your Mission and supporters.

New slides, movies, A-V materials and new methods of presenting the work must be utilized to keep your reports interesting. This may be a problem for those not adept at speaking.

A first term of two years may mean you have just finished language study and have not fully adjusted to your field. (This is why many missions give a choice of length of term only after the first furlough)

If family and supporters are widely separated geographically, you may not be able to see them all. Much time will be spent travelling with little time for rest and relaxation.

ADVANTAGES	DISADVANTAGES
There will be openings to attend camps and DVBS programs for promoting your field and your work.	It is more difficult to obtain deputation meetings during the summer "slump" in homeland churches. Missionary conferences are often scheduled for the spring or fall. You may have to speak in churches where pastors are on vacation. (It is always better to speak where a pastor is present so he can direct the church in giving and concern for you.)
Short term projects can be planned and consummated on the field, thus giving a feeling of accomplishment and success.	Long-term projects cannot be completed before furlough. Unless someone else has your zeal for and interest in it, they can fail.

2. 3 years on the field and 8-9 months at home.

This gives you enough time to see your programs put into action and to plan for their supervision.	Very few programs can be implemented in such a short time. You may try to extend yourself too far to complete a project before furlough.
Your travel support is not as hard-pressed to be replenished.	If you have a large family, it may be difficult to raise this extra travel money every 3 years.
Your first term will see you having "learned" the language and gotten a start into your own work.	Depending on the length of your language study, you may only have been on a station for a year before having to leave.

ADVANTAGES

DISADVANTAGES

It allows ample time to visit friends, relatives and supporters. It should provide at least 2 months of rest, relaxation, rehabilitation, and goal setting. It should also give you an opportunity to be home for the "family" holidays (Thanksgiving, Christmas, New Years).

It often does not provide sufficient opportunity for taking advantage of educational opportunities which could be valuable in your ministry.

It can give the children a summer at home and a semester of school so they do not lose touch with the homeland.

Missionary schools are usually advanced. Thus a child may be put into a higher grade in the homeland resulting in frustration and some adjustments when reentering the M.K. school.

3. 4 years on the field and 1 year at home.

You can become completely engaged in your field work with less attention to packing, unpacking, moving, adjusting, settling in, etc.

You may feel the work on your station is too much "yours" and unintentionally forget the need for a team effort.

It may allow you to settle into your own station for 2-3 years so you will become acquainted with your people and your responsibilities.

You might be a better worker as an itinerant, or as a specialist or consultant moving to new situations every 2 years.

It further alienates you from the conveniences and material benefits which you relied upon in the homeland, but now find are not needed for efficient working conditions.

You may find it difficult to adjust to things as they are in the homeland, preferring the simpler life, thereby offending some friends and supporters.

ADVANTAGES

It helps you to understand better your field authorities and your special niche in the work assigned.

It puts you in a situation where your co-workers become your "family" with special privileges and joys.

There is a wholehearted effort to put permanence into the work and to teach nationals responsibilities, since someone else will probably be taking over your work for your year of furlough.

It gives you the privilege of taking a year of college work in your specialty, take refresher courses in education, medicine, engineering, mechanics, etc.

You have opportunity for at least 3 months of rest—perhaps 2 months at the beginning and 1 month at the end of your furlough.

You can enroll your children in a full year of school in the homeland.

DISADVANTAGES

It may, unconsciously give you the feeling that an appointment giving you greater authority should be given upon return from furlough, whether you are capable of it or not.

You may have met with problems on your station. Going home without finding solutions could result in premature resignation from the work.

Nationals may not respect or respond to the one(s) who is (are) sent to carry on the work in your absence.

It may be that your course will take 2 years to obtain the degree you are seeking. Not wanting to work at it piecemeal, you request a year's leave of absence, thus increasing the personnel problem on your field.

For some, the extra time simply means extra work since they feel guilty about taking an adequate rest break.

Depending on the type and place of the school, it may be better to have the children obtain as much of their education as possible in a Christian School on the field. Christian Schools at home can be expensive.

ADVANTAGES	DISADVANTAGES
You can visit supporters leisurely and make new contacts for yourself and your Board.	If a married man, this may mean a great deal of time will be spent away from your family.
There is time to be with the family in relaxed and rewarding situations.	Children may be taken up with all that could be available to them if they were to stay in the homeland.
You may be asked to be an Assistant Pastor, Youth Director, Child Evangelism worker, Church Secretary, or to take other responsibilities or offices in the church for a year (Men's Club President, Circle Leader, etc.).	There may be apprehension about taking meetings or committing yourself to an office. With a year to spend at home, boredom may set in and questions will arise concerning the advisability of returning to the field.
You may wish to work during furlough to learn up-to-date and efficient methods of doing your work on the field.	Work may involve you to such an extent and the salary look so profitable that the decision is made to continue working rather than returning to the field. The love of money is the root . . .
If there have been difficult problems on the field, there is time to begin to see them and the people involved in proper perspective.	Too much time to dwell on the past defeats may adversely affect your eagerness to return to the situation.
There is sufficient time for those who have had malaria, dysentery, or other debilitating illnesses to become renewed physically before returning to the field.	You may have insisted on completing your 4 yrs of service, thus delaying medical treatment and thereby extending your physical problem.

You will be able to add your own lists of advantages and disadvantages. A great deal will depend upon the type of work you are doing, where you are located, illness which may come upon you, whether you are single or married, if you have school-age children or not, how often you, personally, feel a need for a change such as the homeland can provide, whether you have married an individual from a country other than your own, how well you have adjusted to the field.

Other factors may also enter the picture. You may want a 4-year term in order to take a year of furlough to care for details concerning the adoption of a baby; or you may find you need a shorter furlough after 2 years to locate your aged parents into a Nursing Home. Most missions today try to accommodate the needs of their missionaries in these emergency and unplanned circumstances.

It is, in any case, fair to give your Field Director and your co-workers sufficient notice of your intention for taking furlough. Plans must be made to fill the gap. You, yourself, will need approximately six months to get things in order for a change over of personnel, packing, getting papers in order, and notifying the home constituency of your plans. This is especially important if you are using the 2 years on the field with 3-4 months at home plan.

If your Mission does not have a choice for you for years of service and months of furlough, be assured they have determined a fair length of each for you. Have confidence in their decision, and except in emergencies, do not ask to circumnavigate this rule.

You may be serving under a Board which works in many countries of the world. You may be tempted to question why your term is longer than that laid down for another area. Again, trust your Board. They have looked carefully into the situation and have tried to take all things into consideration before determining your length of service.

Other Missions in your field may have shorter or longer terms than you. They have their good reasons, too. If you think your Board is unfair in this matter, look into the situation very carefully before condemning your Board. If there are injustices or inequities, and others feel this, too, your Board will be glad to communicate with you by letter or in person to see if the matter can be worked out.

If, during your term of service, you have married one who is from a country other than your own, it could well be the determining factor as to the length of your furlough. For example, consider a girl from the United States who marries a man from Australia. Will they visit one homeland during one furlough and the other homeland during the next? Will they decide on a longer term on the field, thus assuring six months at home in each country? Or will the year of furlough be chosen so three months can be spent in one country and 9 months in the other, thus assuring the children adequate schooling without a need for having to adapt to two totally different educational systems? These questions must be weighed carefully, and in the event your mission requires you to take only a 3-month furlough, there must be careful planning for both areas. An unwise and unhappy decision would be for each partner to go his own way for the three months. Except for emergencies arising in the family, this would be the least satisfactory solution to the problem.

Some missionaries opt to stay in their "adopted" land or in an area nearby for their short furlough. Some have even volunteered to help other missionaries in various ways during those short months. But such a plan is often less than adequate for the good of both the missionary and his work.

EARLY FURLOUGH

There may be legitimate reasons for considering an early furlough. In the course of human events, there are trials, disappointments, delays, the unexpected—as well as the joys, happinesses, encouragements, and goals reached. There are times when missionaries must come to grips with factors beyond their control. The result may be a decision to return home sooner than anticipated. In most instances, it is a time of great soul searching and sadness, for the happy candidate goes to the field filled with excitement, and the expectation of a lifetime of service on the field of God's choice.

Among the reasons for early furlough are:

1. Debilitating sickness or accident

2. Psychological factors

3. Illness or death of a relative in the homeland

4. Needs of young people in the family

5. Proper rotation of missionary staff

6. Government restrictions

7. War, riots or rebellions

8. Disciplinary measures

9. Need for help in the Home Office

10. Settlement of business or legal matters

The most common of these is illness. Diseases such as amoebic or other dysenteries, typhoid, typhus, black water fever, yellow fever, and many other tropical illnesses can sometimes be debilitating to an individual who has not previously encountered these illnesses and the causes for them. A Field Director may suggest an earlier than normal furlough so suitable medical treatment may be received and/or proper rest may be obtained.

An unexpected death in your immediate family is another reason to speed up the time for leaving. Although in many cases the missionary cannot put things in order fast enough to attend the funeral, it may be possible to get exit papers, and other legal matters cared for so it is possible to leave in a matter of a few days. This should be considered when there is no one in the homeland to care for matters related to the deceased. Although it must be a personal decision, it may be well to consider staying on the field during the time of bereavement, especially if your loved one is with Christ and other loved ones can care for details. Further consideration may be appropriate if it involves a non-Christian family member, or leaves a parent alone with no family nearby to give comfort or provide necessary help.

A call or cable may come from the homeland stating that a loved one is very ill and not expected to live. Relatives or friends may request that you return home as soon as feasible. This is an easier decision if your furlough time is almost due. It may be difficult if you have recently arrived on the field. In some situations, of course, the trip home may be for a very brief period. In others, where there may be a long-term, lingering illness, there may not be the same urgency. But if there is no one else who can take the responsibility for this family member, it may be necessary to leave for home as soon as possible, for an extended period of time.

Some missionaries face the decision of putting a parent or parents into a nursing home or other type of housing arrangement or institution. You may be an only child and it will be your responsibility to care for these matters. You may be able to wait for your normal furlough time; otherwise you may have to request permission for early furlough.

There may be other occasions when important events will take place three to six months before your regularly scheduled furlough. Not every event may be considered sufficient cause for early furlough, however. You may be given permission to fly home for the actual event, stay two or three weeks, then return to the field to finish your term. Most mission boards try to accommodate their missionaries in these circumstances, but it would be impractical and financially prohibitive to be home for every "event" in your family throughout your missionary career. In all of life, many **good** things must be refused in order to choose the **best** things. God has called you to work in His vineyard.

You were needed on the field or you would not have been accepted for service. You must be absolutely certain in your own mind that the reason for returning home for any given cause outweighs what you will need to give up in ministry on the field, and the work which will fall to others in your absence.

If your trip to the homeland is unavoidable and necessary, you must hurriedly make arrangements for departure. You will be burdened with the pressures of leaving your work unfinished,as well as the cares of whatever forces you to leave the field. It is a distressing time, draining your physical, mental and emotional stability. Your spiritual strength will be lessened as time is compressed. It ought not to be, but you ARE still human and God understands your stress even when you and/or your associatescondemn it.

It is at times like these that God has an opportunity to prove Himself to you. He, of course, was aware of these events from the beginning. They came as no surprise to Him. But what is your reaction? Does your attitude show an implicit and unmoveable faith in the God of Job ("Though He slay me, yet will I trust in Him"—Job 13:15)? Do the "whys?" and "hows?" overpower the knowledge that "He knoweth the way that I take: when he hath tried me, I shall come forth as gold" (Job 23:10)?

Although the human heart cry is for sympathy, our strength and satisfaction must be found in the fact that "Even the Son of man came not to be ministered unto, but to minister, and to give his life a ransom for many" (Mark 10:45).

Few may understand your heartache, the turmoil raging within you, the tears, the frustrations. But if God is not Lord of all, He is not Lord at all. He is sufficient. These are the days to find the reality of His promises . . . No matter what is taken from you, nothing can separate you from the love of God. Yes, the LOVE of God. He has not brought this trial to you in His wrath. There was no other way He could have caused you to grow and mature. You may not be able to comprehend His secret just now, but as He brings you through this dark tunnel, you will be able to see the light on the other side. It may take time, patience and sheer persistence. But He means it for your good—whatever it is.

> What better way to thank my Lord For the life
> that He has lent, Than in whatsoever state I
> am, Therewith to be content.

And, dear missionary friend, if such a trial has not been entrusted to you, be grateful. But also be very understanding of those who must face such situations. They need your love and support as never before. Do what you can to help them through their night of depression or desperation. They may not ask for your help; in fact, they may show very little appreciation for it at the time. But be assured they need a friend who cares enough to be concerned. Just standing by can be of tremendous value.

QUESTIONS—CHAPTER 35

1. What do you feel are the 10 most important reasons for a furlough?

2. How long do you feel a first-term missionary should be on the field before taking a furlough? What is your mission policy?

3. What length furlough do you feel is appropriate for a first-term missionary? Why?

4. What might cause you to consider an alternative to a furlough in your homeland? What might that alternative be?

5. Should an "early furlough" ever be considered? For what reasons?

6. For what reasons may your Board refuse you permission to fly home from Kenya to be with your daughter when she has her first child?

7. How best can you help a fellow-worker whose college-age son has been in a serious accident in the homeland? (The report is that the son will be in a wheelchair for the rest of his life.)

36
Preparations From the Field

Preparations for return to the homeland should be made at least 6 months before leaving the field. Keep in mind that you will have at least 3 major responsibilities while on furlough, i.e., (1) to yourself; (2) to your prayer and financial supporters; (3) to your Mission.

Men in the military service are familiar with the "R & R" leave. You, a missionary, also need Rest and Rehabilitation. Although your home church or supporting church may request that you speak as soon as you get off the plane, unless you have chosen a three month furlough try not to plan extended deputation schedules for your first two months at home. You will need that time to become adapted to the homeland, visit loved ones, obtain spiritual refreshment, and settle into your "headquarters". If you are a single person, you may be moving about during furlough with no "fixed" address for the entire period. Couples with children are usually obliged to stay in one place to enroll the children in school. You will need to decide where you would like to settle to be closest to those whom you love, or those among whom you will worship, or in the area where your children will be attending school. This is a fairly complicated decision if father and mother have different homelands.

Some Missions locate housing for their furlough folks. Some supporting churches provide housing for their missionaries. There are missionary communities set up in various sections of the country. Arrangements for the use of these facilities must be made well in advance of your arrival. The larger your family, the greater will be your problem.

You will want to send a prayer/newsletter from the field telling of your furlough plans, announcing the times you will NOT be available for services. You may plan, tentatively, what areas you will visit and the approximate dates for being in that vicinity. You may decide to put this tentative schedule in your letter.

You will look over the slides and pictures you have taken on the field. You will begin to plan several slide series for use in deputation.

Put your slides together. Are you missing some key shots? You've still got time to get them. Try to think of the various groups you will be reaching at home. Then make series accordingly—for children, for young people, for women's groups, for church services, for general audiences (schools and civic organizations) and others. Unless you expect to pass over your slides in gunshot fashion and leave your audiences gasping for breath and wondering what they saw, use between 40 and 80 slides per series, depending upon your emphasis and what you want to say in pictures. Perhaps you will want to make a taped narration with background sounds from the field. Or you may prefer to speak in person when presenting your slides. You may wish to tape material from the field to assist with other presentations, however. The Muslim call to prayer, the sounds of the marketplace, a group of children singing in their native tongue, the braying of a donkey, the sounds of camel bells—you'll think of hundreds of sounds you'd like to share with the folks at home, or that you will enjoy, yourself, during furlough. (You will be surprised how homesick for the field you can become during furlough.)

Begin gathering little items to present to your supporters. They deserve a token of your appreciation. No matter how small the gift, make sure it is unique to the country in which you serve. Some missionaries have purchased postage stamps to be given to stamp collector supporters. For 50¢ or $1.00, a fine gift can be given, even if most of the stamps are of the lowestdenominations. Coin collectors will appreciate a coin or two from your country (if it is legal to take coins out of your country). Handwoven bookmarks are easily attainable, yet inexpensive. Wood carvings, pictures, calendars, knick knacks of all kinds and descriptions are available to you. Although it will cost you something, give some trouble, and result in precious suitcase room being given to items of this sort, it is worthwhile. You may wish to find inexpensive items you can leave in homes where hospitality is extended to you. Even if you, personally, are not interested in these items, it is courteous to show your appreciation, and what better way than giving a token from your mission field?

There will be several legal matters to be cared for on the field to make sure your residence papers and visas are in order. In some lands you may wish to obtain a "No objection to Return" paper from the local Commissioner to help with your re-entry papers following furlough. Shots and vaccinations should be brought up to date. Tax matters will be cared for. Passage will be arranged. Most of all, you will want to be sure you prepare the way for a national or another missionary to take over for you during your furlough absence. Matters for which you are personally responsible should be cleared up by YOU. Don't leave your work in a position that will doom it to failure after your departure. Don't make nationals so dependent upon you, as a person, that they are unable to take direction from another, or from the Lord.

You may wish to take 8mm or 16mm movies which can be edited and spliced at home. Make sure you have recent material to present. Historical material is one thing; up-to-date missionary presentations are quite another! With movies, too, tape recorded background sounds will improve your presentations.

You will probably have to provide displays during your time at home. Be thinking of items which can be used. Curios, food, newspapers in the national language, a Bible and/or hymnbook, clothes, lamps, decorations, children's toys, pictures in plastic folders, etc., are all useful. Plan your display now and be sure you have all the items you will need to make it effective. Unless you are working with naked tribespeople, be sure to carry at least one native outfit home with you to wear during special meetings. It is often good to take a set of children's clothing, since dressing children in these clothes for a Sunday School or Young People's meeting can be effective.

Some zealous missionaries go to no end of trouble to capture giant spiders, scorpions, baby boas, and other animals and insects, put them in formaldahyde, and carry them from conference to conference. Let's try to avoid this type of presentation! It may be, however, that you, or your children, have been able to build up a beautiful display of butterflies. This is much less alarming for public meetings!

Be sure to look into the principles and practices of your Mission by reviewing its handbook, to find out what your responsibilities will be during furlough. Perhaps there are matters suggested therein which should be cared for on the field.

If you are planning to study during your furlough, be sure to make arrangements with the school and your Mission well in advance.

If personal items are to be loaned, stored, or sold, begin to take care of these matters a month or two ahead of your departure.

Prepare, to the best of your ability, the nationals who work with you for the change in leadership which will take place upon your departure.

Inasmuch as possible, help prepare your children for return to the homeland. Many of them will be unhappy at the thought of leaving their friends on the field. They must understand why it is necessary for them to return to the homeland for a while, and that they will not be away long.

If you are a missionary in the homeland, there may be less need for complex advanced preparations for furlough. But there will still be a gap in the ranks during your absence, so it is essential that someone take over your responsibilities. If a full-time person is unavailable, someone should be placed in a position of supervision as a counselor and resource person. Furlough is no less necessary for "home" missionaries than for "foreign" missionaries.

Don't let the anticipation of "going home" adversely affect the remainder of your term on the field. True, there is much to be done in preparation. Some will have projects to complete and it will mean a grueling schedule. Others may feel they should slacken off their work to prepare others for the impending "hole" which will be left upon their departure. (It's sometimes easy to think, "Now they'll realize just how much I've been contributing to the work!)

One reminder . . . Unless the Lord originally led you out for only one term of service as a specialist for a designated task, or you are on loan to a particular mission or field for a term, or one of your children has developed a disease or malfunction which doctors tell you will need many years of treatment in the homeland never never NEVER decide just before furlough that you are not going to return to the field. Making such a decision amidst the problems and pressures of the situation in which you are located can result in a wrong choice which can be a life-long regret. You may be discouraged, downcast and disgusted. You may have seen others get the credit for your ideas or labors. You may have had personal and legitimate gripes against your fellow-workers. You may be unhappy with the area in which you were placed. You may have expected to be put into an administrative position, but no one realized your potential. On the other hand, you may have been placed in a position of leadership for which you felt completely unprepared and inadequate. You may have struggled over lack of finances. You may have had severe illnesses during your term. The language may have been a formidable foe which you were not able to conquer. So you decide to give it all up—and you prepare NOT to return to the field. Have a conference with your Field Director before you leave, sharing problems and looking for solutions. BUT DON'T MAKE A DECISION TO RESIGN WHILE ON FOREIGN SOIL. Be patient just a little longer and do your work as unto the Lord. Trust Him to keep you. There would not be nearly so many "missionary casualties" if decisions had been made after a time of rest, fellowship, and evaluation in the homeland.

QUESTIONS—CHAPTER 36

1. Insomuch as possible, what details of your furlough plans should be made from the field?

2. How far in advance of your normal furlough time should these plans be made?

3. What training or arrangements need to be considered regarding nationals or missionaries who will take your place during furlough?

4. How will you explain the necessity of your furlough to the nationals among whom you live and work?

37
Furlough Housing

Missionaries planning to be in the homeland for more than three months will, undoubtedly, have a problem locating in an area and in a home that will meet their needs and fit their budget.

We are grateful God has raised up several furlough communities where missionaries can stay for a period of up to one year. Ordinarily, reservations must be made well in advance of arrival in the homeland, although on occasion, a forced cancellation will allow you to be accepted. These communities are well situated, provide all conveniences, and are comparatively inexpensive. The fellowship with men and women from other missions is stimulating. The joy of being closely allied with Christians with the same concerns as yours is strengthening. The social and spiritual environment is energizing. And most are located in areas with good school facilities nearby.

There are supporting churches which provide homes for their own furlough people on a "first come" basis. These may be homes owned and maintained by the church, or apartments in members' homes which are made available for missionary use. This might not work in a church situation which supports only 2 or 3 missionaries, but if there are a good number of you, it would be likely that the home or apartment could be kept filled continually. If such is the case in your home or supporting church, be sure to tell them well in advance of your furlough as to when you will arrive, how many and what ages your children are, and for how long you would like to be accommodated. This is a real ministry for churches. Never take it for granted. Live in and care for the home as though it were your own.

For those on short furloughs, relatives are usually anxious to provide accommodations. Since they may not have seen the children for some time, they (especially grandma and grandpa) may enjoy having them for three months. When your parents are physically able to take on this responsibility, and volunteer to do so, it is of tremendous help when it is essential for both of you to go to meetings or conferences, or to attend extended meetings either near or far. For single folks there is usually little problem in finding housing with relatives or friends.

Even for some who elect a longer furlough, family and friends may desire to have you make your headquarters with them. It will depend upon individual circumstances whether or not this is the best arrangement for you.

Since housing is essential on furlough, you will have given it a great deal of thought before leaving the field. You will have prayed much concerning it and you will have mentioned it in your newsletter so others might join in praying with you. God is very apt to answer those prayers, so be prepared for it! From unexpected sources, you may find God supplying your need. A friend of a friend, an acquaintance of one of your supporters, people you've never met before will offer facilities fully adequate to meet your needs in the area in which you desire to settle. God answers prayer in remarkable ways. And if it seems hard to believe, try to remember the last time you heard of a missionary who had no place to live during furlough!

For some there may be a necessity to find a home in the community in which you have decided to settle. You may be staggered by the rents requested. But you will find something suitable, and the Lord will supply what is needed above normal furlough housing funds designated for that purpose each month.

It makes sense to want to be centered somewhere near your supporting churches, if possible. If your relatives are in the same area, it makes it very handy. Or if you are planning on furlough education, you will live near the school, seminary, or university which you plan to attend. If you are being assigned to work with the Home Office in a special project, you will locate near your Headquarters. For those who have their support pledged through their Board or Denomination and are sent on tour, there is no real crisis as to where to settle, since you will be travelling for a specified time in a specified area.

You should decide whether you want to live in the city, the suburbs, or the country. City living is, of course, most expensive, and for a family of six or eight it can prove prohibitive. Living in the suburbs will usually provide for good schools for the children, lower rents, adequate transportation, Christian fellowship, somewhat less danger due to crime, a place to park your car. Country living is much more relaxing and restful. But there are inconveniences. Children may have to travel long distances to school. Shopping may need to be done several miles away and if the husband is using the car for deputation, unless the mother can find a friend to transport her, or a store willing to deliver, this could become a problem, especially in northern winters.

It is almost certain the majority of furlough folks who must provide their own housing live in the suburbs, then. Apartment houses are being built by the thousands, and are sometimes obtained at a good price. Be sure, however, to ask about the lease. If you have a 9-month furlough and the lease runs for a year, you will be responsible for the extra 3-months unless a special arrangement can be worked out.

The possibility of renting a mobile home should be considered if the space provided is adequate. These, although usually immobile, are often inexpensive and comfortable. It means little or no material things must be purchased to furnish it, they take little time to clean, they cost less to heat and/or air condition. Purchasing a trailer or mobile home is probably not a wise choice since the resale value is inadequate, considering the short time you will be using it.

Furlough housing may appear to be a formidable barrier, but be assured of God's awareness of your need. And once again you will find that where He guides, He WILL provide.

As much furlough housing planning as possible should be done from the field. If it is not possible to finalize preparations yourself, ask a friend, relative, pastor, or your mission board to help you make necessary arrangements. Living in a motel or hotel while seeking adequate housing once you arrive at home is very costly and should only be done in cases of emergency furloughs when there is insufficient time to put things in order in advance.

QUESTIONS—CHAPTER 37

1. What type of financial arrangements does your Board provide for furlough housing?

2. What questions should you ask yourself before deciding where to locate during your furlough?

3. What advantages do single folks have over married folks when it comes to planning for housing during furlough?

4. Is a mobile home a viable option for you? Why?

5. Other than financial consideration, what other things should be considered when seeking furlough housing?

38
Reverse Culture Shock

You expected to face culture shock when you left the homeland for Language School or your term of service overseas. You were, if not wholly ready for it, at least mentally aware that your new environment would provide a total change in standards, values, language, culture, customs, etc. The actual shock level was determined by you, individually, and by the place to which you were sent.

Some folks adapt rather easily to change; others are totally alarmed by it. Fortunately, most missionaries find themselves somewhere in the middle, perhaps not fully acclimated to the new situation, but at least able to cope physically, mentally, emotionally, socially and psychologically with the changes surrounding them.

Now you have been on the field at least a year—perhaps 4 or 5— and you are beginning to enjoy your new style of living. You have learned to communicate in the language of the people you have come to love; you have learned, in a measure, to adapt to their ways of life; it may have been fast-paced and you had to rev your motor; perhaps you have learned to enjoy the serenity of a slower pace; you have come to live by their sun or their clock, their donkey or their bullet train; if something doesn't get done **today**, there may serious trouble, while in other areas one day or the next makes very little difference in what can be accomplished; the sight of raw meat or fish hanging on the roadside has become commonplace; the pungent smells of the marketplace are enjoyed; the lack of a sewerage system is overlooked; the daily hassle with servants is a less tense chore; the lack of privacy no longer troubles you; fellowship with "foreign" Christians, like yourself, is less needed; sharing with national believers and entering into their joys and sorrows has become an enjoyable experience.

But now it is time for furlough. You look forward to it with anticipation. You will be getting some needed physical rest and spiritual renewal, meeting again with relatives and friends, and sharing your work with supporters and other groups. You've had some difficult situations to handle on the field; interpersonal relations were often strained even among your own co-workers, both missionary and national; financial trials have come again and again; sickness has taken its toll; there have been frustrations on every hand in spite of some evidence of advance in the work and joy in service; you've missed having celery and olives on the dinner table because they were too expensive or unobtainable; you're tired of ghee in place of butter; you wonder how your cook can make the food so spicy hot; it will be good to speak your mother tongue all the time; the children may also be anxious to get home.

But now you've just arrived on home soil. All of a sudden you decide you had never realized the full impact of culture shock. You expected it when you left the homeland, but you never anticipated it to be even more forceful upon your return. True to form, things have been changing rapidly at home. You've tried to keep posted on news, but you realize you're out of touch. Relatives are happy to see you, but even they are not quite the same as when you left them. How were you to know that single-breasted suits were out, wide ties were in, long dresses were in, spike heels were out, etc. Styles change too rapidly for a missionary to keep up with them. Or perhaps you laughed at the clothes some kind person or church sent you to make you presentable upon arrival. You grimaced when you saw the violet shirt and mottled green trousers, or the granny gown with long sleeves trimmed with lace. But when you got off the plane and saw the crowded terminal, you felt you were the only one wearing clothes in style—the style you remembered from four years ago. When you reach the automobile which will provide your transportation, you almost die of fright in the heavy traffic . . . eight lanes of it heading out of the airport . . . and all driving on the "wrong" side of the road. (You had forgotten that driving on the "other side of the road" had become as natural as breathing.) You see the people surrounding you. Did they look like that when you left? Could there have been so many cults, sub-cults and mini-societies when you were home before? You are amazed at buildings and homes being razed in the city to make room for larger apartment buildings and condominiums. There is construction everywhere—new housing areas, model cities, urban renewal, roads, bridges, office buildings. You feel lost!

You aren't home long before you see how materialism has spread. The minimal necessity of life is a color TV set in every room of the house. Each family must have two cars—and if there are teenagers old enough to drive, more cars may be needed. You can't get into the rush of life in the homeland. You go to the store for a pint of icecream and discover 120 different flavors. The supermarket leaves you breathless. Every item seems outrageously expensive. Choices abound; decisions must be made quickly. Computers are doing the work you used to do in the company. You visit to say hello to your former boss, but he's been promoted and transferred to an office 1500 miles away. You walk through the section where you used to be employed. Few recognize you. The few who do are not very interested in you. But they are keen on showing you the progress they and the company are making. No one had written since they gave you that going away party, and everything you see is new to you.

Surely in your supporting churches—and in your home church—you will find stability. You've never met the new pastor who came shortly after you went to the field. You find the educational program highly organized. The church people have meetings of one sort or another every night of the week. Along with TV, sports and social obligations, it has drawn families apart so they can no longer plan even one night a week together. It is difficult for them to fit you into their schedule for a meal. You are anxiously willing and waiting to share your field experiences with them, but they are seemingly occupied with their own problems and involvements. There isn't much time for them to spend with you, and your desires for fellowship and sharing, to which you had looked forward so long, are quenched. Then, too, your friends use words you don't understand. They tell jokes that are meaningless. They speak of events, important to them, of which you have not heard.

And you begin to realize you are suffering from culture shock now as you never did when you went to the field. You are finding it most difficult to adjust.

Your children will face kinds of problems you had never even thought of on the field. Their culture shock will depend on how old they were when they left the homeland, how much they remember of it themselves and how much you have told them about things "back home". The school system will have changed. Should they go to a public or Christian School? How involved should you allow them to become in social activities? In an age when dating starts extremely early, where attendance at "good" movies is not only condoned but encouraged, where drugs are as easily obtained as a glass of water, where permissiveness is rampant, where children are almost undisciplined—what are the right answers? And when other children have every material thing they desire, how do you handle the matter of providing things for your own? What about clothing crazes? Music fads? And if your young child was born on the field, he may be frightened by the "foreigners" surrounding him. Can he be expected to "fit right in?" He may not even be able to speak English fluently. And he's never met his close relatives.

You had expected to come home for rest and fellowship, renewal, revitalization, sharing, and a bit of appreciation. But you are lost in the rushing crowd. You've only been home two weeks, but already you are looking forward to your return to the field. You are lonely for your friends out there. Some of them, on occasion, actually **needed** you. Things were so much simpler and less confusing. They miss you, too. You'd love a dish of hot curry, or injera and wat. So often you open your mouth to speak your new language, but no one here would understand. Yet it is so much more expressive. Satan, many times, tried you to the utmost on the field. But he is no less challenging at home.

You go to the Lord and beg Him to give you strength for these furlough days, to give you wisdom in talking with people, to give you a ministry that will be rich and rewarding, to give you adaptability for the changes you face, to give you discernment in dealing with your own family. Culture shock has been met head-on in the homeland, and you were not prepared for it.

God will help you through. Trust Him for it, and remember to pray for those who continue to hold the ropes at home. They find it difficult to live an uncompromising and consistent Christian witness. Stand behind them in prayer even as they attempt to stand behind you. Perhaps you hadn't known how to pray for them any more accurately than they had known how to pray for you. Whether this is your first furlough or your fourth, you will discover culture shock will be awaiting your arrival. You may or may not be able to adjust to it fully or quickly, but it will surely be there, and you must be prepared to reckon with it.

A book which may give you additional insights into reverse culture shock (though written for the secular world) is **The Expatriate Life: A Handbook on Moving and Living Abroad** by Lori Austin, Sandra Albright, and Alice Chu (Hippocrene Books, May, 1985).

QUESTIONS—CHAPTER 38

1. What is culture shock?

2. What things do you feel will not change in the homeland while you are serving overseas?

3. What special problems may children have to face in the homeland?

4. What are some ways of coping with reverse culture shock?

5. How can you seek to understand the changes which have occurred
   in the homeland during your absence?

39
Rest and Rehabilitation

"I don't have time."

"I don't need any." "If I relax, I may never want to work again!"

"How can I?"

"I must see my supporters right away."

"I'm not being paid to rest."

"The Mission expects me to do deputation work."

"My account is in the red. I've really got to work hard to gain additional support."

"I'm too young to slow down."

"It's sort of a compulsion, I guess. I just don't feel right about resting for a month."

"I'm not really sick. I just feel tired."

And with these and a hundred similar statements, missionaries home on furlough rush here and there, filling their days and weeks with work and worry and return to the field less rested than when they arrived home. And some never make it back to the field for a second term because they have pushed their physical or emotional capacities to the limit and their health does not permit them to return.

One of the basic reasons for a furlough is for physical readjustment and rehabilitation. It is an important reason and should be considered very carefully by each individual. Many denominational boards will insist on a set period of rest and adjustment.

Very few missionaries find their first term of service restful. There is too much adjustment to be made. Days are full of language study, work, people. Nights are short. Illness may have taken its toll. And yet when they arrive home, they find they are in high gear, and it is difficult to rest and relax. Perhaps there have been serious problems on the field and keeping busy at home helps to ease the intensity of them.

Rest does not imply sleeping 24 hours a day for a month. This is seldom helpful or necessary unless a person is deeply depressed and wants to block out the world around him. Usually two or three days when you can lounge about and have no responsibilities will begin the process of rehabilitation. This does not mean, however, that you are now ready to go on tour and speak in every church in the country with no further time for rest. Twiddling one's thumbs appeals to very few, but how about a week at a Bible Conference with no assigned responsibilities? Or a week visiting friends in the old home town with no formal meetings planned? What's wrong with a week or two of vacation in a cabin loaned to you, or camping in the mountains or at the seashore? You've been collecting stamps in your country. Why not put them in an album and enjoy them? Spend leisure time with your children.

What you must seriously try to avoid is a mad dash into deputation work with no preparation and no time to evaluate your term of service. Until you do this, you cannot properly challenge people or give them a balance view of your work.

This should be a time when the Word of God and prayer become very real to you. Much time should be spent in the presence of God, seeking direction for your furlough months and committing it all to Him, for in this ministry as well as in all other phases of Christian living, without Him you can do nothing.

Perhaps it is absolutely impossible to arrange for rest as soon as you reach the homeland. This does not excuse you from finding a time as soon as possible for this. And days of travel between meetings cannot be considered a substitute. Nor can Monday and Tuesday do it in the event you have meetings on Sunday and Wednesday. You must set a time aside when you have no other responsibilities—just to enjoy life. This is not being selfish; it's being sensible. Test yourself. See if even a week with no meetings doesn't restore a serenity to you which you haven't known for quite a while. And it's amazing how differently things appear to a relaxed mind in comparison to the way they appear to a tense, tired one. People and things begin to take on new meaning and perspective. Remember that God is no slave driver. He is not yet in the business of striking people dead for taking a day of rest. In fact, He set us an example in this!

Some of you with children will begin to realize how little time you've actually been giving to those little ones. No, your work didn't come before your children. Or did it? Give them some time now. Help **them** to rest, too. Give them time to adjust to their new situation. Let them unwind. Let them be normal children.

If you are single, you have no excuse for not resting. You will have far fewer demands upon your time than married folks. Or if you're planning on schooling during furlough, plan to arrive before school opens to give you an opportunity to become physically and mentally prepared for the days ahead. (If you have been away from formal studies for any length of time, you will be amazed at the change which has entered the academic world during recent days. This, too, will take a great deal of adjustment).

You will find the end of your furlough time will be hectic. Try to plan very carefully so that shopping, shots and social calls can be completed at least two weeks before your return to the field. This will give you at least a few days to relax. Most missionaries say during furlough, "I'll be glad to get back to the field and get some rest," especially just before they are due to return. It ought not to be this way. Why should a missionary exhaust every resource during the time he is supposedly building himself up for another term?

There are many reasons, of course. Poor planning, demands by supporting churches, lack of sufficient support, and mission obligations are among them.

It is common knowledge that a sick missionary can hinder as much as help the work. If you came home with a physical problem, unless you are rehabilitated, you are a poor risk for return to the field. Getting well is a priority consideration. Even getting your support level improved makes little difference if the mission doctor refuses to pass you physically. Rest and rehabilitation, therefore, are of utmost importance. Take every opportunity you can find to renew your spirit, soul, mind and body. It is not wasted time. It is imperative. Even those who feel they can get by very well by pushing themselves night and day on the field and at home will find, under careful analysis, that problems are becoming "muddy", decisions are not as quickly and keenly made, interpersonal relations are not what they once were. Age is blamed for a quick temper and impatience. Everything and everyone gets blamed when the real culprit is your mind. Rest your emotions. You'll be a different person, and far better for it.

QUESTIONS—CHAPTER 39

1. Why is rest and rehabilitation a vital necessity for furlough folks?

2. What are some ways in which you can "unwind" during your furlough ?

3. How soon after arrival in the homeland should you have a complete physical examination?

4. Should all of your furlough time be spent in deputation ministry? In an educational institution? In a church ministry?

40
Ask Yourself Some Questions

A good reason for the furlough period is to take an objective look at ourselves, our work, and our relationship with God and our fellow man. An evaluation of where we have been and a goal for where we are going is of the utmost importance if our lives are to be effective and fruitful in the total ministry committed to the church of Christ. It will also help us to determine our own strengths and weaknesses, giving us an opportunity for readjustment and change where it will prove beneficial.

Perhaps we should have entitled this chapter "Active Learning". We often think of learning as "that which we receive through instruction." But it is a far more active process than that. Some of its other meanings are "to find out", "to acquire knowledge or skill", to "ascertain", "to come to know", "to come to know how", "to fix in mind", "to acquire". Although education tends to take a more formal pattern, learning takes place constantly.

We do not intend to give specific answers to the questions which will be asked in this chapter. But if each of you, in the quietness and honesty of your own heart, will take, several hours, or days, to find your own answers, you will be assured of a fuller knowledge of yourself, a better understanding of others, and more impetus for effective planning for your coming term of service.

A. PERSONAL CONSIDERATIONS

1. How satisfying is my devotional life?

    Of what does it consist?

    What could be done to make it more effective and meaningful?

2. How long has it been since I've set down on paper my personal doctrinal statement?

    Have there been any changes in recent years?

    Am I over-emphasizing one doctrine and neglecting others?

Are there some doctrines which have become meaningless to me?

3. Have I reread my mission's policies and practices?

   Do I still accept and adhere to them, or do I rebel at some of them?

   How does my rebellion come out?

   Have I talked these matters over with my mission leaders?

4. Do love, friendliness, respect, admiration, generosity, encouragement and sympathy rule my personal life and witness?

5. Do I ever have a feeling of rage, fear, frustration, suspicion, being rejected, thwarted, withdrawal, despair, greed, anxiety, hate?

   How do I handle these attitudes?

   How do they handle me?

   What do I do to alleviate the results of these attitudes?

   Can they be changed?

   Do I want them to be different?

6. Do I feel I really have nothing to offer and therefore am not worth much?

   Do I always allow my plans and ideas to be overridden because I'm afraid to speak up?

   Am I insecure in my attitudes concerning my own strengths and weaknesses?

   What are those strengths and weaknesses? What have I been doing with them?

   How much ego-strength do I have?

7. Do I go around in a false state of humility degrading my natural abilities, feeling there is nothing positive which can come from me because "in me dwells no good thing?"

   Do I hide all strengths of my own in order that He might increase and I might decrease?

   Do I feel it is wrong to be able to do something well and admit it?

   Or, on the other hand, am I proud of what I am able to do?

   Am I sure of my ability to carry out my job?

8. Am I enthusiastic about my work or has it become something I have to do?

   Would I be better suited for something or somewhere else?

   Would I be more enthusiastic if certain changes were instituted?

   What changes?

   How can this be accomplished?

9. Am I optimistic in my outlook on life in general, and especially concerning my own problems?

   Or does pessimism creep into every thought I think and statement I make?

   Which is the healthier attitude?

   How can I begin to see the silver lining in the clouds?

10. Am I ready and willing to be flexible in my thoughts, in my work, in all of my relationships?

    Do I willingly offer to go or be or do, and then become very critical because I have been asked to go or be or do?

    Am I subject to jealousy?

    Am I proud?

11. Am I honest with myself?

    Have I correctly analyzed my feelings and the reasons for them?

    Have I covered up an attitude, a sin, an action, a decision, with a Scripture reference taken out of context?

    If I hate or fear something or someone, do I admit it to myself and face it for what it is, or do I cover it over because "Christians are not suppose to have those feelings"?

12. How do I face loneliness?

    Do I determine that Jesus is the only friend I ever need, and therefore suppress my feelings of aloneness?

    Or do I face the fact I am lonely and try to find my own answer for it?

13. Do I find a critical spirit within me?

    Do I feel my answers are usually best when questions arise?

    Do I find myself criticizing everyone and everything?

    How can I deal effectively with criticism?

Do I feel others are criticizing me?

What does this do to me?

What is my reaction?

How do I treat people whom I think are critical of me?

Am I easily hurt?

14. How do I react to sickness?

Do I feel it is a weakness which must be overcome?

Do I follow doctor's orders?

If rest is required, do I rest?

Am I too busy to treat "minor" illnesses?

Do I "keep going" as long as possible without admitting to sickness so as not to involve family or co-workers?

Does physical sickness make me draw closer to the Lord, or does it produce a lethargy with the result that I feel others can uphold me in prayer because I don't feel able to maintain spiritual strength through my own efforts?

Is this a wrong attitude?

How do I react when co-workers become ill and demand time and attention I feel should be given to "serving the Lord"?

15. When pressure comes in upon me, how do I react?

Do I become flustered, incommunicative, "up tight", irrational?

Do I handle it as it comes and thereby maintain a normal boiling point?

Do I feel pressure comes because of a lack in me or in my spiritual life?

Does this become an opportunity for growth in grace, or depression and indecision?

Do I blame other people for pressure?

Do I cause some of it myself?

16. How do I really feel about the lack of privacy afforded me?

The interruptions when I'm studying or resting?

Do I enjoy having people stare at me like an animal in a zoo?

Does it bother me that I can never get away from people?

Do I have an open door policy?

Should I consider closing that door at times?

Do I really want nationals to feel free to come to me 24 hours a day for counsel and Bible study?

Or do I inwardly rebel, but say nothing?

Do I feel I am being exploited?

Where and when do I feel I should be allowed privacy?

Would privacy help my ministry to such a degree that I should demand it at all times?

17.   How much appreciation do I feel I deserve?

How do I feel when others get credit for what I have done?

Is my feeling stronger in this regard if another missionary gets the credit, or if a national gets it?

Can I continue happy in my work without being patted on the back constantly? Occasionally?

18.   How creative am I?

Am I happy doing the same thing the same way all the time?

Could it be done differently?

Could I put new interest and life into my work with a little creative effort?

Is there someone who could help me with this?

19.   How do I feel about money which I have?

Do I cling to it and use it only for myself?

Do I tithe and give gifts to the Lord?

Do I share in needy projects?

Is my pocketbook entirely the Lord's or do I pretty much hold the pursestrings?

Am I generous, or do I withhold?

Could I be considered careful in money matters?

Am I "tight"?

Am I "stingy"?

Do I envy others who seem to have more than I do?

Am I grateful for His continuous supply?

20. Am I a leader?

    Do I have administrative qualities?

    Am I decisive?

    Do I consider the needs of others in an unbiased way?

    Do I lead with authority? Democratically? Autocratically?

    Do I listen with an open mind?

    Do I consider every facet of a problem before making hasty decisions?

    Do I hedge?

    Do I try to push decisions off on someone else?

    Do I join the majority even if I am otherwise minded?

    Do I lead wisely with discernment?

    Do I delegate authority as well as responsibility?

    Do I try to be fair and just in all my dealings?

    Are there things I don't like to do? Refuse to do? Why?

    Am I loved and respected? Only loved? Only respected?

    Should I consider continuing in a leadership position, or should I step down and give someone else the responsibility if he is more qualified?

    What are my feelings when a less qualified individual assumes my place of leadership?

21. Am I a follower?

    Am I critical of the authority of my leaders?

    Do I respect those over me?

    Do I try to make my leader's job easier by conferring with him periodically, keeping him posted on problems and happenings as seen from my viewpoint?

    Do I openly talk against the leadership personnel?

22. Am I dependable?

    When given a job to do, can I be depended upon to complete it to the best of my ability within the specified time?

    Do people depend on me?

    If not, why not?

    If they do, how can I be of more help to them? Should I encourage dependence?

23. Am I ready to learn?

Do I see a need for learning?

What have I learned this week?

Where did I learn it?

How can I use it?

Am I willing to change in any way necessary in order to put this learning into action?

Have I become stagnant in the learning process?

Do I feel I'm too old to learn?

Do I shy away from learning experiences because of my desire to remain a part of the authoritarian establishment rather than a part of the progressive thinking of the younger generation?

Do I feel I know everything I need to know in order to accomplish my task?

Do I feel that active learning will take away my stability and the comfortable feeling of knowing my subject or my people?

24. What motivates me?

Is it my love for Christ that led me to the mission field?

Is it a proper motivation?

Do I feel I have something to offer the world? If so, what?

Am I laboring to get recognition? Make a name for myself?

Do I feel compelled to be a missionary because the Word of God says I should be?

Did my family push me into it?

Would I rather do something else?

Do I need to be more deeply motivated?

Do I feel well qualified for the job I am doing?

Do I feel I must win the world for Christ?

Is my challenge as worthy and heartfelt today as it was the day I committed myself to Christ for full-time service?

25. How do I feel about unity?

What are my feelings about ecumenicity?

How do I support or attack it?

Have I thought it through?

How do I feel Christians can present a more united front?

How do I fit into the picture?

26. Am I outspoken?
    Shy?
    Afraid to speak up?
    Do I speak only when spoken to?
    Do I talk too much?
    Do I feel inferior? Superior?
    Do I always have to be heard?
    How good a listener am I?
    Do I think as much as I could and should?
    Am I happy to be laissez-faire, or do I want a piece of the action?
    Am I interested enough in my part in God's work to contribute all I possibly can to every situation in which I am involved?
    Do I have special talents?
    What are they?
    How am I using them?
    Am I hiding them? Why?
    Am I proud of them?
    Do I volunteer them?
    Could I further develop them?

28. Do I feel comfortable within myself?
    Where could I improve?
    What makes me most uncomfortable?
    How can I overcome this?

29. Do I periodically evaluate myself, my work, my actions and reactions, my need for further learning or education, my attitudes, my behavior, my progress, my spiritual life?
    Am I going forward or backward?
    Quickly or slowly?
    Am I more mature now than when I first went to the mission field?
    Am I ready to put my heart into my deputation work?
    Do I have a message to share?
    Am I looking forward to sharing it?

30. Am I gracious and courteous?
   Do I find myself saying "thank you" more than ever before?
   Is my gratitude genuine?
   Do I take things and people for granted?

31. What is my attitude toward success?
   Do I allow myself the privilege of failing?
   Do I understand that success is relative?
   Do I demand more, or less of myself than of others?
   Is success my only goal?
   Have I failed the Lord when plans do not consummate as I feel they should?
   Who sets my standards for success?
   What does success mean to me?

32. Is my life characterized by humility?
   What does humility mean?
   Is it downgrading?
   Is it necessary for me to refuse to acknowledge all abilities and capabilities in order to maintain an aura of humility?
   Am I aware of being humble?

33. Have I set goals for myself?
   For my devotional life?
   For my family?
   For my work?
   For my co-workers?
   For the nationals?
   For my mission?
   For my term of service?
   For my furlough period?
   Have these been met?
   What difference does it make if they have? If not, why not?

34. Am I a good soldier of Jesus Christ?
   An ambassador without shame?
   A clean vessel for Him to use?
   An unchoked channel?
   A faithful steward?
   An obedient love-slave?
   Are there areas where improvements must be made.

35.   Am I tired to death of being a "saint"?

Do I resent being a missionary? Lacking funds? Raising support? Being nice?

Am I sacrificing time and money on a cause which no longer appeals to me?

Am I ready to give it all up? Why?

What alternate plan do I have?

Will this plan work out better to my liking and keep me in the will of God?

Am I ready to embark on this new plan?

How do I know assuredly that this is God's perfect plan for my life?

B.   MY WORK

1.   Do I feel responsible to speak to every soul I meet concerning the claims of Jesus Christ?

How do I feel when I pass up an opportunity?

2.   Have I felt my parish consisted of 40,000 souls?

Have I tried to reach the masses?

Have I spread myself and the message of the gospel too thin?

Would it be better to put my efforts into training just a few so that they could reach their own people?

Have my efforts been rewarded in salvation and/or growth?

If not, is there a reason for this?

3.   Have I been diligent in language study?

Have I taken every opportunity to learn to

speak idiomatically and intelligently?

Do I communicate understandably in my new tongue?

Do I have the feeling people are laughing at my pronunciation, or my mistakes in grammar?

Or is this secondary to the love I show and concern and care I have for those to whom I am speaking?

Do I really care if I can speak the language well or not?

4.   Have I been able to make decisions which have been required in controversial situations?

Have I been able to counsel a new Christian who finds himself legally married to three wives?

Do I find myself in full agreement that candidates for baptism must wait and be trained for a year or two before receiving baptism?

Do I have the answer for those who fall into sin? For those seeking Scriptural solutions to daily problems? For the backslider?

Am I seeking the answers to these questions and others like them if I have not determined in my own mind and heart what I believe to be correct?

5.   Am I willing to allow nationals to be given positions of leadership in their churches?

In my mission's work?

Within my mission family?

What is my attitude concerning their financial support?

6.   Have I shared my goals for the work with others on my station?

Have we sought to share goals and work to see that they are met?

Have I felt my goals must be met at the expense of anyone or anything?

Have they been attained?

Where have they taken us?

Were they good goals? Attainable?

7.   Have I experimented with new methods?

Have I used audio-visual tools?

In my specialized work, have I been willing to teach others? Missionaries? Nationals?

Did it prove to be helpful?

Have I been reticent about sharing my hard-earned knowledges and skills with others?

8. Have I withheld anything from my national brethren to assure my presence with them for an unlimited time?

    Do I feel it is better if the work remains in the hands of the missionaries?

    How much am I preparing the nationals for my work in the event I should have to leave?

    Do I trust them with responsibility? Authority? Finances?

9. Have I looked for opportunities to expand my ministry and the effectiveness of it?

    Or have I been content to do only what was demanded of me?

    What does the second mile involve?

10. Have I been willing to be moved from my station? Am I flexible?

    If word arrives during my furlough that I will be assigned to a different work or area, what will be my reaction?

    Will it depend upon what work and what area?

    Am I willing for some changes, but not others?

    Is my reaction based upon fear? Dislike for a certain situation? Co-workers? Rumors?

11. Am I willing to take a leadership position when requested, even though I do not feel prepared for it?

    Am I willing to play a lesser role when I feel I should be granted a place of authority?

12. How does my work advance the cause of Christ?

    How does it fit into the entire scope of my mission's work?

    Can I cooperate with other missions in the area? Do I really feel it is my work?

13. As a wife, how much time should I spend in the work?

    Should I give 100% of my time to my family?

    How can I best make my children happy in our adopted country?

    How do I feel about my children having to be separated from us for long periods of time while they are in school?

    How much time do I spend worrying that they will pick up a disease, learn things they shouldn't from national children, or become too nationalized?

Should I take my children with me when I do village visitation?

Should I hire a woman to care for the children in our home so I can continue my missionary responsibilities?

Am I jealous of my husband's work?

How do I feel about the fact he has to go away for several days or weeks on mission business?

14. Is it wrong to take days off from my missionary work?

Do I feel an 8-hour day should be the rule for missionaries?

Is my time for study and research of benefit?

Should I do more of it?

Do I feel others think I am wasting time?

15. Are there items of equipment which I need to obtain during furlough which will facilitate the work when I return to the field?

16. Is my work satisfying to me?

How could it be made more so?

Do I feel I'm doing a good job?

Do I need more help?

Are nationals actively involved in the ministry?

Is this to my liking?

Do I respect them? Resent them?

Do I feel stymied because of lack of finances for the work?

Am I happy doing itinerant work, or would I prefer to stay in one place?

What is best for me, the work, the mission?

17. How do I feel about the country where I serve?

Does their philosophical approach irritate me?

Do I detest reporting every move I make to the local police?

Am I aware of every move I make because I know the CIA or other authorities are closely watching me?

Am I offended by this?

Do I cheat a little now and then on the restrictions laid down for me by my host government?

Do I feel guilty about this?

18. Do I evaluate the work at definite intervals?

    Who helps me with this?

    Do I ever ask for help?

    From whom?

    If we're not reaching our objectives, am I willing to change my approach?

    Or do I merely delay the reaching of the goal?

    Do I set new goals?

    Are these goals made known?

    Are they realistic?

19. How do I feel when nationalism overpowers Christianity in the lives of national believers?

    Am I discouraged? Do I try to make them less nationalized? More Christian?

20. Do I try to make the national church a miniature of the church in my homeland?

    Do I insist on western patterns of culture for all men everywhere?

    How do I feel about drinking from a common communion cup?

    Do I feel illiterates can make a contribution to the local church?

21. Do I preach only salvation, neglecting spiritual food for young Christians?

    Am I interested in a literacy program so these people can come to read the Word of God for themselves?

    Is a Bible School available in my field?

    If not, should we start one?

    What is my personal feeling concerning nationals being sent to my homeland for Bible or technical training?

C. MY INTER-PERSONAL RELATIONSHIPS

1. Am I openly antagonistic?

    Am I set in my ways?

    Am I open to the opinions of others?

    Do I give a strong reaction before hearing out the other fellow?

2.   Am I careful in my behavior?

Do I consider what effect my actions and attitudes will have on others? Missionaries? Nationals?

Am I crushed when others behave in a way which dishonors the Savior?

Do I, in love, speak to my brother or sister, admonishing? Scolding?

Do I have a different set of standards for the missionary and the national?

3.   Do I honestly feel that the Christian nationals with whom I work are on a par with me?

Do I condemn their lack of formal education, their need for money and material things, their discipline of their children (or lack of it), their ways of witnessing?

Do I feel they are somewhat inferior to me in intelligence?

Do I look down on them?

Do I look up to them?

Does the color of their skin have any bearing on my feelings?

Is their way of doing things inferior to mine?

Do they have customs I would like to emulate?

Do I envy them?

Do I try to understand them?

Do I feel they owe me respect?

Do I feel I should be in charge and they should remain subservient to me?

Would I be willing to work under their direction?

4.   How understanding am I?

How insistent am I?

Do I run away from situations I don't understand?

Do I condemn quickly?

Do I look further into those things which I do not understand, or which I feel I may have misinterpreted or misunderstood?

Even when something seems legally, morally, physically or spiritually wrong, do I attempt to find the true motives for the action?

5.   Am I able to communicate with my fellow-workers? Even when I'm upset?

Am I honest in my communications?

Am I able to look someone in the eye and admit I disagree with him?

Do words become heated in discussions?

Am I discerning?

Do I listen?

Am I patient?

Do I feel things inside that I refuse to express?

Does this cause hostility to unleash itself, or build up within me?

When it does, how does it affect my communication?

6.   Am I, as a single person, jealous of privileges given to married couples? (Time away from the station with children, fellowship and sharing with other married couples, family times, etc.).

Do I feel that I, as a single missionary, am expected to be more flexible than they? Be sent from one place to another without being asked? Made to babysit for children of senior missionaries?

Am I certain my senior missionary sees no need for single girls, finds them immature, weepy, unstable, and unfit for their job assignment?

Does my senior missionary really feel that way, or could I be wrong?

Have I felt like an outsider on the station?

Have I been wife- or husband-seeking?

Has my conduct with the nationals always been above and beyond reproach?

Am I jealous of my married co-workers?

Do I have a secret love? A national? A married colleague?

What is my conviction concerning marriage to a national?

7. Am I, as a married missionary careful not to look down on single folks as though there were something lacking in them?

    Do I try to include them occasionally in family plans?

    Do I allow them to fellowship with one another?

    Do I expect more work of a better quality from them than I do from married folks?

    Do I feel they should be free for any task at anytime of the day or night?

    Do I feel that single folks cause many problems on the field because of their insecurity, loneliness, jealousy, shyness or instability?

    How have I tried to help the situation?

    Have I been too critical?

    Have I tried to understand and to put myself in their situation?

    Have I secretly condemned them for their unmarried state? Envied them?

8. Do I feel a missionary should work an 8-hour day, 5-day week?

    Do I rebel at interruptions during my"non-working hours"?

    Do I feel a missionary should work 24-hours a day, 7 days a week?

    Do I bear a grudge against a co-worker who feels differently than I do concerning the work week?

    Do I consider my co-workers before taking time away from my station?

    Do I plan my vacation in cooperation with others who must bear the burden of the work during my absence?

    Do I contrive and make excuses for being away from my station as often as possible?

9. Are there co-workers with whom I cannot get along?

    What are the basic problems?

    What have I done to help the situation?

    To hinder it?

    Am I willing for a reconciliation or working agreement?

    Or do I want to hang on to my grievance(s)?

    Are our personality conflicts beyond the grace of God?

Is the blame as much mine as it is my co-worker's?

10. Have I shown favoritism to certain nationals?

Is this wrong?

Has it produced hard feelings?

Do I prefer to ignore nationals if it is a choice of fellowship with them or with friends from the homeland?

Do I feel at home with nationals?

Can I share with them? Pray with them?

11. Am I interested in the needs of others?

Do I try to give comfort, counsel and consolation when it is needed or requested?

Do I enter into the joys and sorrows of others?

Do I try to become involved, or am I content to remain on the sidelines?

12. Do I respect the training and experience of younger missionaries?

Do I feel they have something to offer me and the work?

Or do I feel they should be seen and not heard for at least the first term of service?

Do I welcome new folks to the field?

Do I try to remember some of the adjustments I had to face, and then seek to understand how the new folks feel and what they are facing?

Do I endeavor to help as much as possible in this adjustment?

Or do I let them grope for themselves as I was made to do?

13. Do I respect the authority and knowledge of my senior missionaries?

Do I automatically label them "outdated"?

Do I accept younger missionaries and weigh and utilize their opinions and contributions?

Do I try to force my opinions on others?

Do I openly rebel when things don't go my way?

Do I downgrade the mission, its workers, and its ministry by refusing to work in harmony with my fellow-workers?

Do I fellowship only with those in my own age group?

Do I feel unaccepted by mission leaders?

14.   Do I respect the confidences of others?

Do I offer fellowship in prayer?

Do I offer my services as freely to my fellow-missionaries as to the nationals?

15.   Do my children know I love them?

Is there any cause for them to feel they are only third or fourth place in my heart?

Do I run to the aid of others when they need me, but insist by attitude and action that my own children should handle their problems with little or no help from me?

Do I allow my children any freedom of decision?

Or is their life a list of do's and don'ts laid down by me?

Have I made them come to understand why we are missionaries?

Do they have any share in the work?

Do they know they are wanted and needed?

Do I openly criticize my work, the workers, and the mission in front of my children?

Do I help them to have a happy relationship with national children, or do I make them feel they are superior and should, therefore, not associate with nationals?

Do my children seek counsel from me or do they go to others for help?

Is our home as free of tension as is possible?

Are there any double standards in my code of morality?

Do my children love me? Respect me?

Are they glad I'm a missionary? Am I?

Do they want to pursue Christian training and work?

Are they allowed to be less than perfect?

Is my discipline of them suitable and carried out in love?

Are they allowed a life of their own when they come of age?

16.   When my fellow-workers do not have as much as I do, am I willing to share with them?

Do I expect to be repaid?

Do I do it out of duty, or concern?

17. Am I willing to take an active part in mission prayer meetings?

Have I been interested in inter-mission activities?

Can I be counted upon to give a hand if needed for a special ministry in my area?

If a co-worker is sick, on vacation, or on furlough, am I willing to fulfill his obligations so that the work will continue to move forward?

Or would I delight to see it collapse?

Perhaps these questions will help in your evaluation of your field experience as well as providing goals toward which you can expect to move during your furlough period and upon your return to the field.

Be strictly honest in your answers. No one else needs to know those answers, but they should help you to become a better person and a more effective missionary. It may even help you to come to know yourself.

May God bless you as you seek to grow in grace and continue to follow the Lord to the ends of the earth.

QUESTIONS—CHAPTER 40

1. List **your** major personal strengths and weaknesses.

2. How does each of **your** strengths and weaknesses help or hinder your ministry?

3. After evaluating your term of service, what changes will you institute for yourself and for your ministry in the days ahead? Why? How?

41
Living Within Your Budget

Your first trip to a store in the homeland will leave you in a state of shock, whether you are buying clothing, food, children's toys, a car, or postage stamps. Were things this expensive two, three or four years ago? No, of course not. But they really haven't increased in price as much as they appear to you. The simple fact of the matter is that the entire economic structure has altered since your last visit home.

Even if you are returning from a country whose economy is on more of a par with the homeland, you will still feel prices are outrageously high. It used to be possible to at least get good hamburger rather inexpensively. But no longer. And unless you want to live on potatoes, beans and rice, the food bill for your family will seem all out of proportion. And with the price of food in restaurants, there will be few meals out in the days ahead. (All of this will, of course, make you appreciate, more than ever, the hospitality given to you in the homes of others).

It will be difficult to live within your limited budget in the homeland, but you will learn to do it just as other families do. The diet will not often include sirloin steaks or legs of lamb. But it is possible to shop for and purchase nourishing food. Watch for sales at the local food stores. Also try, as much as possible, to buy store name brands of tins and jars of food rather than national name brands. The quantity and quality of the food is usually excellent, but the cost is lower. Less expensive cuts of meat can be cooked in such a way that they are tender, tasty, and appetizing. Exotic and specialty foods may not get to your table, but good, wholesome, nourishing food will. If you are fortunate enough to own a freezer, or have access to one, it is possible to get some very good prices on frozen products. Frozen fruits and vegetables are often on sale. Be sure to buy the "family-size" packages which run far less per pound than the smaller packets. Vegetables packed in pouches with butter or cheese sauces are far more expensive than those which are frozen by themselves. Many areas have "day-old", bakery outlets where bread and pastries can be purchased very inexpensively.

During the course of a year of furlough, enough money could be saved by buying food this way to more than pay for a freezer, depending upon the size of your family.

In meal planning, it is good to have only one large meal per day. You will not be able to afford bacon for breakfast every day. Eggs and bulk cereal will be your mainstay for breakfast. Milk purchased by the gallon is less expensive than by the quart. Bulk cheese is less expensive than fancy wedges. Fruit and vegetables can be purchased from farm markets during the season. In some areas, you have opportunity to pick your own tomatoes, cucumbers, beans, peppers, oranges, grapefruit, strawberries or blueberries, paying very little per quart or bag. Canning your own fruits and vegetables can save money.

A woman who can make clothes for her family is most fortunate. The cost of a sewing machine will be repaid after she makes two or three dresses for herself: Or she may wish to rent a machine during furlough. With the many cloth outlets available with very attractive prices for fine materials, clothing can be made inexpensively. Buying a wardrobe at regular retail prices can be devastating to the pocketbook.

There are many discount houses, and stores that through quantity buying or manufacture, are able to offer much better prices than independent stores can offer. Always look for quality in these stores. If you know values, you will be able to do very well. But if you can only compare prices, and you decide on an item just because it is less expensive than advertised somewhere else, you may discover that with very little effort your seams are splitting, your handle is loose or your wheels are coming off!

When looking for transportation for your furlough time, try not to buy the first used car offered to you inexpensively from the lot. You will probably put many thousands of miles on it, and you will do well to get the best car you can afford. Some missionaries are fortunate enough to have friends who loan or buy them a car for furlough use. Others must bear this expense themselves. Some are able to obtain a good used car from a missionary just returning to the field from furlough. Others may feel they will not bother to buy a car for the three months of furlough, if they have chosen the short furlough option.

If you do think of getting transportation, however, there are many things which must be taken into consideration: The size of the family, the size of the car, the make, the cost, the model, the upkeep, a new compact or a used medium size, a car, van or station wagon, 6-cylinder or 8-cylinder, automatic, semi-automatic or standard shift, how much you plan to travel, resale value, etc.

If you are a single girl, and know nothing about automobiles, either buy from someone you know and trust, or take a friend with you who knows what should be under the hood. Remember that even a used-car guarantee will do little good if you have a breakdown in the Arizona desert. Remember, also, that a well-built 4-cylinder car is far more economical than an 8-cylinder one, even though the purchase price may be less for the larger car.

If housing is not provided for you, you may have to add funds from your personal support to stretch your housing allowance to meet your needs. This means even less money available for food and clothing.

Even though it may be difficult to make your dollars purchase all that is needed, you will have many opportunities to see God provide for you in many ways. Missionaries on furlough have not yet had to beg bread. Meals, clothing, housing needs, equipment and travel funds will be provided from unexpected sources. Trust Him for it and He will prove once again that "Faithful is He that calleth you who also will do it." (I Thess. 5:24).

For those who have children, serious considerations must be given to the expense of schooling during furlough. Public schools are available to all. As a broad generalization, private schools on the K-12 level are much less common in the western part of the U.S. In many communities, public schools are quite outstanding, and often have strong Christian student groups for fellowship.

But many missionaries want their children to attend a private or religious (Christian) school. Unless those schools give discounts to Christian workers, the expenses involved may not be available in your budget, unless your Mission allows you to seek specific support for such expenses. Experience in a public school can provide the education your children need, give them an opportunity to witness to children their own age, and allow them to share their overseas experiences. It may also provide new temptations and testings which are difficult to handle. You have committed your children to the Lord overseas. Now you must commit them to Him in the homeland.

If you are considering taking a year of studies during your furlough year, it may be necessary to utilize money from your savings, since costs of education are high. Or your mission may allow you to request designated funds from your supporters for this purpose. Some boards make provision for such training from designated funds which are part of your work fund. It is always wise to contact the college or university you wish to attend, explain in detail your situation and what course of study you wish to pursue. Fewer and fewer institutions of higher learning and technical schools have funds available as outright scholarships. If you are offered a scholarship loan, consider carefully how you may be able to repay it. Also find out if there are restrictions on any funds granted to you (e.g., giving a year of service in practical service). You will need to do some groundwork before leaving the field in order to get into the institution you desire for the course(s) of study you feel you need, or do it immediately upon arrival in the homeland. Be sure you have full permission from your Board before pursuing full-time studies during furlough.

QUESTIONS—CHAPTER 41

1. Write out a budget for a one-month period which will provide for a family of four. (Your cash income is $2,000.00)

2. What should you take into account when considering furlough transportation?

3. Under what circumstances should further education be considered?

4. What are the advantages and disadvantages to enrolling your children in a public school during furlough?

5. What are the advantages and disadvantages to enrolling your children in a Christian school during furlough?

42
Speaking Engagements

There are two kinds of missionaries:

1. Those who thoroughly enjoy deputation work, and

2. Those who thoroughly dislike it.

In the majority of situations, it matters little how the missionary feels about this ministry, for it is expected of him, and therefore it must be done—even the pilot who stutters and the doctor who is quiet and uncommunicative. Of course an alternative could be to schedule a full course of schooling for the entire length of furlough. Your wife could take care of the speaking. Marriage does have certain such benefits! But what of the shy, single bookkeeper? The mechanic who has kept the mission vehicles operating and saved the missionaries thousands of dollars who may be a dud on the market when it comes to speaking in public? Some folks do very well in small groups, chatting over a cup of coffee, or showing slides with a taped narration in a darkened room. But enlarge the group, take away the stimulant, and turn on the lights, and the missionary becomes panic-stricken and speechless.

Among the missionaries who enjoy deputation work, we have three main types:

1. Those who say so little and use such vague descriptions that the minds of their listeners are left totally or partially blank.

2. Those who have a well-prepared message or presentation which has great appeal to the group.

3. Those who feel this is their hour to shine in eloquence, and who, therefore, drone on and on and on—usually leaving their hearers behind after the first 20 minutes.

Let's face it. When did you last sit still and completely absorbed in a long-winded or uninteresting speaker?

As a missionary, you are a very fortunate person. You have something worthwhile to say, you will usually have a sympathetic audience, you will actually have an opportunity to challenge people to share in missions by involvement, you have travelled, you have lived with people about whom your audience knows very little, you have had experiences which they will never face, you have seen problems arise and be solved in unique ways, you have committed your life to Jesus Christ for service in a situation about which your hearers know little or nothing. But you're not a speaker? Do you mean you never converse or communicate with anyone at any time?

Speaking to a group of people, whether many or few, known or unknown, can be a terrifying experience to shy people whose self-image and/or ego strength are less than needed for this type of work. But remember, your audience is made up of individuals just like you. You are sharing with each one in the group your enthusiasm about your work. Among supporting churches, you are sharing their work with them, for they have had a real part in your service by gifts and prayers and personal concern.

Your knees and hands may be shaking, but your listeners will never notice. They aren't against you! They're for you all the way. They're interested or they wouldn't have come. They're interested in you as a person as well as in what you have to share with them.

What do they want to hear? This should not be difficult to decide. When you hear a speaker, what do YOU want to know? What type of presentation do YOU prefer? What appeals to you? What turns you off? Only by speaking in terms of what is relevant and exciting to you can you hope to capture the attention of those to whom you will speak.

Perhaps you feel that what you say is the important part of speaking. Or perhaps you fear that how you say it is most essential. The final answer, will probably involve both of these elements by the effective organization of your thoughts. It is very important that you strive to point to one theme in what you say in each meeting. Don't scatter ideas like buckshot. This type of presentation usually develops when the speaker is not well prepared. The less prepared a person is in anything he undertakes, the less poise he will have and the less impression he will make. An outline of what you are going to say is imperative. You may even wish to share this with your listeners so they can be prepared to follow you. Make your outline simple, but inviting. Don't tell everything you know by means of your outline. It has been aptly stated that to produce the best retention of material, it is best to **tell people what you're going to tell them, tell them, and tell them what you've told them!** It is also true that unless you are an exceptionally capable speaker, lecture-type speaking cannot hold the attention of your listeners for more than 20 minutes. Thus you may wish to use several methods of presentation, breaking off the lecture and showing slides or a movie, or providing for questions and answers.

Your meetings will be mainly of an informal nature. Conversational type speaking will be the order of the day. Although some people say you should speak "just above the heads" of your listeners, others say to pick out a friendly face and speak to it. The truth of the matter is, however, that you must speak in order to reach every individual present, whether you have an audience of 5 or 500.

Part of the attention you receive will be derived from your own involvement in your subject. If you're excited about it and have a desire to share it with others, your enthusiasm will catch on. Try not to scream at your listeners. Don't mumble. Speak as friend to friend. Don't be overdramatic. Try not to adjust your glasses, pull your ear, scratch your nose, or jingle the change in your pocket continually.

In summary, then, be sure to plan well what you are going to say and how you are going to say it; tell your audience what you feel will be most interesting to them; be honest; be yourself; if stories are used to illustrate your lecture, make them short and meaningful (some speakers give the life stories of 3 converts, using 30 minutes to do so, and lose their hearers after the first 5 minutes); be sure your illustrations do not overpower what you are trying to say, but rather enhance your message by stressing the main points; your audience is friendly and appreciative—try not to be afraid of them; maintain rapport with all your listeners. Relax as much as possible and try to enjoy your presentation as much as you hope your listeners will. If you feel you have nothing to say, it might be good to ask yourself some questions as to why you feel that way. Perhaps in such a case your furlough should be spent finding challenge for your own life rather than attempting to challenge others.

Deputation can be a fun thing. Entered into wholeheartedly, it can be rewarding in many ways. The fellowship of those who are interested in you and your work can be a sustaining force in your life.

If you are a married couple, and both are present at a service, perhaps the speaking time can be shared; or one can speak, the other show slides; or one can present in the church while the other is speaking to the young people or Sunday School group. If your children are with you, you may want them to participate in the meetings, or they may be asked to speak or sing, or be introduced. Never force them into a situation that will embarrass them. But if they **want** to be included, don't exclude them.

In your speaking, remember the time limits extended to you. Never go over your time, even when you have been cut back at the last moment from 15 minutes to 2. Return invitations are sometimes not given to those whose "tongue runs completely".

When speaking to a group, avoid controversial issues. There are doctrinal beliefs which are not tolerated in some groups; certain men cannot be mentioned in some churches; certain social issues cannot be upheld or condemned; never take sides in church disputes; do not degrade people, denominations, missions or yourself.

But don't concern yourself unduly with the negatives. The natural, honest, pleasant speaker will avoid unpleasant subjects and will willingly share his field, his work, his people, his hopes, his experiences with those who have come to listen.

Never read a report to your audience. This is the least effective type of presentation.

If you are asked questions, never be afraid to admit you honestly do not know the answer(s).

Because of the many speakers who pass through a church each year, your presentation should be unique. A mediocre meeting will not be a lasting remembrance unless your people already know you and are involved in your ministry. (Even then, you must give it your utmost).

Be sure to give a balanced view of your work and your field. There was a time when it seemed missionaries felt compelled to tell only the bright side of missions. Today your congregation will expect reality. A completely optimistic or pessimistic report will leave many questions unanswered in the minds of your hearers. Young people will not be challenged nearly so much by hearing that your field and work is utopian as they will if you tell it like it is, with its aspects of joy and sorrow, pleasure and disappointment.

Don't apologize for what you have to say. No matter how insecure you feel as a speaker, be positive in what you say. Speak about that in which you are most comfortable and knowledgeable. Picture yourself as a listener rather than a speaker. Especially at missionary conferences, where you have opportunity to hear other speakers, pick out those who appeal to you. What made you listen attentively to them? What was their approach? Usually you will find that the enthusiasm of the speaker in what he is saying far surpasses the words he says in gaining the enthusiastic response of his hearers. If your work does not thrill you, you will never be able to interest others. How sad it is when a missionary comes home after four years on the field and says "I really have nothing to say."

Keep in mind that human interest is of utmost importance in your speaking. An engineer will be thrilled about his amps, ohms and watts. A pilot will be enthused about his rudder, gauges and propellers. A secretary will be ear deep in her typing, transcribing and telephoning. A photographer will be involved with film speeds, lenses and composition. But when these folks come back to the homeland, their audiences will be interested in what happened to **people** because of their use of these components of their daily work.

Although you should involve the emotions of your listeners as well as their minds, it is unfair to play upon the sympathies of congregations. It is not the best way to gain **lasting** support.

When you are asked to speak at any service, be selective in what you present. It is impossible to present a full picture of you, your mission, your field and your work. Dwell on one aspect and deal with it adequately. Decide what you want your listeners to remember more than anything else. Aim for that one focal point. This does not mean that you cannot give background material, but you must be sure to direct your hearers to something they will remember.

If you are in a church for a conference with other speakers, or a week of meetings by yourself, you may find some difficulty in presenting your field to various groups and the same group again and again. Each service should build upon that which you have told before, not a repetition of what you have stated previously. Sometimes your host church will outline what they would like to hear. But often it will be up to you to outline your meetings. Do it carefully after much prayer and preparation.

Be sure to find out before you attend a meeting whether they expect a strictly missionary presentation, a Bible study on the theme of missions, or just a Bible study. This can save a lot of grief.

Some of you will have your personal support pledged. This should not keep you from being prepared to speak and represent your Board. And don't be afraid to be as enthusiastic about a general presentation for your mission as you are about gaining your own support.

Others will be fully supported through their Board and will be asked to go on tour with 2 or 3 missionaries from other fields within their mission's scope of responsibility, appearing primarily at missionary conventions. Although you will present your own work, you will also need to be prepared to give your testimony, to challenge your audiences from the Word of God concerning their response to missions, and to uphold your Mission Board and gain support for it. But since you will travel widely, it will be possible to work out a basic outline of what you wish to present during a week of meetings. When churches are separated by long distances, you will be able to use your messages many times. In doing so, however, be sure that they are, at all times, as fresh and inspiring the tenth time as they are the first. When **you** begin to tire of a certain presentation, change it. Otherwise your boredom will be transferred to your hearers and your team members.

Speaking in deputation meetings is a great privilege. It is one of the important reasons for a furlough. It is the means by which others are encouraged to participate in the greatest work in the world—missions.

May God bless you as you seek to honor and glorify Him in each of your meetings and may He encourage you with a positive response from those to whom you speak.

QUESTIONS—CHAPTER 42

1. What personal characteristics do YOU admire in a speaker?

2. How would you deal with a situation in a missionary conference if another speaker used all of his own allotted time and most of yours?

3. How can you improve your oral presentations?

4. If your message is being taped or broadcast, what special facts should you keep in mind regarding your presentation?

43
Using Slides and Movies in Your Meetings

Missionaries usually take movies, slides or pictures during their term on the field. They may be taken with little prior experience in the art of picture-taking. They have no form or design. They are not the pictures you now wish you had taken, and you regret that you did not have a plan and goal, but merely shot here and there at this and that. You also wish you had taken more pictures upon your arrival on the field when everything engulfed you because it was new and different. After a while, everything was so commonplace that it did not seem necessary to "shoot" it. But whatever you've captured on celluloid, avoid the following in your meetings:

1. You show a picture of your national church group—75 individuals. You then proceed to tell the life story of the 7th man from the left in the next to last row. To make matters worse, the picture was taken from a distance of 50 feet because you wanted to get the entire church building in the background. And unbelievably, after 5 minutes on Raphael's life story, you tell the conversion history of two others in the group. (You not only lose your audience, but you can burn up your film by keeping it in front of a 500-watt bulb for ten minutes)!

2. You didn't have your slides set up before the meeting. Therefore in your rush to put them in the tray, four get in upside down and two go in sideways. This can take away from the effectiveness of what you are trying to present.

3. There is one slide in the midst of the rest which is a double exposure (or overexposed, or underexposed). You explain that this is the only picture you were able to obtain of this individual or thing, and ask forgiveness for it not being a better shot. It's so poor that it would have been far better to leave it out.

4. You weren't really used to setting your new camera accurately. The shots are just a bit fuzzy or blurry. The projectionist tries frantically to bring the scenes into sharpest focus, going from blur to blur. The congregation decides, individually and collectively,

that they really must make that appointment with the eye doctor (especially if they're over 40), and you go merrily on your way describing the pictures as though they had been taken by a professional photographer!

5. You describe your pictures, but don't speak loudly enough for people to hear.

6. You have a tape recording to be played to describe your pictures. So people will be sure to hear, you place the machine in front of a microphone. The quality of the recording and its closeness to the mike make the words unintelligible, and its shrillness and loudness give everyone a headache.

7. You insist on operating the projector yourself. It's a machine with which you are not familiar. The slides jam, or the 16mm film rolls on the floor instead of on the take-up reel. The lights are on and off so many times that it entirely disrupts any continuity that may have been intended.

8. You were able to get some really good shots in the Mission Hospital operating room—close-ups of amputations, bleeding gunshot wounds, weeping sores; you were also fortunate enough to visit a leprosarium where you took close-up views of men and women minus noses, fingers, toes, and other parts of the anatomy. These are best shown, of course, at Medical Conventions. In public meetings, especially with women and children present, either don't show such pictures, or be sure to provide plenty of smelling salts and basins.

9. Naked natives are not usually best shown on wide screen in mixed audiences. You may be working amongst people who do not wear clothes. To you the scenes are natural, typical and true to life. But to pastors of churches, they may not be the the type of films they want shown, and it is up to them to decide where, how and when such pictures should be used. Never show nakedness on the screen without prior approval.

10. Don't show more than 80 slides in a meeting unless many shots are shown rapidly as different angles of the same person or thing or theme. Many times, 40 slides will be sufficient, but it depends upon how much you describe each view and the length of time allotted to you.

11. If you show slides and then speak concerning your field and its work, don't merely repeat what you said during the slide presentation. Build and elaborate on it. Or if you speak and then show slides, don't keep repeating "You'll be seeing this later in the slides or film". What you say, however, should have some sort of recognizable relationship to the visual presentation to follow.

12. Don't depend entirely upon your slides or movies to present your work. You are more important to your audience than your visual presentation.

In spite of all the don'ts we've mentioned, there are some more positive things to remember for you presentation:

1. Limit your presentation to the time designated for it.

2. Have some order to your slides or film so that they focus on a given theme. You may want to have several slide sets or films available, depending upon the emphasis you seek to stress.

3. Explain the scenes, so they will be meaningful to those who watch.

4. Move the program along, spending no more than 15 or 20 seconds on each slide. In rare instances you may wish to spend as long as a minute—but please, no longer. Also, 10 seconds is the minimal time for a slide to be viewed properly.

5. Show your best slides, fewer groups and more close-ups, scenery to set the climate, and then an emphasis upon your ministry.

6. Take into account the type of group to whom you are speaking. Gear your descriptions to them.

7. Consider the size of your group as to how loudly you should speak, how far the projector should be from the screen, how close the tape recorder should be to the microphone. Unless people can see and hear, the meeting is so much wasted time.

8. Try to show your work as thoroughly as possible by means of pictures. Your listeners remember far more of what they see than of what they hear.

9. Use slides or films with which you are familiar.

10. When you are using a projectionist, arrange beforehand what signal you will use when it is time to move on. It is very disruptive to have to say after each scene, "The next slide, please."

11. Be sure you are pictured at work in several of your slides or movie scenes so your audience can actually see you on the mission field.

As you speak from time to time, you will be making mental notes as to pictures you will obtain upon your return to the field. You may even prepare several slide-tape series for next furlough if you didn't do so for this one.

Some missionaries hold their finger across the lens, shake the camera, or become discouraged with mechanical gadgets. These are they who don't take a camera with them to the field. As a last desperate effort, they borrow slides from friends and may not be sure what they have obtained. Or perhaps they have borrowed a series from the Mission Office. Unfortunately, a picture-less secretary ends up with a series on the engineering accomplishments of the mission, about which she knows little or nothing. (Isn't it amazing how cloistered we can become in our own ministry with little or no understanding of what our fellow-missionaries are accomplishing)? As far as effectiveness is concerned, it would be far better to admit to no pictures!

We've spoken of the negatives, and it would not be fair to pass by without congratulating those many missionaries who have realized that up-to-date pictures from the field are important and necessary, those who have taken excellent pictures with inexpensive cameras, have put together a good display of photographic material, and are using it as a means of a vivid graphic, detailed analysis of their country and their work. They have included pictures of themselves on the job; they have thrown away every poor shot; they have planned their slide or film presentation as carefully—perhaps more so—than any message they will give during furlough. They find their presentations are effective, stimulating, descriptive, thought-provoking, informative, and worth all the time and effort put into them.

Your mission may have excellent, professionally filmed, 16mm sound color movies available for your use. Keep these in mind for missionary conferences. It is not ideal, however, to use your Mission's film on Japan if you are working in Zambia, no matter how good the film is. People are interested primarily in YOU and YOUR work unless you have been specifically asked to represent your mission in a general way. The latter is usually left up to the Deputation Secretary or Regional Representatives. If the film happens to depict your own field, use it freely, for it should be well-planned and better organized than your own unprofessional movies which are pieced together.

In using either slides or movies, it is possible to create clever titles without too much difficulty. If filming movie titles, be sure to take enough footage to allow the audience to read it unhurriedly.

It should be kept in mind that slides and films are not an end in themselves. They must be used with care as an adjunct to the speaker, not in place of him. They are an educational tool—not a movie show. Movies, if well taken, put together and presented will give a better picture of actual living scenes since they show motion, cover a large range of subject matter, cover progress and development, bridge time and space, and better put the viewer into the scene.

Pictures tend to clarify some of the false impressions people get when listening to a speaker. When the word "desert" is mentioned, minds think of barren sands spread under a hot sun. Pictures show that a "desert" can have trees, shrubs, grass, canals, villages, railroads, airports, animals and people. One hears the word "equator" and assumes the worker lives in a hot, wet jungle where temperatures are unbearably warm. Pictures show the equator can be 10,000 feet above sea level with snow-capped volcanoes, fertile valleys, and cold days and nights. And we could go on with such analogies. "A picture is worth a thousand words." But be sure it is a **good** picture.

To make slides or a film (which you would narrate) more interesting, involve your audience. Before the showing, toss out several questions which can be answered by the visual aid (e.g. name the animals pictured, what is the name of the school, where is the station located, in what type of homes do the people live, how many teachers do you have in the school, etc.). These questions will be answered in the brief showing of your pictures (not more than 5 minutes and no more than 10 seconds per slide). Then the service will take on an informal pattern, thus alleviating the need for lecturing. The more people you can involve, the more interested they will become. After your specific questions have been answered, allow others to ask questions. To close the meeting, show the same pictures, explaining them, thus making a deeper impression upon the minds of those who watch. This is particularly effective with children and young people.

One further word is necessary. You may be prepared to show an excellent film or series of slides. You have proven by its use in scores of services that it is effective. But do prepare for an alternate program which will cover the same amount of time. For the electricity can go off unexpectedly; your projector can blow its last bulb as you turn it on; you may be given less time in the program at the last minute and you will not be able to show your slides or film (especially if you have a tape recorded message or description); you may drop your slides and get them out of order; or the projector which was promised for your use never arrives. As always, **be prepared to preach, pray, die, or get married at a moment's notice** and go on with your presentation—minus visuals—as though you had planned it that way. Please don't apologize in every other sentence concerning this dire turn of events. Most of all, don't panic. Everyone will live through the experience!

QUESTIONS—CHAPTER 43

1. List at least five things you should avoid when giving a visual presentation of your work.

2. List at least five things which make a visual presentation most effective.

3. Are there variations to the usual visual presentations with slides and films? If so, what are they and when should they be used?

4. What do you do if your slides and/or films are lost in transit?

44
Use of Other Audio-Visual Aids

Often when we think of audio-visual aids for meetings, we think only of 2 × 2 slides and 8mm or 16mm movies. But there are many aids which are just as effective in presenting your missionary ministry to all age and ability groups. Not every group responds to audio-visual stimuli in the same way, so it is necessary to use a variety of means and methods. Films of every kind have been overworked. Much of their glamor has been long since lost through the fact that people have come to expect missionaries to use slides or a film if he isn't going to lecture.

But let's look at a variety of other tools which can be utilized by the missionary on furlough:

1. Flat pictures. These can be obtained on the field from shops, calendars, newspapers, books, advertising, etc. and made into notebooks mounted on heavy paper or poster board, titled, and used in small groups, or be left on the display table for private perusing. They can also be used as a backdrop for a display or literature table, or projected on a screen by means of an opaque projector. Pictures should be colorful, chosen with care, and tell a definite story just as a film or slide series.

2. Photographs. These should be no smaller than 8″ × 10″. They can be used in the same way as flat pictures. They are especially effective in Sunday School classes, home presentations and individual contacts. Be sure that the pictures are properly exposed and developed, with good contrast, depth of field and clear detail. They must tell a story to be effective. Pictures showing unique scenes, or contrasts are good. It is possible to have a series of photographs showing close-ups of various types of people among whom you work.

3. Overhead projectors are an excellent means of showing distinctive materials to any-sized audience. Preparation of materials can be readily accomplished. Transparencies made can be used time and again. Any type of graph, chart, illustration, etc. can be marked on acetate. Colored pictures and other materials can be "lifted"

and used effectively. This projector can be used in an undarkened room which is an advantage for daytime showing.

4. Opaque projectors can transfer to a screen any material you may wish to show a group. Material from books, clippings, maps, post cards, magazines—even objects—can be projected. This takes a fully darkened room, so keep this in mind.

5. Filmstrips. These are inexpensively made by most reputable photographic companies. They can use slides which you have taken or clips from your movies. They are a cross between slides and movies and can be used with a taped or "in-person" narration.

6. Graphs. For small groups, statistical material can be well presented by means of flat drawings employing means to visualize data. For comparisons, analyses, or interpretation, graphs are exceptionally good. There are several kinds of graphs to tell your story quickly and easily:

   a. Bar graphs can suitably show comparative religions, population, Christian community, etc.

   b. Circle graphs show how a whole is divided into parts and can be used to tell what percentage of missionaries are in various professional roles, number of national to missionary worker ratio, division of your total support figure into its proper categories (personal support, housing, transportation, health care, retirement, etc.), divisions of peoples among whom you labor (various tribes, groups, whites, blacks, etc.).

   c. Line graphs can plot the conclusion of trends such as how soon nationals may take over positions now occupied by missionaries, increased funds needed to complete certain projects, number of trained nationals available for the future expansion of the work, etc.

7. Charts. These help your interested friends and supporters to understand better the task you and your Board are undertaking. There are many kinds of charts such as **flow charts** (to show sequence and relationship), **stream charts** (how several events converge, thus forming one large event, e.g. showing why a Bible School became a necessity), **tree charts** (reversing the stream chart, thus beginning with one large event and showing the small events of which it consists), **process charts** (showing how something is made, e.g., the conversion of an unbeliever), **map charts** (dots or symbols indicating your Mission's stations in a given

country or national churches in your area). Charts cannot be used in large crowds, require time and skill in preparation, but can highlight key points, increase interest and attract attention. It is even possible to lightly pencil your chart and then draw it in front of your audience with a black marker pen. There are many varieties of charts including flip charts, slip charts, poster charts and pinboard charts.

8. Posters. Use a single idea and utilize symbolism and slogans. Good for emphasizing what you want from your hearers, e.g., go, give, pray, write, prepare, etc.

9. Diagrams and Sketches. You may wish to show how your hospital is laid out, what your people look like, types of clothing worn, where your radio antennae are located, and areas which you are reaching.

10. Maps and Globes. These are helpful in establishing relative positions and sizes. They pinpoint your area of responsibility. They can show physical features by color. Outline maps may be used so you can mark on them that which is pertinent in a given meeting. Wall maps are very acceptable, but arrange a place for them to be hung, or people to hold them at the time of your presentation.

11. Chalkboards. Any information, drawings, cartoons, or graphic material can be easily placed on a slate with chalk. Be sure to print large and legibly. Use various colored chalk to produce a more professional-looking effect.

12. Phonographs and Tape Recorders. Records from your country can be played for climate setting. You may have taped your national school children singing their national anthem or a Christian song; you may have a national give his testimony (3 minutes is sufficient) and you could interpret. The sounds of your country will be appreciated by your audience—camel or donkey bells, native music or musical instruments, sounds in the market place, the Muslim call to prayer, etc.

13. Flannelgraph Board. Although we think of the use of flannelgraph as being limited to work with children, it is very effective with adults.

14. Objects and Curios. You will have curios which you have brought home with you (lion tooth necklace, national newspaper, dolls, skins, wood carvings, cooking utensils, clothing, etc., etc.). These can be a most effective means of describing your country and work. If the items are drawn from a box or bag so they cannot be seen before being described, attention is heightened. Each article may be placed on a table after being shown.

15. Models. Miniatures of the real item such as the buildings on your mission station, the route from the homeland to your area of service, etc. These can be created from wood, sand, cardboard, paper, clay, paper mache, or other materials. Working models may also be created and used for demonstrating a Persian water wheel or the operation of a hydroelectric plant.

16. Exhibits and Displays. These will often be as explanatory as slides or films. But a great deal of work must go into them. Be sure they say something, are self-explanatory, and well made. Plan on paper what you are trying to accomplish before putting it into more permanent form. Make it easy to handle and set up. Be sure to make good use of color, spacing, lighting, location, lettering, and unique items.

17. Dioramas. These are scenes representing the real thing, shown in a 3-dimensional way in a shoebox or like container. You can utilize curios, or objects made of clay or soap. A bit of the artist and some good ideas are needed to utilize this form of presentation to its best advantage. One diorama or a series of them can be utilized, depending on what you try to get across to your audience.

18. Dramatizing. A husband and wife, or family team can dramatically show what life is like on your field. There is no end to the number of situations which can be worked out in this manner. Dressing in national clothes and utilizing large curios and objects are essential.

19. Puppets. Again we have usually limited the use of puppets to work with children, but they are just as effective with adults. Ventriloquism is an excellent method of presentation if you have the ability to perform in this way.

20. People. Having dressed one or more of your audience in national clothing they can be used to demonstrate some of the traits and customs of your nationals. (Be sure to explain just what you will ask of these people before you dress them and use them as models).

Your audio-visual aids will need to be worked out to suit the size of your audience, the type of meeting, the points you want to stress, and the uniqueness with which you are able to reach your goals. You may wish to utilize several combinations of the forms we have mentioned, or you may be able to come up with new ones of your own. Changing the format of your service will put new life into it, for you and for your listeners. Only be sure that your aids are relevant, visible, portable and subordinate to the message you are striving to get across. Your aids will help to improve your presentation by allowing you to present more statistics, graphic illustrations, concrete details and more vivid "for instances".

In preparation, you will need to analyze what you want to say in order to design the proper aids. You will have more confidence, assurance, authority and poise because good aids multiply your ease of communicating, thus improving your friendliness, enthusiasm and rapport with your hearers. Aids help the hearers and observers by generating curiosity, interest and questions.

If aids are not subordinate to the message you are trying to present, then your lecture becomes a demonstration, and you become nothing but a voice. A good test is to determine that what you have to say would be relevant, meaningful, and interesting if it stood on its own; then use aids to supplement what you are saying.

Visual aids should never be left in plain sight. If they are prepared in advance, keep them covered or hidden until used. Otherwise, it will distract from what you are trying to say. The best aid can be held between the speaker and the audience so that neither is distracted by having to turn aside.

The types of aids available to you are limited only by your imagination and the scope of your message.

QUESTIONS—CHAPTER 44

1. List at least 10 audio-visual aids which you can utilize in your deputation ministry.

2. What makes a visual aid most effective?

3. What are some "dangers" in using visuals?

4. Should visual aids always be a part of your presentations? Why?

45
Question and Answer Sessions

Many times in your meetings you will have an opportunity to answer questions posed by your listeners. This is an informal time when both you and your hearers will feel relaxed, and where you can meet each other's needs.

A question and answer period should not be tacked on the end of a lecture to fill up extra time which you have not been able to fill. It should be announced at the beginning of your program and the amount of time to be devoted to it should be stated. Listeners should be invited to note on paper those items about which they would like further information so they will be prepared when the after-session is opened to them. Often when the question period is announced after the speaker has finished, the audience is so unprepared that it takes several minutes to get them into the mood, and then almost always when they warm up and enter in, the time has expired and they still do not have the knowledge they had hoped to obtain.

There is little preparation you can do for this type of session. Most questions will be concerned with the country, culture, people, language and work to which you have gone. You should be prepared to state facts concerning the political trends, the opportunity for workers, the Christian population, the Missions working in your area, numbers of missionaries, problems young people face, etc. Most of the questions will be relatively simple and your specialized knowledge will be sufficient in most instances.

There are several factors to keep in mind during this type of session:

1.   Getting started. If people do not have questions, seem restless and anxious to get away, close the meeting and let them go. On the other hand, if they feel inhibited or shy, make them feel at ease. There may be occasions where someone will be previously "planted" with a question in the event folks are slow to speak up. This will sometimes get things moving if the "plant" is not too contrived or obvious.

2. Make sure that questions are heard and understood and that your answer is heard. Speak directly to the point without side-tracking.

3. Occasionally a person will ask a personal or "loaded" question, trying to corner you. Answer tactfully, "unloading" it by the best means possible. You may get complex questions requiring several answers. Divide it and simplify it as much as possible.

4. Answer as directly as possible, back up your statements, if necessary, don't be afraid to take a stand, and don't be afraid ever to say, "I don't know" if you honestly do not have the answer. People are willing to accept this answer. Never gloss over or try to make up or venture a guess in order to appear to have expertise in your field. If you do give ideas which may not be valid, be sure to tell your audience it is only your guess.

5. Keep the session moving. Let questions be asked from several sections of the group. Try not to let this lead to a monologue between you and one other person. Involve the whole group.

6. Why not try throwing out a question to your audience such as "How would you feel if . . . ", "What would you do . . . ", "What are your feelings toward . . . ", "How would you solve . . . ", "Suppose . . . "

7. Don't let the session drag on ad infinitum and ad nauseum. Don't give extended, complicated answers to simple questions, especially if they are asked by children.

8. Don't close the session with silence. Many times speakers will ask for more questions when there are none. After a lapse of nothingness, he turns to the pastor, nods, and the session is abruptly finished. When the questions are over try to give some sort of summary, challenge, or other effective statement which will tie loose ends together, and also open the door for folks to approach you following the service.

Questions from the audience indicate effectively whether they were merely casual, uninterested observers, or active participants, involved in your ministry. This feedback information can also help you the next time you speak, for you can incorporate some of the material about which folks seemed especially interested. Because you are so close to the situation, it is sometimes difficult to choose what may be most interesting to those who will hear you. Questions help you to meet their needs, and in turn help to meet **your** needs.

QUESTIONS—CHAPTER 45

1. If a question is asked and you do not know the answer, how will you respond?

2. Of what value are question and answer sessions to you? To your audience?

3. How can you add life to question and answer sessions?

4. If no one asks a question, what will you plan to do with the time designated for this session?

5. How can you make humor work for you?

46
Missionary Conferences

If you are in a mission which sends you on tour, you may be involved **only** in conference sessions, perhaps as little as 2 days, or as many as 8 days in one location. Others of you will, during the course of furlough, be invited to participate in one or more conferences.

Looking at it casually, there will seem to be little difference in providing a single service or a week of conference—but let's look at it in more detail.

In your initial letter of invitation, several facts should be stated, i.e., the name of the participating church(es), name of the pastor, name of your contact person (if other than the pastor), dates of the conference, location, theme of the conference, when you are expected to speak, to what groups, whether a display or literature table will need to be provided by you, what financial arrangements will be made for you and whether audio-visuals are requested, and if so, what equipment will be provided for you. (If this information is not included, write to the inviting church requesting further details).

Your responsibility will be to prepare messages, varying in length, geared to various age groups, and growing out of the Conference theme. You will also fit your audio-visuals into the program to expand your presentations, but still fitting in with the overall theme. Your display will emphasize the theme again. Although seldom mentioned specifically, pastors always appreciate this emphasis.

Remember that you may be the only missionary at a given conference, or you may be one of sixty. In either case, your presentations must be so vital and unique that they will be remembered. To do this, you do not have to be a dynamic, world-renowned personality. You have only to be enthused about your area of service and, by some means, make your enthusiasm contagious. Some will ask "How is this possible? Who wants to hear how I build a church, or how I repair the mission cars, or how I keep the press running, or how I entertain at tea?" Do you have the assurance that your work is vital to your mission's outreach? Are you assured that you are in God's perfect will? Do you have any contact with that which is happening in your area? Do you see the need for others to give their lives in service to the Lord for just the thing you are doing? Perhaps your satisfaction in the service of the King cannot come from the fact that you are winning nationals to Christ and building them up in the faith. But surely, as a member of the team, you **do** have a share in all that is accomplished. It is possible that you, in your supporting ministry, can be identified with by many of those who will hear you speak, for they, too, are in a supportive role by their gifts and prayers on behalf of those who are out on the front lines. You, more than other missionaries, can encourage and challenge those who can help through use of just ordinary talents. You can challenge men and women to short-term service. You can lay before them the need for retired folks to volunteer for a year or two of ministry. Surely you can speak in depth of the type of prayer partners which are needed to uphold the work of the ministry. You can give a clear presentation as to where missionary dollars go and how they are used. Your personal testimony will be used in a wonderful way as you ask God to make it pertinent to your listeners. You can do much to make people in the homeland realize that **missionaries are ordinary Christian people, facing the same problems and temptations with which folks in the homeland have to deal.** You can gently lower the missionary from his pedestal and show him to be merely the Ambassador of Christ which God intends for Him to be. You can be a living proof that faithfulness to Cod is every Christian's foremost responsibility.

So, if you are not the world's greatest speaker, if you feel your ministry is obscured because of the things which are so daily, and you are on the platform with men and women who have worked in more difficult fields, can make their audience weep over the sad state of the poor women and orphans, or who can tell story upon story of scores of conversions—remember that those missionaries will be respected, and looked up to, and admired, and yet in the end, the listeners may actually be better able to identify with you and your work, because they, themselves, are involved in this type of service.

Now many of you will be "born speakers". Words may flow easily and sincerely. You can hold the attention of your group. You can present your field and your ministry in an unforgettable way. You are creative and your presentations are well-planned and long remembered. You are in an evangelistic ministry or a church planting position. You are involved in many areas of the work. You are outgoing and being in an administrative position, you have a far better overall view of the work being accomplished in your field, and throughout all the fields of your Mission. You speak with authority, know your fellow-workers intimately, enjoy your deputation ministry. You can present a challenge that produces response. Be grateful that God has given you special talents.

Missionary conferences are a good opportunity to present your field and work in depth. You can build upon previous sessions. You can also learn from listening to other speakers, viewing others' visual aids and displays. You are with the church group for a sustained period of time, and can, therefore, come to know them while they come to know you.

Missionary conferences can also have drawbacks. It may mean dividing a family for this period of time. Very few churches, using a number of missionaries in a conference, invite children to attend. This means, unless you have friends or relatives in the area, children must be left with others at home, or one parent stays home to babysit while the other goes to the conference. Conferences are usually scheduled for a time when children are normally in school. Thus some churches never meet the "other half" of the missionaries they support.

Then too, conferences can be very wearying to those who tire easily. Not only are there the planned meetings at which you are to speak, but on the spur of the moment you may be asked to say "a word" many times. Extra meetings may be scheduled at the last minute. Other churches may request your appearance during the conference week. Informal Home Bible Classes may ask you to attend and speak. Perhaps you will find yourself being asked for an interview by the local newspapers, radio or television. On some occasions you may be asked to teach classes at the local Christian or Public Schools. You are expected to be at the Men's breakfast, the Women's Missionary Tea, the Young People's banquet, the daily noon luncheons at a local cafeteria, the evening pot-luck suppers with the members of the church, and the daily afternoon prayer meetings. The church somehow feels you are their property 24 hours a day and you are expected to abide by their schedule—or be in danger of losing support or being dropped entirely.

If you are physically able to keep up with the schedule, you will, of course, do your best to comply. But if you are not able to do so, be very frank with the pastor of your host church, share your limitations, ask for time to rest, if need be. Most pastors will be understanding of your needs once they understand the situation.

Since churches often prepare for their conference for a full year, and it becomes the highlight of the church year, when the time actually arrives, they want the most and best they can get from you. Try to understand their position. It will be difficult to keep up such heavy schedules conference after conference. There must be understanding on both sides. Fit in as much as possible. If you must have a day away by yourself, contact the proper authority and get permission to do so. A great deal will be expected of you. Try to take it in stride. Refresh yourself as much as possible through the ministry of others.

By all means, do not go on to your next meeting or conference and brag or complain about how hard you were worked in a previous engagement. Whether condoning or condemning, you are placing your present ministry in jeopardy. So take your conferences as they come, enjoy them to the full, rest as much as possible, prepare and pray as much as necessary, and commit it all to the Lord.

Try not to be disappointed if you are in a conference for a week and receive no financial support as a result. This often happens. Yet God will supply your needs. And you may never know, this side of glory, of those whose hearts were touched by your messages and who have prayed for you daily, although they have never written you or sent you a gift.

When you are competing with many missionaries from many fields, never try to outdo them with sensational or gory tales, jokes, sympathetic appeals, or by trying to "ape" them or their techniques. As in every presentation, be strictly honest, present yourself, your Board, your field and your work as you see them and leave the service with the Lord to speak to the minds and hearts of people. Human persuasion is seldom successful. Stretching points to make them sound clever or productive may be picked up and examined and compared with the truth, to your utter dismay and embarrassment. Make no statements and give no examples which you cannot back up with evidence. And unless you are sure your facts are correct, better omit them. Hearsay evidence will not do.

Conferences can be a great learning experience. You meet folks from several areas of the world. Talk with them about their problems and how they solve them. Find out about their ministries. Discover recent trends in their policies. Learn about their fields. Discuss unique methods of missionary endeavor. Share your field with them. Missionaries can become very cloistered, knowing very little about the world of missions other than the work on their station or among their tribe. At conferences you can take in as well as giving out.

And at many conferences there is sufficient time for rest and relaxation. Happy is the missionary who is invited to a conference in Florida during November or February! Time for boating, fishing, swimming, sightseeing and sunbathing are offered while friends in the north are turning up the heat and shoveling snow. There are compensations for conference speakers!

If you are a missionary in the homeland, your ministry can be made as exciting to your hearers as that of anyone working anywhere in the world. Your service is on an equal with any other missionary. It has as much challenge, it produces as many results, and it needs as many workers as God can supply through those whom you have an opportunity to contact. You are, in no way, "among the least of these". In many instances, Christians are unaware of missionary work in their own country—even though it may be only 100 miles away. You have a unique opportunity to interest others and to challenge them to support such ministries.

QUESTIONS—CHAPTER 46

1. What differentiates a missionary conference from a single speaking engagement?

2. What types of questions should you have answered before becoming part of a planned missionary conference?

3. When you are a part of a conference, is it necessary to attend every formal and informal meeting scheduled for the week?

4. What are some of the ways in which you can receive from a conference rather than simply giving?

5. Should you ever turn down an invitation to be part of a missions conference? Why?

47
Honesty in Presentation

Missionaries are not dishonest people. They are Christians who have felt the call of God upon their lives for service in a full-time commitment either at home or abroad. They have been honest enough to admit to this call and have responded to it. Why, then, must we caution about honesty?

Admittedly, every individual sees a situation from a personal viewpoint. This is why witnesses at the scene of an accident give conflicting testimony. This is what makes debating teams function. This is what gives personality and flavor to human beings. But, in reality, it marks us as liberal or conservative, democratic or autocratic, right or wrong, broad-minded or biased, good or bad.

Sometimes in stressing a point, it is easy to alter statistics, create situations which are more fable than fact, and give false impressions of what is really happening on the field. Part of this is demanded by church groups. People in the homeland do not always understand why one missionary comes home boasting of thousands of converts and scores of churches while another comes home to confess the conversion of three souls, two of whom have backslidden and turned back to their former religion because of the pressures brought to bear upon them. If these two missionaries are scheduled to speak on the same platform or at the same conference, it is a temptation to make the one convert appear to be a giant of the faith, witnessing without reservation, and surely a jewel for the missionary's crown. Because facts have to be focused on such a small area of the work in order to magnify the one convert, many false impressions can be given.

For those who work in out-of-the-way places, it is easy to dwell on one tiny fragment of a small tribe, which is not especially typical of the rest of the country in which you work but you neglect to mention this. Urban workers speak of the city and neglect the rural work.

When showing slides, try to avoid the expression, "This is a typical . . . " It is confusing to supporting churches when you show a grass hut as being typical of your country and the next missionary from your area shows a brick house, declaring it is typical. The truth is, that depending upon what area you happen to be in, a certain scene is typical. But it may be entirely atypical when considering the entire country of which you are a part. Show your pictures and explain them, but try not to show "typical shots".

A missionary is, of course, supposed to be desperately unhappy in the homeland, and hardly able to wait for the day of return to his people. This may or may not be true. If you are enjoying the refreshment and rest of furlough days, you don't have to try to convince people you are out of your element away from the mission field. If you stress your desire to be back on the field openly and too often, it can embarrass the people or churches among whom you are presently fellowshipping, for they will feel that you find a lack in them. On the other hand, it could show a lack in you. Perhaps by stressing your longing to be back on the field, you are trying to convince yourself that you really feel that way when you don't. Analyze your attitude toward this matter and be sure that you honestly and conscientiously miss your work, your co-workers, and the nationals with whom you serve, or say nothing.

Some missionaries feel that when asked, even privately, if they have a need for additional support or equipment, their reply should be that "God has always met my needs, and He will continue to do so." This is your side of the picture, but this is no answer to one, who in all sincerity, wishes to enter into financial fellowship with a missionary. If, indeed, you have everything you need for support, travel and equipment, is it possible that you would appreciate a magazine subscription (Christian, general or technical), or some item of equipment which you hadn't mentioned to anyone, but had previously hoped to be able to obtain? It is not strictly honest to say you have everything you need if there is something you feel would be helpful in your ministry. If asked, give a truthful answer.

How do you describe your new country? What do you mention about the people? How do you speak about their present religions? Missionaries often give the impression that the natives lined the streets when they arrived, waiting with open arms to welcome these Christian workers, ready to give up their unsatisfying religion to accept the foreigner's good news of Jesus Christ. Is it wrong to confess to your prayer partners in the homeland that your arrival went unheralded (as did your recent departure); in fact, there was open opposition to your intrusion, and the "natives" were completely happy and satisfied with their own religion?

Why do missionaries insist on telling only of the victories they have encountered? Were there no defeats? Are you really telling it like it is, or are some facts hidden behind a facade of strength in and devotion to the Lord? Is He, in truth, the only thing that matters to you? Has it been easy to go where He has led? To say what He would have you say? To do what He asked you to do? To be all that He wanted you to be? Or perhaps you have dwelt on the despairing negatives and you have left your audiences with such a dark view of the work that they feel sorry for you and are assured that only failure can result from missionary efforts in your area.

A wise missionary doesn't tell everything he knows. He doesn't condemn his mission or his fellow-workers, or his own inability to adjust and get along with people. Discernment must be exercised along with honesty in deciding what should be said, and what should not be stated.

If you are involved in a missionary conference in a large city church, it is very possible that there will be one or more nationals from your field in your congregation. If you are not aware of their presence, you may give a very biased view of their country. If you sense their presence, you will do everything in your power to speak the truth in love and present a well-rounded picture. You can never be sure such people will not be among your hearers—another reason you should seek always to give a fair, accurate and truthful picture of your work.

You may also discover that one or more of your hearers has visited or worked in the country to which you have gone. They will already know the truth. If you are not completely honest, you are being unfair to your audience.

If a missionary asks another missionary, "What is your greatest problem on the field?", the answer 9 times out of 10 will be, "Getting along with people." If a lay person asks the same question, he can expect to hear "Lack of time", "Dishonest servants", "Lack of adequate transportation", "Illiteracy of the people", etc., etc. With whom are we honest? What was YOUR greatest problem on the field? Do not prayer partners deserve to know the truth so they can better pray intelligently?

Let's not try to fool ourselves in this matter of misrepresentation of facts. It can be dangerous and devastating. Honesty is, after all, the best policy.

QUESTIONS—CHAPTER 47

1. What is your definition of "honesty"?

2. In what areas of your life is there a temptation to be dishonest?

3. Should you bare your inner self to every group to whom you speak? Why?

4. How honest should you be if you are asked specific questions concerning an incendiary political issue, problems of a personal nature, or opinions concerning events which may be about to occur (church splits, electronic media problems, denominational differences, etc.)?

48
Courtesy and Gratitude

To remind missionaries of the need for gratitude and courtesy may appear to be unnecessary. Yet it affects so many vital relationships, it seems appropriate to emphasize it again and again. Unfortunately, there are those who feel they deserve the funds they receive from individuals and supporting churches since "the laborer is worthy of his hire." Therefore, little is said or done to show appreciation for the gifts which supply every need according to God's promise. If a supporter tires of this attitude of ingratitude, support may be dropped. By this it is not meant to be implied that missionaries should thank people merely that their support will be maintained at the proper level. This would be adding insult to injury. One could rationalize and determine that tithe money is due the Lord, and therefore, there is really no personal involvement just because it happens to be designated for your support. A good test of your appreciation for those who support you comes when, if you are under a mission which pools its support funds, you receive only 50% of your normal salary allowance. Do you fuss or complain? Do you find it more difficult to get through the month? Do you have to go without a few items you had planned on purchasing? Without a doubt, some thought is given to the fact that you have had an insufficient salary. But, on the other hand, when your full support is given month after month, are you as knowingly grateful as you were openly complaining? Think about this, and then be grateful for those who faithfully support you. Some of them will invest many thousands of dollars in you and your ministry through the years. They would like some response from their investment. If you are too busy to say "thank you", you are too busy! Now you are home does not relieve you of the responsibility of thanking your supporters for their continuing gifts.

You will be asking for meetings in various churches, or will be invited by pastors to take services during your furlough. If you are to speak at an evening service some distance from your home, it is never out of place to ask if overnight accommodations will be arranged. Along with this, be sure to specify how many individuals this will involve, along with the age and sex of children who may accompany you. If a church offers accommodations, but you have made previous arrangements, be very frank about explaining this. It is usually good, however, to stay with folks from the church you are visiting if at all possible since it gives you a closer tie with them. But, it may be necessary to stay with relatives or friends in the area whom you would otherwise not be able to visit during furlough.

When staying in homes providing hospitality for you, be as considerate as possible of your hosts. Don't make a shambles of your room by hanging, draping and dropping clothing, etc. on the bed, chairs and floor. If space is provided, hang clothing in the closet. Many articles can remain in your suitcase. If an iron is needed, ask your hostess for one and be sure to use it on her ironing board, not on her dresser. If you need to wash out a few articles, ask where you should hang them. Again, don't hang a wet shirt or dress in your room and let it drip all over the floor or rug. If you must have food snacks in your room, don't get the crumbs on the floor or in the bed. And in the morning, be sure to make your bed, or strip it at the request of your hostess.

If you are expected to arrive at a certain hour, and you are delayed en route, let your hosts know. Be sure to find out what arrangements have been made for your meals. If your host does not tell you what time breakfast is to be, ask. Be sure to carry an alarm clock with you when you travel. It is an essential part of furlough equipment. If you are arriving by plane or train and must be met, try to arrive and depart at reasonable hours to accommodate those responsible for your transportation.

Never complain about food which is served to you. If there must be restrictions in your diet, specify this in your original letter telling the time of your arrival. No one objects to leaving onions or salt out of their food, but no one condones complaints about items when there was no idea that these could not be tolerated favorably by you. Of course, if parsnips are served, and you just can't "go them", it's always polite to leave them untouched on your plate if they are served to you, or to pass them by if you have a choice. The usual complaint of furlough folks is that too many people feed them too well too often. If you are a guest in one home at noon and in another home for the evening meal, normally the family will serve their big meal when you are with them. This does not mean, however, that you must eat a huge meal at each sitting. Discipline in the matter of eating must be exercised. It will be a struggle because most things will be very tempting, and some of them you will not have been able to get on the field. Nevertheless, one helping should be the rule.

If you are travelling with your children, be sure your children are suitable houseguests. They should not be allowed to roam throughout the home, picking up and handling every item in sight. Small children cannot be expected to sit for four hours with their hands folded. Be sure to take games, coloring books, dolls, etc., for them to play with. If the children are undisciplined, you'd better plan not to bring them.

Most families who accommodate you, knowing your children will be with you, will make them feel at home. They may even spoil them. It is your privilege to specify the limits allowed.

In some cases, families will give up their own bedroom, or ship their children off to the neighbors to make room for you and your family. Be sincerely appreciative of all they do for you. Above all, remember that these people are sharing the best that they have with you. It is never in order to boast to them that "the last church we went to provided accommodations in a local Motel and it was fantastic." Or "a family in one of the churches we visited let us stay in their beautiful home for a week. They let us use their Cadillac, and the kids sure enjoyed the swimming pool and the boat on the lake." Nor, by the way, do you ever mention in meetings your visits to other churches, criticizing or commending them, nor do you describe people in those churches. Even though it may be hundreds of miles distant, someone in the congregation may just happen to know of whom or what you are speaking. When you are in a given community, your attention should be focused positively on the people there. Sides should never be taken in church disputes. Controversial subjects should not be discussed.

If you are taken to a restaurant for a meal, unless you are certain your hosts mean for you to do so, try to refrain from ordering the $14.50 steak. If possible, try to determine what they are going to eat, and limit yourself to that approximate price range. Some hosts will insist upon the most expensive meal, and if you are in agreement with their choice of the main dish, let them order it for you. But in other cases, if you do not know your hosts, it is far better to order what you really like in a lower price category. If your children are with you, be sure to order something they enjoy. Order a child's plate if a full meal contains too much food. And never discourage a hamburger or hot dog if this is what the child enjoys most.

If you are invited to a church, and already have other meetings in the area, be sure to tell the pastors of each church. Sometimes you will arrive in an area for one meeting and the church will ask you to stay for another service. The courtesy of telling your plans beforehand will help your host church to plan more adequately and intelligently.

You have been out of the country for quite some time. You now live "out there" in a land where people are brutally frank and outspoken. Remember when you return home that it is not at all polite to admire someone's suit or dress and then ask how much they paid for it. Try to remember the courtesies of your own culture.

Some of you will have friends who send out your prayer letters for you. This involves keeping your address list updated, preparing envelopes, getting your letter typed, printed, stuffed, sealed, stamped and mailed. If you've been taking this friend or these friends for granted, be sure to put out your own letters during furlough—especially if you have over 500 on your mailing list. You will discover how much work and expense is involved, and it will make you appreciate this service to a far greater extent. Be sure to give an indication as to how many times a year you expect to send out a letter. Also, if your friend should be moving, save your letter until the move is completed. Never send a letter less than a month before Christmas and expect it to be in the mail before the holiday. Be helpful and courteous in these details.

If someone has offered to pay for your prayer letters, you may find a church or an organization which will do the actual sending. Even in this case, don't send a letter every month just because someone else is paying for it. Four times a year is maximal. Once a year is minimal.

If, during furlough, you have special favors done for you, be sure to give a token of appreciation to the one(s) responsible by means of a gift or a sincere note of thanks. But do not overlook these blessings bestowed upon you. Some of these favors might include care by a doctor, dentist or lawyer; discounts in stores; mechanical work on your car; housing; food; use of a gasoline credit card; courses at local educational institutions; admission to refresher workshops and seminars; toys for the children; gifts of equipment for yourself or your mission, etc.

Each time word reaches you that support or personal gifts have been received for your account, write a brief card or note of thanks.

No one is obliged to support you, but their willingness to do so should receive a response of gratitude from you. Perhaps close friends have a part in your support. Don't neglect to thank them, too. It's even easier to take their gifts for granted than those received from strangers.

Always thank a church publicly for allowing you the privilege of being with them. People like to be appreciated. It takes little effort, but it can encourage an otherwise disinterested group.

Sometimes Christians expect more from the preacher's kids than they do from other children. They also seem to expect more from missionaries than from other Christians. Although we may have gone too far in that direction, nevertheless, it stands to reason that missionaries need both to receive and to give a fair share of gratitude and courtesy. If these do not come naturally to you, be sure to work at it. Without them, your furlough ministry will be thwarted and unfruitful. With them, people will be attracted to you and the Lord will be glorified in your life.

QUESTIONS—CHAPTER 48

1. What kinds of treatment deserve gratitude?

2. How can you show courtesy to a host/hostess when you are in his/her home?

3. What special courtesies should you observe concerning meals which are served to you?

4. Should young children be included in your deputation travels? Why?

5. In what ways can you show your gratitude for those who support you financially?

49
Communication With the Field

During your furlough time, it is extremely important to keep up with happenings on the field. If you are in a leadership position, this is imperative, since you may be responsible for making important decisions affecting the work on the field. If you are not in an administrative capacity, you will want to keep the field informed concerning your definite plans for return and ideas you would like to investigate. Depending upon the type of control within your Board, you will be expected to comply with orders from the field and the Home Office, or be able to write very freely concerning your goals for your next term of service. You should keep in contact with your co-workers to receive up-to-date news from your area. You may wish to correspond with nationals.

Correspondence will never take the place of actually being in a situation. It can be very biased and one-sided. If you are on the scene, you know all the "little" things that surround each happening affecting you. But when such events are put on paper by a fellow-missionary or a national, they can appear warped and twisted; overly optimistic or pessimistic. You must take into consideration that letters can only give you a general ,one-person opinion about any given situation.

Your own role in communication should be to encourage and enlighten. No matter how you think your station must be run in your absence, be sure to give a fair amount of freedom in the work. Furlough time should not be a continual worry about how poorly your station is being handled in your absence. Do not write remarks to nationals which degrade the work or the workers. Do not try to have them lean heavily upon you, but encourage them to trust the Lord, each other and their missionary partners.

If you have grudges against anything or anyone, do not let your feelings out on paper to avoid a direct confrontation with the person or persons involved. Communications via the written word are easily misinterpreted.

There are countries today where letters can, at the discretion of the ruling government, be censored or confiscated. There must be a great deal of discretion used in written communications, especially in troubled countries of the world. Your personal feelings—even your ideas of your country's feelings about the land in which you work—should not be stated. Criticism of your adopted country, no matter how slight, should be avoided. When this type of information falls into the wrong hands, it can cause missions to be in jeopardy of losing their entry privileges. Magazine and newspaper articles concerning extremely sensitive areas should not be sent to friends in those countries. Until you return, it is probably best for the U.S. Information Service to relay their interpretation (or interpolation) of these matters.

Even though a national may be a very close friend in whom you feel you may confide, never write in criticism of your mission or its missionaries. Even among strong Christian national believers, it is a temptation to destroy the effectiveness of the ministry of the foreigner. Nationalism can be very strong to these believers. They may have every right to believe that their own people can do the job as well as, if not better than, the missionary.

On the other hand, do not ignore your national brethren just because you are away from them. You can continue to have a ministry to them through this means of communication. It may be difficult for you to understand their language. It may be even harder for you to write a meaningful letter in their language. But this contact can be profitable as they understand you have not forgotten them even though you have parted for a while. If nothing better can be arranged, send a letter to a missionary colleague which can be read to specific national friends or to a group of believers.

Many of our problems come from lack of communication—even when we are in a group and can speak face to face. Often very serious situations can be avoided if you will take the time to keep in touch with the field. If you are not a writer, become one. Determine to become involved. Perhaps you need to clarify an issue, or receive clarification of an event or policy. Perhaps you merely want some word concerning a project you began or how the building is progressing, or how many attended the deeper life conference. By all means, do not lose contact with the field while you are away from it. You may not be told all the struggles and problems, but you can obtain information. You do not have to become personally involved in other's trials except through the ministry of prayer. Seek honestly to have this continuing fellowship.

Some of you may be fortunate enough to have a friend or neighbor who is a ham radio operator. If it is possible to contact your field in this way, ask for the privilege of doing so through your friend. Although business matters cannot be handled in this fashion, it is a convenient way to get routine news items concern what's going on in your work, on your field and at your station.

If you are in the homeland for a full year, much will be happening on your station which needs to be updated in your furlough presentations. If you receive no news from your colleagues overseas in any given month, be sure to contact your Board to ask for the latest news from your area.

QUESTIONS—CHAPTER 49

1. What types of communication should you expect to receive from your field during furlough?

2. What types of communication should you plan to send to your field during your furlough?

3. What kinds of situations should be avoided in your overseas communications?

4. Why is communication with your field important during your absence?

50
Prayer Cards

When you were first accepted by your Board, you hastened to have prayer cards printed for distribution. This is no less necessary during your furlough period. You have changed! You may have had additions to your family. Interested prayer partners and supporters will appreciate an up-dated reminder. And while you are having a picture taken for your prayer reminder cards, be sure to obtain a copy for the Home Office of your Mission. These are often used in the annual prayer bulletin, or in other literature. Some missions use a picture in their periodical when you return to the field. Many Home Offices keep a bulletin board with pictures of missionaries. Perhaps you have noted annual prayer bulletins from other missions (or perhaps your own) where some of the pictures, even of the administrative and home staff, have not been changed for ten years. Don't let this be the case with you.

When preparing your prayer card, be sure it contains the following information:

1. Your picture

2. Your name

3. Your address (on the field)

4. Your Mission's name

5. Your Mission's address

6. Where you will be serving

It is possible that you know exactly what your work will be upon your return to the field. If so, this can be included in print or by means of a line drawing or graphic art.

As upon your acceptance, your prayer card will need to be well-planned. The color(s), type of stock (heavy, light, coated), style (wallet size, bookmark, 2- or 3-fold, stand-up, special cut such as praying hands, airplane, nurses cap, map) formal invitation type, flat, printed on one or both sides, must be decided. Do you want a Scripture verse imprinted? A map? In these considerations, remember that you are to produce something that will cause people to think specifically of YOU and YOUR ministry. It must be uniquely yours. Set your goals as to their purpose(s). Find a good printer who will work with you to communicate exactly what you desire through the finished product.

Perhaps you have proper facilities on your field to have the cards printed before you reach the homeland. If so, you may wish to enclose them with a letter from the field announcing your forthcoming furlough. Or you may wish to carry them with you for distribution in your early meetings. This would be most appropriate if you have only a short furlough. Some Boards have a set pattern for their prayer cards. If so, it may be necessary for you to correspond with the Home Office to make arrangements. If a recent picture is sent to them, they may be able to have the reminders ready for you upon arrival at home.

You must decide on the method of distribution of your reminders. Consider:

1. Enclosing one in a prayer letter sent upon your arrival in the homeland.

2. Put them on the display or literature table in you meetings for general distribution.

3. Have people sign up for one, allowing you a confirming letter to them after your departure from their presence, enclosing the card. This is good follow-up procedure and maintains an otherwise casual contact.

4. Send them in letters to pastors requesting speaking engagements.

5. Enclose one in each thank-you letter written to those who provide hospitality during your tour of deputation.

6. Give them only to those who promise prayer and financial support.

7. Send them in a letter in a general mailing just prior to or upon your departure for the field.

You will want to leave a supply of cards at your Home Office. There are occasions when churches request the names of missionaries for whom they can pray or in whom they can have a financial interest. The Board will then be able to supply a reminder of you which helps cement their decision. Supporting churches will sometimes request a number of cards for a missionary conference or special emphasis meeting. Always leave at least a dozen copies with your Home Office. If you have a packet left over when you return to the field, leave them, too. You have no further use for them. If your Board cannot use or store them, they may discard them after a reasonable time, but in the meanwhile, they are available if requested.

In many instances, the cost of prayer cards is a legitimate expense which can be taken from the work account set up for you. Some Boards take the expense from General Funds if it is mission policy to require cards. For a few, the expense will be borne from the support account, personal funds, or by the gift of an interested friend.

Prayer cards are an effective communicative aid in maintaining the interest of God's people in you and your ministry. Distribute them carefully and prayerfully.

QUESTIONS—CHAPTER 50

1. Because of the expense of prayer cards, is it essential for you to utilize them? Is there an alternative?

2. What does a prayer card do for you? For those to whom they are given?

3. How do you plan to distribute these visual reminders of you and your ministry?

4. What suggestions can you give to friends concerning the use of your prayer cards?

5. Design a sample prayer card which you will be able to use during your furlough time.

51
Legal, Medical and Dental Matters

Be sure all your papers are in order before leaving the field, since your return may depend upon this. Some countries give a "No objection to return" document. Others demand it. All income tax should be cleared. Residence papers updated, health certificates signed, passports put in order, visas renewed and departure papers duly signed by the appropriate officials. Upon arrival home, these papers should be kept in a safe place so they can be taken with you upon your return to the field.

Upon arrival home there are papers which need to be checked and brought up to date as necessary.

Your WILL should be considered. Perhaps you went to the field single and are now coming home married with a family. Codicils may need to be added or a new will made (the latter probably being the best method). Some Boards have a mission lawyer, or may undertake to provide this service to missionaries. Or your home church or a supporting church may have a lawyer who would be willing to provide this service to you. For some, there may need to be changes in beneficiaries or executor. If, for some reason, you went to the field originally with no official will on file, be sure to take care of this matter at once. For those with children who are not yet of age, it is imperative, for your peace of mind, to specify a guardian in the event they should be orphaned. Some states require that a will be made out in your legal state of residence with an executor named from that state. Be sure to look into these specifics and abide by them so your will becomes legal.

Consider your INSURANCE policy(ies). Do you have living beneficiaries named? Do you want to change your beneficiary(ies)? Do you have sufficient insurance to meet your needs? If your Mission carries insurance on your life, decide whether or not you need additional coverage. If you are a doctor, nurse, or other sueable professional, be certain you have obtained LIABILITY INSURANCE before you depart for the field. It may seem unnecessary, but it is absolutely imperative in the day in which we live and serve.

If you gave your POWER OF ATTORNEY to an individual when

you departed for the Field, have you been satisfied with your choice, or should a change be made? In any event, it should be given to one in whom you trust so that legal matters concerning you can be cared for in your absence without the delay, bother, or possibility of loss which comes from sending legal papers to the field to be signed and returned.

Look at your PASSPORT to see when it expires. It is usually far easier to renew it in the homeland than on the field. Don't leave this until your last month of furlough!

VISAS AND ENTRANCE PAPERS will probably be cared for by your Board at the appropriate time so they can be cleared before your furlough is finished. Early attention to this important matter will expedite your return on time. Visas for many countries are being delayed or withheld. Pray much that God will overrule in the obtaining of these vital affidavits.

You will probably have questions concerning SOCIAL SECU-RITY and INCOME TAX. If your Home Office cannot answer your questions concerning these matters, be sure to have a conference with your nearest Social Security Office and/or your Internal Revenue Service Agency.

If you have neglected to keep up a DRIVER'S LICENSE in the homeland, do not drive until it is legal for you to do so. Some States allow renewal in spite of a lapse. Others may require a written examination and/or road test. Many renewals now also require a picture for identification and a sight and hearing test. Check with your local Office of Motor Vehicles concerning this matter.

PROFESSIONAL LICENSES must also be kept in force. If, through error or carelessness, you have allowed your license to lapse, be sure to find out the procedure for becoming reinstated. Contact the Board of Registration in the state(s) in which you are currently licensed. Never practice on a lapsed license! If you are a teacher, you may need to obtain recertification (which may require taking a course of study at a local college). These professional responsibilities are extremely important to care for.

Your HEALTH CARD will continue to be a constant companion to your passport. Keep your immunizations up-to-date.

If you had no need for a BANK ACCOUNT upon your initial departure for the field, you may wish to open one now. It may be best to have your Home Office treasurer's name on your account. In this way he can transact business for you at your request. (Or you may prefer to have a relative or friend care for banking matters for you). It is important to have an account if you need to pay bills, purchase items to be sent to you, or you wish tomake deposits toward your children's education, etc.

Have a copy of your BIRTH CERTIFICATE, ORDINATION PAPER, COMMISSIONING, and/or RECOMMISSIONING PAPER and MARRIAGE CERTIFICATE (if applicable) available.

Caring for these legal matters is essential. Check on them periodically to make sure they are properly cared for.

Most missions require their missionaries to have a complete physical examination, including lab work, just before leaving the field (if there is a good medical set-up in your area) or immediately upon arrival in the homeland by an appointed mission doctor or your own physician (with reports sent to your Home Office). It is a testimony to the grace of God that these reports are often remarkably normal. If, however, there is a physical problem, prompt attention should be given to it. Other problems may be discovered which will require extensive treatment or surgery. Discovering this at the beginning of furlough helps in planning for the days and weeks ahead. This is especially essential for those who have chosen the short term, short furlough. It is also wise to have a complete check-up before returning to the field—especially if you are home for 9 months or a year.

Although the physical examination is usually a must, a dental examination may not be required. For your own health and the preservation of your teeth, be sure to have your dental needs cared for early in your furlough with a final check just before leaving for the field. Good dentists are few and far between on many fields unless you are stationed in a large, modern city.

Unless your Board is responsible for your medical and dental bills, you will be shocked at the expense of a complete physical or a partial plate. If you receive personal salary of $500 per month, and you have a tooth capped for $350, you may be tempted to despair. Your bills may run to $2000 or more for a family of four in a very short time, and your medical insurance covers none of it. You might want to obtain dental insurance, but may find it very costly, considering what it covers and the short time you will be at home. You will be tempted to get the most work for the lowest price. But unless a Christian doctor or dentist is willing to provide such services at greatly reduced prices, or as a contribution, it is probably wisest to get the best care for the price asked. It will mean truly trusting the Lord for funds to cover the expense, but He never says, "I will provide all your needs except for medical and dental expenses!"

It is always in order to ask professional men if they give a discount to those in the ministry. Many have such a policy. But never demand this. And in good faith, pay your bills as promptly as possible. Few doctors or dentists complain if you make arrangements beforehand to pay $5 or $10 per month on your bill. But be sure to follow through on this. It may be necessary for you to arrange with your Home Office to withhold the required amount from your support each month which will be sent to fulfill your obligation.

If an operation is necessary and you carry appropriate insurance, the doctor may be willing to charge only the amount covered by insurance for his services. Again, do not demand this, and if you are left with a large personal bill, it is your responsibility to pay it by whatever means possible. Professional men deserve to be paid for their services and it is up to you to honor their bills with payment. Your Board may allow you to request special funds from supporters to help meet your medical, surgical, and/or dental needs.

Those of you with children will be tempted to get their teeth checked by an orthodontist. Remember that the straightening of teeth can be a long process. Before opting for braces, check to see how often they have to be checked and approximately how long they will be needed, as well as the cost of the entire project. Parents and children appreciate straight teeth, but other factors must be taken into consideration. How long is your furlough? Is the work worth the time and expense involved? Will it make a major improvement? Is it a necessary procedure? Is there opportunity for follow-up on the field to which you are assigned?

Some individuals put off required treatment because (1) they are too busy; (2) it is too expensive; (3) they feel it isn't essential; (4) they're scared. (What will the biopsy show? What if the anesthesia has an adverse effect? What if it's worse than it appears? I don't like to take medicine). None of these reasons seems valid when you measure the preventive or curative factors of treatment with a long and physically successful missionary career. Certainly your children deserve the very best treatment in this regard, too.

Some of you are frail and always will be. Others are strong and feel nothing will change that. But it is the responsibility of each individual to look to his Heavenly Father for health and strength in the greatest degree possible. Your body is the temple of the Holy Spirit. It is your body which makes it possible for you to take the Gospel to those to whom God has sent you. Make sure, then, this temple is in the best possible condition physically, mentally and emotionally, as well as spiritually.

QUESTIONS—CHAPTER 51

1. What legal matters do you need to care for during your furlough?

2. For how many years is a U.S. passport valid?

3. How is a U.S. passport renewed?

4. Why is it important to have a valid professional license if you are in a profession that requires licensure?

5. Why is a complete physical and dental examination important when you arrive for furlough?

6. If surgery should be indicated, what arrangements will you need to make in regard to your original furlough plans?

52
Records, Reports and Financial Affairs

Paper work is an essential part of the present world system, and missionaries, too, must comply with the rules. It is time consuming, sometimes frustrating, often monotonous. But it is still necessary. Therefore, the best way to attack it is to keep your records and reports up-to-date. If you let a month lapse and then try to figure out how many miles you travelled, how much toll was payed, how much was received in your meetings, etc., it will be an impossible job. The easiest way to keep accurate records, of course, is to carry a small notebook in your pocket, purse, or the glove compartment of your car. Jot down pertinent information when it happens. Then it is simply a matter of transferring this information to report sheets supplied by your mission, or to plain typing paper. JUST A REMINDER! **Make someone very happy. TYPE YOUR REPORTS, IF POSSIBLE!** Otherwise, be sure to write or print legibly.

Most missions ask for a monthly report of meetings, expenditures and offerings. Whenever you send checks to the Home Office to be receipted, be sure to identify specifically where the receipt should be sent, i.e., name, full address, zip code, and name of the church or group. Be sure it is properly designated, also. Always ask for this essential information whenever you are presented with funds. You may wish to send the offerings to the office as soon as you receive them rather than waiting to send your monthly report. This assures the donors of prompt receipting. It also means you are not responsible for a large number of checks. Never send cash to the Home Office. Usually you will have a checking account while on furlough. If possible, deposit the cash and send your personal check to cover it. Or you may wish to use the cash and send the check from your account. Always be sure you indicate to your Home Office complete information concerning the donor and the designation of the gift when you send your own check in place of cash.

When sending reports to the office, be sure the amount of your report and the total of your checks tally. If funds have been expended, write a letter explaining this. There are occasions when money has been used for a legitimate item of equipment, and although it is not available as cash, it must be receipted. Try to avoid a situation of this nature since legally the mission should not receipt funds not passing through its hands. The usual procedure is to send the funds for receipting and ask for a mission check by return mail. If it is imperative that you spend funds, you might send the mission a personal check, asking them to return it by mission check to your account.

Sometimes people give you gifts through the church. In that case, a receipt is sent to the church. If a personal receipt should be issued, indicate this, giving full name, address and zip code of the donor. It is not possible to send a receipt to a donor when the church has already received a receipt for that gift. For income tax purposes, the donor must get evidence from the church, not the mission, in such cases.

If funds are needed for travel, equipment or reimbursement, send a letter, or a form to your Home Office indicating how much is needed and why. Ordinarily you will not be able to receive funds if those funds are not in your account. The only exception would be that support and housing will be given even though the account is in the red, but is is understood that the missionary cannot return to the field until his account is in the black and sufficient support funds have been promised for his coming term of service. (Not every Board makes this exception).

Medical reports should be submitted to the Home Office upon arrival in the homeland. If there are items to be cared for, the missionary will not be allowed to return to the field until he has medical clearance.

If an extension of furlough or leave of absence is anticipated for health, family or educational purposes, be sure to obtain approval from the Home Office well in advance of your previously designated date of return and notify the Field office. There may also be times when a missionary is assigned to special service in his homeland to fill a need in the Office or in representation. This should have both field and Home Office approval, as well as the full approval of the missionary.

In your reports, be sure to give addresses where you may be reached most quickly during furlough. Sometimes this will consist of your tentative itinerary. At times your home address will be the best contact. But it is essential that you apprise the Home office of your location at all times, for forwarding mail, sending monthly checks and reimbursements, and for emergency purposes.

You will, from time to time, meet those who have a general interest in your mission and will want to be placed on the mailing list to receive mailings. Be sure to obtain the proper title (Mr., Mrs., Miss, Ms. Rev., Dr., Prof., etc.), full name, correct address (including Box or Route number where applicable) and correct zip code. Your Home Office will have their files set up by zip code, so this is an essential item. Ordinarily, donors to the mission will receive mission literature on a regular basis.

Mission offices are usually in the market for articles or news from your field. Don't be afraid to submit copy and pictures for possible publication. Often you will be asked for such information upon your arrival in the homeland.

In your personal report notebook, it is good to make a notation of what you spoke about, what scripture you used, and what audio-visuals were utilized at each meeting. It is possible that before furlough is over, you may be asked to return to the same church, and how embarrassing it would be to repeat your previous message!

Among reports which are necessary are the prayer or newsletters. Even though you are at home, it is essential to keep friends and supporters informed as to your location, work, needs and prayer requests. And, of course, these "form" letters will not take the place of personal "thank you" notes to those who contribute to your support.

Your Home Office must be kept informed as to your support standing. Before return to the field is approved, a list of all donors and amounts pledged must be sent to the office. If support is below par, confer with your Board concerning it. In most cases today, missions must insist on minimum support being fully pledged before return to the field.

If personal gifts are given to you and the donor requests no receipt, they do not have to be reported to the office. Personal gifts can be receipted, but must be clearly identified as not being deductible for income tax purposes. It is your responsibility to explain this to those who insist on giving personal gifts. Many do not understand what is and what is not tax deductible.

Usually, if you take a full-time position for your furlough period, you are allowed (1) to keep the money you receive from your work for salary and living expenses and not accept monthly allowance from the mission, or (2) live on your monthly mission allowance, sending each pay check from your work to be credited to your account. The latter method is usually used when a account is in the red and must be built up before return to the field, or when a missionary is mainly self-supporting. It is also employed when a missionary insists on working rather than becoming involved in deputation work.

If you are requested to do deputation on behalf of the mission, you are usually reimbursed for travel, but funds received from your speaking go to the mission rather than to your support account.

If you are planning to visit the Home office, and this should be a requirement, let the staff know of your arrival well in advance so they can make arrangements for transportation and housing.

If you notice from monthly reports sent from the Home Office that your funds seem to be depleting faster at home than they did overseas, it is probably due to the fact that your monthly allowance has been increased during your time of furlough. This means additional funds from deputation must be obtained to keep your account solvent.

Financial and medical clearance will be required before you will be allowed to prepare to return to the field. Close communication with the Home Office, therefore, is vital.

Some of these matters will seem trivial and unimportant. But so that the mission can carry on in a business-like manner, it is absolutely essential for each missionary to bear his part of the paper work.

Don't let it discourage you.

QUESTIONS—CHAPTER 52

1. When checks are given to you at deputation meetings, should they be made out to you, or to your mission board? Why?

2. Make up a sample financial sheet to send to your Home Office. Include all monies received as well as all expenditures for the month of October.

3. Why is it important to keep a complete record of each of your meetings, your presentation, audio-visuals utilized, and the dates of your engagements?

4. Should a missionary be required to do deputation work? If not, what kinds of reports need to be sent to the Home Office?

53
Seeking New Workers

You will have many opportunities to be with and talk with people—Christian people—during your furlough time. It was once thought that if you wanted to interest workers in the field, you had to challenge high school and college-age young people. This is no longer true in the strictest sense. Missions no longer look only for the Bible College graduates and those just out of other institutions of higher education. Men and women in their late 20's and 30's, and even older, are now being sought to fill positions of need on the field. Short-term workers are found among young and old.

Voluntary services are being rendered by countless numbers of retired individuals. As a knowledgeable member of your Mission, and representative from your field, you should have, at your finger tips, a list of personnel needs. You will speak of these in your meetings and in your conversation with individuals. You will be able to explain the type of work which needs to be done. You will stand by your Mission and its policies, not condemning. You will emphasize to those who may be interested that age is no longer an all-determining factor. (Some missions have found older workers more ready and eager to adjust than some younger ones. They have not been severely handicapped by not learning the language in their younger years. And the very fact that they have several years of experience in their specialized training in the homeland can be of inestimable value on the field.)

Young people want a challenge. They do not expect an easy life. They want to know there is a place they can fill, a need for them as individuals and as Christian workers, and a task that they can do.

As you talk with young people, you may be amazed at their intelligent and academic approach to the matter of missions. Depending upon your own age and background, you may be surprised at the simplicity, reality, truthfulness and forthrightness of today's inquiring young man or woman. And, by the way, their appearance will not determine if this is an interested inquirer who should be encouraged to approach your Board concerning service!

Young people are looking for reality in the world, and they are especially looking for it in you. No longer can you gloss over the hardships and even the mistakes missions have made. Youth want answers which are straight from the shoulder and true to fact. They are not interested in pretty Christian cliches. They are not primarily impressed with stories that have happy endings. They are less concerned with material benefits and salary than the fact there is a work for them to do, they are needed to do it, and they can find satisfaction in their role.

Young college people are going to expect certain things from you. They want to be heard. They have questions, and will expect you to have an awareness of their problems, and the issues which are vital concerns to them (social reform, race relations, women's rights, the new morality, war, etc.). They will also expect you to be fully apprised of the work of your own Mission, the conditions (political, social, religious) in the country where you serve, your mission's strategy, your personal philosophy of missionary endeavor, and the theological implications of ecumenicity. They will ask about open doors, closed doors, unreached people. They will ask what work needs tobe done, and how much financial remuneration they will receive.

Although you may not be an intellectual or have expertise in the knowledge of world affairs, you will be expected to have, and voice, an opinion on a wide range of subjects. To today's young people, a missionary must be more than a dedicated worker who preaches the Gospel of Jesus Christ.

The message you give to young people in seeking workers, must be Bible based, but related to things as they are. The matter of becoming personally involved in a cause which gives meaning both to the missionary and to the work which he does cannot be stressed too much. You must be bold and honest in your approach. You will want to explain "old" and "common" Christian words in new ways so they lose none of their effectiveness, but are also meaningful to youth. Remember, many of the young people you talk with will not be members of a local church, and may have their own reasons for not joining one. This will need to be discussed in a loving and scriptural manner.

You have the possibility of seeking out a number of qualified workers for your agency. Some may be just now deciding on their life's work. Others may be finishing college and deciding what mission would best meet their needs. Some may be long out of school, but experienced in the pursuit of their profession. Others may have retired from business but still have a number of years of service to give to the

Lord. Some may have abilities which would be extremely helpful in the Home Office. Answer questions which are put to you and then be sure to emphasize the need for them to contact your Candidate or Personnel Secretary for full details and an application blank. You may even have an opportunity to direct individuals to other mission agencies, thus increasing the missionary force among specific people groups. Next to leading a soul to a saving knowledge of Jesus Christ, helping to turn a life toward the mission field is probably the greatest joy for a Christian.

QUESTIONS—CHAPTER 53

1. How much responsibility should you, a missionary on furlough, take upon yourself to seek qualified workers for your Board and/ or your field?

2. In what areas of overseas ministry can retired persons become involved?

3. List the 10 most important things you would tell a college student who is inquiring about service with your Mission.

4. What direction would you give to a girl in her senior year of high school who asks, "What can I do on the mission field and what kind of training should I get to prepare myself to become a missionary?"

5. What advice would you give to a young man with a B.A. in History, whose only real interest is in boating?

54
Additional Studies

Now that you have actually been in your missionary situation for a while, you are better able to determine the educational requirements demanded of you. Some of you went to the field with a minimum of one year of intensive Bible School training plus a minimal degree in your specialty because it was required by your Board. Now you find (1) the government of your host country demands a higher degree for you to continue receiving entry papers, or (2) your work demands more extensive training in a specific field of knowledges and skills. You are not keen on further studies, nor are you merely looking for initials after your name, but you realize the necessity for up-dating and furthering your educational capabilities. Continuing education (life-long learning) is a necessity in the day in which we live.

Let's take, for example, the case of an engineer working in communications on the field. The store of scientific and technical knowledge and techniques involved in applying it have changed and expanded rapidly. Most engineers find it difficult to cope with these ever-increasing development. Technological obsolescence is making retraining of engineers imperative.

Although it seems reasonable that engineers could keep up with progress in their field through literature, because of new breakthroughs in mathematics and physics with which the engineer is unfamiliar, he is not able to comprehend the methodologies and technologies which are built thereupon. He may not have studied Matrix Algebra or Set and Ring Theory. He may need to learn a great deal about computers and computerized operations. No longer can an individual be fully trained for a lifetime of engineering service.

If an engineer seeks to delve into Research and Development, his needs for additional education will be increased over those who are employed in Operations, although the latter would need periodic refresher courses in mathematics and/or the physical sciences. If engineers do not keep pace with the movement of their profession, they may be forced to alter their role and become skilled technicians, working under younger men who are better trained in engineering. If the entire engineering staff suffers from technical obsolescence, the work being done will suffer severe setbacks, few new ideas will be instituted, and advance will be impossible. Thus continual professional education must be the norm for successful engineers and the advance of missionary communication media.

Medicine is another field in which progress is so rapidly producing new medicines, new surgical procedures, and new techniques, that a doctor cannot hope to keep up with his field through literature alone. If he were a specialist and could stay within the confines of his specialty, he would have the benefits of his specialty magazines and taped series which are being produced constantly to up-date him. But missionary doctors, in most field situations, are general practitioners and/or general surgeons, treating not only all kinds of diseases and symptoms, but often having to deal with situations in which they have had no prior training (leprosy, elephantiasis, dysenteries, black water fever, etc.). Time is limited for gaining knowledge through literature on the field, too.

A nurse often finds she is ill-equipped for the many-faceted responsibility of caring for patients. She may be in a place where she must undertake minor surgical procedures, diagnose in place of a doctor, supervise a training school for nurses, institute in-service programs, administrate a hospital, set up an intensive care unit, a cardiac unit or special care nursery, become an anesthetist or be involved in radiology. Some nurses will go to the field with a 2-or 3-year Nursing education background and others with a 4- or 5-year B.S. in Nursing, or an M.S. specialization. But with the shortage of staff, the nurse is forced into situations beyond those in which she is knowledgeable and comfortable. She is forced to think in terms of additional training. In some cases, the host country is demanding more qualified nurses to take leadership roles in training and supervising national nurses, while general nursing is being cared for by trained nationals.

Other professionals will find the same need for advanced or further training in their specialties. Missions are aware of the fact that if they are going to provide a service in the areas where they work, their missionaries must be as fully trained as possible. Technology from various parts of the world is filtering or flooding into smaller nations which once needed whatever small help the missionaries could give them. Today, help is more easily and readily available. Thus it is imperative that missionaries maintain the highest possible standards in every field, not only as a testimony to the Lord, but to uphold their place of respect in world evangelism.

Since more and more the place of the missionary is becoming that of one who trains national leadership, it is imperative that adequate knowledge be transmitted to qualified nationals. Thus, when a missionary is on furlough, there is time for seeking God's will concerning further education. You must ask yourself some questions: What are my specific needs? Where and how can they be met? How long will it take? How much will it cost? Are refresher courses available? Will short seminars serve my purpose? Will working in my professional capacity in the homeland update me in processes and procedures sufficiently to prepare me for further service? Am I in a training capacity? Is my basic knowledge sufficient in the field in which I am engaged?

Some will feel the answer must be a leave of absence for educational purposes. Others will feel they are highly enough qualified for their positions. Perhaps one of the areas of missionary work which is most neglected is that of administration. Very few men and women in places of leadership have had training in administration, counseling, interpersonal relations, management, supervision, psychology, or other related fields. There are excellent short courses, training programs, and workshops/seminars being held throughout the world today in these subject areas. Anyone in a leadership role on the field should take advantage of some means of understanding their responsibilities. Too long, untrained personnel have been given administrative responsibilities without their roles and functions ever being defined and with no training being offered. One problem is that the nature of management is significantly different in a mission organization. The annual IFMA Mission Administrators Seminar is outstanding in the help it offers.

It is becoming increasingly apparent that there is a need for individuals with advanced studies in missions itself (i.e., missiology), and its mission-oriented components such as anthropology, cross-cultural studies, biblical and theological education by extension, church growth, unreached peoples, and all areas of communication. It would be well to look into programs of this nature which are offered by The U.S. Center for World Mission, Missionary Internship, The Billy Graham Center, Columbia Graduate School of Bible and Missions, as well as (increasingly) at many of the standard evangelical seminaries such as Trinity Evangelical Divinity School, Dallas Theological Seminary, and Fuller Theological Seminary. BIOLA University now has a graduate School of Intercultural Studies. Bethel College and Seminary (Minneapolis) have an unusually large number of faculty members with mission field experience. Be on the lookout for new developments everywhere. Do not overlook workshops and seminars in any of these specific fields just mentioned, or other short term courses.

A most welcome trend is for U.S. evangelical schools to offer graduate courses to missionaries while they are still on the field (e.g., Wheaton College and Azusa Pacific). One school, founded and headed up by experienced missionaries, which emphasises field-based education, is The William Carey International University, associated with The U.S. Center for World Mission. Even its undergraduate program sends students overseas six months each year. The greater proportion of its Ph.D. candidates are overseas; all are missionaries or national leaders.

Again, many things must be considered when thinking of further education, whether formal or informal learning. Your length of furlough, home base, need for active deputation work, health situation, family needs, as well as the needs of your Mission as a whole must be considered. Consider it carefully. Pray about it. Discuss it with your mission leaders, and act in the best interests of the Lord's work through you, in your mission, on your field.

QUESTIONS—CHAPTER 54

1. What would you now suggest to your Board should be the minimal educational experience for a candidate applying to your Board as a nurse?

2. What are the advantages of taking a leave of absence for educational purposes? The disadvantages?

3. Is it important for those in mission leadership positions to obtain formal academic education in administration? Why?

4. What do you feel is appropriate educational preparation for a church planting missionary?

55
Return Outfit Allowance and Purchases

Many Mission Boards have set guidelines concerning the amount of money which the returning missionary is allowed to spend on equipment and outfit. Unfortunately, in too many cases, these allowances have not been revised periodically and the amounts listed may be quite unrealistic when purchasing is begun. If the guidelines do not take individual fields and living conditions into consideration, you may need to request the expenditure of more funds for your particular circumstances. On the other hand, you may find you are able to get by with far less than you are allowed.

As one who has been on the field, you are aware of items which cannot be purchased there. You already have items which will not need to be replaced. (Some missionaries hold to the policy that they will sell all their goods to other missionaries before leaving the field. This means they can purchase everything new for their next term. It also means if they should, for some reason, not be able to return to the field, they would have no unfinished personal business overseas.)

Except, however, for items which are obsolete or not useful to you, those which would deteriorate during your absence, or those which are ready for replacement, it seems quite impractical to dispose of all your material possessions. The price of your items will have increased significantly. Duty on getting items into your field will be expensive. Staying within your weight and financial limits set down by your Board for returning missionaries will cause hardships.

But many factors must be weighed. Will that 5-year old Jeep be good for another term, or should it be replaced? Should the reel-type tape recorder be sold so a cassette-type can be purchased? Should your plain plastic dishes be replaced with a prettier setting? Should a more expensive camera be purchased, or a movie camera to replace the 35mm? Should furniture be stored, loaned, or sold? Answers to these questions must be decided before leaving the field, but always with the consideration that replacement is expensive and funds must be raised to cover their cost.

Clothing, unless hand-made at home, will be an exceedingly expensive item. Quality and cost must be carefully considered before purchasing. Items essential in your work must then be considered (books, audio-visuals, tools, instruments, supplies, etc.). Household items which were lacking previously should then be considered. Finally, there should be a consideration of various non-essential, but important and time-saving items.

There are discount houses and organizations available which obtain the best possible equipment at the lowest possible price for missionaries needing equipment. Check with your Home Office if you do not know the names and addresses of such outlets. They can save you hundreds of dollars, depending on the items you may wish to purchase. Take advantage of these discounts.

If you are purchasing items in general or clothing stores, ask about their discount policies. Many well-known stores give a 10- 20% discount to Christian workers, but they may not advertise the fact. In some cities, your Mission Board will be allowed a discount for its workers as a non-profit organization. Some states waive the sales tax on items purchased by qualified non- profit organizations.

In the event the store in which you intend to purchase items does NOT give a discount, do not demand one. They are under no obligation to do so. Remember that the owner's or manager's profits go down with each discount sale. Be grateful for those who are willing to do this, but also be understanding toward those who cannot limit themselves by this means.

Most missionaries find a church or group of individuals who want to hold a shower of one type or another to provide necessary items for your return. If they speak to you about this in advance, be sure to give them at least this much information: (1) Plan the shower no less than a month before your return to the field so items can be packed adequately for shipment; (2) Give them a list of items which would be most helpful to you, in order of preference; (3) Supply a list of items which are NOT needed or which are NOT allowed into your country if there are restrictions; (4) Sizes for each member of the family if they are interested in providing clothing.

When purchasing for your children, sizes will need to be approximated for the length of your expected term. This is, perhaps, one of the most difficult tasks of all, but must be done if adequate clothing and shoes are not available on your field.

Fortunately, in a day of increasing technology with its supply and distribution, fields which once could offer little or nothing of conveniences, clothing, household goods and food items which were considered necessities in the homeland, are now being sold widely and sometimes less expensively than items purchased in the homeland. This is especially meaningful to returning missionaries.

Your outfit should be more easily produced upon your return to the field than when you first left the homeland. You know what you need and can afford. You know what is available overseas. Thus you can plan wisely and early—sometimes hitting sales on needed items, sometimes mentioning needed items in your newsletter and sometimes by the offers of interested friends and churches.

Do think twice about some items. Is that freezer or dishwasher essential, or do you merely want to keep up with or surpass your co-workers? Will those inexpensive dresses and shirts hold up under the rigors to which they will be subjected, or would it prove less expensive to pay for better quality?

Many of you have found that being encumbered with a great amount of material possessions has been a hindrance to you and your work. This may be especially noticed by those who live and work down-country or in the bush. Others have found that for your ministry among the higher classes of people in your city, you need more material possessions than you had anticipated. Thus one cannot fairly estimate for another what items are essential. But you can determine this fairly and honestly for yourself. God will supply all your **needs**, so look to Him to fulfill His promise to you.

QUESTIONS—CHAPTER 55

1. What general categories of equipment and purchases need to be considered as you plan your return to the field?

2. What are the advantages of taking a vehicle with you to the field? Disadvantages?

3. What kinds of books should you take to the field for you, your spouse, your 6-year old daughter and your 12-year old son?

4. What are the advantages of taking a dishwasher, a freezer, a computer, and a stereo system to the field with you? Disadvantages?

5. What request(s) would you make of an individual or church which contacts you regarding their desire to provide you with an outgoing shower of gifts?

56
Packing and Shipping

Moving will no longer be a new experience for you. It is possible, however, that you will need to be reminded of a few details you may have forgotten since leaving the homeland previously.

You now have a knowledge of your field (if you are returning to the one on which you have previously served) and can better plan on how many containers and what kind need to be found or purchased to accommodate your baggage. You will, of course, choose your containers according to the method by which your excess baggage is to be shipped. Stronger, heavier containers may be used for large items which must go by sea. Lighter fiber barrels and foot lockers may be utilized if items are to be airlifted. Convenience and cost will usually determine the method of shipping. If arrangements are made with the airline(s) ahead of time, you can almost always be sure your luggage will arrive on the same plane as you do. It may be much more expensive to ship this way, but it may also mean less expense on the field end, and the assurance that your things have arrived safely and are available immediately for your use.

If some items are sent by surface mail (by sea), be sure the luggage you take with you contains sufficient supplies to maintain you (and your family) until the rest of your things arrive. In the event of a plane or dock strike, considerable delay may result in obtaining necessary clothing or toilet articles.

Even when you carry your luggage with you on the plane, never pack your passport or other important papers. Carry them with you at all times.

You may wish to commit your equipment to a packing company. Keep in mind the cost. Some items may be ordered from stores which cater to overseas shipments. Give accurate details as to how items should be addressed.

It is wise to pack several types of items in each container, i.e., some clothing, some bedding, some books, some kitchen utensils, etc.

In the event a piece is lost or delayed, you will not suffer the loss of all you have of any one item.

Each container must be well identified. Make a list of the items in each piece of luggage, and be sure the number on your list corresponds with the identically numbered container. When listing items for customs, do not list each separate sock or shoe. Lump items by categories. For insurance purposes, however, an itemized listing is essential. Use the replacement value for each item. For customs purposes, list the fair wholesale value of the items. Clothing should be worn and/or laundered before being packed, and thereby conform to the category of used clothing.

If larger items of equipment need an import license, be sure to apply for it well ahead of your departure date (or request that your Board do so for you, if that is their policy). Pianos, cars, trucks, organs, guns, etc., require special papers.

You will want to find the quickest, easiest, and best way of transporting your goods to the port of embarkation. For some it may mean hiring a trailer to-pull behind your car. For others it will be a trucking company, moving van company, plane, bus, or in some cases an overnight delivery company such as Federal Express or United Parcel Service.

If your items are sent to the plane or dock, be sure your forwarding address is clearly indicated on each piece. A letter must always be sent, stating how many pieces will arrive, the approximate arrival date, how they are being sent, and explicit instructions as to how, when, and where the shipment is to be transshipped. If additional pieces are to be added from stores, packers, or by you at a later date, be sure to inform the transshipper. If the same shipper is used by all members of your mission, you will find a very helpful agent to make matters go smoothly.

If your country of destination requires that you actually be in the country before your items arrive, carefully plan your shipping date. (You may be planning to stop enroute, and this must be taken into consideration).

Make sure your insurance coverage will cover any loss of items either in the homeland or on its way overseas. Carry your bill(s) of lading, including insurance coverage, with you.

You may be asked to transport items to the field for your Mission and/or fellow missionaries. This should be done only with your permission and your prior written approval.

Upon debarkation, be sure to state to customs officials the exact number of pieces to arrive as unaccompanied baggage, when they were sent, when they are expected to arrive and by what means they will reach you.

Securely lock each item sent as accompanied or unaccompanied baggage. If a vehicle is sent, remove windshield wipers, mirrors, hubcaps, and other "loose" items. Lock the spare tire in or on the vehicle, and lock the hood. Items such as the battery, gas tank cover, etc., can easily disappear in transit if not securely "tied down".

Items of personal or intrinsic value can be broken, lost, or stolen at any time. Be grateful for all you have, but if any or all of your material possessions should be taken from you, be content in the knowledge that even then, God is able to make all grace abound toward you and HE will supply all your need in Christ Jesus.

QUESTIONS—CHAPTER 56

1. Should you pack your own equipment and purchases for shipping overseas, or pay a packing company to do it for you? Why?

2. If you want to take a hunting rifle to the field with you, list the steps you would take to procure permission to do so.

3. If your Mission asks you to take three small crates of electronic equipment to your field along with your personal outfit, what questions should you ask and what papers should you have in hand, if you agree to take them?

4. What are the advantages to taking all your outfit and equipment items as accompanied baggage? Disadvantages?

57
Extended Furlough and Leave of Absence

There are those who, having been home for furlough, find their return to the field must be delayed. The reasons for this, though varied, may include:

1. Inability to obtain financial clearance

2. Inability to obtain medical clearance

3. Care of aging parents

4. Problems related to your children

5. Uncertainty as to God's leading

6. Visa unobtainable

7. Adoption of a child

8. Request by the Home Office for special service (administration, deputation, or other representation)

9. Need for additional education

10. Death of a spouse or child

It may be a disappointment to see your anticipated date of departure for return to the field delayed. But God sometimes allows responsibilities to come into our lives, unexpectedly, and they must be cared for as diligently as the work on the field. One's own health and family must be given consideration. Many single women find themselves at home for many years, tied down with the care of ill and/or aging parents. Married couples find themselves with a rebellious teenager who feels his mother and dad think more of the mission field than they do of him. Visas for many countries are delayed in being granted. Parents who arrange for an adoption of a child are almost always required to be in the homeland for at least a year. Because of a shortage of workers at home, furlough folks are sometimes asked to assume mission responsibilities in the homeland for a year or two, or longer. Thus furloughs must be extended to cover such emergencies and exigenci es.

To some it is apparent after a 3- or 6-month extension of furlough that a leave of absence will be necessary. Obtaining this status allows the missionary to maintain a relationship with the mission so that a resignation is not necessary. Certain benefits may be kept active (e.g., retirement fund, health insurance). In most instances, however, payment of housing and allowance, insurance, travel, etc., cannot be continued beyond a limited period of time set by the mission and strictly stated in its by-laws or policies. It does mean that any funds which come in designated for your account are credited properly and your account builds up for the time when you may be able to resume your missionary work on the field.

Some missionaries take a leave of absence during the time their children are in high school, especially if there is no secondary school education available on the field. Education during furlough may require a leave of absence. A physical condition may necessitate a leave. Some want time to reconsider their whole missionary commitment. Most missions are lenient about allowing a leave of absence if they feel you are sincere and they want to preserve your service for the Mission.

Certain facts must be faced if you decide on a leave of absence. Ordinarily, support from the Board will not be available. Thus you will be responsible for earning your livelihood through other work. This may be a very real concern if you must care for someone who is ill, for you will not be free to go out and find work. God, however, has a way of meeting your needs, although you cannot see it now. It may be through your family, an agency, or friends. But He will work in each situation and make provision.

A leave of absence may cause you to feel as if you are in "no-man's land", being neither a missionary nor anything else for the time being. People may have questions if they ask "What is your work?" and you reply, "I'm a missionary on leave of absence." An explanation as to the reason(s) for such leave is appropriate in such cases.

As soon as plans have been completed, the problem has been worked out, or the crisis has passed, change your status with the mission. Keep in close contact with the Home Office at all time, informing them of your progress and keeping up on news from your field. In most missions, a leave of absence status must be voted upon annually. If they vote against granting the LOA for an additional period of time, you will be asked to submit your resignation.

Extended furloughs and leaves of absence make adjustments in the field staff necessary. Therefore, it is important that they be taken only when no other solution can be found to problems which present themselves to you, and that they be terminated as quickly as possible and/or feasible.

QUESTIONS—CHAPTER 57

1. List at least five factors which could cause a missionary to request an extended furlough.

2. Under what circumstances might a Leave of Absence from the mission be indicated?

3. When on Leave of Absence, what responsibilities does the missionary have to his/her supporters, field, mission field, self?

4. What problems must co-workers on the field (both missionary and national) face if you must take an extended furlough or leave of absence?

58
Changing Missions During Furlough

There are circumstances brought to bear upon certain mission aries which necessitate their becoming connected with a mission other than the one with which they were originally affiliated. There are many reasons for this. We will discuss but a few. (No matter the reason, it is best, whenever possible, for this change to take place during the furlough period so official matters can be legally finalized and supporters can be informed, in person, of this new association.)

1. You marry, or plan to marry a member of another mission working in your field. (Most often it is the girl who joins the fellow's Mission, but occasionally the opposite is true. This is, obviously, an uncomplicated reason for changing missions.)

2. You have been loaned to another mission during your term of service. Having become involved in that work, you feel you could become a more vital part of it if you were to become a member of that Mission rather than continuing on loan to them.

3. You may feel led to assume a specific ministry in which your mission has not felt led to enter (e.g., orphanage work, Bible Training School, film ministry). A sister mission is willing to allow you to assume this special work. Some missions also set rules as to where single girls can work and where they feel the ministry should be carried on by a man or married couple. This may be true if a girl wants to work in an isolated tribal area or an especially dangerous zone.) Another mission may not put restrictions upon its members.

4. After a term on the field, you may become increasingly concerned with another area where you feel your abilities can be better utilized. There may be no change in language, but your present mission does not work in that area.

5. Closing of a field due to government or mission controls and restrictions may cause you to seek another Board which has agreed to abide by the appointed restrictions and has been given permission to continue operations in your field.

6. You have found good Christian fellowship with members of another mission. Your interpersonal relations with your own fellow-missionaries have fallen short of expectations. You feel a happier situation will exist if you join the other group.

7. Doctrinal problems may arise which will serve to direct you to another Board. It may be that your group has become liberal, or involved in tangent doctrines, or perhaps it is you who have changed in these areas, but you still want to serve in your chosen field.

8. Denominational missions, because of lack of funds, may cut down on the number of missionaries in a given field, or close the field entirely. Some of these missionaries will apply for service with other Boards.

9. Perhaps you just don't like the mix and make-up of your Board now that you have come to see it at close range. You feel you do not have sufficient freedom to go or say or be or do. Rules and regulations with which you are not happy seem to tie your hands as you seek to serve. You thought the situation could be worked out, but there seems to be no common ground. Another mission appears to be, if not utopian, at least more to your liking. Be very careful about the "grass seeming to be greener on the other side of the fence"!

10. You may be requested not to return with your Board because of your actions or attitudes. But you, and many of your supporters, home church, etc., feel it is God's will that you return. Thus you go about to find a mission which will accept you for further service in spite of your history

Before changing missions, you must remember that no organization is perfect. Each one has its unique strengths and weaknesses, although not always known on the outside.

Also consider the fact that returning to the same field under a different mission will cause many questions to be raised, especially if you return to the approximate area to do a similar work as previously. If your new mission adheres to comity, you will probably not be serving at the same station, but it IS possible that you will be in the same city (which may be "open" with no comity rules). Nationals may ask for an explanation. Your former co-workers will feel awkward about the situation if they do not understand both sides of the situation. Therefore, it is essential that you be strongly convicted by the Lord that you are in His best will. Never condemn or criticize your former mission or work, especially to nationals. Don't blame a mission or a co-worker for that which has taken place in your life. Your call to a different mission must be as certain as the Lord's call upon your life for service. Once convinced yourself, you will be able to share this with others.

Since missions, as a rule, work very closely with one another, your past performance will be considered carefully before you are accepted by another group. In most cases, a missionary does not simply transfer from one mission to another. Usually a mission will not consider the application of an individual who already is a member of another group. This means that you must resign from your present mission before beginning your new candidate procedure. Often you will be required to attend Candidate School and follow all procedures required of other prospective candidates. And it is even possible you may be rejected after due consideration by the Board.

There are truly legitimate and wise reasons for changing missions. There are also immature, selfish and unworthy reasons for doing so. Determine, with God's approval, to accomplish His highest and best in and through your life. He will give light for your pathway as you seek Him with all your heart and mind and soul and strength.

There may be some of you who feel you could have a broader and more effective ministry if you were serving independently of any organization with its rigid rules and policies. You could live less expensively. You could serve in the area of **your** choice. You would have free reign with the nationals to whom you minister. You could choose your length of service and your length of furloughs. You would not have to fit in with co-workers who disagree with you and your methods since you would work alone. If it seemed necessary, you could choose others from the homeland to work with you in this venture of faith. You would not have to fit "the mould" of those in authority because you would be the sole authority. You could even go back to the place where you previously served, rent a home on "the other side of town", and bring up new believers according to your personal policies and beliefs. You do not have to give an accounting of your ministry to a board or an administrator. You simply do your work as unto the Lord.

Your greatest need will be to find a church (or churches) or interested individuals whom you can "sell" on the idea of your planned ministry to such an extent that they will willingly provide you with your complete prayer and financial support needs. Many missionaries have done just that, which is the easiest part. Relatively few missionaries, however, succeed on the field independently. Thus before moving ahead with such a plan, you should seriously consider many things, including:

1.   Is it possible you have needed **more** supervision rather than less?

2.   Will you be able to return to your field of service, having received the necessary visa(s) and residence papers as an individual who is not affiliated with an organization recognized by the government of that country? (In most countries, mission boards must be registered with the government before visas are granted.)

3.   What will happen if you are on the field and those who are supporting you decide they can no longer do so? (This is an especially important question if you get support from only one church.)

4.   If you have occasion to ask questions or seek counsel, to whom will you go?

5.   Is it proper to break mission comity by entering a field designated for a certain mission?

6.   Will it be confusing to young, national believers when you insist on their church maintaining independence from all other churches in the area?

7.   Since you have no co-workers, and perhaps no adequate means of travel or communication with other expatriates, what will you propose to do when your wife becomes very ill with a fever of 106°?

8.   What kind of support group(s) do you intend to maintain in the homeland which can assist you with projects and special needs in times of crisis?

9.   Should any thought be given to the future, i.e., such things as insurance, pension plan, Social Security, health care, etc.?

10. If your ministry is effective and your work expands, what plans do you have for its administration and control?

11. Who will take over your work if there is a need to return to the homeland, especially if the nationals have not yet been trained to take over the work?

12. What kind(s) of relationship(s) will you maintain with those who are serving under traditional mission boards, whether denominational, non-denominational, or interdenominational?

13. What are the major reasons why you feel that serving independently will be more pleasing to the Lord, to yourself, to your supporters, and to those among whom you minister?

14. If you were not able to function adequately in your missionary work under the auspices of a mission board, will you be able to cope better in a position of being entirely on your own? Can you expect others to join you and work under your leadership?

Independence does not always imply complete liberation from the forces which seem to work against you. It implies creating new problems with which you must cope . . . alone. Be sure of God's will, and look carefully before you leap!

QUESTIONS—CHAPTER 58

1. List at least five reasons why a missionary might seriously consider affiliating with a different mission organization as he returns for another term of service.

2. When a man and woman under two Boards fall in love and contemplate marriage, what questions should be taken into consideration in deciding under which Board they will serve?

3. List several reasons for wanting to return to the field under a different board or returning as an independent entity.

4. You served your first term with The Win Some Mission. During your furlough you resigned from the WSM and have been accepted by The Golden Opportunity Mission. Write a one-page letter to those who have been supporting you, explaining the change of boards and requesting continuing support.

5. After resigning from your original board, you candidated with another mission. You are rejected by that board. What will be your next step?

6. What are the advantages of serving as an independent missionary? Disadvantages?

59
Suppose Your Field Closes During Furlough

There is little need to emphasize the uncertainty of the days in which we live. In many nations it is difficult to determine how long missionaries may be allowed entry into certain countries.

What steps should you take if your field of service should close while you are on furlough? You might consider one or more of these alternatives:

1. Wait two or three years to see if the doors will open to missionary service again. (This has happened in many fields). Perhaps you could teach missions in the meantime. Dozens of Christian colleges are adding mission courses.

2. Give up foreign missionary work and stay in the homeland as a worker in the Home Office, or as a Regional Representative for your Mission.

3. Determine that you will go into secular work in the homeland.

4. Decide to be a "missionary" at home by working in a ghetto, coffee house, or as a Christian Education Director or Youth Director or Church Secretary.

5. Enter the field of Home Missions, working with an Indian group, with Jewish people, or with immigrants from abroad.

6. Take a church pastorate.

7. Volunteer for another field in which your mission works where you can utilize your present language.

8. Volunteer for a field where a different language is spoken.

9. Apply to a different Board for another field.

10. Consider working at your profession in the land to which you were originally called, or study in one of their universities, hoping to be a witness by living as a Christian.

11. Destroy your effectiveness in any future ministry by tenaciously holding to something that can never be.

It is no light thing to be told you are not welcome to return to a country and a people whom you have come to know and love, especially when your whole life has been geared toward that specific field and people.

If you decide to wait a while to see if the doors will open again, your support will suffer after several months at home. You will, undoubtedly, have to work until such time as you can return to the field, or the field appears definitely to be unreachable for you. If you can serve your mission at home, some of your support may be salvaged. If you take a secular job, support will be lost.

If an entire field closes, your mission may not be able to put you on the payroll as a home worker. If, however, there are few people involved, they may be able to use some extra hands in the office, writing their promotional materials, or in deputation ministry.

Some will feel this action was ordained of God and a sign they should seek work in the secular field, perhaps to earn money in order to support missions and other Christian work.

There is a great deal of Christian work to be done in the homeland, even in the cause of missions. There will be little difficulty in locating a satisfying ministry, even though your heart may be overseas with the people among whom you have served.

Men who have been ordained may decide to pastor a church in the homeland, by which means they can emphasize missions and interest young people in Christian work. Having had experience on the field should make them prepared to promote this aspect of the church to a large extent.

If you accept an appointment to another field in which your Board operates, and the same language you have learned for your first appointment is used, there is less adaptation needed. The people may have different culture, mores, customs; the country may be desert rather than mountainous; the work may be more or less advanced than your former field. But at least you will be able to communicate with the people—and the rest comes far easier.

If you decide on a completely new field of service, you will have to consider yourself a "new" missionary. Although many fine workers have done this very thing, it is always difficult not to say, "When I was in such-and-such a place, we did it such and such a way," expecting because it worked there, it will work the same way here. It will take time to learn the new language(s) and become acquainted with the country and its people. You may become very frustrated if the people are opposite to your former contacts. Perhaps you came from a spiritually fruitful field; this one is barren. Previously you were in charge of a station; now you are not even consulted in decisions concerning your own ministry. Did you make the wrong decision? Or can these problems be worked out to such an advantage that you will come to love this field as much or better than your first? To a large extent, YOU will determine the answer.

Perhaps your Board has no work in a field in which you have a particular concern. It would then be in order to consider joining a Board which works in the areas of your interest. If this second Board is of the same caliber as your previous affiliation, and your reasons for the change are sound, most, if not all of your supporters will continue to stand behind you financially.

Some of you will feel that your whole life and ministry has gone down the drain if the door closes to your field. You bemoan this irreversible fact so greatly that it adversely affects any other work you may decide to do. Thus your life becomes wasted and useless. It, of course, comes as a shock and disappointment. But it comes as no surprise to the God whom you serve. You can, therefore, be confident that He has good, acceptable, and perfect reasons for these seeming impossibilities.

The choice now is whether this is a call for you to look to another field of service, or an open door for you to enter a different sphere of ministry. The most important responsibility is to be faithful to Him wherever you choose to serve.

It may be a more complicated and difficult situation if you are under a Board which has determined that for safety purposes, or because of increasing tension with nationals in the administration and carrying out of the work, or because of prohibitions against openly preaching the Word, they must close that field. Another mission or other missions have decided to stay in the land. Do you quit your mission and go with another? Do you try to get involved with a health, education, or government agency working in that country? Do you storm the gates of your administrative board and accuse them of making a wrong decision? How you act, react and interact in such a situation can be the making or breaking of your Board as well as of you as an individual mission ary.

In this day of ever-changing political positions, we may see more and more missionaries having their re-entry permits and/or visas refused. If, on the other hand, doors to your work are wide open, prepare to return and be grateful for further opportunity with your people.

Plan well, for there may come a day when YOU will have to face the unhappy situation of not being able to return.

Some missionaries have opted to return to a "closed" field as a "tentmaker" or as a student. Visas are sometimes available for these purposes. But such a step must be considered very thoroughly. Some countries require a signed statement assuring them that you will not practice or propagate a religion foreign to the country. Open worship services may be forbidden. The only means of witness is the life that is lived without words to back it up. Great care must be taken to abide by the laws of the land, or arrest or expulsion can result.

QUESTIONS—CHAPTER 59

1. List YOUR options for continuing in missionary service if your field should close and you are unable to return.

2. What will you need to consider if you decide to apply for service in a country other than the one in which you were originally assigned?

3. According to your present thinking, what would you opt to do if your mission allowed YOU to decide whether or not to return to a dangerous, war-torn, politically charged overseas situation? (State whether you are single, married, or married with a family.)

4. Are there advantages/disadvantages to serving in a non-missionary capacity in an otherwise closed field? Explain.

60
Resignation

If you have come home with the thought that you are through as a missionary, furlough is a good time to work it out and get it straight. Refresh yourself for several weeks. Pray unceasingly. Share your thoughts and feelings with your closest friends and prayer partners in the most unbiased way possible. Do not state your intentions from the pulpits of supporting churches!

Arrange for a conference with the administrator(s) or Board at the Home Office and bring up the problems you are facing. Gain expert advice from those who are neutral in the situation but perceptive in their thinking. If your health or a family situation is the problem, allow time to see if it can be worked out satisfactorily. Perhaps an extended furlough or leave of absence will solve the problem for you. In any case, your furlough is a time of special consideration of God's call upon your life. Be very sure Satan does not blind you to the perfect will of God.

If, after due consideration and counsel, and an honest leading from the Lord, you feel you must resign from your Mission, be sure to take care of all necessary details with your Home Office. Decide with them whether you or they should write to your supporters. Often support is salvaged for another missionary if the supporting church or individuals are contacted in a way which gives them an opportunity to transfer their support to another missionary or a project in which you are especially interested or in which you have been involved.

Supporters are usually very lenient in their feelings toward those who resign because of personal or family health problems, your inability to adjust to the demands placed upon you, a take-over of the work by nationals, or expulsion from the country for reasons beyond your control (even if you might be able to go to another area or country under the same mission). They are less lenient of those who become embittered, speak disparagingly of the work, the country, the nationals, the mission, or who decide they can be happier or make more money in the homeland. Fortunately, most supporters never know when their missionary has been requested to turn in his/her resignation because of bad attitudes, open sin, or pressure from fellow-missionaries who feel they could work in harmony apart from this individual. Reversals or changes in doctrine resulting in resignations must be carefully considered by the individual and the Mission. In some cases, the missionary will not feel he can work any longer within the restrictions of his Board's statement of faith. In other cases, the missionary feels no constraint to resign, but is forced to do so because his/her views are not those firmly established by his Board. Problems in the area of doctrine in recent years have been in questions concerning healing, baptism, speaking in tongues, the view of the Holy Spirit, inerrancy, and the social implications of the Gospel. A most unsatisfactory answer is when a Board says, "You can believe it, but you can't practice or teach it," and the individual is allowed to remain in the Mission.

A missionary should be truthful, but in many cases, the truth concerning a resignation is very one-sided and therefore strongly biased. Condemning a mission for a few isolated and unintentional instances is hardly fair. Although you may not have found your niche with your Board, or feel you have been treated unfairly, others have found a very happy relationship serving under the same Board. There is always the possibility that you were responsible in a slight way for the dissolution of your affiliation! At any rate, it is always best to tell the brightest side of the true story.

For those who find they must resign for acceptable and legitimate reasons, have you looked into the possibility of serving your Board in the homeland? There may be some who even now are undecided about the future. The facts seem to indicate that resignation is the best answer. But you are beset with fears: What will the Board think? How will my home church feel? How can I explain to my supporters? What will it do to my children? Will my unsaved loved ones understand? Isn't my faith enough to get me through another term? Is it better that I live out my few remaining days on the field with the possibility my illness will increase and other workers will need to care for me? What will I do if I stay home? What will people think of me?

There is really only one answer to your problem. It comes by laying the facts on the table, evaluating the pros and cons, obtaining the best counsel possible, and committing your decision to the Lord before, between, and at the end of your prayerful deliberations. He will show you HIS answer. Once you have made your decision and are assured that the reasons for it are valid, stick by it. There is no need to go back and worry about it. Making the right choice and being sure of it is far more important than wondering what people may think of you for what you have done. Resigning from a ministry does not mean you are resigning from life! Obedience to your Lord must be your prime consideration.

QUESTIONS—CHAPTER 60

1. List at least five reasons why a missionary might consider resigning from his Board.

2. With whom should you consult before writing your resignation letter?

3. Write a short, sample newsletter to your supporters and prayer partners to tell them of your resignation.

4. What are some of your options if you, a single missionary, are fully supported by a denominational church which insists you return to the field under their denominational Board rather than serve with the interdenominational Board with whom you presently are affiliated?

5. If you are a family, what are your options if you and your wife are committed to overseas missionary work but your two teen-age daughters rebel against returning to the field?

61
Return to the Field

The weeks and months have flown by. Is it possible you've travelled so many miles to conduct meetings and to be involved in missionary conferences? You still marvel at God's supply of your every need, in spite of the fact you had prayed unceasingly for this to be true! Every bill has been paid or arranged for. Your full support has been pledged. Equipment has been purchased, packed and forwarded for shipment. Shots and immunizations have been obtained. Medical clearance has been given. Social calls have come to an end. Most problems have been solved, questions answered, and personal needs met.

Adjustment to the homeland was difficult, but at least you were able to cope. You appreciated the hospitality and comforts which friends provided for you. You're grateful for renewed fellowship with supporters and the opportunity to speak in places where you and your mission had not previously been known. There were many along the way who seemed to be interested in learning more about applying for service. There were occasions when special ministries were honored with spiritual results. Souls were saved and built up in the faith for you were no less a missionary just because you had returned to the homeland for furlough.

Perhaps you and your children began to get a taste for material things. You may miss some of the niceties of life when you return to the field. Or, on the other hand, you may look forward to returning to the field and to your friends, both national and expatriate.

It is never easy to say farewell to those whom you love dearly. Perhaps you must leave a Mother or Dad still unsaved, or secure in Christ but physically incapacitated. Or for the first time, your family will be separated as you leave a son or daughter in the homeland to enter a secular or Christian high school or college. You know you must be strong in the Lord and you're assured that His grace is sufficient. But these are difficult hours.

Yet, in spite of the heart ties and cries, you are looking forward to another term of service, determined by the grace of God to be a more effective witness, a more mature counselor, a more loving co-worker, a more obedient steward of talents and time, a more fully informed administrator, a more faithful child of God.

No one can be sure how much time he will have to work in his field. Plans must be carried out as quickly as possible to meet goals which have been set. Nationals must be trained and given authority and a voice in decisions. There must be more teamwork between missionary and missionary, between missionary and national between your Mission and other Missions, between the Field Office and the Home Office. You are a vital part of this program of advance, and there is much to do, and no assurance how long is left to you for doing it.

So with "Goodbye" and "God bless you" ringing in your ears, you head through the gate and board your plane. As you taxi to the end of the runway, then speed ahead faster and faster until you hear and feel the wheels leave the pavement and fold themselves under your feet, you take a last look at the homeland, grateful for the opportunity you've had of returning for this short while, knowing it will be greatly changed before you see it again, but anxiously awaiting your arrival on the field to take up the work to which God has called you. Whether you return to the exact location of your previous term, or are assigned to another station and work in a different area; whether you are in the same country, or in another; whether you serve with the same Board or with another; whether you have similar responsibilities or are called upon for new outreach and service; you will be grateful that you are a co-laborer with God in the soul-satisfying ministry of missionary endeavor.

QUESTIONS—CHAPTER 61

1. What were the most important lessons you learned during your furlough?

2. What are your three primary goals for your ministry when you get back to your field?

3. What are your greatest fears about entering upon this new term of service?

4. What scriptural promise(s) have you chosen for encouragement, challenge and/or spiritual stability and strength during this coming term?

PART IV
FINISHING THE RACE
Retirement

62
Thinking Ahead to Retirement

It has been a long time since the Lord laid it upon your heart to consider missionary service. As you look back over the years, you are heartened by all the way He has led you. You have known what it is to "soar on wings like eagles . . . run and not grow weary . . . walk and not faint" (Isaiah 40:31). You have experienced the elation of victories and the disappointment of defeats. You have come to love the people among whom you have worked for so long. You feel a part of the bone and marrow of the country in which you have served. You have made strong friends among both national and expatriate co-workers. Perhaps you have had a part in the organization of a church—or several churches. Or it may be that when you went to the field there was a need for a radio ministry, and you saw it through from a 50-watt whisper to a 500,000 watt witness. You may have taught or administered in a Christian school which trained thousands of boys and girls in the Word of God. Or served in a hospital which met the physical needs of individuals so that they later had an opportunity to have their spiritual needs met. You may have trained hundreds of men and women in Bible schools, and seen many of them go forth as missionaries to their own people or to neighboring peoples. You may have merely gossipped the Gospel to any and all who would listen, or been involved in evangelistic efforts among children for 35 years.

If you were to recall all of your experiences during these years of ministry, you could write several books! Some things will be best forgotten so that bitterness does not erupt. (Yes, missionaries **can** become embittered. Suppose you have been jailed for a deed you did not commit; or interned by a foreign government in time of war; or been widowed through the merciless act of murder; or those who professed to be believers have turned against their Lord and God's ambassadors; or been betrayed by those who said they were your friends.)

Most of your experience—though looking back at it you might think of ways in which you could have improved upon it—will remain forever in your memory and be an encouragement to you—and through you to others—for as long as you live. When you left for the field, you believed that "Faithful is He that calleth you who also will do it" (I Thessalonians 5:24). Now you can aver assuredly that He Who called you has been faithful and has done it!

With the passing years there has remained a willing spirit, though the body may no longer be able to take as much of the rigor required of today's missionary. There are times when you feel you want to continue your ministry, or perhaps retire on the field and give additional years of volunteer service. But in almost all situations, your mission board will be the final decision-maker concerning retirement requirements.

Boards often have an "either-or" statement in their policies which will indicate that you may retire after serving 30 years (or another designated time span) with the mission, or automatically retire at age 65 (which, in the case of married couples, may mean their average age or whichever spouse reaches 65 first). Because many in the United States are fighting to push back the retirement age to 70 or beyond, many missions are reconsidering the mandatory 65 retirement age. New types of "senior" ministry are being developed. But because of the intenseness of the work and the physical stamina needed in many overseas situations, many boards will give only annual or biennial extensions for active missionaries over 65. It is then up to the Board to decide when actual retirement is mandated and whether or not part-time work can be assigned thereafter (unless retirement is requested previously by the missionary).

Eventually the day of retirement will approach. It can be a day of dread, or a day of anticipation. The attitude with which this eventuality is accepted will mean the difference between wasted years or continuing usefulness.

When you realize retirement is just around the corner, there is one first important step to take. At least three months before your 65th birthday, see your nearest Social Security office to sign up for benefits as well as for Medicare. Be sure to carry a supplemental medical policy which will provide for the costs which Medicare will not cover. You are very fortunate if your Mission carries the full cost of your medical insurance as part of your retirement benefits. If it does not, carefully consider your need for coverage. In the event you are going to be on the field when you turn 65, you should be in contact with your Board and have them help you in your contact with a local Social Security office in order to put things in order with them. (Those from countries other than the U.S. should contact their appropriate pension office to see what proper procedures are upon retirement.)

Perhaps the greatest fear of the retiring missionary is that he/she will not be able to adjust to the home country which has not, except for furloughs, been his home for many, many years. So many changes have been noted during those furlough times, but not all of them had to be absorbed, because return to the field was always assured. But now there is so much to have to learn and get used to. The thought of becoming a part of the materialistic, TV-oriented, politically motivated society which is your homeland has little appeal to you! Yet it will be undesirable to live at church 24-hours a day or watch only Christian television in your home. There will be the necessity to become a part of the homeland you love. And as you stand at the gateway of retirement, you may feel like a fish out of water—being neither a part of the country where you served or a part of the nation to which you pledge allegiance.

Another large problem which looms up before the retiring missionary concerns finances. You may raise many questions as to where your sustenance will come from. And you may ask, with the Psalmist, "From whence cometh my help?" (Psalm 121:1).

If you do ask such a question, you must, of course, read the remaining verses of Psalm 121, and you will discover that God will not depart from you when you enter retirement! Your help will continue to come from Him. He isn't about to fall asleep as far as your needs are concerned. He'll continue to protect and watch over you—forever! This being so, you can be sure your financial needs will be met.

He Who hath taught you to trust in His Name,

Wouldn't thus far have brought you to put you to shame!

Perhaps your Mission has a pension plan which, added to Social Security retirement benefits, will provide for your needs. Some missions require retirees actively to solicit continuing support funds. Others provide housing accommodations and monthly stipends to retired missionaries and home office workers. Such provisions may not have seemed important when you signed on with the Mission 35 years ago. But today they loom large before you.

Housing for retired persons will be another consideration which must be faced. In some cases, individuals have received monies through bequest or inheritance, or by carefully saving through the years. This will provide for rented facilities—or perhaps a small home of your own—for the years ahead. Many retirees like the independence of having their own home and becoming part of a larger community.

Some Missions have made provision for their retirees in the form of simple, but fully adequate, housing in small mission-related communities. Few Boards fully pay for these apartments or homes, but do offer them at subsidized cost—with or without a monthly maintenance fee. Many of these retirement centers are completely booked, so plans should be made at least two years in advance if you are interested in becoming a resident of such a missionary community.

There are different ways of financing such residences, so be sure to check into these details. You may have to pay for half the cost of constructing a home. You may be asked to turn over certain assets to the Board to make you eligible for lifetime housing and health care. You may pay a monthly rental and/or a maintenance fee (which may include upkeep of your lawn, painting of your home or apartment, or even one meal a day in the community dining room).

Much prayer and thought should be given to where you want to live, how much you can afford to pay, and the advantages and disadvantages of living in what is an "in-grown" community. There are, of course, good reasons for being in a place where similar interests, work experiences and fields of labor can be fully shared with those who care and understand. Yet many individuals prefer a less cloistered setting.

There are missionary communities available which accept workers from any Mission. There are also "villages" which are controlled by a denomination or church board, but the residents are not required to have served with that group—in fact, non-Christians are as welcome to live in the "village" as are Christians.

In many areas it is possible to find adequate, yet inexpensive housing near a missions-oriented church, or in a community where Christian workers are well-accepted and also utilized in ministries. Mobile home retirement villages are prevalent throughout the warmer climates of our country and many choose this kind of leisure lifestyle for their retirement years.

Single retirees are sometimes invited to share a home with a friend. Couples are sometimes provided for by their children. Mission-minded churches have occasionally provided retirement facilities for those whom they have supported on the field for many years.

If you are with a Board which allows or requires retirement after 30 years of service, and you were 25 when you went to the field, you may decide to retire to some other type of work/ministry for another 10 years. In such instances, you will probably rent or purchase your "retirement" home in an area which most appeals to you, and which will continue to be your retirement area permanently. (Or you may volunteer as a representative or deputationist for your Mission if your financial means are already sufficient for later retirement).

You will soon discover that your lifestyle may not be able to match that of your neighbors because of the high cost of living in the day in which we live. On the other hand, by shopping carefully, taking advantage of discounts and sales, and by living a life not given to excesses in any area, it is possible to live a very happy, comfortable and enjoyable life of retirement, with all the necessities of life provided, and with enough left over to support the work of the Lord! Always keep in mind that financial problems may concern **you**, but the Lord of the universe surely has the answer to every question.

When considering retirement housing, you must decide if you want to be near your parents, your children, friends, your home church. Do you want to be in the mountains, near the seashore, in a drier desert area, in a humid spot, in the country, in the city? Do you prefer the cold or the heat? Do you want to be in the North or the South; the East or the West? Do you prefer to be near a certain doctor or hospital? Have you been willed property upon which you could build? Do you have physical impairments which would be helped or hindered by your geographical location? Be sure you are certain in your own mind where you will best be able to enjoy your retirement years.

If you are married to one who is native to a country other than your own, it must be mutually decided where you will retire. If one of you is English, Welsh, Irish, Scottish, Australian, New Zealander, Canadian—consideration must be given to the social welfare benefits available in such countries. On the other hand, your family and children may live in the U.S. which makes retirement there more to your liking. There are many pros and cons to consider in the choice of a geographical retirement location. Decisions should be made well in advance of your actual cessation of missionary work.

There are some who are completely content in their country of service overseas. Because they are now at the age of normal retirement (or forced retirement, if demanded by the policies of their Board), many—perhaps all—of their close family is deceased. Their children live their own lives and are not dependent upon them. They no longer have deep roots in their home country. After much thought, they decide to retire in their country of service. This has worked well in some situations—especially so in cases of Britishers retiring in India, Kenya, or Singapore. But serious consideration must be given to such a choice. Does the government allow expatriates to own property? How will it affect your retirement income (pension, stipends, Social Security, interest on foreign accounts, taxes, etc.)? Are there medical, dental, legal, and other necessary services readily available to you? Are wills enforceable in this country? To whom would you leave personal items and property owned overseas, or is that of no concern? Will you be accepted as a legal, life-time resident of that country? How stable is this country? Is there a local church and Christian community where you can worship and enjoy fellowship? Can you live a disciplined life so that you do not become entangled in your former missionary concerns and become a disruptive force in the policies and procedures of missionary organizations working in your area? Are there things in which you **can** become involved so that you do not simply cease to have any usefulness? What would your plan be if your area became war-torn? Do your thoughts of retiring on the field stem from completely unselfish motives? Is your family in agreement with your decision?

The word RETIREMENT, itself, may be difficult to accept. There should be a word which more accurately describes the anticipation of coming years in which heavy loads are transferred to younger shoulders for the long climb yet ahead. The dictionary gives the impression that retirement is complete withdrawal from and conclusion of one's position, profession, occupation or career. There are times when the mind pictures a life of unmitigated ease—when you can do exactly what you want to, when you want to—or not do anything at all . . . just as the fellow said when asked what he expected to do in Heaven. "I guess I'll just sit in my rocking chair for the first thousand years," he replied. "After that I might start rocking!"

Unfortunately, too many individuals think of retirement as the end of productive living. Too few consider this new period in their life as REVITALIZATION. Yet this is what it can and should be if you are to be happy, have a ministry, and fulfill the work and will of God for your life.

The most positive aspect of retirement will be your zest for living. Always planning reachable goals, anticipating special events, and looking forward to the future with hope and expectation will be motivation to lead a normal, active, meaningful life which will be fulfilling to you and a blessing to others.

All your life you may have felt the constraint of time. Now you will be able to slow down—an adjustment which may not come easily. But gradually your lifestyle will begin to reflect this new attitude of leisure—and you should find it therapeutic. Your body will slow more quickly than your mind and you will come to truly understand the meaning of the phrase, "the spirit is willing but the flesh is weak." The Lord was extremely wise in seeing that we wind down as we age. Enjoying the process, rather than fighting it, is a key to good physical and emotional health.

Do you fear that retirement will mean you will lack things to do? Have you asked retired people if they have found this to be a problem? If so, you have probably found that most retirees are busier today than they were before they retired. But they are, to some extent, doing the things they **want** to do—the things they never had time to do while they were engaged in full-time work responsibilities.

You will discover, after settling into retirement, that there are open doors of ministry opportunities available to you in many areas. For example you might serve in one of the following ways:

—Interim pastor

—Pastor of visitation

—Chairman of Men's/Women's Prayer Groups

—Teacher of Home Bible Study Class(es)

—Personal witness

—Hospital/Nursing Home/Convalescent Center Visitor or Volunteer

—Tract distribution

—Musician (soloist, choir member, organist, pianist, music director)

—Special representative/Deputationist for your Mission

—Conference speaker

—Missionary Chairman/Member in local church

—Sunday School teacher

—Home Department teacher

—DVBS teacher/helper

If you want to share your expertise in other areas as a help to your community, why not consider being:

—A volunteer worker at a local library
—A teacher's assistant in a public/Christian school
—A provider of food for the ill
—A comforter to the lonely/bereaved
—A volunteer worker for a political campaign, or to collect
   funds for the United Fund, Muscular Dystrophy campaign,
   Heart Association, etc.
—A teacher for adult education courses at a local school
   (utilizing your skills in sewing, carpentry, mathematics,
   writing, electronics, typing, or other area of expertise)
—Involved in local government

As a retired missionary, you have a unique investment of yourself over many years which you will want to keep your eyes on. Your children, as they grow up, may never quite find they have no need for the fellowship and encouragement of their living parents. You will probably also have many "children of faith" in whose progress you will never lose interest.

You may find that while other retirees keep track of the great games such as the Super Bowls and the World Series, you will keep on with growing interest in the quiet, spectacular power of the Gospel at work all across the world. You may find that retirement gives you your first real opportunity to get a breath-taking view of the overall situation.

But, of course, you will share many of the same experiences with all other retirees. You may be located in a rural area where opportunities for involvement may seem fewer than if you were in an urban setting. But there is no lack of things to do. A garden is a wonderful way to enjoy yourself, grow foods which you can utilize, and watch flowers come into being before your eyes.

House plants can be a joy to sow and propagate. A study of plants, and some concern for them is all it takes to provide you and your friends with a houseful of colorful blooms and greenery. Even tomatoes, peppers and other vegetable and fruit plants are available inexpensively for inside growing.

Making things keeps the mind and hands busy and the heart happy. Make things you can use, things you can give to others—even things you can sell to earn a little extra income. There is no end of afghans, sweaters, shawls, baby blankets, slipper, dresses . . . that can be knitted or crocheted. Cross-stitch is very popular as well as all kinds of needlework (which is enjoyed by both men and women today). If you are handy with a sewing machine, clothing can be made easily and inexpensively (compared to clothing purchased at retail). Sea shells can be turned into necklaces, paper clip holders, or Christmas tree ornaments. Wood can be made into bird houses, toys, picture frames . . . A visit to a nearby Craft Shop—and they are located in almost every shopping mall—will convince you that you can make something different every day of the year and never run out of things to do. (If you are in a missionary community which provides occupational therapy facilities, you will become involved in scores of activities of this kind). Photography can be fun, also.

A hobby can be fun and educational. Hobbies are not just for children! Stamp and coin collecting are two of the most popular hobbies. But many people collect cups and saucers, salt and pepper shakers, clocks, owls, cats, dogs, spoons . . . The list goes on and on. Think of something common,inexpensive, but not usually collected. Then work at your hobby. Some collect match covers, others recipes, still others versions of the Bible.

Collecting and clipping discount coupons will consume time, but save money. Newspapers carry coupons; they arrive in the mail; they can be picked up at grocery stores; they are included in boxes of cereal and on packages of cake. Trading coupons with a neighbor may be of mutual help. Just one caution—use coupons to purchase only those items you would ordinarily use. Do not buy something just because the price is reduced (doubly so on double coupon days). Yet utilizing these free coupons may reduce your total food bill by as much as 5-10% on each visit to the store.

Senior Citizen Centers offer the retiree many opportunities to become involved with others. Fishing, golfing, biking, hiking, or other leisure time activities will fill your days and hours. Many retirement communities band together and take busloads of people to ball games, a symphony, an organ recital, the beach, to local attractions, to shopping malls, and on longer trips—all at the lowest possible cost.

Letter writing should become a part of your retired life. Keeping in touch with friends and acquaintances at home and overseas is a privilege. It is encouraging to those who hear from you (remember how much you looked forward to getting mail when you were overseas)? You will be glad to have their responses, as well. But letter writing should be something to look forward to. Too many retired missionaries let their mail pile up to such an extent that every three months when they send a letter, the first paragraph always apologizes for a late response because "a pile of 100 unanswered letters is stacked on my desk." With some, letter-writing becomes a fetish. They lose sleep if they do not respond immediately. They feel pressure if letters pile up. Be sure you write letters, but don't worry about your mail build-up.

In these days when postage is so expensive, it may help to set aside a "stamp piggy bank." Perhaps the change from your trips to the grocery store can be placed in this special place to be used only for postage. You may decide to set a goal of writing one or two letters a day—or you may decide to send out a form letter with a personal note attached once every 3-4 months. A friend may have a computer with print-out capabilities, and will be willing to run off a quantity of letters for you.

Keep in mind that usually only your closest friends and relatives become truly concerned when they do not hear from you by return mail. In other words, letters to most people on your list can be put off a week, or a month, with no adverse outcome. In almost every case, concern over unanswered correspondence primarily affects **you!** Bills must be cared for, of course. Other correspondence may need immediate attention. But to be in a constant "flap" about owing so many letters can produce paranoia, panic, or other problems!

Now that you are retired, it would be well to devote more time and attention to prayer than was possible when job expectations and daily duties took so much more of your prime time. Having been a missionary you know how to pray, in depth, for missionaries and for national Christians. You will be receiving letters from former colleagues requesting specific prayer requests. Literature will flow into your home concerning missionary and other Christian ministries. Each piece will be a call to prayer. (Be sure to get your name on the mailing list of a good number of Missionary/Christian organizations to keep informed of what God is doing through His servants **worldwide**.) If you live in a missionary retirement center, prayer requests will be shared with like-minded pray-ers. Your local church may have a prayer line and you will be called upon to take part. Your personal prayer list will be extended and you will see more answers to your requests. It will be encouraging to see God at work through your prayer ministry.

Be sure you always have something to look forward to—guests for tea, dinner out, a visit with friends, a luncheon date, game times, a drive into town, a trip to visit a friend or relatives, Christmas with your children, a visit from the grandchildren . . . it may be something seemingly insignificant to others, but you will glory in the anticipation, doing, and memory of it. (And try not to be too disappointed when plans do not work out exactly as you schedule them.)

Retirement may put you into more immediate contact with more of your own countrymen than you have had during all your furlough years at home. Then you saw people only briefly. Now you will have longer contacts. In retirement, as in active mission service, the greatest gift you can give to anyone, old or young, is to share with them your own excitement and "glow" concerning the immense global enterprise of God and His intimate concern for every single person. By contrast to your non-missionary friends, your global experience will have made you enormously more "wealthy", and retirement is when you can have your most luxurious ministry by giving away that "wealth"!

Doing things for others is a wonderful ministry during your years of retirement. Yes, others will do things for you—and that will always be appreciated. But it is still "more blessed to give than to receive" (Acts 20:35). And you will have hundreds of opportunities to prove this truth. Bake a loaf of bread. Invite your neighbor in for hot bread with jam and a cup of coffee. Did you realize one tomato plant per person in the family will produce an ample supply for your household? Why not share the rest with those who have no garden. (May as well include some cucumbers, peppers and squash while you're at it.) Does someone need a ride to church? Too many spider plants at home? Share them with a friend, or put one in a hanging pot and take it to the Nursing Center. Just had a grandson? Knit him a pair of booties. A neighbor has pet ducks? Give him your leftover bread. Mrs. Smith needs help with her income tax. The Mens/Womens Society at church needs a faithful telephone voice to call each member before each scheduled monthly meeting. Just look around and you will discover ever so much to do for others. It will not be overtaxing on your time or energy, but it will give you a feeling of worth and usefulness. You will have received more than you have given.

During these years of declining physical abilities, there can be a world of satisfaction. The activities which constitute your daily life can be enjoyed—no matter how limited they may seem to be. You have wonderful memories of your past life. You can be grateful for reaching several major goals in your lifetime. You should maintain a positive self-image, and maintain an optimistic attitude toward yourself, others, and the world around you. You will come to appreciate the faithfulness of a loving Heavenly Father and will long to enter an ever closer relationship to Him as you anticipate the future.

Aging often produces loneliness and the need for social exchanges. You may note this in others, yet not recognize it within yourself (or not be willing to admit to it). Maintaining a close personal relationship to the Father is imperative. Then do things for others. Discover the sheer joy of giving. Share heart concerns with a friend. Try new things, or new ways of doing old things. Reach out a helping hand to a needy world. Live with an open-palm policy. Laugh. If you haven't been used to doing it, learn! Don't be critical. Maintain a healthy mind and body. Enjoy the fellowship and companionship of those whom God sends your way. Spend time with younger people. (You have much which they admire). Think on things that edify.

As the years of retirement lengthen, the process of aging will take its normal course. There may be decreased mobility (perhaps the inability to drive, to utilize public transportation, or to get about conveniently). There may arise the need for using safety devices (hand rails, walkers, wheelchairs, firm, flat flooring),a need for dignity, a need for self-determination, a need for self-actualization—much of which can be neutralized by well-meaning but insensitive bystanders! There will be a desire for privacy, autonomy and personal space. These may or may not be available to you.

The physical aspects of life will seem to become priority concerns. There is so much that could be said about these matters, but let us consider just a few:

—Be faithful in getting 8 hours of sleep. If you can sleep only 6 hours at night, don't feel guilty about taking a 2-hour nap after lunch. (Wait at least an hour after lunch before succumbing to the bed or couch to avoid the discomfort of developing a hiatal hernia.)

—Watch your diet. Low far, low cholesterol, high fiber, low salt . . . whatever your doctor recommends. On the field you may have had breakfast, coffee break, lunch, teatime and dinner. But at home, unless specifically prescribed by your doctor, there is no need for a snack break every hour. It puts on weight and serves no real purpose other than financial expenditure. Indulge in teatime once a week, or for a special occasion—but dispense with the pies, cakes, cookies and crackers which once were available on a daily basis.

—Eat slowly! Enjoy your meals. Make them uncomplicated. Try always to make mealtime a time of relaxed fellowship, or time of leisure (reading mail, a book or magazine if you are alone).

—Exercise insofar as you are able. Again, your doctor will set your limits. Walking is probably the best and safest way to exercise.

Swimming is also excellent. Pumping iron or daily jogging is far too strenuous for the average retiree, and the possible physical harm it can do probably far outweighs its justification.

—If you find 18 holes of golf are a bit strenuous, leave the course after 9 holes, or 14 holes. Don't overdo something you truly enjoy.

—Friendships are important. Lonely individuals are more prone to a variety of physical and emotional disorders than those who have strong links with those who care for them, or for whom they care. As Christians we have a "Friend that sticketh closer than a brother" (Proverbs 18:24). But friends "with skin on their face" can bring comfort and solace when we need it most.

—Companionship produces a calming effect within an individual which is difficult to duplicate. A life companion is a tower of strength and much to be desired. For those who do not have close ties with another, seek a friend (or friends) with whom you are able to share your heart when necessary.

—If you are age 65 or older, be sure to see your physician at least once every six months. There is no need to become a hypochondriac—imagining every ache and pain becoming a life-threatening disease. Regular checkups should allay any fears of an unknown entity destroying you unexpectedly.

—If you are seeing more than one doctor, be openly honest with each one concerning drugs which may have been prescribed by the other doctors. Drugs may interact with or counteract one another. Sharing your drug intake (including such common, over-the-counter medicines as aspirin, laxatives, or cough medicines) with all tending physicians will result in a healthier you!

—Don't play doctor. If you have always put yourself on and off medicines, stop doing this immediately. Follow only your doctor's advice.

—Never take medications which have been prescribed for or used by others who have symptoms similar to yours. Always let your doctor diagnose, prescribe, and treat—not a friend or neighbor, no matter how well-intentioned.

—If your doctor puts you on medication for high blood pressure, you will need to remain on that medication until he takes you off of it. Don't stop taking your medicine if you feel better, or if you find your pressure reads "normal" at the machine in your corner drugstore. (Drugstore blood pressure machines are often inaccurate!)

—As aging continues, you may develop signs of arthritis, diabetes, changes in heart rhythm, high (or low) blood pressure. Aches and pains will appear and disappear. Contact with your doctor and use of prescribed medications will usually bring relief.

—Sometimes a doctor will prescribe a medication which give you an adverse reaction. Phone your physician **immediately** and explain the difficulty. Often a simple change of medicine or dosage will do away with the problem(s). Never suffer needlessly from a medication which may not agree with you.

—Have an annual dental checkup. Did you know that chewing well enhances your entire well-being? It does!

—If you are missing out on a full life because of hearing difficulties, don't be ashamed to admit it, or don't be offended if a friend mentions it to you. Go to an audiologist (hearing specialist) for a hearing test. Practically invisible hearing aids are available today. Hearing properly can be a great morale booster and will certainly enhance your self-image and ability to communicate.

—Eyesight can be a problem. Have it checked regularly. Stronger glasses or surgery may be indicated. For those who have difficulty seeing well enough to read, there are many Christian and secular organizations which make taped books and magazines available to the visually impaired at no cost.

—Scientific research has been showing that healthy pets can be of significant importance to the well-being of people. A dog or cat can be a faithful companion. It gives you something to care for. It gives you attention in return. Of the two, cats are probably easier to care for— especially in communities with leash laws. Food every day, a lot of love, and a clean litter box will provide the necessities of life for an indoor cat. And he/she will reward you with a special kind of kitty gratitude. If you prefer canaries, parakeets, goldfish, or guppies, they are also easy to care for and will provide entertainment. Admittedly, you cannot form the same loving relationship with a guppie as you can with a dog or cat, however! Consider having a pet (if your housing situation allows you to have one).

—Use vitamins and minerals to help maintain health and prevent disease. Use only as recommended by your doctor, however. Purchase Generic prescription and over-the-counter drugs in order to conserve financial resources.

If you are far away from your closest relatives, try to see your family on very special occasions, or invite them to visit you.

Take advantage of senior citizen discounts available to you at retail stores, pharmacies, restaurants, motels, car rental agencies, airline offices, etc. These were designed especially with you in mind. It is part of your financial provision.

If you are married, retirement does not give you an excuse for sloppiness. Always strive to look your very best for your spouse. Dress up when you go to church or out to dinner or to visit a friend. Although you may be limited financially, you can still look nice by buying a few flattering items of clothing, by making them yourself, or by allowing a friend the privilege of producing something special for you. Single folks should not become slovenly in their dress, either. For your own ego-strength, self-esteem and for the affirmation of others, habits of good dress should be maintained. (Of course you can wear those shorts, that ragged shirt, those baggy trousers—even that old pith helmet—when you are fishing, gardening, mowing the lawn, or lounging in your hammock!)

Retirement communities put individuals in close contact with one another. It is even possible to live in a duplex or in an apartment next to a retiree who is a considerable nuisance—walking in at mealtimes, asking personal questions, inviting himself/herself to private social events, etc. If such an annoying person is your neighbor, your first responsibility is to speak to him/her very frankly concerning what you consider to be the problems. Set up guidelines as to your right to privacy and insist that those rules be adhered to. (This might consist of refusing entry except upon invitation, or in an emergency. Or it might include placing notes on your door indicating when you are unavailable. If you do not face the individual with the facts, you will have to put up with the nuisance and keep your silence about it. If it is a cause of stress, it must be brought into the open. If you suspect mental or emotional instability is the root cause of the disturbing influence, share the situation with the Director, Manager, or other person in charge, and request a prompt solution.

You may be faced with having to care for one who is becoming debilitated from a stroke, diabetes, blindness or other physical impairment or handicap. Consideration should be given to finding someone to care for your loved one on occasion to allow you the privilege of getting away to shop, to go for a swim, to visit a friend, or to treat a neighbor at a restaurant. Constant responsibility for one in quickly failing health can be detrimental to both parties when there is no relief given in the situation.

Widows, widowers, and single retirees may find retirement more difficult than couples. Although it should be a period of far greater liberation than ever before, many people, now considered part of the large body of singles, find it difficult to cope with aloneness. Those once married feel strange in an environment where only couples are present. Those never married may feel they are invited to fellowship with others out of pity. But this is your problem, not that of those who give an invitation. Even if you are invited out of pity, accept gladly, behave naturally, enjoy yourself, and reciprocate the invitation. If you stay aloof from people, you will miss out on many happy times. Being with others is healthy. If you do not receive invitations from others, invite others to be with you—for a meal, for an outing, for a walk, for prayer, for chats—for whatever reason. Avoiding cliques can be helpful. Have a large number of friends. Just be careful not to intrude upon their own plans or privacy.

There may come a time when you will need to consider institutionalization. If you become mentally incompetent, such a decision will fall to others. But if you are, in the aging process, unable to care for your home, prepare your meals, or ambulate safely, it may be time to consider entering a nursing facility, extended care facility or full-care hospice type of arrangement (unless you live with someone who is willing and able to care for your adequately in your home). Such institutions are readily available, but much care should be taken in choosing one which is accredited, has adequate and properly trained nursing personnel, which is clean, quiet, comfortable, and affordable. Because there may be a need for such facilities late in life, it would be well to consider a retirement community where there are nursing facilities available within the complex, and where services are provided free of cost to all residents of the village. Lifetime care communities may cost more to enter, but the benefits will almost always far outweigh what you pay for your financial investment.

If your Mission Board has established its own retirement facilities, you will probably find you will be well-provided for in the way of various planned fellowships and functions. You may choose to take part or not, but they are available to you.

You have had a lifetime of service overseas and have much to offer younger Christians. That knowledge and experience is most often shared in a local church. It is not recommended that you volunteer to be on every committee of that church, or seek to sway its pastor or members concerning matters which need to be decided by the entire fellowship. But your expertise will be much sought after and utilized if you are patient and seek to counsel rather than dictate.

Many retirees live long, active, healthy lives until the Lord calls them home. Not everyone ends up bedridden or in a nursing facility. Both men and women have a longer life expectancy than ever before—especially those whose health has not been ruined by smoking, drinking, drug addiction or serious disease. And those who retire in an environment conducive to busy, but leisurely living, live longer and stay in better health than those who feel their usefulness and zest for living has been taken from them.

An active mind aids a healthy body. Never give up your quest for learning. Read books and magazines. (If you find it too expensive to purchase all the books and magazines you would like, meet with a group of people and decide what subscription or book club each individual would like to pay for. If 10 people join together in this project, the books and magazines can be passed from one to the other after they are read, and the cost for each individual becomes minimal.) Go to lectures; read the newspaper; learn from others; visit places you've never seen before; ask questions; find answers; research material. Dig into the Word of God and discover new truths. Never stagnate. Enroll in a continuing education course in cake decorating, creative writing or bookkeeping. Many colleges and universities offer courses without tuition charges for those who are 65 or older. And many are taking advantage of these learning opportunities, with profit. Keep up on missions! Take some Bible Correspondence courses. Above all, never become a TV addict!

In many ways, the years to come can be some of the very best of your entire life. You have turned over responsibilities to younger missionaries who, though they will not do things as you would have, will be used of God to fulfill the Great Commission. You are free from the responsibility of raising your children or caring for your aged parents. You are free to enjoy life to its fullest without the pressures of time and space limitations.

Make your home a happy place to be and a refuge into which you can invite your friends. Keep it simple so you are not tied down to excessive housekeeping chores. Choose comfortable furniture. Wall to wall carpet can be easily kept, and helps insure against falls on slippery floors. Beware of scatter rugs! Put anti-slip material in your tub or shower to reduce the hazards of falling. Utilize items from your field of service to make your home unique—wood carvings, paintings, knick knacks. Even the colors you utilize for painting your home and decorating it can make a difference in your long-term outlook (e.g., yellow suggests sunlight and laughter, orange suggests brightness and activity, red is passionate, blue promotes an aura of reserve and restful security, green produces coolness and rest, while gray is depressing, black is somber).

For those who are now thinking of retirement, several questions need to be answered:

1. When should you be making plans for retirement?

2. What questions will you need to answer in regard to retiring? (Example: geographical location).

3. What sources of income will be available to you for retirement living?

4. In what ways can you continue to have a vital ministry in retirement?

5. What hobbies do you want to pursue in your leisurely retirement living?

6. What physical changes are a normal part of aging? How should you respond to these changes?

7. What benefits will you be able to enjoy as a retiree?

8. Under what circumstances must institutionalization be considered?

9. How can "singles" best adjust to retirement living?

10. How can a zest for living be continued throughout your retirement years?

As a new retiree, you may find it will take time to adjust to this period of your life. But you are not alone in the Senior Citizen category of our country. The National Council on the Aging has found that in the year 1900, only 3 million people were over 65 years of age. Today, 27 million (12% of our total population) are over 65. Two million are over 85. The Council also predicts that by the year 2020, one of every six Americans will be 65 or older. You have a long way to go and much yet to accomplish!

As a retiree, it will be to your advantage to become a member of the American Association of Retired Persons (AARP). A very minimal fee (just a few dollars) per year (sent to AARP, 215 Long Beach Blvd., Long Beach, CA 90801) maintains your membership. You receive a monthly copy of Modern Maturity magazine, discounts on travel, free booklets, discounts at motels, eligibility for group health insurance,

discounts of up to 50% on prescription drugs and pharmaceutical supplies, and other benefits.

There is one final consideration to be mentioned. At this juncture,
some thought must be given to a very real part of life, namely death. As
Christians we do not fear death—but if asked if you are ready to die,
you would probably reply, "Yes—but I'd rather not do it today!" You
have plans for the future—things to do, places to go, people to be with,
life to enjoy, perhaps a book to write about your field experience . . .

But death is a reality and must be faced. A will should be updated
in accordance with the state in which you reside. You may wish to give
away certain pieces of jewelry or special mementos to special friends or
relatives. You may also want to make funeral arrangements, buy a
cemetary lot, and/or make arrangements for being an organ donor. The
more you do in these regards, the less will need to be left for the decision of others.

Those who lose a lifetime partner will need to make many adjustments living alone. Even in these circumstances, a loving Heavenly
Father will not leave you nor forsake you.

> It is of the Lord's mercies that we are not con-
> sumed,
> because his compassions fail not.
> They are new every morning:
> great is thy faithfulness.
> The Lord is my portion, saith my soul;
> therefore will I hope in him.
> The Lord is good unto them that wait for him,
> to the soul that seeketh him.
> It is good that a man should both hope
> and quietly wait for the salvation of the Lord.
> It is good for a man that he bear the yoke
> in his youth.
> Lamentations 3:22-27

Now may God richly bless you and give you a full, happy and
productive retirement.

Bibliography

The books listed on the following pages in their various categories are not, by any means, the only ones available for your reading. Your Mission Board will be able to advise you concerning books which they feel will be especially beneficial to you in preparation for your particular field. But this selected list will give you an overall view of the various facets of missionary life which will help you obtain a fuller understanding of your part in the Great Commission.

HISTORY OF MISSIONS

Beaver, R. Pierce. ALL LOVES EXCELLING: AMERICAN PROTESTANT WOMEN IN WORLD MISSION. Pasadena: William Carey Library, 1968.

Chaney, Charles L. THE BIRTH OF MISSIONS IN AMERICA. Pasadena: William Carey Library, 1976.

Hulbert, Terry C. WORLD MISSIONS TODAY. Wheaton: Evangelical Teacher Training Association, 1979.

Kane, J. Herbert. A GLOBAL VIEW OF CHRISTIAN MISSIONS FROM PENTECOST TO THE PRESENT. Grand Rapids: Baker Book House 1971 (The bibliography included in this book is excellent.)

Latourette, Kenneth Scott. CHRISTIANITY THROUGH THE AGES. New York: Harper & Row, 1965.

Neill, Stephen. A HISTORY OF CHRISTIAN MISSIONS. E. Rutherford, NJ: Viking Penguin, 1964.

MISSIONARY PREPARATION

Beals, Paul A. A PEOPLE FOR HIS NAME: A CHURCH-BASED MISSION STRATEGY. Pasadena: William Carey Library, 1985.

Beyerhaus, Peter and Lefever, Henry. THE RESPONSIBLE CHURCH AND THE FOREIGN MISSION. Grand Rapids: Eerdman, 1964.

Cable, Mildred and French, Francesca. AMBASSADORS FOR CHRIST. London: Hodder and Stoughton, 1937.

Conn, Harvie N. (ed.). REACHING THE UNREACHED: THE OLD-NEW CHALLENGE. Phillipsburg, NJ: Presbyterian & Reformed Publishing Co., 1984.

DuBose, Francis M. THE GOD WHO SENDS. Nashville: Broadman Press, 1983.

Eliott, Elisabeth. A SLOW AND CERTAIN LIGHT. Waco: Word Books, 1977.

Engel, James F. and Norton, H. Wilbert. WHAT'S GONE WRONG WITH THE HARVEST? Grand Rapids: Zondervan Publishing House, 1975.

Ford, Leighton. THE CHRISTIAN PERSUADER. New York: Harper & Rowe, 1966.

Gallagher, Neil. DON'T GO OVERSEAS UNTIL YOU'VE READ THIS BOOK. Minneapolis: Bethany Fellowship, Inc., 1977.

Haggai, John. HOW TO WIN OVER LONELINESS. Nashville: Thomas Nelson Publishers, 1979.

Hansel, Tim. WHEN I RELAX I FEEL GUILTY. Elgin, IL: David C. Cook Publishing Co., 1979.

Hepler, Thom. A WORLD OF DIFFERENCE: FOLLOWING CHRIST BEYOND YOUR CULTURAL WALLS. Downers Grove, IL: InterVarsity Press, 1981.

Howard, J. Grant. THE TRAUMA OF TRANSPARENCY. Portland, OR: Multnomah Press, 1979.

Kane, J. Herbert, UNDERSTANDING CHRISTIAN MISSIONS. Grand Rapids: Baker Book House, 1974.

_____, WINDS OF CHANGE IN THE CHRISTIAN MISSION. Chicago: Moody Press, 1973.

Lockerbie, Jeannie. BY ONES & BY TWOS. Pasadena: William Carey Library, 1985.

Loss, Myron. CULTURE SHOCK: DEALING WITH STRESS IN CROSS-CULTURAL LIVING. Winona Lake: Light and Life Press, 1983.

Luzbetak, Louis J. THE CHURCH AND CULTURES: AN APPLIED ANTHROPOLOGY FOR THE RELIGIOUS WORKER. Pasadena: William Carey Library, 1976.

McGinnis, Alan Loy. THE FRIENDSHIP FACTOR. Minneapolis: Augsburg Publishing House, 1979.

Morgan, Helen. WHO'D STAY A MISSIONARY? Fort Washington, PA: Christian Literature Crusade, 1972.

Mostert, John. THE PREPARATION OF A MISSIONARY. Wheaton: Accrediting Association of Bible Colleges, 1968.

Narramore, Clyde and Ruth. HOW TO HANDLE PRESSURE. Wheaton: Tyndale House, 1975.

Nida, Eugene A. and Smalley, William A. INTRODUCING ANIMISM. New York: Friendship Press, 1959.

Reed, Lyman E. PREPARING MISSIONARIES FOR INTER-CULTURAL COMMUNICATION. Pasadena: William Carey Library, 1985.

Rust, Brian and McLeish, Barry. THE SUPPORT RAISING HAND-BOOK: A GUIDE FOR CHRISTIAN WORKERS. Downers Grove, IL: InterVarsity Press, 1984.

Seamands, John T. TELL IT WELL: COMMUNICATING THE GOSPEL ACROSS CULTURES. Kansas City: Beacon Hill Press, 1981.

Sine, Tom. MUSTARD SEED CONSPIRACY: YOU CAN MAKE A DIFFERENCE IN TOMORROW'S WORLD. Waco: Word Books, 1981.

Stafford, Tim. THE FRIENDSHIP GAP: REACHING OUT ACROSS CULTURES. Downers Grove, IL: InterVarsity Press, 1984.

Strachan, R. Kenneth. THE INESCAPABLE CALLING. Grand Rapids: Eerdmans, 1968.

Sweeting, George. CATCH THE SPIRIT OF LOVE. Wheaton: Victor Books, 1983.

Tuggy, Joy T. THE MISSIONARY WIFE AND HER WORK. Chicago: Moody Press, 1966.

Wagner, C. Peter. ON THE CREST OF THE WAVE: BECOMING A WORLD CHRISTIAN. Oxnard: Regal, 1983.

Weber, James M. LET'S QUIT KIDDING OURSELVES ABOUT MISSIONS. Winona Lake: Don Wardell, 1982.

Wicks, Doug (ed.). FORGET THE PITH HELMET: PERSPEC-TIVES ON THE MISSIONARY EXPERIENCE. Chicago: Moody Press, 1984.

Yancy, Philip. WHERE IS GOD WHEN IT HURTS? Grand Rapids: Zondervan Publishing House, 1978.

MISSIONARY PRINCIPLES AND PRACTICES

Allen, Roland. MISSIONARY PRINCIPLES. Grand Rapids: Eerdmans, 1964.

CHANGING MISSIONARY METHODS

Brock, Charles. PRINCIPLES AND PRACTICES OF INDIGENOUS CHURCH PLANTING. Nashville: Broadman Press, 1981.

Cook, Harold R. STRATEGY OF MISSIONS: AN EVANGELICAL VIEW. Chicago: Moody Press, 1963.

Conn, Harvie M. ETERNAL WORD AND CHANGING WORLDS: THEOLOGY, ANTHROPOLOGY AND MISSION IN TRIALOGUE. Grand Rapids: Zondervan, 1984.

Howard, David M. STUDENT POWER IN WORLD EVANGELISM. Downers Grove, IL: InterVarsity, 1970

Huston, Perdita. THIRD WORLD WOMEN SPEAK OUT. New York: Praeger Publishers. 1979.

McGavran, Donald A. BRIDGES OF GOD. Cincinnati: Friendship Press, 1955.

UNDERSTANDING CHURCH GROWTH (Fully revised). Grand Rapids: Wm. B. Eerdmans Publishing Co., 1980.

Mayers, Marvin K. CHRISTIANITY CONFRONTS CULTURE. Grand Rapids: Zondervan, 1980.

Mellis, Charles J. COMMITTED COMMUNITIES: FRESH STREAMS FOR WORLD MISSIONS. Pasadena, CA: William Carey Library, 1976.

Needham, William L. CHRISTIANITY IN THE FUTURE. Monrovia, CA: World Vision International, 1978.

Rees, Paul S. DON'T SLEEP THROUGH THE REVOLUTION. Waco, TX: Word Books, 1970.

Wilson, J. Christy, Jr. TODAY'S TENTMAKERS. Wheaton: Tyndale House Publishers, Inc., 1979.

Winter, Ralph D. and Hawthorne, Steven C. (eds.). PERSPECTIVES ON THE WORLD CHRISTIAN MOVEMENT. Pasadena: William Carey Library, 1981.

MISSIONARY PROBLEMS

Institute in Basic Youth Conficts. THE PINEAPPLE STORY. Oak Brook, IL, 1978.

Isais, Juan M. THE OTHER SIDE OF THE COIN. Grand Rapids: Eerdmans, 1966.

Schaffer, Francis A. THE GREAT EVANGELICAL DISASTER. Westchester, IL: Crossway Books, 1984.

Sweeting, George. HOW TO SOLVE CONFLICTS. Chicago: Moody Press, 1973.

Taylor, Rhene. ROUGH EDGES. Leicester, England: InterVarsity Press, 1979.

MISSIONARY BIOGRAPHIES

Note: At best, this is a partial listing of biographies available to you. Search out these and others concerning your special field of service.

Brumberg, Joan Jacobs. MISSION FOR LIFE (The Story of the family of Adoniram Judson). New York: The Free Press, 1980.

Canfield, Carolyn. ONE VISION ONLY (Isobel Kuhn). Sevenoaks, Kent, England: Hodder and Stoughton Limited, 1959.

de la Haye, Sophie. TREAD UPON THE LION (Tommie Titcomb). New York: Sudan Interior Mission, 1980.

Dortzbach, Karl and Debbie. KIDNAPPED. New York: Harper & Row, Publishers, 1975.

Edwards, Jonathan, ed. THE LIFE AND DIARY OF DAVID BRAINERD. Chicago: Moody Press, 1949.

Elliot, Elisabeth. SHADOW OF THE ALMIGHTY: THE LIFE AND TESTAMENT OF JIM ELLIOT. New York: Harper & Rowe, 1958.

Goforth, Rosalind. GOFORTH OF CHINA. Grand Rapids: Zondervan, 1937.

Grubb, Norman. C. T. STUDD: CRICKETER & PIONEER. Fort Washington, PA: Christian Literature Crusade, 1982.

Hefley, James and Marti. NO TIME FOR TOMBSTONES. Harrisburg, PA: Christian Publications, Inc., 1974.

_____. UNCLE CAM. Waco, TX: Word Books, 1974.

Houghton, Frank. AMY CARMICHAEL OF DOHNAVUR. Fort Washington, PA: Christian Literature Crusade, N.D.

Latourette, Kenneth S. BEYOND THE RANGES. Grand Rapids: Wm. B. Eerdmans Publishing Co., 1967.

Magnusson, Sally. THE FLYING SCOTSMAN: A BIOGRAPHY OF ERIC LIDDELL. Quartet Books, 1981.

Mueller, J. Theodore. JOHN G. PATON: MISSIONARY TO THE NEW HEBRIDES. Grand Rapids: Zondervan, 1941.

Neely, Lois. COME UP TO THIS MOUNTAIN (Clarence W. Jones). Wheaton: Tyndale Publishers, Inc., 1980.

Olson, Bruce. BRUCHKO. Wheaton: Creation House, 1982.

Paton, William. ALEXANDER DUFF, PIONEER OF MISSIONARY EDUCATION. New York: George H. Doran Co., 1923.

Petersen, William J. ANOTHER HAND ON MINE (Dr. Carl Becker). New York: McGraw Hill, 1967.

Rasooli, Jay M. and Allen, Cady H. DR. SA'GGD OF IRAN: KURDISH PHYSICIAN TO PRINCES AND PEASANTS, NOBLES AND NOMADS. Pasadena: William Carey Library, 1983.

Roseveare, Helen. LIVING SACRIFICE. Chicago: Moody Press, 1979.

Scherer, James A. JUSTINIAN WELZ: EARLY PROPHET OF MISSION. Grand Rapids: Wm. B. Errdmans Publishing Co., 1959.

Taylor, Mrs. Howard. THE TRIUMPH OF JOHN AND BETTY STAM. Philadelphia: China Inland Mission, 1935.

Taylor, Dr. and Mrs. Howard. HUDSON TAYLOR IN EARLY YEARS: the growth of a soul. China Inland Mission, 1911.

Wilson, Dorothy Clarke. TEN FINGERS FOR GOD (Dr. Paul Brand). Nashville: Thomas Nelson Publishing, 1983.

Wilson, J. Christy. APOSTLE TO ISLAM; A biography of Samuel M. Zwemer. Grand Rapids: Baker Book House, 1952.

SPECIALIZED MISSIONS

Cook, Frank S. SEEDS IN THE WIND. Quito, Ecuador: The World Radio Missionary Fellowship, Inc., 1961.

Kane, J. Herbert. FAITH MIGHTY FAITH. Missionary Aviation Fellowship, 1956.

Wallis, Ethel E. TWO THOUSAND TONGUES TO GO. New York: Harper, 1959.

SPECIFIC MISSION FIELD AREAS

Anderson, Lorna. YOU AND YOUR REFUGEE NEIGHBOR. Pasadena; William Carey Library, 1980.

Bollinger, Edward. THE CROSS AND THE FLOATING DRAGON: THE GOSPEL IN RYOKYO. Pasadena: William Carey Library, 1982.

Carmichael, Amy, MIMOSA. London: Society for Promoting Christian Knowledge, 1949.

Chamberlain, Margaret. REACHING ASIANS INTERNATION-ALLY. Wayne, NJ: International Missions, 1984.

Collins, Jodie. CODE WORD: CATHERINE (Ethiopia). Wheaton: Tyndale House Publishers, Inc., 1984.

Crawford, David and Leona. MISSIONARY ADVENTURES IN THE SOUTH PACIFIC. Rutland, VT: Tuttle, 1967

Dawson, David, M.D. NO FEAR IN HIS PRESENCE (Zaire). Ventura, CA: Regal Books, 1980.

Davis, Raymond J. FIRE ON THE MOUNTAINS (the study of a miracle—the church in Ethiopia). Grand Rapids: Zondervan, 1966.

_____ THE WINDS OF GOD. Toronto: SIM International Publications, 1984.

Dretke, James P. A CHRISTIAN APPROACH TO MUSLIMS: REFLECTIONS FROM WEST AFRICA. Pasadena: William Carey Library, 1979.

Duff, Clarence. CORDS OF LOVE (Ethiopia). Philipsburg, NJ: Presbyterian and Reformed Publishing Co., 1980.

Eby, Omar. WHISPER IN A DRY LAND (Somalia). Winona Lake, IN: Herald, 1968.

Elliot, Elisabeth. THE SAVAGE MY KINSMAN. New York: Harper & Brothers, 1961.

Forsberg, Malcolm and Enid. IN FAMINE HE SHALL REDEEM THEE. Cedar Grove, NJ: Sudan Interior Mission, 1975.

Gabre-Tsadick, Marta. SHELTERED BY THE KING (Ethiopia). Lincoln, VA: Chosen Books, 1983.

Gaye, Pippa. BETTER THAN LIGHT (Botswana). London: Mowbray, 1983.

Gonzales, Justo L. THE DEVELOPMENT OF CHRISTIANITY IN THE LATIN CARIBBEAN. Grand Rapids: Eerdmans, 1969.

Groves, C.P. THE PLANTING OF CHRISTIANITY IN AFRICA 1840-1954. 4 volumes. London: Lutterworth, 1948-1958.

Gunther, Peter F., Ed. THE FIELDS AT HOME: STUDIES IN HOME MISSIONS. Chicago: Moody Press, 1963.

Imasogie, Osadolor. GUIDELINES FOR CHRISTIAN THEOLOGY IN AFRICA. Achimoto, Ghana: Africa Christian Press, 1983.

Johnson, Harmon A. THE GROWING CHURCH IN HAITI. Coral Gables, FL: West Indies Mission, 1970.

Kraft, Marguerite G. WORLDVIEW & COMMUNICATION OF THE GOSPEL: A NIGERIAN CASE STUDY. Pasadena: William Carey Library, 1978.

Kuhn, Isobel. NESTS ABOVE THE ABYSS. Philadelphia: China Inland Mission, 1947.

_____STONES OF FIRE. Philadelphia: China Inland Mission, 1951.

Lageer, Eileen. NEW LIFE FOR ALL (Nigeria). Chicago: Moody Press, 1970.

Lam, Wing-Hung. CHINESE THEOLOGY IN CONSTRUCTION. Pasadena: William Carey Library, 1982.

Lawrence, Carl. THE CHURCH IN CHINA: HOW IT SURVIVES AND PROSPERS UNDER COMMUNISM. Minneapolis: Bethany House Publishers, 1985.

Lee, Robert. STRANGER IN THE LAND—A STUDY OF THE CHURCH IN JAPAN. London: Lutterworth, 1967.

Liao, David C. E. THE UNRESPONSIVE: RESISTANT OR NEGLECTED? Pasadena: William Carey Library, 1979.

McGavran, Donald. CHURCH GROWTH IN MEXICO Grand Rapids: Eerdmans, 1963.

_____ETHNIC REALITIES & THE CHURCH: LESSONS FROM INDIA. Pasadena: William Carey Library, 1979.

McCurry, Don. GOSPEL AND ISLAM (revised edition). Monrovia, CA: MARC, 1985.

Mbiti, John S. AFRICAN RELIGIONS AND PHILOSOPHY. London: Heinemann, 1969.

Miller, William M. THE BAHA'I FAITH. Pasadena: William Carey Library, 1984.

Neill, Stephen. THE STORY OF THE CHRISTIAN CHURCH IN INDIA AND PAKISTAN. Grand Rapids: Eerdmans, 1970.

Nickel, Ben J. ALONG THE QUICHUA TRAIL. Smithville, MO: Gospel Missionary Union, 1965.

Nida, Eugene. UNDERSTANDING LATIN AMERICANS. Pasadena: William Carey Library, 1974.

Parshall, Phil. BRIDGE TO ISLAM: A CHRISTIAN PERSPECTIVE ON FOLK ISLAM. Grand Rapids: Baker Book House, 1983.

NEW PATHS IN MUSLIM EVANGELISM. Grand Rapids: Baker Book House, 1981.

Parvin, Earl. MISSIONS USA. Chicago: Moody Press, 1985.

Patterson, George N. CHRISTIANITY IN COMMUNIST CHINA. Waco, TX: Word Books, 1969.

Porterfield, Bruce E. COMMANDOS FOR CHRIST (Bolivia). New York: Harper & Row, 1963.

Read, William R.; Monterroso, Victor M., and Johnson, Harmon A. CHURCH GROWTH IN LATIN AMERICA. Grand Rapids: Eerdmans, 1969.

Richardson, Don. LORDS OF THE EARTH. Glendale, CA: Regal Books, 1978.

————. PEACE CHILD. Glendale, CA: Regal Books, 1974.

Rin, Ro-Bong and Nelson, Martin L. (eds.) KOREAN CHURCH GROWTH EXPLOSION: CENTENNIAL OF THE PROTESTANT CHURCH (1184-1984). Los Angeles: Word of Life Press, 1984.

Sales, Jane M. THE PLANTING OF CHURCHES IN SOUTH AFRICA. Grand Rapids: Eerdmans, 1971.

Sinclair, John H. PROTESTANTISM IN LATIN AMERICA: A BIBLIOGRAPHICAL GUIDE. Pasadena: William Carey Library, 1976.

Spain, Mildred W. AND IN SAMARIA. Dallas: The Central America Mission, printed by Banks, Upshaw and Co., Dallas, 1962.

Sundkler, Bengt. THE CHRISTIAN MINISTRY IN AFRICA. London: SCM Press, 1962.

Wall, Martha. SPLINTERS FROM AN AFRICAN LOG. Chicago: Moody Press, 1960.

Wallis, Ethel E. THE DAYUMA STORY. New York: Harper & Rowe, 1960.

MISSIONARY IMPACT

Bavinck Dr. J. H. THE IMPACT OF CHRISTIANITY ON THE NON-CHRISTIAN WORLD. Grand Rapids: Eerdmans, 1948.

Dayton, Edward R. THAT EVERYONE MAY HEAR. Monrovia, CA: MARC, 1979.

Kraemer, Hendrik. THE CHRISTIAN MESSAGE IN A NON-CHRISTIAN WORLD. New York: Harper and Brothers, 1947.

McGavran, Donald. UNDERSTANDING CHURCH GROWTH. Grand Rapids: Eerdmans, 1983.

McQuilkin, J. Robertson. MEASURING THE CHURCH GROWTH MOVEMENT. Chicago: Moody Press, 1974.

MISSIONARY AGENCIES

Kane, J. Herbert. A GLOBAL VIEW OF CHRISTIAN MISSIONS FROM PENTECOST TO THE RESENT. Grand Rapids: Baker Book House, 1971

Wilson, Samuel, ed. MISSION HANDBOOK. Monrovia, CA: MARC, 1980.

MISSIONARY BOOKS FOR CHILDREN AND YOUNG PEOPLE

The Jungle Doctor Series authored by Dr. Paul White, published by Moody Press, are highly recommended books. Basil Miller books, published by Zondervan, include: NINETEEN MISSIONARY STORIES FROM THE MIDDLE EAST, TWENTY MISSIONARY STORIES FROM AFRICA, TWENTY MISSIONARY STORIES FROM INDIA, TWENTY MISSIONARY STORIES FROM LATIN AMERICA, ANN JUDSON: HEROINE OF BURMA and WILFRED GRENFELL; LABRADOR'S DOGSLED DOCTOR.

BIBLE REFERENCE BOOKS

It is strongly suggested that the following reference books (or others of equal content and caliber) be taken with you to the field:

Halley, Henry H. HALLEY'S BIBLE HANDBOOK. Grand Rapids: Zondervan, 1962.

Jamieson, Rev. Robert, Fausset, Rev. A. R., Brown, Rev. David. COMMENTARY ON THE WHOLE BIBLE. Grand Rapids: Zondervan (n.d.)

Packer, J.I., Tenney, Merrill C., White, William, Jr. THE BIBLE ALMANAC. Nashville: Thomas Nelson Publishers, 1980.

Strong, James. STRONG'S EXHAUSTIVE CONCORDANCE. Grand Rapids: Guardian Press, 1976.

Thompson, Frank Charles, comp. & ed. THE NEW CHAIN REFERENCE BIBLE. Indianapolis: B. B. Kirkbride Bible Co., 1934.

Unger, Merrill F. UNGER'S BIBLE DICTIONARY. Chicago: Moody Press, 1965.

Larson, Gary N. THE NEW UNGER'S BIBLE HANDBOOK. Chicago: Moody Press, 1984.

Walvoord, John F. and Zuck, Roy B. THE BIBLE KNOWLEDGE COMMENTARY. Wheaton: Victor Books, 1984.

Be sure to take a good English dictionary, and an encyclopedia, if one is available to you. (This is especially helpful if you plan to teach your own children on the field.)

THE MISSIONARY FAMILY

Buffam, John C. THE LIFE & TIMES OF AN MK. Pasadena: William Carey Library, 1985.

Danielson, Edward E., MISSIONARY KID--MK. Pasadena: William Carey Library, 1985.

Dobson, Dr. James C. LOVE MUST BE TOUGH. Waco: Word Books, 1983

Kenney, Betty Jo. THE MISSIONARY FAMILY. Pasadena: William Carey Library, 1984.

Schaffer, Edith. WHAT IS A FAMILY? Old Tappan, NJ: Fleming H. Revell,

Co., 1975.

Werkman, Sidney, M.D. BRINGING UP CHILDREN OVERSEAS. New York: Basic Books, 1977.

DEVOTIONAL BOOKS

Take a variety of devotional books. Among those which you may choose are:

DAILY LIGHT ON THE DAILY PATH
MY UTMOST FOR HIS HIGHEST by Oswald Chambers
MORNING AND EVENING by C. H. Spurgeon
STREAMS IN THE DESERT by Mrs. Charles E. Cowman
SPRINGS IN THE VALLEY by Mrs. Charles E. Cowman
EDGES OF HIS WAYS by Amy Carmichael (or any of Amy
  Carmichael's books)

Take several Versions of the Scriptures for both study and devotions.

For your prayer time for missionaries world-wide: Johnstone P.J. A HANDBOOK FOR WORLD INTERCESSION. Bromley, England: STL Publications, 1979.

GENERAL REFERENCE BOOKS

Those who will be serving in specialized fields in a professional capacity will take up-to-date reference books pertinent to your sphere of service. This may include music books, a Secretary's Handbook, books on engineering, bookkeeping, administration, photography, radio, medicine, television,education, children's work (including a good Bible story book), building, mechanics, or cookbooks with simple, basic food recipes.

Every doctor and nurse should have the latest copy of the PHYSICIAN'S DESK REFERENCE (PDR). Each household should have a good First Aid Book and the following inexpensive Manuals: WHERE THERE IS NO DOCTOR by David Werner, HELPING HEALTH WORKERS LEARN by David Werner and Bill Bower, and NUTRITION FOR DEVELOPING COUNTRIES by King, Morley and Burgess. These can be obtained from Dr. David Morley, Institute of Child Health, University of London, 30 Guilford St., London, WClN lEH, ENGLAND, (medical visual aids and simple textbooks for overseas use in tropical lands are available at the same address) or from The Hesperian Foundation, P.0. Box 1692, Palo Alto, CA 94302.

For those who will be involved in Christian Education ministries, THE MODERN PRACTICE OF ADULT EDUCATION by Malcolm

S. Knowles (New York: Association Press, 1970) will prove to be invaluable.

Because you will be writing prayer/newsletters to your constituency, the following books may help you to write more understandably and effectively:

Burack, Abraham S. THE WRITER'S HANDBOOK. Boston: The Writer, Inc., 1970.

Holmes Marjorie. WRITING THE CREATIVE ARTICLE. Boston: The Writer, Inc., 1973.

Nichols, Sue. WORDS ON TARGET FOR BETTER CHRISTIAN COMMUNICATION. Richmond, VA: John Knox Press, 1970.

The books, FEARFULLY & WONDERFULLY MADE (Dr. Paul Brand and Philip Yancey, Grand Rapids, Zondervan, 1980) and IN HIS IMAGE by the same authors and publisher (1984) should be read by all.

Because some may have to face death and dying in their years of service, the book, GRIEF, DYING, AND DEATH (Theresa A. Rando, Champaign, IL: Research Press Company, 1984) is recommended.

A last minute browse through your local Christian Bookstore may prove to be profitable. Seek out books which may be of particular help to you or your children as you set your face toward the field. You will not want to take hundreds of volumes with you. Many will be read in the homeland and passed on to others. You may want to take some of your favorite novels, classics, or lighter reading material to the field with you for sheer recreation.

To keep in touch with the latest published books in the area of missions, be sure to keep in contact with the William Carey Library, P.0. Box 40129, Pasadena, CA 91104.

If you are interested in correspondence courses, there are many available to you. Moody Bible Institute and Back to the Bible Broadcast are among those offering excellent courses.

There are also several good Book Clubs. You might want to contact one, such as the Global Church Growth Book Club (William Carey Library, P.O. Box 40129, Pasadena, CA 91104), and ask how you may become involved while you are preparing for service as well as after you arrive on the field.

Bible courses on video tape are available from Biblical Education by Extension, Columbia Bible College, P.0. Box 3122, Columbia, So. Carolina 29230.